The Ultimate
Guide
To the SDLC

Victor M. Font Jr.

A FontLife Publication, LLC
Raleigh, NC 27603
Email: info@ fontlifepublications.com
http://fontlifepublications.com/

A FontLife Publication, LLC

A FontLife Publication, LLC is a North Carolina Limited Liability Company. All Rights Reserved. No part of this book shall be reproduced, stored in a retrieval system, or transmitted by any means, electronic, mechanical, photocopying, recording, or otherwise, without written permission from the author and publisher, except for the inclusion of brief quotations used in a review.

International Standard Book Number: 978-0-9855666-4-7
First Printing

© 2012 Victor M. Font Jr. and A FontLife Publication, LLC—All Rights Reserved

Trademarks

Trademarked names may appear in this book. All terms mentioned in this book that are known to be trademarks or service marks have been appropriately capitalized. The author cannot attest to the accuracy of this information. Use of a term in this book should not be regarded as affecting the validity of any trademarks or service marks. Rather than use a trademark symbol with every occurrence of a trademarked name, we use the names only in an editorial fashion and to the benefit of the trademark owner, without intention of infringement of the trademark or service mark.

Warning and Disclaimer

Every effort has been made to make this book as complete and as accurate as possible, but no warranty or fitness is implied. The information provided is on an "as-is" basis. No patent liability is assumed with respect to the use of the information contained herein. The author and publisher shall have neither liability nor responsibility to any person or entity with respect to any loss or damage arising from the information contained herein.

This document is an original work of the author. It may include reference to information and materials commonly known, freely available to the general public or provided by contributing third parties. Any resemblance to other published information is purely coincidental. The author has in no way attempted to use material not of his own origination or that contributed by third parties without their express written consent.

Bulk Sales

The author offers excellent discounts on this book when ordered in quantity for bulk purchases. For more information, please contact the author at info@fontlifepublications.com.

Printed and bound in the United States of America by Lightning Source, Inc., La Vergne, TN USA 37086.

Register Your Book

Register your book today at http://fontlifepublications.com/register/ to get access to exclusive member benefits:

- Free Lifetime Access and Updates to eBooks
- Email notification and discounts on new editions
- Special member discounts on books, videos, and events available only to FontLife customers

Acknowledgements

Cover design by Victor M. Font Jr.

The images that appear within this book are either the original work of the author, public domain, or third party provided used with permission and attribution.

This work is dedicated to my wife Susan and daughter Victoria
...the loves of my life.

About the Author

Victor M. Font Jr. is an award winning author, entrepreneur and high performing executive with global Information Technology experience in application development, project management, business analysis, quality assurance, and leadership development. A Founding Board Member of the North Carolina Executive Roundtable, Victor has served as a member of the International Institute of Business Analysis, Association of Information Technology Professionals, and Toastmasters International. He is author of several books including the popular Winning With WordPress series.

Victor entered Information Technology when he bought and operated Bayonne Computer Center, the first computer retail store in Hudson County, New Jersey. He served as a general partner and the Chief Information Officer of SGL Data Systems, a computer consulting and custom software development house located in Greenwich, Connecticut. SGL Data Systems was first to market with LawCruit®, a software package designed to assist legal recruiters in their role of tracking and communicating with candidate attorneys. As a consultant, he worked for JP Morgan Bank, NJ Special Olympics, S. B. Thomas, AT&T Consumer Sales Division, Austin & Merritt, Warner-Lambert, Porzio, Bromberg and Newman, and the US Government.

His corporate career began as a manager in Human Resources Information Systems where he worked his way up through the ranks to become an IT Director for a major global pharmaceutical company, serving on a variety of enterprise-level IT governance councils including Architecture and Engineering Council, Information Security Council, Active Directory Governance Board, Identity and Access Management Governance Board, and IT Process Improvement Council. He founded and led a Business Analysis Center of Excellence and a Business Analysis Community of Practice. Victor is fluent in more than a dozen programming languages and holds certifications in ITIL Foundations, Six Sigma Green Belt, Capability Maturity Model Integration and People-Capability Maturity Model.

Prior to entering IT, Victor was a licensed Mobile Intensive Care Paramedic working for large inner city trauma centers in northern New Jersey where he responded to over 25,000 calls for assistance and delivered 16 babies. He taught Emergency Medical Technician and Cardio-Pulmonary Resuscitation training courses for the New Jersey State Department of Health and American Heart Association. While working as a medic, he taught himself how to program in BASIC on a Timex Sinclair 1000 and never looked back.

Table of Contents

Forward

"The Ultimate Guide to the SDLC" is a collection of best practices, activities and processes gathered from leading industrial nations and the minds of some of the greatest thought leaders in Information Technology that ever lived. It consists of a history and comparison of a dozen system development methods, from waterfall through agile; and many of today's recognized best practices and standards all the way to continuous improvement and performance metrics. Its concepts, principles, practices, disciplines, guidelines and models are proven to help deliver successful Information Technology projects and mature organizational practices from ability to capability.

Many authors say their books are a labor of love, but I'll only admit to the labor part. Yes, I love writing, but writing a book is an arduous task and one of the hardest projects I've ever undertaken. In all, I've invested well over a year bringing this project to fruition. This includes over ten months researching, reading and studying and about three and half months writing eight to ten hours a day, six days a week; all the while keeping up with family and parental responsibilities and service to the community. Believe me, it is labor! And it's a labor undertaken with absolutely no assurance of financial reward. So why did I do it? I did it because there is a great need in the Information Technology world for this kind of book. I saw the need and had the availability, wherewithal, passion and drive to fulfill the need; and as far as I can tell, there isn't anything else like it on the market. Even though it's a labor, it is a labor well worth the effort and one that provides a deep satisfaction in knowing this is a job well done.

When I was writing a SDLC for a former employer, I searched high and low and could not find a single reference source that brings everything required into view of what an organization needs to know to guide the development of a SDLC which is exactly what this book does. I don't believe there's anything like it that's ever been written before that uses modern best practices, at least not that I can find. Maybe you know better, but I really believe, or perhaps am self-deceived, that this book is the first of its ilk. When I shared what I was doing with Larry Zucker, a former co-worker and owner of Z Brand Ventures in Raleigh, NC, he said, "Interesting…lots of books out there to tell you where you should be, but not many to tell you how to get there." Larry's comment is spot on! This book is a GPS roadmap for building or maturing a best practice based System Development Life Cycle. Everything you need to know to arrive at the final destination is right here.

If you were to hire a consultant to bring to your organization what this book delivers, you could easily spend $500,000 or more in fees in today's marketplace. Don't believe it? Let's examine a few facts. The estimate is based in US Dollars at a prevailing contractor rate in the range $125-$250 per hour or higher in some cases. You do the math. To cover the broad knowledge areas presented in this book, you would have to contract someone with an expert background and experience with the SDLC at a very high cost. Experts don't come cheap and you probably won't find anyone who intimately knows all of the topics covered in this book. You may find experts in some of the disciplines, but no one who knows it all without charging billable hours for doing at least some research. You may end up needing to hire multiple contractors to cover all of the information in this book.

Let's consider for a moment that you have found someone who can do it all at the mid-point of the scale or $187.50 / hour. The expert begins by researching your company culture, as-is processes and interviewing key personnel. S/he drafts an SDLC, an organizational change management plan, templates, manuals and other artifacts and leads the organization through its vetting, acceptance and adoption. Optimistically, it takes anywhere from six to twelve months to complete the project. For argument's sake, let's again use the mid-point of nine months. Assuming 4 week months, nine months at 40 hours per week is 1,440 hours at $187.50 per hour which equals $270,000. For the full twelve months at the same rate the cost is $390,000. If the contractor is at the high end of the range ($250/hour) a full year costs $520,000. This is only for the cost of the contractor! When you factor in all the overhead of employee participation, the cost for creating and implementing an SDLC and its deliverables and training, the bill can easily be two to three times that amount.

This is an extremely optimistic estimate when you consider some of the alternatives. The Software Engineering Institute published statistics in 2005 that show that since 1992 it has taken organizations a median of 75 months to move from maturity Level 1 to Level 5 with its older software Capability Maturity Model. Imagine paying a contractor at the high rate for 75 months to bring you the collective knowledge that this book brings you. In 6 ¼ years you could easily spend over $3,000,000! Don't misunderstand, I am not guaranteeing that you can achieve a CMMI Level 5 designation by implementing the details of this book. That's not what I'm saying at all. What I am saying is that for the price you'll pay for this book, you will derive incalculable business value from it; and that's not a bad investment at all.

Appreciations

Something that has always been a mystery to me is the number of individuals authors thank in the forwards of their books. I used to wonder how so many people could be involved in writing a single volume. Now I know. As the author, I am a researcher and documentarian of information. As a researcher, I need to confirm facts; confirming facts means reaching out and verifying them with their original sources. Most of the information I gathered originates in the minds of others. I simply collect it and weave it together like a tapestry forming a complete and comprehensive story that makes sense to the reader. Even so, you will encounter original thinking in Chapter 1 where I present my theory of the inextricable linkage and synergies of IT Governance, Project Management and the SDLC—the three-legged stool of IT business value. But before I get into thanking individuals, allow me to acknowledge some of the major reference sources used to frame my thinking as I wrote:

Organizational change management activities and practices are based on materials developed for the Accelerated Implementation Methodology (AIM), a proprietary approach to organizational change management published by Implementation Management Associates (IMA).

Business Analysis activities are grounded upon the foundations established in the *"Business Analysis Body of Knowledge Version 2.0"* (BABOK) published by the International Institute of Business Analysis (IIBA), 3605 Sandy Plains Road, Suite 240-193, Marietta, GA 30066

Project Management activities are based on the *"Guide to the Project Management Body of Knowledge, Fourth Edition"* (PMBOK) published by the Project Management Institute (PMI), 14 Campus Boulevard, Newtown Square, Pennsylvania 19073-3299

Some development and continuous improvement practices are based on public domain sources available through several United States Government entities including, the United States General Accounting Office, the United States Department of the Treasury, the United States Army, the United States Navy, United States Air Force, National Institute of Standards and Technology (NIST) and the National Aeronautics and Space Administration.

Ralph Waldo Emerson is credited with saying, "The glory of friendship is not the outstretched hand, nor the kindly smile, nor the joy of companionship; it is the spiritual inspiration that comes to one when he discovers that someone else believes in him and is willing to trust him with his friendship."

As we turn to recognizing individuals, there are many people I want to express my gratitude to for believing in me and inspiring me with their phone calls, emails and comments attached to my postings on LinkedIn, Facebook and my blogs. You'll never fully understand how much of a comfort and encouragement it is to me to know that you've kept me and this project in your thoughts and prayers. You've helped motivate and focus me when the work became a real chore and I began to lose sight of my goals. You've been honest with me, attentive and adaptable. You've shown that you believe in this work, care for me and accept me for who I am even when my behavior is less than stellar. I'd love to list your names individually so the entire world can know the source of the profound joy you bring. But to do so, I run the risk of unintentionally omitting someone deserving. Please accept this blanket acknowledgment of my appreciation. You all know who you are and I thank you from the bottom of my heart.

This book would not be complete without the influence of others. I have personally communicated with all of these scientists, scholars, academicians and corporate representatives and they have all expressed their gratitude for being included and sometimes offered additional facts that they have allowed me to incorporate within the book's chapters or on the accompanying CD. It is with grateful appreciation that I thank the following for their thought leadership, input or contribution of materials to include either in the book or on the accompanying CD:

- Kara Joiner, Director Client Solutions, Implementation Management Associates (IMA)
- Jacqueline Hansson, IEEE Intellectual Property Rights Coordinator
- John Petlicki, DePaul University's College of Computing and Digital Media
- Dr. Barry W. Boehm, TRW Professor of Software Engineering, Computer Science Department Director, USC Center for Software Engineering
- Arnold George, IABG
- Germany's Federal Office of the Bundeswehr for Information Management and Information Technology and the Federal Ministry of the Interior, Central Office for Information Technology Coordination in the Federal Administration (BMI-KBSt)
- Dr. Kevin Forsberg and Harold Mooz, Co-Principals for the Center for Systems Management
- Jo Ann Lane, Principal at the University of Southern California Center for Systems and Software Engineering
- Craig Larman and Bas Vodde, The Lean Primer
- Keith Ellis, Vice President Marketing & Strategic Alliances, IAG Consulting
- Mike Buckley, Department of Computer Science and Engineering, University at Buffalo, The State University of New York

Finally I want to thank my wife Susan and daughter Victoria to whom this book is dedicated. You are my reason for living. If we were to lose everything in life and you are still there, then all is well and life is good. Susie, you are a great support to me. Thanks for your love and all that you do to keep us happy and comfortable.

I believe with every fiber of my being there is a God and my life is in His hands. I encourage readers to do what I did at the age of twenty-one, invite Him into your heart to take control…then see what He does to get you through life's challenges. I'm thankful to Him for the blessings He has bestowed upon us and the gifts and talents He has given us in order to be munificent to others. Writing is one of these gifts and I hope this book is profitable to you and to your career.

Warmest regards,

Victor M. Font Jr.

This page left intentionally blank

Introduction

Early in 2009, my boss asked me to do something I had never been asked to do before in my 25 year career in Information Technology (IT). A yet to be delivered strategic goal on his plate for the prior two years was to distribute a Systems Development Life Cycle (SDLC) to his organization that is based on current industry best practices. Determined to accomplish this long awaited objective, he asked me to write it. Along with the document, he expects me to develop course materials, an organizational change management strategy and instruct my colleagues in the new practices. In addition to the SDLC, he asks me to develop training materials to establish a Business Analysis Community of Practice. Our Business Analysts need to learn the processes, skills and techniques for the requirements practices documented in the SDLC. This is a huge assignment and my first thought is, *"Where do I begin?"*

At the time, I held the title of Corporate Director of Human Resources Management Systems (HRMS). My team and I supported Oracle HRMS and Payroll for a company of approximately 18,000 employees in the US and Canada. Over the two years we worked together as a team, we became known for process improvement and innovation. The company is a global leader in the automotive aftermarket industry, not only in sales and product variety, but in technology as well. If you don't know what the automotive aftermarket is, it is the business of providing replacement parts and supplies for any kind of vehicle. If it moves and it breaks down, the automotive aftermarket has a part to repair it.

One of the most interesting and important automotive industry metrics used as a forecaster of potential future sales is miles driven. Year over year, sales shadow this vital metric. When miles driven goes down because people aren't traveling as much due to the high price of fuel or the impact of the recession on their lives, it negatively influences sales, margin and net profit—the three-legged stool of shareholder value. With fewer miles driven, fewer parts wear out which means there are less vehicle repairs. With less vehicle repairs, sales decrease. To remain competitive, prices and margins are reduced resulting in declines in net operating income. When net operating income goes down, capital budgets are slashed. Our Chief Information Officer (CIO) often quips, "Friction is our friend."

Even with the vast number of vehicles on the road, the automotive aftermarket is not immune to the impact of the worst worldwide recession since The Great Depression. Whenever there is a downturn in the economy, two corporate groups that seem to bear the brunt of fiscal conservatism are Human Resources and Information Technology. Unless you are actually in the business of IT to generate revenue, in the corporate world, both of these departments are cost centers. Although they are both productivity enhancement enablers, it is often argued that they produce little to no direct bottom line value through their work. For some, they may have been fortunate enough to develop a marketable product or training for resale beyond their corporate boundaries to supplement the revenue stream. Unfortunately for the rest, that's not the case. As senior executives maneuver to address ever changing market conditions, increasingly scarce capital funding is diverted from IT projects into strategic higher priority revenue generating opportunities.

In stark contrast to traditional business management theory, Dr. Howard Rubin[1] said in a presentation given at an October 2009 Gartner Symposium, "The most opportunistic time for technology investment is during an economic downturn; it is the only area in which investment can change the operating profile of an organization—doing so effectively can create an insurmountable competitive gap. Bad IT economics will put you on the wrong side of this gap and may even be creating advantage for your competitors."

To gain competitive advantage during an economic downturn, smart executives invest in IT if they have the confidence in the IT organization to deliver that which is promised; quality products that meet or exceed customer expectations, on time delivery and well managed budgets. For IT organizations to be successful today and tomorrow, they must evolve into values-based cultures that drive high performance, low turnover, and increased productivity without impeding creativity and innovation. The organization must embrace defined, managed, measurable, repeatable and reusable practices that form the blueprint for their overall systems delivery strategy. The blueprint feeds the continuous improvement cycle. It's said in the Six Sigma world, "If you can't measure it, why are you doing it?"

This is why the SDLC is so important. The SDLC provides a framework that describes the activities performed during each phase of a system development project; activities that are defined, managed, measurable, repeatable and reusable; just what the doctor ordered! It endorses standards and practices to ensure consistency across projects and tasks undertaken by different groups within IT such as Telecom, Data Center, System Administration, Quality Assurance, Network, Applications Development and others.

Let me point out that I'm being very careful at this juncture not to use the word "software" when discussing the SDLC. I use the term "system" to emphasize the SDLC's broader impact across all of IT. Undoubtedly, a major focus of any SDLC is software, but when you think of all the projects that are undertaken in an IT organization, every project team has a responsibility to:

---

[1] Gartner Senior Advisor, Founder Rubin Worldwide, MIT CISR Associate, howard.rubin@rubinworldwide.com

- Elicit and analyze requirements
- Develop systems specifications
- Define success metrics
- Produce clear, consistent and unambiguous artifacts
- Deliver products that comply with the highest quality standards that meet or exceed customer expectations
- Transfer knowledge to operational support and maintenance personnel, sometimes to outsourced, off-shore locations
- Train end users and support resources
- Offer post deployment support and maintenance

Are these statements true or false? If true, then consistent reusable processes and practices across the entire IT organization are critical for an organization's absolute success.

You may or may not be familiar with an organization known as SEMAT. SEMAT is an acronym for Software Engineering Method and Theory. The group formed in October 2009. Its purpose is to "support a process to refound software engineering based on a solid theory, proven principles and best practices.[2]" Its 31 founding signatories include such Information Technology luminaries as Ivar Jacobson, Bertrand Meyer, Scott Ambler, Watts Humphrey, Capers Jones and Alistair Cockburn to name but a few. These industry movers and shakers all believe "Software engineering is gravely hampered today by immature practices." And I agree with them!

In an abstract of an article[3] found on the SEMAT website (http://www.semat.org) authored by Ivar Jacobson, Pan Wei Ng and Ian Spence entitled "Enough of Processes - Lets do Practices" we read,

> All modern software development processes try to help project teams conduct their work. While there are some important differences between them, the commonalities are far greater - and understandably, since the end goal of them all is to produce working software quickly and effectively. Thus, it doesn't matter which process you adopt as long as it is adaptable, extensible, and capable of absorbing good ideas, even if they arise from other processes.

> To achieve this kind of flexibility things need to change. The focus needs to shift from the definition of complete processes to the capture of reusable practices. Teams should be able to mix-and-match practices and ideas from many different sources to create effective ways of working, ones that suit them and address their risks.

---

[2] Source: http://www.semat.org
[3] Ivar Jacobson, Pan Wei Ng, Ian Spence: "Enough Process - Let's Do Practices", in Journal of Object Technology, vol. 6, no. 6, July-August 2007, pp. 41-66, http://www.jot.fm/issues/issue_2007_07/column5

This is exactly what this SDLC accomplishes. Researching nearly full time for ten months, I looked at IT best practices recognized by leading industrial nations and some of the most well-known IT thought leaders from the latter half of the 20th and the beginning of the 21st centuries. Vetting these best practices with over 50 people within our organization, we debated and agreed to a best in breed SDLC model that provides the kind of flexibility needed to drive business value in rapidly changing and competitive environments. The model is based on commonalities found extending across a host of different methods and approaches.

With all the books read and websites visited, I found one general theme that troubled me. All of them assume that an organization has a SDLC in the first place. Experientially, I know this isn't always the case. Many of the books written address a single area of competency focus such as requirements, quality assurance or metrics. Or the books are so theoretical and academic in nature; no IT professional that I know would be interested in purchasing them unless they are studying at a post-graduate level. They certainly don't make handy desk references.

The websites also focus on single methods. There are sites that provide SDLC documents that are nothing more than giant policy and procedure manuals or process diagrams for a specific development philosophy. I never came across one book or website that gives you a complete SDLC that can be adopted for your own internal use. Nor did I find anything that teaches the steps necessary to build a SDLC. That is what differentiates this book. The research brings together best practices from a variety of sources to give you a ready-to-go blueprint for an organizational SDLC framework that is flexible, reusable and "capable of absorbing good ideas" to improve it over time.

For most of my corporate life, I've worked in HR systems, as a developer, technical manager, and director, progressing through the ranks in influence, scope, authority, and responsibility. For 9 years, I worked for a major global pharmaceutical company. In the 13 years prior, I was an independent contractor and entrepreneur, working for major companies such as JP Morgan Bank on Wall Street, AT&T Consumer Sales Division in Liberty Corner, NJ, SB Thomas (the English muffin people), Austin and Merritt Insurance and Warner-Lambert.

To the best of my knowledge, none of these companies had a written SDLC at the time I worked for them, at least none that I had ever had the privilege of reading. It wasn't until I was promoted to Director at the pharmaceutical company and moved to their research and development division, that I ever saw a documented SDLC. That was after almost 18 years in the IT business! While there, I joined a continuous process improvement team to help further distill the division's best practices and refine the SDLC with continuous improvement metrics

It doesn't matter if you're in a small mom and pop IT shop or a multi-divisional international entity. You have certain processes and practices you follow when you develop and deliver a system to a customer. Whether you realize it or not, those practices and processes are the foundation of your SDLC. It doesn't matter whether they are documented or not and whether you follow them for every project or not. These form the basis of how you do things to deliver a product. In many circumstances they are habitual in-grained behaviors you inherently follow.

Please ask yourself three questions:

1. Does my SDLC help me achieve a successful project and deliver a product that meets or exceeds my customers' demands every single time I try?

2. Are my processes and practices perfect in every way?

3. Am I measuring what I am doing?

I can think of a host of other questions to help you discover the efficacy of your practices. But for now, if you answered yes to all three questions, you probably don't need this book. Put it back on the shelf you're browsing from and walk away and enjoy the fruit of your labor. You are to be celebrated as the IT professional we all should emulate. But if you're anything like the rest of us who acknowledge we have room to improve and desire to keep our customers coming back to us time and time again, this book is for you. Learning is a lifelong process and sharing our knowledge with others is a privilege.

Let's examine a case study. A small company began experiencing explosive growth in early 2004. At the time, the IT department consisted of approximately 30 people. The singular focus of the company's senior leaders had been sales growth, not building out the technology infrastructure. They made minimal investments into IT and the IT staff did everything, from custom programming to hardware support, data entry and report generation.

In subsequent years, as the company matured, senior management decided to fortify their infrastructure to support future growth. They heavily invested major capital in Supply Chain, Demand Planning and Forecasting, Distribution, Enterprise Resource Planning, Human Resources, Payroll, Financial Systems, Point of Sale, and Business Intelligence. The IT staff grew to over 300 with departments for telecom, network, data center, database administration, system administration, quality assurance, project management, help desk and technical communications. They formed a Program Management Office which helped define their IT governance practices and managed their project management staff. They put tools into place to allow their project management and reporting to be more efficient and meaningful.

Despite these successes and growth, there was no documented SDLC! Ask for any kind of system documentation and you get blank stares or nervous giggles because everyone is so busy meeting the needs of the business that nobody ever has the time or inclination to focus on developing consistent, managed, measurable and repeatable processes for IT's sake. The majority of projects never reach a state of total completion. Turnover documents? What are they?

Over time, each system development group created their own method for doing things. All of the different methods eventually converged on their only documented and measured process: change control. Doing things differently resulted in project delays and failures. Projects pervasively overran budgets. The organization became the target of major criticism from the company's senior most executives. The executives lost their faith and trust in the organization to deliver. The IT organization worked very hard, but they weren't working very smartly.

Even something that should be consistent across an organization like business requirements documentation is handled differently by the various groups. In many cases, it's difficult if not impossible to understand the artifacts being produced unless you are an integral member of the project team. The documents are rife with ambiguous thoughts and requirements, and undefined acronyms and business terms. Key success metrics and traceability might as well be foreign concepts. What is called a business requirements document in one group is a detailed system design to another. A requirements workshop consists of inviting business users to a meeting and asking, "What are your requirements?" This is their primary notion of facilitated requirements elicitation.

Defective systems and code roll into production regularly causing production outages and business disruptions. This results in the generation of a high number of emergency and exception change requests. An emergency change request is apropos when production is down and the system needs to be brought up rapidly. When production deployments are the root cause of business interruptions, there is a BIG problem in the process that needs to be addressed.

Exceptions are change controls that are implemented in less than the 5-day lead time required by the company's internal change management procedure. The most common reason for emergency change requests is poor planning on the part of either the business or the project team. Sometimes exceptions are legitimate as in the case of a newly issued tax patch for payroll or some other regulatory compliance issue, but poor planning as the stimulus for exceptions is unacceptable.

In the first of a three-year monitoring period, emergency and exception change controls accounted for 49% of the company's change requests. During the year their development teams submitted 1,111 changes with an average success rate of 92%, 545 of them were emergencies or exceptions. If we count the emergencies and exceptions as first try failures, the true success rate is 51%.

The statistics didn't change much by the third year; in fact, while a slight overall improvement is noted, one of the metrics actually got worse. In that third year, they had 1,979 changes submitted with an 88% success rate, a 4% drop over the first year. The 12% failure rate is disturbing. It means that 237 changes didn't work the first time a system or code was implemented in production! On the bright side, the number of emergencies and exceptions are reduced to 36% which is better, but still exceeds the strategic goal of 30% (10% emergency and 20% exception). Even so, it means 712 changes fell outside of the defined process metric. If we count these exceptions and emergencies as first failures as we did in the first year example the real success rate is 52%. At least the company is consistent!

You would think that after measuring these processes for three years, there would have been a significant improvement observed. The lack of a SDLC is squarely to blame for the poor results. You can't improve processes, even if you can measure them, if everyone is doing something different.

You might be thinking to yourself, "Yes, but that's a small company with a growing and under developed staff. That wouldn't happen with big corporations."

How wrong you are! Think again.

Company size and maturity do not correlate to the need for standards. Moving from ability to capability maturity requires them regardless of structural construct. If you want to do IT right in any size organization, the adoption of consistent, measurable, repeatable and reusable standards and practices is compulsory.

The pharmaceutical company consisted of 120,000 employees spread across 5 divisions located in 80 countries. There is a central Corporate IT group that is responsible for the overall common architecture, infrastructure and distribution of discretionary IT funds. The other divisions are Sales and Marketing, Manufacturing and Distribution, Research and Development, Consumer and Confectionary. Consumer and Confectionary were eventually divested, but were still part of the mix when I worked there.

Historically, each division had their own unique needs that weren't met by Corporate IT. They responded by forming their own divisional IT departments with autonomous business unit funded budgets. These organizations grew fiercely independent from each other. Each IT group developed processes so varied that you would never believe they were all part of the same company. Communication across divisional boundaries was virtually non-existent. Business users were frustrated because of the lack of consistent IT practices. Each division built or bought applications and systems apart from Corporate IT. Redundancy and duplication of effort ruled the day. Shadow IT organizations staffed by contingent workers popped up everywhere. It was chaotic! It was impossible to accurately account for IT spend because there were so many sources of outbound money.

To give you an idea of just how bad things were, when I became a lead architect representing Corporate HR to the Identity and Access Management project, there were 17 distinct corporate directories deployed around the organization. Each one received their data from different source systems. None of them were in sync and all of them displayed different information. My goal was to reduce that number to one directory fed directly from PeopleSoft, our enterprise HR System and the only source of truth for people data.

We had just finished completing the global deployment of PeopleSoft and knew the data was accurate and current. Because we went global with a single HR system, we also had Safe Harbor compliance to deal with which means no forward transfer of data apart from the central source system. The interfaces from all the ancillary systems feeding these directories had to go. If the company wanted a people directory, the various support teams were given no choice but to come to the single source of truth for their data feeds.

In the end we compromised on three directories all fed from the HR system. It fell short of the goal, but was acceptable. We managed to retire 14 of the 17 systems at considerable savings to the company. If we had had a common core set of consistent and manageable IT practices across the divisions in the first place driven from the corporate level, we may not have ever ended up with so many directories.

Several things happened to change the picture. We got a new CIO who focused on building process and consistency across the company. We still had the divisional CIOs to deal with, but this is the first time we had a strong leader in Corporate. He was determined to break down the barriers of communication that existed across the divisions. He commissioned a number of "Just Do It" teams composed of divisional IT leaders to focus on various aspects of process improvement. I was assigned to work on the team that designed and chartered the IT Architecture Council. After the Council was commissioned, I became the first representative from Corporate HR to serve on its board which was composed of representatives from every legitimate IT group from throughout the company. We eventually eliminated shadow IT.

At first, we focused on architecture across the enterprise. Every project any division was undertaking had to be vetted by the Council. We assessed impact, cost, infrastructure fit and whether other business units could benefit from the project. For the first time, all the divisions were communicating and we were successfully able to reduce redundancy and lower the cost of operations. That was the first year.

The second year our role changed somewhat. The CIO shifted gears and had us focus on the overall IT budget and distribution of $70 million in discretionary project dollars. We literally functioned as a PMO and IT Governance Council rolled into one. We were so busy maintaining financial order that we couldn't focus on architecture and IT began to suffer again because of it.

The CIO recognized this weakness and commissioned a sister council to handle the financials so we could return to our first calling: technology architecture and standards.

Regardless of our successes with architecture and program management, we did not have common practices across the enterprise. The divisions, while now communicating, maintained their independence. One thing we learned through better communication was that people were beginning to stand up and notice the Research and Development Division. They became recognized as a model for sound IT practices. An opportunity arose for me to take a Director position with the division's Functional Support Lines. Then I found out why they became so successful. They are the only division in the company that implemented and documented a SDLC. For the first time in my career, I had access to one.

The division's enterprise architect authored it and it was very impressive. She and her group built an enterprise architecture model based on the Zachman framework. Her SDLC is structured around her architecture model. She is also the first person I have ever worked with who established a quality assurance group reporting into her department. Her introduction of consistent, manageable, repeatable and reusable processes to the organization, policed by a top notch QA team, resulted in tremendous benefit. I can't think of one project that ran over budget or schedule after we assimilated the practices.

The key factor in the success of the SDLC deployment is organizational readiness. At the R&D division, the organization wanted it. The organization asked for it. It was delivered as promised guided by a superb organizational change management strategy. It succeeded. A strong organizational change management strategy is absolutely necessary when deploying a SDLC.

In contrast, here is another case study highlighting one company's readiness to deploy a SDLC. The CIO commissioned a survey to "test the waters" for deploying a SDLC. To protect the respondents' anonymity, the survey was deployed to the entire IT organization through Zoomerang.com. It consists of four closed questions. The questions and their responses are:

- Have you ever worked in an organization with a defined SDLC?
    - Yes – 46%
    - No – 44%
    - What's an SDLC? – 10%

- Have you ever participated in the roll out of a SDLC?
    - Yes – 29%
    - No – 71%

- What is your commitment level to the SDLC?
  - High – 61%
  - Medium – 29%
  - Low – 10%

- Do you believe the SDLC will impose a rigorous, restrictive engineering methodology to guide and govern the system development process?
  - Yes – 15%
  - No – 85%

Out of the 250 people to whom this was sent, only 87 responded. This is a disappointing response rate, but statistically significant nonetheless representing 35% of the organization. One reason this result is so unsatisfactory is because the SDLC is the CIO's response to the results of an earlier employee satisfaction survey.

A year earlier, the company went through a reduction in force and IT was hit pretty hard. Morale was at its lowest point ever. Everyone knew it, but no one liked to talk about it. The CIO wanted to do something to boost employee perceptions about the company and improve the atmosphere in the general working environment. First, he needed to understand what everyone was thinking so he could respond appropriately. In that survey, which had a 70% response rate, the #1 dissatisfier across the organization is the lack of consistent IT processes. "Lack of process is killing us," some wrote. Second to the lack of process is the lack of communication across the various IT groups.

From the first survey, you could almost believe the organization is ready for change. It sounds like they are asking for it. The CIO addressed the #1 issue by deploying a SDLC and what happens? A whopping 39% say they have medium to low commitment. Another 15% believe the SDLC imposes a rigorous, restrictive engineering methodology to guide and govern the system development process. And finally, 54% have either never worked for an organization that had a SDLC or doesn't even know what a SDLC is to begin with. This last metric is okay because people can learn what they don't know. On the other hand, this could very well become an organizational change management nightmare if the right steps aren't observed early in the process.

Organizational Change Management and the SDLC

Since we've touched on the topic of organizational change management, let's shift gears and discuss it briefly. There are many organizational change management methods out there. Do a search on Google for "organizational change management method" and you'll return 18,900,000 web pages! The website 12Manage.com lists 155 different organizational change management methods. As I reviewed their list, I quickly observed that there are at least two others that I know of that aren't in their directory. But that's okay; they have a link to click if you want to add missing change management methods to their listing page.

I am a student of the AIM Methodology of organizational change management. AIM is an acronym for the Accelerated Implementation Methodology, a proprietary approach developed and perfected by Implementation Management Associates, Inc. (http://www.imaworldwide.com). The pharmaceutical company included me in a pilot AIM training program after their Learning and Organizational Development group decided to deploy the methodology to the Research and Development Division. I became a vocal advocate and champion of the process, even sending one of my direct reports to school to become an instructor.

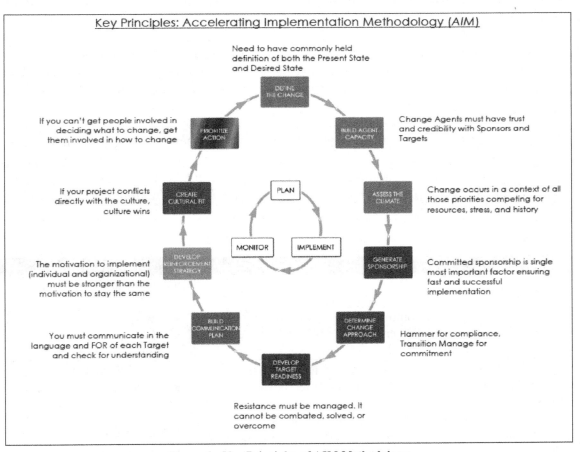

Figure 1 - Key Principles of AIM Methodology

Don't confuse this AIM, with the other popular AIM, Oracle's Application Implementation Methodology. Oracle's AIM is essentially a legacy SDLC for the Oracle applications platform. The two AIMs couldn't be more different. Also, don't confuse organizational change management with project change management. Change management in a project context is very different from organizational change management. Project change management is a process by which changes to projects are formally introduced, vetted, approved, tabled or denied. An organizational change management method is not typically part of a SDLC or project management method although elements of organizational change management, such as communications plans, may be.

Organizational change management is about people's behavior. Organizations are comprised of people and their behaviors formulate the accomplishments of the organization. Organizational change management explores behaviors to achieve greater results in performance which in turn drive bottom line value.

Just as development methods share commonalities, so do change management methods. Regardless of the method you choose to follow, the core fundamentals of organizational change management are the same and must be observed if you want to achieve a successful SDLC implementation.

IMA Worldwide has graciously granted their permission to extract the content of their materials to use in this book. They've also provided a host of change management related materials on the accompanying CD including *"The Mini Guide to INSTALLATION VERSUS IMPLEMENTATION: How to Avoid the Trap of Premature Project Completion and Accelerate Return on Investment."*

AIM Element	What	Deliverable(s)
Define the Change	Create alignment with a clear and commonly held definition of both the Present State and Desired State.	Business Case for Action • What • Why • Consequences of not implementing
Build Agent Capacity	Develop competence and distribution of Agents in impacted business areas.	• AIM Introductory Program • AIM Project Workshop • Coaching
Assess the Climate	Identify implementation strengths and barriers as they exist in current organizational climate.	Data generation and appropriate action planning
Generate Sponsorship	Make sure leaders are demonstrating	Sponsor Strategy

AIM Element	What	Deliverable(s)
	the proper expressed, modeled, and reinforced behaviors down and across the organization.	• Key Role Map • Assessment • Contracting
Determine Change Approach	Determine which components of the change are compliance or commitment driven and identify others' Frame of Reference (FOR).	Sponsor reinforcement of compliance and commitment elements.
Develop Target Readiness	Identify, measure and manage the sources of resistance to the change among those that are most impacted.	Readiness Strategy • Individual Readiness Assessment • Data feedback and action planning • Impact mapping
Build Communication Plan	Communicate the right message to the right people using the right vehicles.	Communication Strategy • Multiple vehicles • Two-way • Open, honest, and direct • Feedback loop (content and process)
Development Reinforcement Strategy	Alignment of reinforcement mechanisms with performance expectations.	Reinforcement Strategy • Reward • Negative consequences • Effort
Create Cultural Fit	Align the change with the culture.	Awareness of effective and ineffective cultural elements relating to implementation success
Prioritize Action	Involve people throughout. Even in compliance driven change when people cannot be involved in what the change is… involve them in "how" it gets implemented.	Implementation Plan • At a minimum, this must include a Business Case as well as Sponsor, Readiness, Reinforcement and Communication strategies

Figure 2 – Source: AIM Methodology Quick Reference[4]

The results of the earlier mentioned case study survey are not really out of line with typical change management statistics. As poor as we may think they are, they're much better than what you can typically expect when implementing a change. Studies show that for any organizational change 20% of your employees will be for it no matter what that change may be. Another 20% will be against it because some people don't like change no matter how beneficial. They are

---

[4] Materials © 2008 IMA. Used with Permission

comfortable where they are and loathe stepping out of their comfort zone. The other 60% are the fence sitters. These are the ones who adopt a "wait and see" or "what's in it for me" attitude. This is the target of your change management strategy, the 60% who can go either way. In the case study, the company had 60% in favor. That's a significant approval rating, but as human beings we have a tendency to focus our attention on the negative and overlook the fact that a 60% approval rating is a job well done.

Unfortunate as it may be, the 20% who are always opposed to change may very well find themselves at the bottom of the performance evaluation heap. They may have developed a reputation for not being a team player. They might find themselves being placed on performance improvement plans or worse, managed out of the organization. The perception they exude is that they aren't happy working where they are.

It is certainly okay to vocalize concerns you have about a particular change during the vetting process. You might instinctively see something about the change that others may be blind to. Be a leader! Anytime you seek to influence the thinking, behavior or development of people, you are taking on the role of a leader. Make sure your opinion is heard. Your influence on a particular situation could save your company the cost of making a drastic mistake. But once the company decides upon a strategy, be prudent and support it even though you may personally disagree. That's a fundamental attribute of effective teamwork. Supporting an idea you may have initially disagreed with means you become a promoter for the change. Never let your direct reports see you waver in your support of your company's values and strategic direction. It's a career limiting move.

Change management starts at the very top of the organizational structure. For IT, this starts with the CIO or CTO as he or she defines the strategic vision and goals. The CIO's goals are aligned with the overall strategic goals of the organization as determined by the Board of Directors and the CEO with his/her senior staff. To successfully deploy a SDLC, it must be a strategic goal of the senior most leaders. As strategic goals cascade throughout the organization, it creates alignment with a clear and common language and understanding for the change.

Once goals are defined and distributed, assessing the organization's readiness for change is the next step. How do you do that? Surveys like the one highlighted in the case study are a good method. The goal of an organizational readiness survey is to uncover the barriers that exist within your organization's climate, both current and historical. Barriers that may have impeded the progress of previous changes must be discussed to capture lessons learned. You will also want to uncover implementation strengths. What has gone right in the past that we can do again?

Referring to our case study once more, the greatest barrier the company faces is the need for education. That's crystal clear because 54% have either never worked for an organization that had a SDLC or don't even know what a SDLC is to begin with. What do you think would happen if the SDLC were implemented without understanding this critical need? For one thing, the company might invest funds into developing the wrong training program, for all the right reasons, but the wrong program nonetheless. Never underestimate the value of the organizational readiness survey.

Identifying the approach you'll take to implementing change follows the readiness assessment. You really only have two choices here. You can force your hand and generate compliance using the hammer approach or you can choose to build commitment and buy-in by managing the transition. On the surface, you may think the hammer approach is a little heavy handed and it may not be a good fit with your personal values. There are reasons where the hammer approach is the right approach. What if the change is due to regulatory, HR or safety compliance?

Do you remember Sarbanes-Oxley in the US, Basel II in Europe, AS 3806 - Compliance Programs in Australia and the Data Protection Act 1998 in the UK? Complying with regulatory agencies is a worldwide concern and protecting your human assets from missteps is obligatory. Before you start doing business in countries other than your native home, you must understand those countries' regulatory compliance issues and effect the change in your own organization. Where compliance is concerned, telling your people they must perform a certain action by a specific date is the right thing to do. But it must be communicated effectively; otherwise, you face the prospect of finding yourself on the receiving end of some unwelcome resistance.

Let me share a personal example. As a young man, I worked as a quality control inspector for a company in Jersey City, New Jersey that manufactured miniature gold wire used to connect integrated circuit chips to their boards. I didn't know it at the time, but the company employed lead in their manufacturing processes. At one point during my employment, the HR ordered all employees to get mandatory blood tests. They never explained why the blood tests were necessary; they just said you had to go get one. They used the hammer approach and threatened that if we didn't comply with the order by a certain date we would get fired.

Normally, I would have fallen into the 20% who would comply with the change. This time, I fell into the 20% (actually more like 80% company-wide) that opposed the blood testing. A few months earlier I had become certified as an Emergency Medical Technician in the State of New Jersey. I knew from my Medico-Legal training that no one has the right to force medical procedures on anyone without informed consent unless the person is unconscious or at risk of death. And I was neither. Unless I knew why, I wasn't going to have my body violated by a forced blood test, even under the threat of losing my job. Besides, back then I used to pass out when I got needles and I was afraid of embarrassing myself. Thankfully, I've outgrown both the passing out and fear.

Questions flew through my mind, "What is the company exposing us to that they don't want us to know?" When I and others began to refuse the blood testing for the same reasons, HR decided to soften the hammer approach and began conducting walking tours around the campus pointing out the dangerous chemicals on-site and explaining to everyone what the blood testing was for and why it was important. The compliance rate shot up to nearly 100%. Some people did get fired for non-compliance which was sad. The company had chosen the right method to address the safety concern, but executed it poorly. Effective communication acquires buy-in and commitment especially with the hammer approach.

The second approach, transition management, requires more time to adapt a change. The organization becomes increasingly focused and the additional time allows for course correction along the way before implementation. You'll gain greater buy-in, produce less waste and achieve greater precision in your implementations. Transition management is particularly effective when implementing changes in customer service, quality assurance and developmental paradigms such as the SDLC.

Organizational change will not happen efficiently without the right sponsorship. We've already talked about strategic goals cascading from the top down. Sponsorship is making certain the right people are doing the right things at the right times to demonstrate their commitment and ownership of the change. You'll need an Executive Sponsor who has sufficient authority to authorize the change and commit the resources to make it happen. Then you'll need Champions who can influence the organization's commitments levels and Change Agents who'll plan and execute the implementation.

When my boss told me to write the SDLC, I knew there wasn't any way I could ever accomplish all of that work in six months by myself. I no longer had direct reports so I knew I was going to need to draft volunteers to work with me to get the job done. I served as the Champion and lead Change Agent. The true change agents are the army of volunteers supporting me. The first thing I did was hold an organization wide meeting where I unveiled my approach. I asked for feedback and then formed eight teams, one each for Requirements Maturity, Development Guidelines and Standards, Organizational Change Management, Documentation Quality, Deployment and Implementation, Quality Assurance, Technology Tools and Continuous Improvement Reporting. Forty-three people volunteered to fill the teams.

I also facilitated a team of SDLC Governors to oversee the activities. This team is composed of the heads of Quality Assurance, the Program Management Office and Directors of several other areas in the organization such as Application Development and Infrastructure. This temporary body would eventually evolve into a permanent review team after the implementation to assure the SDLC continued to service the company's needs in the best ways possible. The team's mandate is to review continuous improvement metrics and existing practices at least twice a year. They are authorized to adapt the SDLC to meet changing business needs and recommend policy and procedure changes to the CIO.

To fully realize your change management strategy, you need to make sure your change fits your culture. You'll also need detailed reinforcement and communication plans. Cultural fit is as individual as companies themselves. Every organization has its own variety of cultures and sub-cultures. Most businesses establish a target company-wide culture through their mission statement, vision, values and leader behaviors. Senior management demonstrates the cultural norms as they interpret these tenets. How these creeds flow down and become the organization's cultural norms may differ from group to group within a company just as strategic goals start at the top and evolve to fit each group's contribution to the overall strategy. There is no one-size fits all approach to cultural fit. There are tactics however that can guide your moves.

First, define the cultural dimensions of each group impacted by your change. For the SDLC, this is your entire IT organization, senior management and your business users and customers. The SDLC represents a broad sweeping change. It is important to first focus on the "low hanging fruit." Exploit the aspects of the change that produce the highest yield and lowest risk. Take advantage of any opportunity to lead with results rather than rhetoric. Altogether avoid or reduce the initiatives that are more about image and not reality.

Each of your target groups need to have sponsors who are capable of identifying the cultural characteristics that support the change as well as the values, behaviors and "unwritten rules" that resist the change. Positively reinforce and emphasize the behaviors that support the change. Provide high visibility rewards and recognition for attaining the desired state.

Regardless of how effective your positive reinforcement is, you will face cultural resistance. Someone once asked me, "Why is it necessary to have a company-wide SDLC? We all do things now that are effective for us, why change?" This individual was a member of one of the working teams building and vetting the SDLC processes. His question caught me off guard. He didn't understand the big picture even though he was serving as a change agent and involved with the very construction of the SDLC. As I thought things through, I realized this question is a direct result of my failure to effectively communicate the vision to the change agents.

For each major source of cultural resistance, you need to discover the answers to these three questions:

1. What are the values, behaviors and "unwritten rules" that are motivating the resistance?
2. What is it about the culture that reinforces the "unwritten rules?"
3. What is it about our system that rewards the "bad" behaviors?

Armed with this intelligence, you can then work to define and implement specific changes that reduce or eliminate the cultural dimensions that reinforce change adversity and execute those that reward the new behaviors. Develop a positive reinforcement plan that is stronger than the motivation to keep the status quo. It requires significantly more sponsorship attention, discipline and stamina to inspire a group to move from "discomfort and resistance" to "opportunity and need." The sponsors must "walk the talk" and visibly display the new behaviors even if they are individually painful.

Consider offering financial rewards as part of your positive reinforcement plan such as a salary increase, bonus, prize or perk for demonstrating the new behaviors. Apply the positive rewards immediately after observing the performance of the new behaviors. Celebrate early successes and wins. Do whatever you can to make it more difficult to continue to operate in the old state.

Build an effective communication plan that explains the objectives and rationale, the time frame and the cost of not changing. Implement the communication plan early and communicate often. Send out frequent progress updates. Focus the organization's attention forward and generate an excitement about the new changes to the SDLC. Commission surveys or walk around the floor to learn if people understand the message. Are they getting it? Keep your communications credible, comprehensive and clear.

We've only touched upon a few aspects of organizational change management. There are a lot of moving parts to rolling out a SDLC. An organizational change management strategy is much broader than the few examples I've presented here, but for a SDLC implementation, it is absolutely essential.

You might be thinking to yourself right now, "Wow! Organizational change management is a lot of work. Why should I bother?" Or, you may be thinking as my change agent did, "I already have practices that work for me even if they aren't best in breed."

The answer is simple. The Balanced Scorecard Collaborative published the following statistics:[5]

- 90% of all companies fail to execute strategy successfully
- Only 5% of the workforce understands their company strategy

The Gartner Group said, "$75 billion spent annually on failed IT projects and poor management is the culprit."

An 11 year study by Kotter and Heskett[6] demonstrates the correlation between change adaptive companies to their revenues and stock value. The results of the study revealed:

---

[5] Source: IMA Worldwide
[6] John P. Kotter & James L. Heskett, Corporate Culture & Performance (Free Press 1992),

	Revenues	Net Income	Stock Price
Change adaptive companies	602% up	756% up	901% up
S&P Index			265% up
Companies not adaptive to change	166% up	1% up	74% up

What this tells us is that the shareholder value of companies practicing sound organizational change management principles outpaced the S&P Index over the 11 year period by 340%. Think of the possibilities when a sound change management strategy is used to implement sound IT practices. Do you think you can match these results? That's a good reason to bother and it also leads us to our first principle.

> **Principle #1: "An effective organizational change management strategy is essential to the success of the SDLC."**

IT Governance and the SDLC

What has the SDLC got to do with IT Governance?

It has long been the tradition of board-level executives to defer all key IT decisions to the company's IT professionals. The truth is that many board-level executives don't understand IT well enough to manage IT effectively; and IT professionals don't understand business initiatives well enough to decide how to invest in them. Deferring key decisions to the IT staff often leads to disconnects between the board's strategic goals and real business initiatives and the investments IT makes. It leads to frustration at all levels.

IT governance is a business-driven function which focuses on the investment and prioritization of IT systems, their performance, risk management and enhancing a company's competitiveness. It's about ensuring IT investments harmonize with the enterprise's strategic priorities. It's about IT demonstrating to senior leadership they are receiving acceptable value in return for making IT investments.

In June of 2005, I attended a summer session on IT Governance and Leadership at the MIT Sloan School of Management Center for Information Systems Research (CISR) in Cambridge Massachusetts. The course was facilitated by Peter Weill and Jeanne W. Ross. Peter is the director of CISR and Jeanne is a Principal Research Scientist. Together they authored the book *"IT Governance"* published in 2000 by Harvard Business School Press. The book is about "How

Top Performers Manage IT Decision Rights for Superior Results." It is written for "concerned officers of the enterprise (CEO, CFO, COO, and other senior managers) looking for practical guidelines to improve their returns from IT investments."

According to Weill and Ross, "Top-performing enterprises succeed where others fail by implementing effective IT governance to support their strategies. For example, firms with above-average IT governance following a specific strategy (for example, customer intimacy) had more than 20 percent higher profits than firms with poor governance following the same strategy."

All companies have some sort of IT governance. Effective IT governance includes well defined and documented processes for work uptake, decision making, budgeting and estimating resources, approvals, IT value realization, project reporting and change management. Many IT governance committees are comprised of the senior most leaders from all strategic areas of the business, not just IT leaders. With a finite enterprise budget, there is competition for capital project dollars. There must be a governance process in place to assure that the right projects are getting the right amount of investment at the right time to improve bottom line profitability and shareholder value.

Weill and Ross assert that effective IT governance answers three questions:

1. What decisions must be made?
2. Who should make these decisions?
3. How will we make and monitor these decisions?

To further explain the first question, they say, "Every enterprise must address five interrelated IT decisions: IT principles, IT architecture, IT infrastructure, business application needs, and IT investment and prioritization."

The SDLC figures prominently in executing the answers to all of the interrelated decisions above with the lone exception of IT principles. IT principles are subordinate to corporate principles established at the enterprise level. They support or enable strategic company business goals, guide the development and implementation of the SDLC and steer the decision making process in the other four areas.

Questions surrounding IT investment and prioritization cannot be fully answered until at least one practice area of the SDLC is executed and at least partially concluded. That area is performing the processes and practices governing requirements elicitation and analysis. We're going to talk about the requirements process in detail in the Chapters 3 through 6, but for now let it suffice to say that we've discovered our second principle:

When discussing investment opportunities at governance meetings, senior managers invariably ask: "How much will the project cost us?" In the early phases of opportunity talks many IT leaders respond with the "SWAG" (Scientific Widely Aimed Guess) based on experiential supposition. Later, after governance approves a deeper investigation into the cost, IT leadership returns to governance with a slightly more predictable estimate known as a ROM or Rough Order of Magnitude, based on nothing more than the research they've done from talking to vendors and presuming what their resources will be needed. They don't even have enough information at this point to distribute a formal Request for Information (RFI). Returning to governance, they supply a statement of work documenting what they believe is required, a Return on Investment (ROI) calculation based on the ROM, resource plan and projected schedule. If all goes well, governance is impressed with the projected derived business value and ROI and approves the project.

Nobody up to this point has gathered any of the actual requirements from the business users. The discussions thus far have all been very high level. This is highly ineffective IT Governance in action. You may also say this is IT Governance inaction. Ineffectual governance processes often lead down the path of conducting requirements elicitation and analysis early in the project lifecycle but only after the project is approved and funded. This is a bad decision and one that leads to more problems for IT leadership down the line. Hopefully, your governance processes don't follow this line of thinking.

When Business Analysts start the requirements process after the project approval and kick-off, it doesn't take too long to discover the original investment estimates were way too low. Now that the true business requirements are known, the project team realizes the scope to deliver the necessary functionality to the business is much broader than they thought. What happens as the project proceeds several months down the road is that IT leadership goes back to governance and asks for more money to complete what they started and explains why the original timeline has to be extended. Governance either reluctantly responds to the increase in funding or trashes the project altogether. Whatever the case, IT leadership loses credibility with senior management.

Do you think this scenario is farfetched? It's not. I've worked in organizations that have followed this exact process and have witnessed it time and time again. Senior leadership's loss of trust and credibility in the IT organization is always the result. It is a difficult if not nearly impossible obstacle to overcome. Trust and credibility can be regained over time, but it takes a lot more than continuing with the same processes that got you into trouble in the first place. It often requires replacing the senior IT staff and embarking upon a long journey of IT business process transformation.

An effective approach to governance includes performing some requirements elicitation and analysis before submitting the final project proposal/request. This is a little tricky because it requires investment. Depending on how large the project, the requirements process may require a few weeks or months to conclude. When you present your initial project proposal to governance include an estimate to conduct the analysis or a feasibility study. Argue if you have to for the importance of this step. Once the analysis is carried out there is enough empirical data to more accurately estimate the investment. But the question now is, "How much of the requirements do I need to gather during this first pass? Do I have to document everything?"

Vilfredo Federico Damaso Pareto was an Italian industrialist, sociologist, economist, and philosopher born in Italy in July 1848. He made a number of important contributions to economics, particularly in the study of income distribution and the analysis of individuals' choices. He introduced the concept of Pareto efficiency and helped develop the field of microeconomics. He also was the first to discover that income follows a Pareto distribution, which is a power law probability distribution. The Pareto Principle was named after him and built on observations such as that 80% of the land in Italy was owned by 20% of the population. The Pareto principle (also known as the 80-20 rule, the law of the vital few or the principle of factor sparsity) states for many events roughly 80% of the effects come from 20% of the causes.

What has the Pareto principle got to do with IT governance, requirements elicitation and investment decisions? If we apply the Pareto principle to investment value and requirements, the resulting theorem says, "80% of the business value of an investment comes from 20% of the requirements." This tells us that we don't have to capture all of the requirements in the initial pass. We only need to capture the major requirements in a quantity sufficient to extrapolate a fairly accurate resource allocation projection. A general rule of thumb of IT investment estimation is to pad the estimate with contingency funds anyway. I've seen contingency budgets account for as much as 25% of an overall project estimate. Those are the projects where there was no upfront requirements analysis performed and those projects ended up running over budget regardless. Capture the requirements early and you have a much better chance of project success. We're going to spend quite a bit of time looking at requirements practices in later chapters.

The Project Management Method and the SDLC

Many people are confused over the difference between a project management method and the SDLC. Some believe a project management method is a subset of the SDLC and some believe the inverse, that the SDLC is a subset of a project management method. The truth lies somewhere in between. In terms of importance to a project, the SDLC and a project management method are co-equals which complement each other. Together they harmonize to form a complete methodology for delivering high quality products to our customers that meet or exceed their expectations. Neither can stand on its own to deliver high value to the business. They each have different roles in support of business initiatives. Throughout the life cycle both of these methods work together to achieve business goals, drive the value equation and progress organizational maturity. Though their activities differ greatly, they interrelate and harmonize to produce superior results.

A project management method provides detailed instructions for the discipline of planning, organizing, controlling, reporting and managing project resources to successfully complete project goals and objectives. It includes all of the activities for managing a project. A project is temporal in nature. It has a defined beginning and end. The project management method begins with project inception and closes when its product is delivered. When a project is over, the project manager moves onto something new.

The SDLC provides a framework that describes the activities performed during each phase of a systems development project. The SDLC is about quality, consistency and product delivery. It is about the realization of a product's requirements. Products are of a more permanent nature than a project because products continue to exist long after the projects that delivered them have closed. Therefore, the SDLC's framework provides guidelines for supporting the product post production. Guidelines include practices for knowledge transfer, training, document turnover, maintenance and on-going support. When a product is to be retired, the project management method takes over to sunset the system. It is a full circle in a system's life cycle.

Project management is often expressed in terms of the constraints of scope, time and cost. This is also known as the project management triangle. Each side of the triangle represents a constraint. No side can be changed without affecting the others. At one time, "quality" or "performance" was considered a component of scope. The model has since been refined to delineate quality as a fourth constraint.

Time is the period available to complete a project. Cost is the project's budget. Scope is what must be done to complete the project's deliverables. The three constraints often compete with each other: scope creep means increased time and higher cost, a tight time frame may mean higher costs and less scope, and a tight budget may mean less time and reduced scope. Quality may be at risk if there are changes to any of the constraints.

To demonstrate the complementary nature of the SDLC to project management, I've invented the SDLC triangle. Earlier I said the SDLC is about quality, consistency and product delivery. Quality, consistency and product delivery are the outputs of a defined, managed, measurable, repeatable and reusable set of processes and practices. The processes and practices form the core framework of the SDLC. Where a project is defined by its constraints, the SDLC is defined by its freedoms and empowerment. The SDLC empowers a project team to choose from among several approved pathways to deliver the highest quality products possible in the shortest amount of time and at the lowest possible cost.

Scope is a constraint that SDLC processes liberate by managing scope creep. Scope creep is a project killer. In this SDLC, I provide simple, practical examples on how to manage scope creep during requirements workshops. Let's be clear, project scope will change during the course of a project. That's because business priorities are fluid and may drive changes in projects so that evolving current needs are met. It's how we manage scope that's important. We'll never be able to eliminate scope creep, but we can manage it effectively so it doesn't become the constraint that kills our project. In most cases, managing scope creep begins with the project's business analyst.

Consistency of process helps keep the cost constraint under control by practicing repeatable, measurable and defined algorithms. Let's be pragmatic. Whenever we practice something, we get good at it. It doesn't matter if we're talking about music and the arts or sports or anything else. The old adage is "Practice makes perfect." If we do something the same way over and over again, not only will we get good at it; we'll find ways to improve what we are doing so we can do it faster, better and cheaper.

The schedule constraint is complemented by the SDLC's timely delivery of a quality product that meets or exceeds customers' expectations. If we manage scope creep effectively and are consistent in our ability to repeat and improve our processes, not only will we deliver a product on time, there may even be enough wiggle room in the schedule to address lower priority items or deliver the product ahead of the due date.

The central attribute of each of these triangles is quality. In the project management method, quality is constrained by changes to any of the other three dimensions. In the SDLC, quality processes are built in from day one and remain a continuous activity throughout the various phases of the life cycle. As SDLC processes become second nature to development teams, quality is enhanced because the processes are being measured to support a continuous improvement cycle. Continuous improvement is an on-going effort to improve our products, processes and services. The SDLC framework provides methods in which we can constantly evaluate and improve our processes and practices in terms of their efficiency, effectiveness and flexibility.

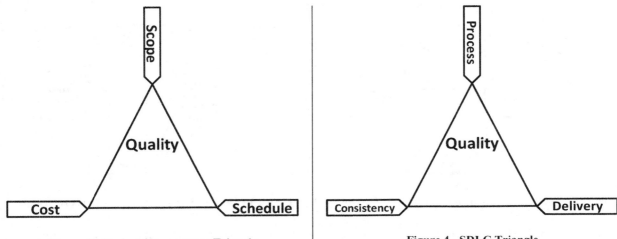

| Figure 3 - Project Management Triangle | Figure 4 - SDLC Triangle |

A strong relationship exists between the activities within the stages of the project management method and the phases of the SDLC. Most every project manager is familiar with the Project Management Institute (PMI) based out of Newton Square Pennsylvania. Established in 1984, PMI offers a range of services to the project management profession that include the development of standards, research, education, publication, networking-opportunities in local chapters, hosting conferences and training seminars and maintaining multiple credentials in project management. The Project Management Professional certification (PMP) is one of the several credentials offered by PMI. It is a highly regarded asset. PMI reports that as of June 2009, there are 359,379 PMP certified professionals world-wide.

The standards developed by PMI are collectively published in a book entitled *"A Guide to the Project Management Body of Knowledge"* (PMBOK). PMBOK recognizes 44 processes that fall into five basic process groups and nine knowledge areas that are typical of almost all projects. The best-in-breed SDLC that we'll be exploring in this book also has five basic process groups that approximate the five basic process groups of PMBOK.

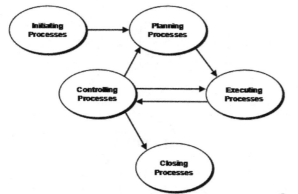

Figure 5 - Project Management Basic Process Groups[7] | **Figure 6 – Best-in-Breed SDLC Basic Process Groups**

The complementary relationship between the basic process groups of the SDLC and a project management method cannot be denied.

> **Principle #3: "The Project Management Method and the SDLC are complementary. They do not compete with each other."**

Tying It All Together

Let's recap what we've discussed so far. We understand the critical importance of an organizational change management strategy to break down communication barriers, drive alignment, build commitment and develop a common vernacular between the business and IT.

We learned that just as the three-legged stool of business profitably is driven by a balance of margin, sales and net profit, the success of an IT organization to deliver high business value is driven by the three-legged stool of IT Governance, the Project/Program Management Method and the Systems Development Life Cycle. The three are inextricably linked and together form a trilogy that are foundational to IT success and the business value IT provides.

---

[7] Source: PMBOK 2000 Edition

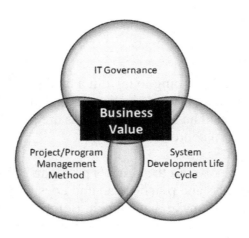

Figure 7 - Three-legged Stool of IT Business Value

We realize that ineffective IT Governance crushes an organization. It leaves senior leaders with a bad taste in their mouth. They lose confidence and trust in the IT group to deliver what they've promised. A poor project management method leads to project failures, cost overruns and delays. An immature SDLC results in poorer quality products, increased defects and lower customer satisfaction. All three must work in concert and all three must be effective to produce the desired results. Effectiveness is measurable and can be continuously improved. If any one component is out of balance, our projects may topple and fall; and like Humpty-Dumpty, we may not be able to put all the pieces back together again.

We've also discovered our first three principles:

Principle #1: "An effective organizational change management strategy is essential to the success of the SDLC."

Principle #2: "Investment opportunities cannot be estimated accurately until the requirements are known."

Principle #3: "The Project Management Method and the SDLC are complementary. They do not compete with each other."

What to Expect

As we progress through this book, I'm going to lay out a ready-to-go best in breed SDLC that you can either implement in your own IT organization or study to understand its principles to mature your existing SDLC further. The recommendations are based on current best practice and thought leadership from a variety of sources.

Is this the perfect SDLC that will solve all the world's problems? No—not by a long shot! No SDLC is ever perfect. Every process and practice can and does improve over time. You will discover ways to do it. Only you can make that happen. Before you can make it happen however, you have to have the processes in place. In our discussion about organizational change management, we talked about cultural fit and how cultural fit is unique to every organization. This SDLC can be tailored to fit the inimitable dimensions of your culture.

In the following chapters we're going to learn about and compare twelve different historical System Development Models, dive into Requirements Elicitation and Analysis, System Analysis and Design, Development, Quality Assurance, Implementation and Maintenance, Continuous Improvement and Metrics. We're also going to take a look at some best practice companies and their achievements and discuss technology and tools you may want to consider as your SDLC matures. There may even be a few surprises along the way. You can look forward to experiencing a couple of "AHA" moments just as I did as I was writing the book.

There is an accompanying CD loaded with information, templates, white papers, guidelines, checklists and studies that I hope you find useful. Many of the companies mentioned in the book have provided something for you on the CD. All of the PowerPoint slides and Visio diagrams that I created to illustrate some point or activity may be found on the CD, the most important of which can also be found in the Handy Desk Reference of Chapter 11. Please feel free to use and modify them for your own personal, non-commercial purposes internally within your organization. The content of the CD can be downloaded by registering your book at http://fontlifepublications.com/register/. By purchasing this book, you are also entitled to download the .pdf version.

System Development Models

Search the internet and you'll eventually come across a page[8] that displays a generous list of systems development approaches, styles and philosophies. As of February 2, 2010, there are 62 titles on this list as well as a caveat at the bottom of the page that says, *"This list is incomplete; you can help by expanding it."* Some of the items are well known and mainstream such as:

- Agile software development
- Agile Unified Process (AUP)
- Dynamic Systems Development Model (DSDM)
- Evolutionary Model
- Extreme Programming (XP)
- Iterative and Incremental
- Joint Application Design
- Lean software development
- Microsoft Solutions Framework (MSF)
- Model-driven architecture (MDA)

- Rapid application development (RAD)
- Rational Unified Process (RUP)
- Scrum
- Spiral model
- Structured Systems Analysis and Design Method (SSADM)
- Test-Driven Development
- Unified Process (UP)
- V-Model
- Waterfall model
- Wheel and spoke model

Others are a bit more esoteric:

- Big Design Up Front (BDUF)
- Cathedral and the Bazaar
- Cowboy coding
- Don't repeat yourself (DRY) or Once and Only Once (OAOO), Single Point of Truth (SPoT)
- Hollywood Principle

- KISS principle (Keep It Simple, Stupid)
- Quick-and-dirty
- When it's ready
- Worse is better (New Jersey style, as contrasted with the MIT approach)
- You Ain't Gonna Need It (YAGNI)

With the multitude of methods out there, it's no wondering why the SEMAT dignitaries conclude software engineering is "gravely hampered today by immature practices." They illuminate specific problems they observe which they encapsulate in these thoughts:[9]

---

[8] Source: *http://www.wikipedia.com*, s.v. "Software Development Philosophies," (accessed February 2, 2010)
[9] Source: http://www.semat.org

- The prevalence of fads more typical of fashion industry than of an engineering discipline.
- The lack of a sound, widely accepted theoretical basis.
- The huge number of methods and method variants, with differences little understood and artificially magnified.
- The lack of credible experimental evaluation and validation.
- The split between industry practice and academic research.

SEMAT's founding members are scientists and their concerns focus on software engineering. However, immature practices are more pervasive than to limit their discussion to software engineering alone. As a result, SEMAT's comments may be extended to all IT systems development areas. Our best in breed SDLC addresses these shortcomings. It is not another obscure boutique method to be added to the esoteric internet list to be lost among the countless varieties in vogue at any given time. It is a set of concepts, principles, practices, disciplines, guidelines and models for delivering Information Technology projects and maturing organizational practices from ability to capability.

We're going to travel back into history and take a look at the evolution of some of the traditional mainstream development models to examine shared commonalities and best practices. Understanding what the scientists and thought leaders believe to be best practices helps us begin to frame our own best in breed development model. Our SDLC does not force developers to use any specific methodology such as Waterfall or Agile. Instead, it empowers project teams to decide which practices to use, within acceptable guidelines, for each project. Once the choice is made the teams remain on that pathway until production deployment.

Team empowerment is a greatly misunderstood concept. Empowerment does not mean senior leaders have abdicated their responsibility to lead their organizations. To the contrary, empowerment requires stronger leadership and accountability at the team level. Empowerment means allowing people at all levels of the organization to extend their decision making scope in order to furnish them with the latitude to more fully exploit their intrinsic resourcefulness, talents and skills. Empowerment leads to greater innovation, creativity, commitment and motivation; it broadens the breadth of individual and team contributions. Since the team has made the choice of which development practices to pursue, there is greater cohesiveness among its members.

Empowerment cannot be endowed without constraints. The last thing you want or need is for teams to select from any development model they desire. They might randomly choose any of the multitudes of models to be found on the net; or they may come up with their own model and call it "Because We Can." If that's allowed to happen, chaos becomes the rule the day. Restraint is found in limiting choices to among a preferred few. The select few are those practices that have been elected through management prerogative because they most closely align with IT strategy. Management continues to lead the organization, but has granted privilege to the project teams to choose how they control their implementations.

Having several practice models to pick from does not mean that everyone is going to be doing their own thing. That would defeat the purpose of the SDLC. The permitted models are subordinate to the overall SDLC framework. They are subsets of the grander design to achieve project success. They all have common deliverables and processes that bind them together to ensure consistency across the enterprise. They have to be agile enough to adapt to the organization's culture and supple enough to be able to assimilate process improvements through the test of time. Depending on the team's choice, the artifacts are flexible in terms of quantity of content, but are steadfast in the type and quality of content required, the documents needed, their naming conventions, their format and continuous improvement metrics.

We're going to take a look at twelve different historical models including iterative and incremental varieties, RAD, agile, a hybrid and at least one that isn't a model at all but a philosophy. Let's begin by analyzing the granddaddy of all software development models, the Waterfall.

Waterfall Model

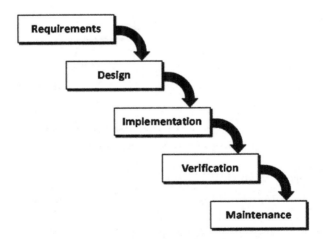

Figure 8 - Classic Waterfall Model

The Waterfall model is a linear sequential approach to systems development in which progress is perceived as flowing steadily downward through the various phases. It is called Waterfall because the model reminds one of water cascading over the edges of a multi-stepped ridge. In the Waterfall approach, one phase must be completed in its entirety before the next phase can begin.

For example, requirements must be completed before design begins. Design must be completed before implementation, etc. Once requirements are completed under Waterfall, they are engraved in stone. In the pure Waterfall sense, there is no re-visiting a phase after you've moved beyond it.

Dr. Winston W. Royce (1929-1995) is attributed with being the first computer scientist to formally describe the Waterfall model for systems development. He is a recognized leader in software development within the latter half of the 20th century. He worked as director of Lockheed Software Technology Center in Austin, Texas. For years his assignments were largely related to developing software for spacecraft mission planning, commanding and post-flight analysis. In 1970, he published a paper expressing his personal views about managing large software development projects. The document, named *"Managing the Development of Large Software Systems,"* appeared in *Technical Papers of Western Electronic Show and Convention*[10] (WesCon) August 25-28, 1970, Los Angeles, USA.

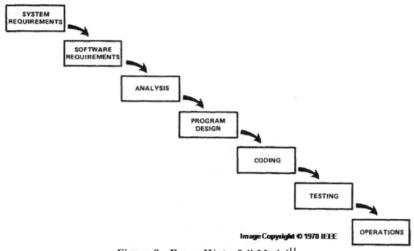

Figure 9 - Royce Waterfall Model[11]

Dr. Royce never used the term "Waterfall" in his article; nor did he invent the term in reference to his model in Figure 9. In some texts he is accredited with inventing the model which he did not. Both linear and iterative and incremental methods can be traced as far back as the 1930s to the work of Walter Shewhart,[12] a quality expert at Bell Labs who devised a sequence of "Plan-Do-Study-Act" cycles for quality improvement. Shewhart's work was expounded upon in the 1940s by William Edwards Deming, the father of the post-war Japanese industrial renaissance.

---

[10] *Proceedings, IEEE WESCON*, August 1970, pages 1-9. Copyright © 1970 by The Institute of Electrical and Electronics Engineers, Inc. Originally published by TRW.
[11] Source: IEEE. Used with permission.
[12] W. Shewhart, *Statistical Method from the Viewpoint of Quality Control*, Dover, 1986 (reprint from 1939).

Surprisingly, Royce never advocated for the use of Waterfall as a viable methodology. He called the model "grandiose" and argued that it doesn't work because requirements change over time. He presented it as an example of a model that is flawed and non-practicable. It is a process that simply does not compute. Referring to his drawing in Figure 9 he said,

"I believe in this concept, but the implementation described above is risky and invites failure...

...required design changes are likely to be so disruptive that the software requirements upon which the design is based and which provides the rationale for everything are violated. Either the requirements must be modified, or a substantial change in the design is required. In effect the development process has returned to the origin and one can expect up to a 100-percent overrun in schedule and/or costs...

...However, I believe the illustrated approach to be fundamentally sound. The remainder of this discussion presents five additional features that must be added to this basic approach to eliminate most of the development risks."

Royce proposes five modifications necessary to make the Waterfall model effective. They are:

1. Complete program design before analysis and coding begins
2. Documentation must be current and complete
3. Do the job twice if possible [iterative]
4. Testing must be planned, controlled and monitored
5. Involve the customer

Note well Royce's five modifications; we may discover some or all could be commonalities we find in other methods as we move through this chapter. Royce concluded his paper with the drawing in Figure 10 summarizing the improvements he suggested to the Waterfall model. It's a far cry different from where he started in Figure 9, isn't it?

At first I didn't fully appreciated Royce's point #1: "Complete program design before analysis and coding begins." It doesn't jive with my world view of system development. I've always believed analysis is the process by which system and business requirements are synthesized into a preliminary system specification and program design. I thought step one is either a misprint or stated wrongly. But if it's not a mistake, it makes no sense to me why a man of Royce's stature would put forward the notion of crafting the program design before the requirements are analyzed. As I studied the summary drawing (Figure 10), the steps are clearly laid out as showing the program design coming after analysis which is the opposite of the statement and more in line with traditional thinking. I must be missing something, but what is it?

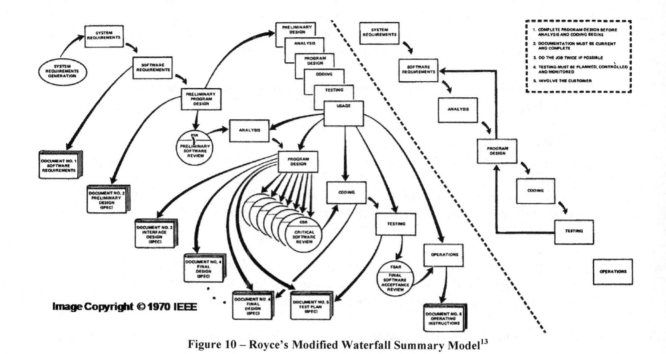

Image Copyright © 1970 IEEE

Figure 10 – Royce's Modified Waterfall Summary Model[13]

The disconnect is not understanding what Royce means by the terms "analysis" and "program design" in the context of *his* world view. Don't be thrown off by the language as I was. He isn't talking about analysis as in my definition above. Remember, he really is a rocket scientist writing to a mainframe audience in the 1970s. Here is what he said about analysis,

> *"In my experience there are whole departments consumed with the analysis of orbit mechanics, spacecraft attitude determination, mathematical optimization of payload activity and so forth, but when these departments have completed their difficult and complex work, the resultant program steps involve a few lines of serial arithmetic code. If in the execution of their difficult and complex work the analysts have made a mistake, the correction is invariably implemented by a minor change in the code with no disruptive feedback into the other development bases."*

The analysis Royce is discussing is aerospace engineering which results in the detailed design and coding of system subroutines. Without that frame of reference, the concept of program

---

[13] Source: IEEE. Used with permission.

design before analysis is lost. He describes program design as all the steps necessary to document the system overview and describe the operating procedures. When he talks about completing the program design first, he's talking about what I would call the requirements analysis phase to produce system design specification artifacts.

Since his specific sphere of reference is a mainframe world, he includes the steps of database and processor design, allocate subroutine storage and allocate subroutine execution times. These may not be familiar concepts to many growing up in the age of the internet, distributed networks, server farms and cloud computing unless they have specific experience with mainframe program design, logical partitions (LPARs) and virtual machines which is the general Big Iron[14] archetype.

So if the position of the man whom many wrongly believe created the Waterfall model is that it is a busted process, how then did it become so ubiquitous? I've worked for several places where senior leaders mistakenly entertain no other development paradigm except pure Waterfall. If you scrutinize some of the scientific articles written about systems and software engineering, particularly software engineering, many writers say something like "Waterfall is a proven method (Royce, 1970)." They cite the paper we've now investigated which makes no such claim at all.

One reason unsubstantiated claims become quoted as "facts" is that an author cites a reference because some other author did so in his/her publication. Then another author picks up on it, and then another and another, multiplying the effect when not one of them ever read the document they are citing. They each trust the other person corroborated the specifics and got it right. There is no single source of "citation checks" for authors to verify the facts of their references. They either do the verification leg work themselves, depend on a research assistant or risk damaging their credibility by placing their confidence in someone else's work even if that person is considered a trusted source.

By the early 1980s the Waterfall model began to fall out of fashion because people struggled with it and learned the hard way it is not sufficient to deliver high quality products on time and within budget in an environment where business requirements are fluid. After all, what business environment doesn't change to meet the challenges of the day? We can squarely blame mis-citing authors and the Department of Defense (DOD) for Waterfall's resurgence and persistence.

On June 4, 1985 the DOD issued Military Standard DOD-STD-2167, *"Military Standard Defense System Software Development."* Folklore credits an unnamed official with going to the Institute of Electrical and Electronics Engineers in the late 70s to search for articles on the subject of software development best practices. The military was seeking to adopt best practices

---

[14] Colloquial for mainframe computer systems

to drive higher efficiencies and lower the cost of systems development. So what did this mysterious individual's research uncover? Dr. Royce's article of course, *"Managing the Development of Large Software Systems: Concepts and Techniques."* As the story goes, this person flipped to the Waterfall drawing (Figure 9) and said, "Well, if it's good enough for Royce, it's good enough for the military." He allegedly never read the article and went off and wrote DOD-STD-2167.

I've repeated the tale here for the tongue-in-cheek aspect and to hopefully bring a little smile to your face. I don't buy for one second the military would base an entire 95-page system development specification on a single drawing in a short article even if it was written by the distinguished Dr. Royce. The risk is too high not to deliberate the issues and discuss what works and what doesn't. Nevertheless, considering the widespread use of the Waterfall model in the 70s and the fact that many mistakenly believed in its capability, it is not surprising to see the DOD-STD-2167 model possess certain characteristics hauntingly familiar to Dr. Royce's drawing. Figure 11 is a rendering of DOD-2167.

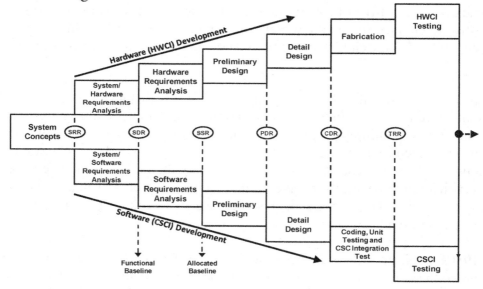

Courtesy of the United States Department of Defense. DISTRIBUTION STATEMENT A. Approved for public release; Distribution is unlimited.

Figure 11 - DOD-STD-2167 Systems Development Model

DOD-STD-2167 is a double waterfall design with bifurcating tributaries for the simultaneous implementation of hardware and software. You may imagine this resembles a V-model laid on its side but it is not. The V-Model came along a couple of years later. We'll discuss V-models in more detail further along in the chapter.

If the unadulterated Waterfall model doesn't work well, a double Waterfall model brings twice the pain. What's more, if you look at the hardware tributary, the water flows uphill as does the

"Wrong Garden" water feature invented by James Dyson for the United Kingdom's 2003 Chelsea Flower Show. Not an impossible task if you depend on capillary action, a hydraulic ram or an optical illusion as in Dyson's fountain. Alright, I'm being a little silly but as a US taxpayer, I am grateful to the Department of Defense for superseding DOD-STD-2167 with DOD-STD-2167A and MIL-STD-498. In 1998, the DOD altogether got out of the business of designing systems development models. The memo[15] canceling MIL-STD-498 says:

"Information regarding software development and documentation is now contained in the Institute of Electrical and Electronics Engineers (IEEE)/Electronics Industries Association (EIA) standard, IEEE/EIA 12207, "Information technology-Software life cycle processes". IEEE/EIA 12207 is packaged in three parts. The three parts are: IEEE/EIA 12207.0, "Standard for Information Technology-Software life cycle processes"; IEEE/EIA 12207.1, "Guide for ISO/IEC 12207, Standard for Information Technology-Software life cycle processes-Life cycle data"; and IEEE/EIA 12207.2, "Guide for ISO/IEC 12207, Standard for Information Technology-Software life cycle processes-Implementation considerations."

What do we do with the Waterfall model then? Many IT organizations still use it today and have a number of projects in motion depending on it. They simply can't extricate it from their toolset. The pain would be like a dentist pulling a bad tooth without any anesthetic and the cost would be astronomical. Do companies continue to use it, modify it or abandon it in favor of some other model? The answer is "it depends." I know that's not a definitive answer so let's revisit our Chapter 1 discussion on organizational change management.

Change takes time and transition management is the preferred approach for changes to development paradigms. If the Waterfall model is ingrained in your culture, you need to change it gradually. If you hammer it away and tell your teams, "Next month we completely stop using the Waterfall model and begin doing all of our development in some agile method," nothing will prepare you to handle the ensuing resistance. A better approach might be to introduce a level of iterations and the types of modifications such as Dr. Royce suggests. At least it assists in maturing your process. You may also think about how to measure your processes to collect statistics that feed into your continuous improvement planning, provided you aren't doing so at present. Whatever you do, it's good to be able to explain the relative strengths, weaknesses and selection criteria for using Waterfall in your communication plan.

---

[15] Source: http://www.barringer1.com/mil_files/MIL-STD-498-Cancel.pdf

Strengths:[16]	Deficiencies:
<ul><li>Easy to understand, easy to use</li><li>Provides structure to inexperienced staff</li><li>Milestones are well understood</li><li>Good for management control (plan, staff, track)</li></ul>	<ul><li>All requirements must be known upfront</li><li>Deliverables created for each phase are considered frozen–inhibits flexibility</li><li>Can give a false impression of progress</li><li>Does not reflect problem-solving nature of software development–iterations of phases</li><li>Integration is one big bang at the end</li><li>Little opportunity for customer to preview the system until it may be too late</li></ul>

Royce contends the Waterfall model doesn't work because requirements change. If business requirements remain static or change only minutely, it may not be a bad choice. It can produce a quality product if executed in alignment with other best practices. Use the Waterfall model when requirements are very well known at the beginning of the project and there is little chance of them shifting as the project progresses. If the requirements aren't subject to change, the product definition or system design specification remains stable throughout the project. What's more, there cannot be any surprises in the technology platform you are using to build the system. Use the tried and true rather than introducing the latest craze or language. Make certain you understand your tools and their limitations. Two projects particularly well suited for Waterfall are upgrading an existing system to a newer version or porting an existing project to a new platform such as moving an application from UNIX or Windows to Linux. Waterfall is not recommended for a project where you are delivering a new, unproven design.

Given that we are seeking commonalities across various development models to glean our own best-in-breed SDLC, let's begin to build a comparison grid before moving on to the Spiral model. From reviewing Royce's Waterfall recommendations, we recognize the attributes of linear vs. iterative, risk management, customer collaboration, quality control and big bang delivery. We'll add new characteristics to the chart as we discover them at the conclusion of each model's discussion.

Characteristics	Linear Waterfall	Modified Waterfall				
Date	1930s	1970				
Linear	✓					
Iterative		✓[†]				

[16] Source: Session2.ppt, Author: John Petlicki, DePaul Univ. lecturer, indep. consultant and former supervisor for app dev at AT&T, URL: http://condor.depaul.edu/~jpetlick/extra/394/Session2.ppt. Used with permission.

Characteristics	Linear Waterfall	Modified Waterfall				
Manages Risk		✓				
Customer Collaboration		✓†				
Quality Control	✓	✓				
Big Bang Delivery	✓	✓				

Figure 12 - Waterfall Comparison Table 1   †Limited capability

The Spiral Model

Barry W. Boehm[17] is a mathematician and TRW Professor of Software Engineering, Computer Science Department Director, USC Center for Software Engineering. He started working as a Programmer-Analyst at General Dynamics in 1955 and switched to the Rand Corporation four years later where he was Head of the Information Sciences Department until 1973. From 1973 to 1989 he served as Chief Scientist of the Defense Systems Groupworked at TRW. Afterward he served until 1992 within the U.S. Department of Defense as Director of the Defense Advanced Research Projects Agency (DARPA) Information Science and Technology Office, and as Director of the Department of Defense Research & Engineering Software and Computer Technology Office.

He is known for his many contributions to software engineering including the Constructive Cost Model (COCOMO), the Spiral Model of the software process, the Theory W (win-win) approach to software management and requirements determination and two advanced software engineering environments: the TRW Software Productivity System and Quantum Leap Environment. He defined the Spiral Model in his 1986 article *"A Spiral Model of Software Development and Enhancement."* The Spiral Model is a risk based approach which combines characteristics of evolutionary prototyping with the Waterfall Model. As envisioned by Boehm, the Spiral Model is intended for large, complex projects with durations of 6 months to 2 years. This iterative model influenced Model-Based Architecture and Software Engineering (MBASE) and Extreme Programming.

The United States Army adopted the Spiral Model for the development and upgrades of its Future Combat Systems (FCS) modernization program. Officially launched in 2003, FCS was foreseen to equip troops with manned and unmanned vehicles connected through an extraordinarily fast and flexible real-time battlefield network. The project was apportioned to four 2-year development spirals. Spiral 1 was scheduled to begin in FY2008 and deliver

---

[17]http://sunset.usc.edu/Research_Group/barry.html

prototypes for use and evaluation. Following a successful Spiral 1 evaluation, Spiral 2 was scheduled to commence in FY2010. Production deployment was planned for 2015.

In August 2005, Boeing announced the completion of the project's first major milestone, the Systems of Systems Functional Review. Boeing Company and Science Applications International Corporation (SAIC) we're co-leads for the systems integration, coordinating more than 550 contractors and subcontractors in 41 states. By October 2005, the Pentagon recommended delaying the FCS project due to the high cost impact of the Iraq War, Hurricane Katrina relief efforts and the anticipation of future budget reductions. Budget cuts did arise and the project was canceled in June 2009. While the Spiral Model is suited for large projects, it never had the chance to prove its benefits in the intricate $3B interoperable, distributed combat related mission.

Today the Spiral Model has found a welcome home in the gaming industry. The large (>$3M) projects and continuously shifting goals of gaming systems development and resolutions achieved through evolutionary prototyping has created a demand for the process. For every spiral's iteration, there are four activity quadrants which are:

1. Determine objectives, alternatives and constraints:
    a. System requirements are defined in as much detail as possible and include artifacts for functionality, performance, hardware/software interfaces, key success metrics, etc.
    b. Alternatives such as build vs. buy, can we reuse existing components or do we sub-contract are examined
    c. Constraints such as cost, schedule and interfaces are addressed

2. Identify and resolve risks, evaluate alternatives:
    a. All possible and available alternatives for developing a cost effective project are evaluated and strategies developed to determinate their use
    b. Identify and resolve all the possible risks in the project such as lack of experience, new technology, tight schedules, poor process, etc.
    c. Resolve any found risks and uncertainties. Subset reviews may be commissioned to investigate other process models until all high risk situations are resolved

3. Development and test: Prototype the system from the preliminary design. Follow the usual pattern of create and review design, code, inspect code and test

4. Plan the next iteration:
    a. Review the first prototype for strengths, weaknesses and risks
    b. Elicit the requirements for the second prototype
    c. Plan and design the second prototype:

<ol type="i">
<li>Create the project plan</li>
<li>Document the configuration management plan</li>
<li>Construct a test plan</li>
<li>Devise an installation plan</li>
</ol>

As the spirals progress and development intensifies, increasingly detailed system elaborations are defined, culminating in incremental releases of the system's operational capability. A couple of the major problems with this approach are that spirals may continue indefinitely and each spiral is its own waterfall. It is iterative in terms of the delivery of evolutionary prototypes and linear in terms of how those prototypes are evaluated for risk and constructed. For the most part it's best to avoid long-term project commitments due to potential changes in business priorities.

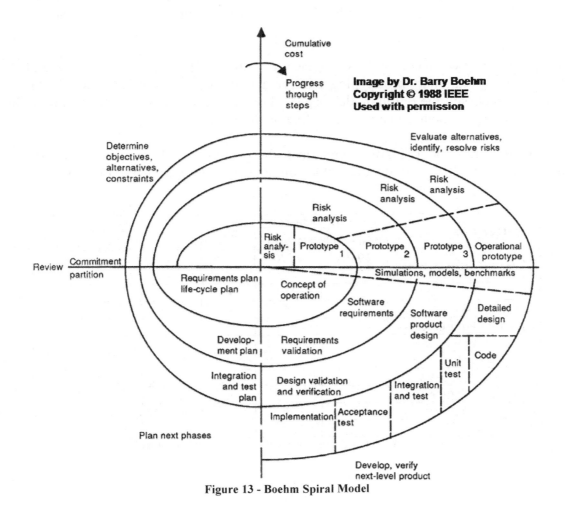

Figure 13 - Boehm Spiral Model

Strengths:	Deficiencies:
• Balances all of the risk elements, i.e. the high-risk elements/functions are developed first • Provides early indication of insurmountable risks, without much cost • Users see the system early because of rapid prototyping tools • Users closely tied to all lifecycle steps and provide early and frequent feedback • Cumulative costs assessed frequently	• Demands considerable risk-assessment expertise • Time spent planning, resetting objectives, evaluating risk and prototyping may be excessive • The model is complex. Spirals may continue indefinitely • May be hard to define objective, verifiable milestones that indicate readiness to proceed through the next iteration

Use the Spiral Model when cost and risk management are high priorities. You may want to consider it when evolutionary prototyping is important although there are alternatives. Medium to high-risk projects suit the Spiral model, especially where risks include: users unsure of their needs, complex requirements, a new product line or significant expected changes.

Let's insert the Spiral Model into our comparison chart adding the characteristics of evolutionary dynamic requirements albeit limited, reusable components, prototyping and incremental delivery.

Characteristics	Linear Waterfall	Modified Waterfall	Spiral			
Date	1930s	1970	1986			
Linear	✓					
Iterative		✓†	✓			
Manages Risk		✓	✓			
Dynamic Requirements			✓†			
Reusable Components			✓			
Prototyping/Modeling			✓			
Incremental Delivery			✓			
Customer Collaboration		✓†	✓			
Quality Control	✓	✓	✓			
Big Bang Delivery	✓	✓				

Figure 14 - Waterfall Comparison Table 2   †Limited capability

The V-Model

German V-Modell 97 and V-Modell XT

A funny thing happened on the way to the V-Model. In the late 1980s two countries, Germany and the United States, simultaneously but independently developed a V-Model. While the two models are similar in concept, they differ enough to be considered alternative approaches. The German V-Modell was developed in part by Industrieanlagen-Betriebsgesellschaft mbH (IABG) in Ottobrunn, near Munich in cooperation with the Federal Office for Defence Technology and Procurement in Koblenz for the Federal Ministry of Defence. IABG was founded in 1961 as a central analysis and testing organization for Germany's aeronautics industry and the Ministry of Defence. Their focus was aeronautics industry testing and security and defense analysis. Today, IABG is a leading European technology and science service provider[18] and is involved with the Airbus development programs.

Development of the V-Modell occurred over a 4-year period beginning in 1986. Pilot project trials started in early 1990. It was made obligatory for the defense area by the Federal Ministry of Defence in February 1991. The V-Modell proved so successful in Germany's defense industry that in the summer of 1992 it was taken over by the Federal Ministry of the Interior for the civilian public authorities domain to provide a uniform systems development standard for the whole range of public authorities. With the publication of the *"Development Standards for IT Systems of the Federal Republic of Germany"* in 1997, the V-Modell 97 entered into force as the standard for all civil and military federal agencies. It was used throughout Germany by banks, insurance companies, car manufacturers, the manufacturing industry and energy producers.

The V-Modell gained traction in Europe. An English translation was completed for use in international projects. It is the subject of a European Commission (EC) project started in 1989 with the goal of surveying software engineering methods and harmonizing them. The German representative to the EC Committee is the Federal Ministry of the Interior. In view of the Ministry's own use of the V-Modell, it was nominated as the German standardization contribution at the European level.

The German V-Modell was structured into four functional parts called sub-models. The sub-models are:

- Software Development (SWD)
- Quality Assurance (QA)
- Configuration Management (CM)
- Project Management (PM)

---

[18] Source: http://www.iabg.de/

These four are closely interrelated and mutually influence one another through the exchange of products/results. Since the focus of our SDLC is systems development, let's decompose the software development sub-model. The sub-model comprises the following nine primary activities:

1. System Requirements Analysis and Design:
   a. Describes the system requirements its environment
   b. Conduct a threat and risk analysis; develop a security concept
   c. Deliver a user level model of functions/data/ objects
   d. Structure the system into subsystems, segments or configuration items
2. DP Requirements Analysis and Design
   a. Describe the DP segment requirements and its environment
   b. Development of a security model, structuring the segment into its SW and HW configuration items
3. SW Requirements Analysis
   a. Describe the SWCI requirements and its environment
4. Preliminary Design
   a. Structure the SWCI in SW components/modules/database, specification of the interfaces and interaction of its elements
5. Detailed Design
   a. Describe the components and modules with respect to the real implementation of their functions, the data administration and error handling up to a programming specification
6. Implementation
   a. Convert the programming specifications to statements of the programming language
   b. Perform informal assessment of developed code and implementation of a database (if required)
7. SW Integration
   a. Integrate modules to components and components to the SWCI
8. DV Integration
   a. Integrate the different SW and HW configuration items to a DP segment
9. System Integration
   a. Integrate the subsystems (if existing) and segments to the system

V-Modell 97 met with obsolescence in 2004. It no longer reflected the state-of-the-art of information technology and its use declined. New methods and technologies—as for example component-based development or the test-first approach—are considered only to a limited degree in V-Modell 97. It is superseded by "V-Modell XT," completed in 2006. The V-Modell XT is a standard developed on behalf of the Federal Office of the Bundeswehr for Information

Management and Information Technology and the Federal Ministry of the Interior, Central Office for Information Technology Coordination in the Federal Administration (BMI-KBSt).

US Vee Model

The US Vee-Model was first discussed at a joint conference sponsored by the National Council on Systems Engineering (NCOSE) and American Society for Engineering Management (ASEM) in Chattanooga, TN on October 21–23, 1991. A paper named *"The Relationship of System Engineering to the Project Cycle"* written by Dr. Kevin Forsberg and Harold Mooz, Co-Principals for the Center for Systems Management, formerly of Cupertino, California, now located in Vienna, Virginia. The paper was also presented at The 12th INTERNET World Congress on Project Management held in Oslo, Norway on June 9–11, 1994.

Both Forsberg and Mooz are involved in the aerospace industry. At the time of the document, Forsberg had 27 years of experience in Applied Research, System Engineering, Program, and Proposal Management, followed by seven years of successful consulting to both government and industry. He received the NASA Public Service Medal for his contributions to the Space Shuttle program. Mooz had 22 years of experience in System Engineering and Program Management, followed by ten years of successful consulting to government and industry. Mooz has won and successfully managed highly reliable, sophisticated satellite programs from inception to operations. It's a fascinating coincidence that both the German and US V-Models were parented by the aerospace industry.

Forsberg and Mooz believe their Vee-Model addresses the system engineering deficiencies of Linear Waterfall, Modified Waterfall and DOD-STD-2167A, the immediate successor to DOD-STD-2167. They mention Boehm's Spiral Model in their paper and say,[19] "While Boehm's spiral representation (Exhibit 4) achieves his objective, the system engineering role is still obscured." The "(Exhibit 4)" in the quote refers to an image of Boehm's model reproduced in their document.

As all the other models we've discussed thus far, the Vee-Model is Waterfall based with notable exceptions. They said, "In our approach, the technical aspect of the project cycle is envisioned as a 'Vee,' starting with User needs on the upper left and ending with a User-validated system on the upper right." Notice the deliberate use of the word "user" implying end users are involved in all aspects of the development cycle.

---

[19] *"The Relationship of System Engineering to the Project Cycle"* Copyright © 1995 Center for Systems Management

The model recognizes the changeability of requirements and provides for the establishment of six baselines: User Requirements Baseline, Concept Baseline, System Performance Baseline, "Design-To" Baseline, "Build-To" Baseline and "As-Built" Baseline. The process is iterative and allows for incremental development and concurrent engineering within any phase until that phase's stage review. After a stage review successfully completes, a new phase is initiated and the old phase is not revisited as in the Waterfall design. Major emphasis is placed on Verification and Validation activities, risk identification and risk reduction modeling. Verification and validation mean that all requirements are testable and agreed to by the stakeholders. We'll discuss verification and validation in detail in the requirements chapters.

The Forsberg and Mooz Vee-Model consists of nine phases:

- Understand user requirements, develop system concept and validation plan
- Develop system performance specification and system verification plan
- Expand system performance specification into CI "Design-to" specifications and CI verification plan
- Evolve "Design-to" specifications into "Build-to" documentation and inspection plan
- Fabricate, assemble and code to "Build-to" documentation
- Inspect to "Build-to" documentation
- Assemble CIs and perform CI verification to CI "Design-to" specifications
- Integrate system and perform system verification to performance specification
- Demonstrate and validate system to user validation plan

Much of the risk analysis and concurrent systems engineering occur in "off-core" activities. Forsberg and Mooz said, "While technical feasibility decisions are made in the off-core activities only decisions at the core-level are put under Configuration Management at the various Control Gates. Off-core activities, analyses, and models are performed to substantiate the core decisions and to ensure that risks have been mitigated or determined to be acceptable."

Figure 15 is a detailed view of the Vee-Model showing key off-core activities and highlighting the "Time Now" bar, which moves monotonically to the right. The off-core activities focus on opportunity and risk investigations

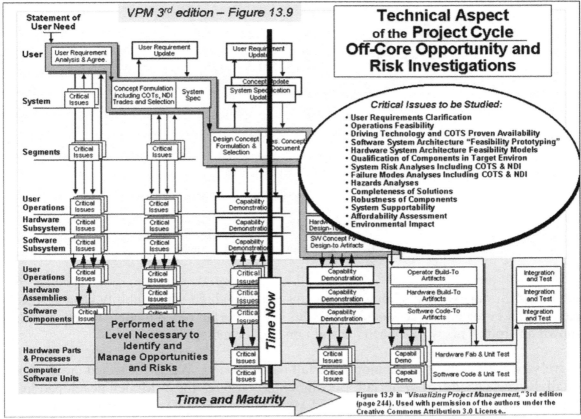

Figure 15 - Forsberg and Mooz Vee-Model Off-Core Activities[20]

Figure 16 is a detailed portrayal of another evolution of a Vee-Model demonstrating the significance of quality assurance best practices.

Strengths:	Deficiencies:
• Emphasizes planning for verification and validation of the product in early stages of development • Every requirement must be testable • Project management can track progress by milestones • Easy to use	• Does not easily handle concurrent events • Does not handle iterations or phases after the stage review • Does not easily handle dynamic changes in requirements after baselining

---

[20] Image first appeared as Figure 13.9 in *"Visualizing Project Management,"* 3rd edition (page 244), Copyright © 2005 Wiley. Used with permission of the authors under the Creative Commons Attribution 3.0 License.

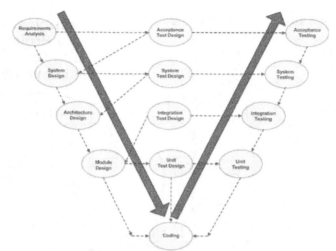

Figure 16 – Quality Assurance Based V-Model

The Vee-Model is an excellent choice for systems requiring high dependability because risk mitigation is a key aspect of the model. Since this is a Waterfall based model, all requirements are known up-front. This works when the solution and technology are known.

So far we've taken a look at five major Waterfall based models. We've inspected the Linear Waterfall, Royce's Modified Waterfall, Boehm's Spiral Model, the V-Modell developed in Germany and the Vee-Model by Forsberg and Mooz in the US. We've examined relative strengths and weaknesses and discussed the type of projects suitable to them. The Vee-Model adds the characteristics of concurrent engineering (off-core), verification and validation and testable requirements.

Characteristics	Linear Waterfall	Modified Waterfall	Spiral	Vee-Model		
Date	1930s	1970	1986	1991		
Linear	✓					
Iterative		✓†	✓	✓		
Manages Risk		✓	✓	✓		
Dynamic Requirements			✓†	✓†		
Reusable Components			✓			
Verification & Validation				✓		
Testable Requirements				✓		
Concurrent Engineering				✓††		
Prototyping/Modeling			✓	✓		
Incremental Delivery			✓	✓		
Customer Collaboration		✓†	✓	✓		

Characteristics	Linear Waterfall	Modified Waterfall	Spiral	Vee-Model		
Quality Control	✓	✓	✓	✓		
Big Bang Delivery	✓	✓				

Figure 17 - Waterfall Comparison Table 3   [†]Limited capability   [††]off-core activity

The Dual Vee-Model

Recognizing insufficiencies with all Waterfall based models including their own the Vee-Model, Forsberg and Mooz continued to refine their thesis. They presented a Dual Vee-Model in a 2006 paper titled *"The Dual Vee – Illuminating the Management of Complexity."* In the abstract they say:

> The Waterfall, Spiral, and Vee models are reminder models that guide us to less perilous paths when developing solutions to problems. Dr. Royce's Waterfall (Royce 1970) provides an orderly approach to software development. Dr. Boehm's Spiral (Boehm 1988) provides emphasis on solving known software risks before proceeding with Royce's Waterfall. The Forsberg/Mooz Vee Model (Forsberg 1991) embraces full systems development by including details of integration, verification, and validation and opportunity and risk management in the symmetry of the Vee development sequence. However, all of these single solution development models fail to address the necessary concurrent development of a system's architecture with the entities of that architecture.

While the original Vee-Model allowed for off-core concurrent engineering, the Dual Vee moves those off-core activities into core processes. In discussing the shortcomings of the Waterfall variants, they said:

"All of these popular development models, while quite accurate in their contributions to solution development, fail to adequately address the real life challenges of concurrently developing the system's architecture while at the same time creating the architecture entities that are in various stages of their development especially when COTS,[21] NDI[22] and new development are all part of the architecture. Since our original Vee model did not clearly provide this aspect we have developed the Dual Vee…"

The Dual Vee Model recognizes two types of system development maturation in an Architecture Vee and an Entity Vee. The system architecture is defined as a "complement of entities that are to be realized at all architecture levels." Entity development is "the creation of each entity within

---

[21] COTS = "Commercial Off The Shelf"
[22] NDI = "Network Deployment and Integration."

the architecture complement." These two Vee models represent separate but concurrent paths that intersect at various points along the development life cycle culminating in system realization.

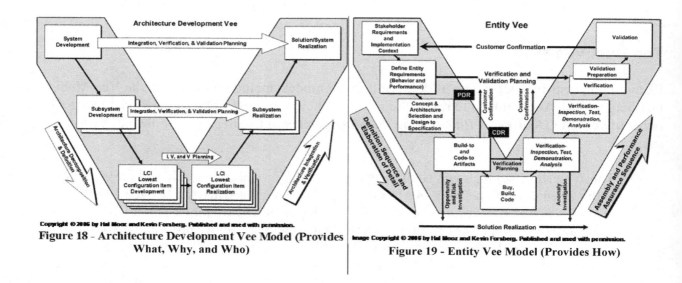

Figure 18 - Architecture Development Vee Model (Provides What, Why, and Who)

Figure 19 - Entity Vee Model (Provides How)

In concluding their paper, Forsberg and Mooz said,

> "Development of systems and system of systems requires the concurrent development of complex architectures and the entities of those architectures. A model has been needed to depict the required multi aspect decisions required to ensure correct and progressive development of both architecture and entity baselines. The Dual Vee Model offers the features of concurrent development, in parallel opportunity and risk management, integration, verification and validation planning, and anomaly resolution. It is a comprehensive reminder model that can remind us of our industry's best practices, if we allow it to."

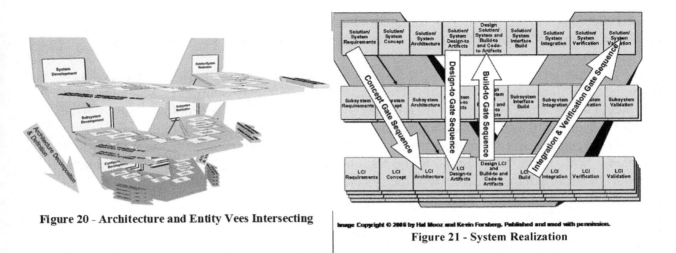

Figure 20 - Architecture and Entity Vees Intersecting

Image Copyright © 2005 by Hal Mooz and Kevin Forsberg. Published and used with permission.

Figure 21 - System Realization

Let's add the Dual Vee and its core concurrent engineering to our comparison chart.

Characteristics	Linear Waterfall	Modified Waterfall	Spiral	Vee-Model	Dual Vee	
Date	1930s	1970	1986	1991	2005	
Linear	✓					
Iterative		✓†	✓	✓	✓	
Manages Risk		✓	✓	✓	✓	
Dynamic Requirements			✓†	✓†	✓†	
Reusable Components			✓			
Verification & Validation				✓	✓	
Testable Requirements				✓	✓	
Concurrent Engineering				✓††	✓	
Prototyping/Modeling			✓	✓	✓	
Incremental Delivery			✓	✓	✓	
Customer Collaboration		✓†	✓	✓	✓	
Quality Control	✓	✓	✓	✓		
Big Bang Delivery	✓	✓				

Figure 22 - Waterfall Comparison Table 4   †Limited capability   ††off-core activity

Incremental Commitment Model

Let's examine one last model before we move onto adaptive software development. The Incremental Commitment Model (ICM) was presented in 2006 in a paper titled *"Using the Incremental Commitment Model to Integrate System Acquisition, Systems Engineering, and*

Software Engineering" written by Barry Boehm (Spiral Model) and Jo Ann Lane, a Principal at the University of Southern California Center for Systems and Software Engineering.

The ICM model emerged primarily as a result of recommendations from two independent studies. The first is the October 2006 Defense Software Strategy Summit in which Dr. James I. Finley, Deputy Under Secretary of Defense (DUSD) Acquisition, Technology, and Logistics (AT&L) sought to find ways of better integrating software engineering into the systems engineering and acquisition process. In the second initiative which ran concurrently with the Defense Software Strategy Summit, the National Research Council addressed the problem of better integrating human factors into the systems engineering and acquisition process.

In their paper, Boehm and Lane propose the ICM model to organize "systems engineering and acquisition processes in ways that better accommodate the different strengths and difficulties of hardware, software, and human factors engineering approaches. It also provides points at which they can synchronize and stabilize, and at which their risks of going forward can be better assessed and fitted into a risk-driven stakeholder resource commitment process."

Boehm and Lane's analysis surfaced five problems common across current development models, including Boehm's Spiral Model, relative to integrating their hardware, software and human factor aspects. The problem areas are:

- Complex, multi-owner systems of systems
- Emergent requirements
- Rapid change
- Reused components
- High assurance of qualities

They said, "The most important conclusion, though, was that there were key process principles that address the challenges, and that forms of the models were less important than their ability to adopt the principles."

These key principles are:

- Stakeholder satisficing
- Incremental and evolutionary growth of system definition and stakeholder commitment
- Iterative system development and definition
- Concurrent system definition and development
- Risk management – risk driven anchor point milestones

ICM draws on the strengths of existing models such as the early validation and verification of the Vee, lighter-weight concepts such as Agile and Lean, Spiral risk management and the Rational Unified Process (RUP) phases and anchor points. We have not discussed RUP in detail but it is an adaptive approach originally developed by Rational Software which was purchased by IBM in February 2003. RUP's foundation is a set of building blocks that consist of Roles, Work Products and Tasks. The project life cycle consists of the four phases of Inception, Elaboration, Construction and Transition. There are six engineering disciplines that include Business Modeling, Requirements, Analysis and Design, Implementation, Test and Deployment. Three supporting disciplines are Environment, Configuration and Change Management and Project Management. As for Agile and Lean, we're going to inspect lighter-weight concepts in the next section of this chapter.

Compared to the Waterfall variants we've seen so far, ICM advocates for the concurrent engineering of requirements and solutions. Feasibility rationales are expressed as simple pass/fail milestone criteria. Certain risks are mitigated by avoiding unnecessary documents, phases and reviews. Emergent requirements are handled through change processing and rebaselining activities to stabilize development for the next increment.

The life cycle is divided into two stages: Incremental Definition and Incremental Development and Operations. Incremental Definition is the three phases of Exploration, Valuation and Architecting. Incremental Development and Operations comprises two phases: Development Architecting and Operation Development Architecting. Timeboxing is employed to regulate iterations.

In concluding their paper, Boehm and Lane said:

> The Incremental Commitment Model described in this article builds on experience-based critical success factor principles (stakeholder satisficing, incremental definition, iterative evolutionary growth, concurrent engineering, risk management) and the strengths of existing V, concurrent engineering, spiral, agile, and lean process models to provide a framework for concurrently engineering system-specific critical factors into the systems engineering and systems development processes. It provides capabilities for evaluating the feasibility of proposed solutions; and for integrating feasibility evaluations into decisions on whether and how to proceed further into systems development and operations. It presents several complementary views showing how the principles are applied to perform risk-driven process tailoring and evolutionary growth of a systems definition and realization; to synchronize and stabilize concurrent engineering; and to enable simultaneous high-assurance development and rapid adaptation to change.

A natural extension and enhancement of the Waterfall variants, ICM is a true evolutionary prototypical hybrid inculcated with the characteristics of Waterfall, RUP and adaptive processes.

CrossTalk, The Journal of Defense Software Engineering is an approved Department of Defense journal. In articles published in CrossTalk (2002-2005) called the "Top Five Quality Software Projects," well over half of the best documented government software-intensive success stories, when analyzed for the use of critical success factors, explicitly applied ICM principles.

For our comparison study, we'll add ICM to the Waterfall Variants chart with the characteristics of full capability for handling dynamic requirements, timeboxing and quality assurance. The distinction between quality control and quality assurance are discussed in Chapter 9—Quality Assurance & Implementation.

| Characteristics | Waterfall Variants | | | | | Hybrid |
	Linear Waterfall	Modified Waterfall	Spiral	Vee-Model	Dual Vee	ICM
Date	1930s	1970	1986	1991	2005	2006
Linear	✓					
Iterative		✓†	✓	✓	✓	✓
Manages Risk		✓	✓	✓	✓	✓
Dynamic Requirements			✓†	✓†	✓†	✓
Verification & Validation				✓	✓	✓
Testable Requirements				✓	✓	✓
Concurrent Engineering				✓††	✓	✓
Reusable Components			✓			✓
Timeboxing						✓
Prototyping/Modeling			✓	✓	✓	✓
Customer Collaboration		✓†	✓	✓	✓	✓
Quality Control	✓	✓	✓	✓	✓	
Quality Assurance						✓
Incremental Delivery			✓	✓	✓	✓
Big Bang Delivery	✓	✓				

Figure 23 - Waterfall Comparison Table 5   †Limited capability   ††off-core activity

Adaptive Software Development

Adaptive Software Development (ASD) embodies principles that teach continuous adaptation to the work at hand is the status quo. ASD was created to replace traditional Waterfall variants such as the six models we've previously discussed. In a general sense, ASD processes represent a repeating series of *speculate*, *collaborate*, and *learn* cycles.

"**Speculate**" refers to the planning paradox—outcomes are unpredictable, therefore, endless suppositions on a product's look and feel are not likely to lead to any business value. Some important dimensions are more than likely wrong. Hypothesize a rough idea of what you need and plan to adapt. The big idea behind speculate is when we plan a product to its smallest detail as in a requirements up front Waterfall variant, we produce the product we intend and not the product the customer needs. In the ASD mindset, planning is to speculation as intention is to need.

Paraphrasing Highsmith,[23] he said, "**Collaboration...** portrays a balance between managing the doing and creating and maintaining the collaborative environment." Speculation says we can't predict outcomes. If we can't predict outcomes, we can't plan. If we can't plan, traditional project management theory suffers. Collaboration counterpoises speculation in that a project manager plans the work between the predictable parts of the environment and adapts to the uncertainties of various factors—stakeholders, requirements, software vendors, technology, etc.

"**Learning**" cycles challenge all stakeholders and project team members. Based on short iterations of design, build and testing, knowledge accumulates from the small mistakes we make due to false assumptions, poorly stated or ambiguous requirements or misunderstanding the stakeholders' needs. Correcting those mistakes through shared learning cycles leads to greater positive experience and eventual mastery of the problem domain.[24]

An adaptive software development process was first described in 1974 in a paper written by Dr. Ernest A. Edmonds named *"A Process for the Development of Software for Non-Technical Users as an Adaptive System,"* General Systems, Vol. XIX, pp.215-218. Dr. Edmonds is Director of Creativity & Cognition Studios, University of Technology, in Sydney, Australia. He writes in an abstract of the paper on his website[25] and says:

---

[23] Source: James A. Highsmith III, "Adaptive Software Development: A Collaborative Approach to Managing Complex Systems," Dorset House Publishing Company, Incorporated (December 1999); ISBN: 0932633404
[24] Derived from: *"MESSY, EXCITING, AND ANXIETY-RIDDEN: ADAPTIVE SOFTWARE DEVELOPMENT"* by Jim Highsmith Copyright 1997 by Jim Highsmith. All rights reserved. Source: http://www.jimhighsmith.com/articles/messy.htm
[25] Source: http://www.ernestedmonds.com/, accessed February 8, 2010

"The aim of the paper is to describe the process of software development as it often occurs unintentionally, in a way that might make it easier to recognize what is happening…

…It is suggested that the solution proposed may also allow users to adapt their methods at the same rate as the development of the software, giving a smooth and well understood change in the system."

Edmond's subsequent works further describe his approach to iterative adaptive processes. The idea apparently caught on. In the mid-1990s a number of adaptive processes sprang up throughout the IT industry. Prominent early methods include Rapid Application Development and Scrum (1991), Crystal (1992), Extreme Programming, Adaptive Software Development, Feature Driven Development, and Dynamic Systems Development Model (DSDM) (1995). These are now collectively referred to as Agile Methodologies, after the Agile Manifesto published in 2001.

It's hard to define exactly what an agile software process is. There are so many approaches to agile software development; there is no one size fits all. Yet, as we'll learn they share common best practices. Scott Ambler, author of *"Agile Modeling: Effective Practices for eXtreme Programming and the Unified Process,"* Wiley; 1st edition (March 21, 2002), puts it this way:

"Disciplined agile software development is: An iterative and incremental (evolutionary) approach to software development which is performed in a highly collaborative manner by self-organizing teams within an effective governance framework with 'just enough' ceremony that produces high quality software in a cost effective and timely manner which meets the changing needs of its stakeholder."

It's welcoming that Mr. Ambler says agile software development must fit into "an effective governance framework." I'm convinced many of the agile methods don't take a corporate IT governance framework into account. But that's neither here nor there at this point; we're going to examine this concept more deeply later in the chapter. To get a better understanding of what agile is supposed to be about, let's peer into the Agile Manifesto.

The Agile Manifesto

Jim Highsmith is one of the authors of the Agile Manifesto and its official historian. Highsmith said:[26]

---

[26] Source: http://www.agilemanifesto.org/history.html, Copyright ©2001 Jim Highsmith

"On February 11-13, 2001, at The Lodge at Snowbird ski resort in the Wasatch mountains of Utah, seventeen people met to talk, ski, relax, and try to find common ground and of course, to eat. What emerged was the Agile Software Development Manifesto. Representatives from Extreme Programming, SCRUM, DSDM, Adaptive Software Development, Crystal, Feature-Driven Development, Pragmatic Programming, and others sympathetic to the need for an alternative to documentation driven, heavyweight software development processes convened."

The 17 authors of the Agile Manifesto are:

Kent Beck
Mike Beedle
Arie van Bennekum
Alistair Cockburn
Ward Cunningham
Martin Fowler

James Grenning
Jim Highsmith
Andrew Hunt
Ron Jeffries
Jon Kern
Brian Marick

Robert C. Martin
Steve Mellor
Ken Schwaber
Jeff Sutherland
Dave Thomas

The Agile Manifesto[27] is a statement of principles that support agile software development. This simple, 68-word statement says:

> We are uncovering better ways of developing software by doing it and helping others do it. Through this work we have come to value:
>
> - **Individuals and interactions** over processes and tools
> - **Working software** over comprehensive documentation
> - **Customer collaboration** over contract negotiation
> - **Responding to change** over following a plan
>
> That is, while there is value in the items on the right, we value the items on the left more.

The twelve principles behind the Agile Manifesto are:

- Our highest priority is to satisfy the customer through early and continuous delivery of valuable software.
- Welcome changing requirements, even late in development. Agile processes harness change for the customer's competitive advantage.
- Deliver working software frequently, from a couple of weeks to a couple of months, with a preference to the shorter timescale.

---

[27] Source: http://www.agilemanifesto.org, Copyright © 2001, the above authors. The authors grant: this declaration may be freely copied in any form, but only in its entirety through this notice.

- Business people and developers must work together daily throughout the project.
- Build projects around motivated individuals. Give them the environment and support they need, and trust them to get the job done.
- The most efficient and effective method of conveying information to and within a development team is face-to-face conversation.
- Working software is the primary measure of progress.
- Agile processes promote sustainable development. The sponsors, developers, and users should be able to maintain a constant pace indefinitely.
- Continuous attention to technical excellence and good design enhances agility.
- Simplicity—the art of maximizing the amount of work not done—is essential.
- The best architectures, requirements, and designs emerge from self-organizing teams.
- At regular intervals, the team reflects on how to become more effective, then tunes and adjusts its behavior accordingly.

The framers of the Agile Manifesto emphasize the human aspect of systems development and rightfully so. All the planning in the world is not going to lead to a successful project if the people aren't engaged. You can spiral iterations into oblivion, but if the stakeholders aren't actively collaborating with the project team you not going to produce a product the customer needs. With the lone exception of the hybrid ICM, this is one of the weaknesses with the early Waterfall variants, the human factor falls short.

As we did with the Waterfall variants, we'll now examine five of the most historically significant Agile methods in the order of their introduction to the world as well as one easy to adopt development philosophy. We're going to look at their commonalities and understand their best practices. We're going to chart them as we did with the Waterfall variants and then compare to two families.

Rapid Application Development

James Martin is a British Information Technology consultant and author, nominated for a Pulitzer Prize for his book, *"The Wired Society: A Challenge for Tomorrow."* Computerworld's 25th anniversary issue ranked him fourth among the 25 individuals who have most influenced the world of computer science. He invented Rapid Application Development as a software approach. Starting with the ideas of Brian Gallagher, Alex Balchin, Barry Boehm and Scott Shultz, Martin developed the Rapid Application Development approach during the 1980s while working for IBM. In 1991, he published the process in his book *"Rapid Application Development."*[28]

---

[28] Publisher: Macmillan College Textbook Division (May 1991)

RAD uses minimal planning, iterative development, the rapid creation of prototypes and continuous customer collaboration to produce quality products. According to Whitten, [29] it is "a merger of various structured techniques, especially data-driven Information Engineering, with prototyping techniques to accelerate software systems development."

RAD's structured techniques and prototypes are used to define users' requirements and design the final system. The process starts with the creation of the first round of data and business process models. Next, user requirements are verified using the prototypes. The prototypes and user collaboration help refine the data and process models. The stages are repeated until a component or final product is delivered.

RAD may be used when requirements are reasonably well-known and the users can be involved throughout the life cycle. It is particularly suited for projects that can be modularized, timeboxed and where there are low technical risks, high performance not required and functionality that can be delivered in increments.

Today the term "RAD" has evolved into a generic meaning for any of the variety of techniques used to speed application development, such as beginning with a web or application framework. The RAD community recognizes there is no single RAD approach that can provide order of magnitude improvements over any other method. It's also interesting to note that although RAD was developed at IBM, two of the world's largest software vendors; Microsoft[30] and IBM[31] rarely utilize RAD techniques in the development of their products, opting instead for traditional Waterfall variants with some spiraling.[32]

Strengths:	Deficiencies:
<ul><li>Promotes strong collaborative atmosphere and dynamic requirements</li><li>Reduced cycle time, improved productivity, lower costs</li><li>Timebox approach mitigates cost and schedule risk</li><li>Business participates in prototyping, writing test cases and unit testing</li></ul>	<ul><li>Accelerated development process must give quick responses to the user</li><li>Risk of never achieving closure</li><li>Hard to use with legacy systems</li><li>System requires modularization</li><li>Stakeholders must be committed to rapid-fire activities in an abbreviated time frame.</li><li>Dependency on strong cohesive teams and</li></ul>

[29] Whitten, Jeffrey L.; Lonnie D. Bentley, Kevin C. Dittman. (2004). "*Systems Analysis and Design Methods*". 6th edition.
[30] Andrew Begel, Nachiappan Nagappan. "*Usage and Perceptions of Agile Software Development in an Industrial Context: An Exploratory Study, Microsoft Research*"
[31] E. M. Maximilien and L. Williams. (2003). "*Assessing Test-driven Development at IBM*". Proceedings of International Conference of Software Engineering, Portland, OR, pp. 564-569, 2003.
[32] M. Stephens, Rosenberg, D. (2003). "*Extreme Programming Refactored: The Case Against XP.*" Apress, 2003

Strengths:	Deficiencies:
• Collaboration minimizes risk of not achieving customer satisfaction and business needs • Uses models to capture business rules, data and processes • Decision-making empowered teams	individual commitment to the project • Success depends on disciplined developers, their exceptional technical skills and ability to "turn on a dime" • Lesser degree of centralized PM and engineering authority

To begin our Agile variant chart, let's start with the characteristics of team empowerment, iterative development, dynamic requirements, verification and validation, testable requirements, timeboxing, prototyping/modeling, customer collaboration, quality assurance and incremental delivery.

Characteristics	RAD					
Date	1991					
Team Empowerment	✓					
Iterative	✓					
Dynamic Requirements	✓					
Verification & Validation	✓					
Testable Requirements	✓					
Timeboxing	✓					
Prototyping/Modeling	✓					
Customer Collaboration	✓					
Quality Assurance	✓					
Incremental Delivery	✓					

Figure 24 - Agile Comparison Table 1

Scrum

Hirotaka Takeuchi is dean of the Graduate School of International Corporate Strategy at Hitotsubashi University in Tokyo and was a visiting professor at Harvard Business School in 1989 and 1990. Ikujiro Nonaka is Professor Emeritus, Hitotsubashi University Graduate School of International Corporate Strategy; the First Distinguished Drucker Scholar in Residence at the Drucker School and Institute, Claremont Graduate University; the Xerox Distinguished Faculty Scholar, Institute of Management, Innovation and Organization, University of California, Berkeley.

In 1986, these distinguished scholars described a holistic approach to new commercial product development. The paper titled *"The New New Product Development Game"* published by

Harvard Business Review presented a method to increase speed and flexibility in systems development. They said:

"Under the old approach, a product development process moved like a relay race, with one group of functional specialists passing the baton to the next group...

...Under the rugby approach, the product development process emerges from the constant interaction of a hand-picked, multidisciplinary team whose members work together from start to finish."

Merriam-Webster's Collegiate Dictionary (Eleventh Edition) defines the word "Scrum" as "a rugby play in which the forwards of each side come together in a tight formation and struggle to gain possession of the ball using their feet when it is tossed in among them."

In their paper, Takeuchi and Nonaka titled one of the topics "Moving the Scrum Downfield" in which they talk about interviews they conducted with CEOs and engineers which taught them "leading companies show six characteristics in managing their new product development processes." They go on to describe the characteristics of built-in stability, self-organizing project teams, overlapping development phases, multi-learning, subtle control and organizational transfer of knowledge. In 1990 Peter DeGrace and Leslie Hulet Stahl named[33] the entire Takeuchi and Nonaka process Scrum after their use of the word in the document.

Scrum was formerly presented as a software development approach at OPPSLA[34] 1995 by Ken Schwaber and Jeff Southerland. Schwaber is a software developer, product manager and industry consultant and operates scrum.org. He is president of Advanced Development Methods (ADM) and with Southerland, co-author of the definitive Scrum Guide. He is one of the leaders of the agile software development movement and a founder of the Agile Alliance. Southerland is a Distinguished Graduate of the United States Military Academy, a Top Gun of his USAF RF-4C Aircraft Commander class and flew 100 missions over North Vietnam. He is currently CEO of Scrum, Inc. in Boston, Massachusetts and Senior Advisor to OpenView Venture Partners. Schwaber and Southerland are two of the authors of the Agile Manifesto.

Scrum theory is founded upon the three pillars of empirical process control: Process Transparency, Inspection and Adaptation. Transparency means facets of the process affecting the outcome must be visible to those managing the outcomes. Inspection means processes must be examined often enough so undesirable variances can be detected. Adaptation means adjustments

---

[33] *"Wicked Problems, Righteous Solutions: A Catalog of Modern Engineering Paradigms,"* Prentice Hall PTR (1990)
[34] International conference on Object-Oriented Programming, Systems, Languages and Applications

must be made as quickly as possible when out of bound variances are discovered through inspection to minimize further deviation.

The Scrum framework consists of Scrum Teams and their associated roles; Time-Boxes, Artifacts, and Rules. Every Scrum team has a ScrumMaster responsible for making sure Scrum practices are followed and impediments to progress removed. The ScrumMaster does not manage the team. Teams are self-organizing with no more than 7 members. There is a Product Owner representing the customer to ensure the team addresses priorities from a business perspective. The Product Owner sits with the team. Team members are called "pigs" and everyone else is called "chickens." The pig and chickens idea originated from a fable. The earliest written version I could dig up is from June 13, 1950 published in the Titusville, Pennsylvania Herald in the column "Try and Stop Me" by Bennett Cerf, pg. 4, col. 4. Cerf said:

> A hen and a pig were sauntering down the main street of an Indiana town when they passed a restaurant that advertised "Delicious ham and eggs: 75¢."
>
> "Sounds like a bargain," approved the hen. "That owner obviously knows how to run his business."
>
> "It's all very well for you to be so pleased about the dish in question," observed the pig with some resentment. "For you it is all in the day's work. Let me point out, however, that on my part it represents a genuine sacrifice."

Schwaber and Southerland use a variation of this fable to illustrate two types of project members. Pigs are totally committed to the project and liable for its outcome. Chickens consult on the project and are informed of its progress. Chickens do not tell pigs what to do. By implication, a rooster is defined as a person who struts around offering uninformed and disobliging views. We all know a few roosters, don't we?

The notion of a Product Owner as a dedicated business liaison to the project team is a great idea and an important concept to grasp. I've worked on jobs where a legacy system didn't even have a clear business owner. These projects were put into production a long time ago and the business problem they solve has since drifted into the twilight zone. For new projects, we typically have an Executive Sponsor and a Project Sponsor who attend status update and progress review meetings. Other than their concern for schedule and cost, they usually have little other involvement in systems development.

Sometimes the Project Sponsor serves in the capacity of subject matter expert and does get involved with high level design and business rules. But business people want and need to focus on the business. IT projects are secondary issues to them. After all, isn't that what IT is supposed to do? They told us what they needed in a couple of design meetings and expect us to deliver to their specification. Their first priority is always the business. Try and schedule meetings with all of the subject matter experts after a project is underway post requirements workshops and you'll find it's very difficult to coordinate everyone's schedules and gain the commitment you need.

Unavailable business users are often the cause of project delays. It's an age-old, catch 22 type of excuse. In a fictional conversation, IT Governance asks: "Why didn't you get that system delivered according to schedule?"

IT answers, "Because the business isn't available to verify the requirements. Our process doesn't allow us to proceed without their approval."

The business responds, "We couldn't verify the requirements because we're too busy manually running operations because IT can't deliver the system we need." See the catch-22? Around and round it goes.

What Schwaber and Southerland propose is a deeper solution to address the described dilemma. The Product Owner is an integral member of the project team responsible for maintaining the Product Backlog and making decisions that affect the outcomes of the project. As the representative for the stakeholders, the Product Owner is empowered to serve as their voice and speak authoritatively on their behalf.

Scrum iterations are called sprints. Sprint durations are one month or less. Timeboxes are used to manage the regularity of sprints as well as the Release Planning Meeting, the Sprint Planning Meeting, the Daily Scrum, the Sprint Review, and the Sprint Retrospective.

Four artifacts are produced in Scrum: the Product Backlog, the Sprint Backlog, Release Burndown and Sprint Burndown. The Product Backlog is a project-level artifact that prioritizes all backlog items by business value. The Sprint Backlog is a task list detailing steps the team is going to turn the output of the sprint into a deployable component or product. The Sprint Burndown shows remaining Sprint Backlog items across the sprint's timeline. The Release Burndown is pretty much the same as the Sprint Burndown except it shows the remaining Product Backlog items across the Release Plan's time dimension. Figure 25 is a sample Scrum Burndown chart.

Rules are the guidelines that tie Scrum's timeboxes, roles, and artifacts together into a managed process. For example, the rules that guide the Daily Scrum or daily stand-up meeting as it is also called include:

- Meeting starts precisely on time.
- All are welcome, but only "pigs" may speak

- Meeting is timeboxed to 15 minutes
- Meeting scheduled for the same location and time every day

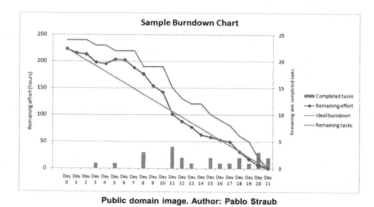

Public domain image. Author: Pablo Straub

Figure 25 - Sample Scrum Burndown Chart

Strengths:	Deficiencies:
<ul><li>Improves productivity over heavy process</li><li>Work prioritization</li><li>Backlog for completing items in a series of short iterations or sprints</li><li>Daily measured progress and communications</li></ul>	<ul><li>Reliance on Scrum master who may lack the clout to remove impediments and deliver the sprint goal</li><li>Reliance on self-organizing teams runs the risk of creating paralyzing internal power struggles</li></ul>

Scrum adds the daily stand-up, shared workplace, work prioritization and dedicated business delegate to the characteristics comparison chart.

Characteristics	RAD	Scrum				
Date	1991	1991				
Daily Stand-up		✓				
Team Empowerment	✓	✓				
Shared Workplace		✓				
Business Delegate		✓				
Iterative	✓	✓				
Dynamic Requirements	✓	✓				
Work Prioritization		✓				
Verification & Validation	✓	✓				
Testable Requirements	✓	✓				
Timeboxing	✓	✓				
Prototyping/Modeling	✓	✓				

Characteristics	RAD	Scrum				
Customer Collaboration	✓	✓				
Quality Assurance	✓	✓				
Incremental Delivery	✓	✓				

Figure 26 - Agile Comparison Table 2

The Crystal Family

Alistair Cockburn (pronounced Co-burn) is an internationally known self-described "project witchdoctor" and IT strategist, best known for describing software development as a Cooperative Game, helping write the Agile Manifesto and the PM Declaration of Interdependence, inventing the Cockburn Scale for categorizing software projects, for finally defining Use Cases and developing the initial response technique relaxation/massage form. Cockburn was hired by the IBM Consulting Group in the early 1990s to construct and document a methodology for object-oriented development. His research led to the formulation of Crystal. In the 2nd edition of Agile Software Development (Addison-Wesley Professional, Oct. 2006) he said:

"A named methodology is important because it is the methodology author's publicly proclaimed, considered effort to identify a set of practices or conventions that work well together, and when done together, increase the likelihood of success...

...Crystal is my considered effort to construct a package of conventions that raises the odds of success, and at the same time the odds of being practiced over time."

Crystal is different from other Agile practices because it is a family of methodologies, not just one. The Crystal family of methodologies started in 1992, before Extreme Programming, Feature Driven Development (FDD) etc. It was named "Crystal" in 1997, before the agile manifesto. It was one of the founding 'agile' methodologies.

The Crystal family is a group of lightweight methods related by their dependence on people, effective communication and frequent delivery of production-ready code. The family tree branches into vertical stripes distinguished by color. Crystal Clear is the methodology for 2-6 person projects, Crystal Yellow for 6-20 person projects, Crystal Orange for 20-40 person projects, then Red, Magenta, Blue, etc. depending on how large of a project team is required. Large projects which have consequences that involve risk to human life use the Crystal Sapphire or Crystal Diamond methods.

In Cockburn's words[35] the Crystal family is:

---

[35] Source: http://alistair.cockburn.us/Crystal+methodologies, accessed February 11, 2010

...a family of human-powered, adaptive, ultralight, "stretch-to-fit" software development methodologies.

- "Human-powered" means that the focus is on achieving project success through enhancing the work of the people involved (other methodologies might be process-centric, or architecture-centric, or tool-centric, but Crystal is people-centric).
- "Ultralight" means that for whatever the project size and priorities, a Crystal-family methodology for the project will work to reduce the paperwork, overhead and bureaucracy to the least that is practical for the parameters of that project.
- "Stretch-to-fit" means that you start with something just smaller than you think you need, and grow it just enough to get it the right size for you (stretching is easier, safer and more efficient than cutting away).

Crystal is non-jealous, meaning that a Crystal methodology permits substitution of similar elements from other methodologies.

Cockburn defines the term methodology as "...nothing more than 'the conventions a group of people adopt.'" He says, "[This is] a nice, simple definition that allows it to drift over time and be easily documented and easily changed." His philosophy is not to define the conventions that every team on the planet should use. Instead, he documents the parameters and principles he understands to help people work together and tell whether their conventions make sense.

Crystal Clear is the most well-known of the Crystal family of methodologies. It is documented in Cockburn's book "*Crystal Clear, A Human-Powered Methodology for Small Teams*," (Addison-Wesley Professional, October 2004). In Chapter 2 he explains seven properties the best teams put into practice when using the Crystal approach. Crystal Clear requires the first three:

- Frequent Delivery
- Reflective Improvement
- Osmotic Communication (Crystal Clear only)
- Personal Safety
- Focus
- Easy Access to Expert Users
- Technical environment with automated tests, configuration management, and frequent Integration

Five of these seven properties are self-explanatory, but osmotic communication and personal safety require a bit more exploration. When I first heard the term "personal safety" associated with the Crystal development methodology, I thought "What is Cockburn getting at?" My mind immediately jumped to the scenario of making sure cabling is secure and that nobody trips over a keyboard or pizza box left on the floor from a late night programming expedition. I envisioned a ridiculous cartoon image of a bunch of broken developers walking into work the next morning all trussed up with bandages and casts supported by crutches. This is not what Cockburn means by personal safety.

Personal safety fosters communication and trust. Cockburn said, "Personal safety is being able to speak when something is bothering you, without fear of reprisal. It may involve telling the manager that the schedule is unrealistic, a colleague that her design needs improvement, or even letting a colleague know that she needs to take a shower more often." The principle of personal safety extends far beyond the Crystal family methodologies and I couldn't agree with Cockburn more.

Personal Safety as Cockburn describes it is a principle of authentic leadership I have long embraced in my life. Whenever I've had direct reports, I share my Leadership Framework with them. When I'm finished, they know who I am as a leader, what my expectations are of them and what they can expect of me. They learn what my hot buttons are and what lines not to cross. Everyone in a leadership position should be able to share those facts with their subordinates. You may not be familiar with the concept of a Leadership Framework, so let me explain. The Leadership Framework is an individual's response to the following challenge:

"Imagine for a minute that you have to prepare a resume where you can't highlight the college you attended, what degrees you hold, your work experience or the project achievements you have had up to this point. The only data you can put on your resume pertains to who you are as a leader and what you have demonstrated. How would the resume read?"

This thought provoking question has stopped many a candidate dead in their tracks during a job interview. I say in my Leadership Framework, "Bring me bad news when it's fresh, when we can still act on it. Bad news is still good data. I don't like being surprised with information when it is within someone's power to let me know what's going on. Communication is the key to smooth operations and to building trust. We must make our concerns known and share feedback throughout the organization. We shall be honest, and we shall not indulge in personal attacks."

This is the essence of personal safety. Nurturing an atmosphere where people feel safe to speak their minds without fear of retribution is every leader's responsibility without regard to rank, title or sphere of influence. This principle has never failed me. In contrast, I know of one true situation where a boss asked a subordinate for her opinion on the manner in which the boss intended to handle a new business challenge. When the subordinate gave her opinion which was contrary to what the boss thought, the boss became incensed and wrote her up with Human Resources for insubordination. This is not an example of personal safety and certainly not a boss that I would ever want to work with. If that boss ever reported into me, he/she wouldn't last very long with that attitude. Personal safety trusts the opinions of others and doesn't punish them for disagreement.

In reference to osmotic communication, osmosis means "a usually effortless often unconscious assimilation" as in the sentence "I learned a new language by osmosis." Live in a foreign country for a while and you may pick up a few words or phrases just by watching television or being in the environment and having to survive in your surroundings. Osmotic communication in the Crystal Clear methodology means developers sit close to each other, frequently in the same room so that rapid communication and rich feedback can flourish. When people work closely together, they'll begin to communicate almost unconsciously. Questions and ideas flow naturally between them.

I witnessed an excellent demonstration of osmotic communication in action at the dentist's office. The two office workers behind the desk were seated about six feet apart. One was scheduling a follow-up appointment for a patient who had just concluded his time in the chair. The other worker was recording insurance payments on her computer. The phone rang and the first worker answered it. We could hear her directing the caller to visit the doctor's website to download a form. She paused momentarily as she began to give out the website's address as if she couldn't recall it. Without a bit of hesitation, the second worker recited the web address from memory and the first person repeated it to the caller. The second worker never looked up from her pc, yet responded at exactly the right moment. Even though she focused on her work, she tuned into the conversation and the first worker immediately picked up on her input.

It was once thought that osmotic communication couldn't be a norm for team communications unless people are sitting in the same room. That may no longer be the case, especially when working with the millennial generation. The millennials have been brought up in the age of social networking, instant messaging and texting. It's a fact that most millennials don't care as much about money, status or jobs as they do about staying in touch. Many companies are adjusting their computer use policies to retain young workers by allowing them to access social networking sites while in the office.

Cockburn said, "Herring[36] (2001) reported the use of high-speed intranet with Web cameras, microphones, and chat sessions to trade questions and code, to simulate the single room to (some) extent. With good technology, teams can achieve some approximation of close communication for some purposes, but I have yet to see osmotic communication achieved with other than physical proximity between team members."

---

[36] Charles Herring, Department of Computer Science & Electrical Engineering, The University of Queensland Brisbane, QLD 4072 Australia, Internet-based Collaborative Software Development Using Microsoft Tools, 5th World Multiconference on Systemics, Cybernetics and Informatics (SCI'2001). 2001. Orlando, Florida

Charting Crystal on our comparison chart is difficult because the methodologies are principle based not process grounded. Cockburn said, "I don't believe that any prescribed procedures exist that can assure that projects land in the safety zone every time. Nor, with the exception of incremental development, do I show up on a project with any particular set of rules in hand, even though I have my favorites. This is why Crystal Clear is built around critical properties instead of specification of procedures."

Development teams define their own procedures to allow maximum variability across different teams and avoid hampering the enthusiasm of individuals. The processes are refined through the Reflective Improvement principle. Let's assume however, that since Crystal is considered an agile method, by inference the characteristics of any generic agile method apply. Of all the methods we've examined thus far, Crystal is the first to make any mention of automated testing and configuration management as a best practice.

Characteristics	RAD	Scrum	Crystal			
Date	1991	1991	1992			
Daily Stand-up		✓				
Team Empowerment	✓	✓	✓			
Shared Workplace		✓	✓			
Business Delegate		✓				
Iterative	✓	✓	✓			
Dynamic Requirements	✓	✓	✓			
Work Prioritization		✓				
Verification & Validation	✓	✓	✓			
Testable Requirements	✓	✓	✓			
Timeboxing	✓	✓	✓			
Prototyping/Modeling	✓	✓	✓			
Customer Collaboration	✓	✓	✓			
Automated Testing			✓			
Configuration Mgmt			✓			
Quality Assurance	✓	✓	✓			
Incremental Delivery	✓	✓	✓			

Figure 27 - Agile Comparison Table 3

Extreme Programming

Extreme Programming is the brainchild of Kent Beck, an American software engineer and another author of the Agile Manifesto. Beck pioneered software design patterns, the rediscovery of Test-Driven Development (TDD) and the commercial application of Smalltalk. Beck's 1999 book, *Extreme Programming Explained: Embrace Change"* (Addison-Wesley), was chosen a runner up in the 10th annual Jolt Awards contest presented by Dr. Dobb's Journal[37] and received a Jolt Productivity Award plaque under the category of Books and Computer-Based Training. The Jolt Awards are considered the "Oscar" of the IT industry.

Software design patterns are object-oriented, domain-level architectural designs that show the relationships and interactions between objects and classes. They are utilized in building reusable software components and frameworks. Test-driven development is a design technique where the developer writes automated unit tests before writing one single line of code. We're going to discuss TDD in greater detail in Chapter 7—Design & Development. Smalltalk is an example of an object-oriented language first made publically available in 1980.

Beck helped popularize Class-Responsibility-Collaboration (CRC) cards with Ward Cunningham. CRC cards are a brainstorming tool used in object-oriented design when determining which classes are needed and their interactions. They are typically created from index cards and list the class name, super and sub-classes (if applicable), the responsibilities of the class, the names of other collaboration classes and the author. Finally, in collaboration with Erich Gamma, he created the JUnit unit testing framework.

Extreme Programming was born out of the Chrysler Comprehensive Compensation System (C3) project which Chrysler Corporation commissioned to replace several payroll applications with a single system to support payroll activities for 87,000 employees. Beck was hired as the project leader in March 1996 for the task of optimizing C3's performance. When Beck took over he found the project running behind schedule and cost projections showing it way over budget. He determined the code base was too complex and riddled with redundancy to ever work reliably in production. His recommendation was to trash the current code base and start over. Chrysler management agreed. In rebuilding the project, Beck created a new process by observing what worked and what didn't. He mixed best practices together from several emerging agile processes with things he had learned while working with Ward Cunningham.

In a January, 2000 interview conducted by Nicolai Josuttis for Overload Journal[38] #35, in response to the question "Who are the people that 'invented' XP?" Beck said:

> I am the one who put all the pieces together, and the one who coined the name. However, the ideas in XP come from many sources. I'm lucky if an original thought happens through my head once in five years, so generally I have to make my living putting together ideas that other folks haven't thought to put together. So, for example:

---

[37] Source: Dr. Dobb's Journal, June 1, 2000. (http://www.drdobbs.com/architect/184414615, accessed February 13, 2010)

[38] Source: ACCU professionalism in programming, http://accu.org/index.php/journals/509, accessed February 13, 2010.

- The testing strategy in XP comes from Christopher Glaser, a compiler writer I worked with at MasPar
- The iteration schedule comes from Jon Hopkins (in my opinion the most under-rated thinker in the world of objects)
- The strict separation of business decision making from technical decision making comes from the architect Christopher Alexander
- The evolutionary design philosophy comes from my long-time colleague Ward Cunningham
- The idea of making change in small steps where you always keep the system running comes from my dad, Doug Beck, who wrote process control software in assembly language for 8-bit micro processors

Don Wells is an expert in object technology and GUIs who worked on the C3 project. In the same interview Beck said, "I came up with all sorts of complicated schemes. Don Wells, one of the original Chrysler payroll people who went on to rescue a project at Ford using XP, set me straight."

Extreme Programming is a compilation of what Beck considers best practices. It is a literal jig saw puzzle of parts that he assembled. The name Extreme Programming comes from the idea of taking favorable elements of traditional system engineering practices to "extreme" levels. This is based on the premise that if a little is good, then more is better. (Kind of like eating ice cream right?)

The Extreme Programming methodology consists of five values and either twelve to fifteen core practices depending on to whom you are listening. Everyone seems to agree on the values. The five values are Simplicity, Communication, Feedback, Respect and Courage. The core practices are: Whole Team, Planning Game, Small Releases, Customer Tests, Simple Design, Pair Programming, Test-Driven Development, Design Improvement, Continuous Integration, Collective Code Ownership, Coding Standard, System Metaphor, Sustainable Pace, Refactoring, On-site Customer, Open Workspace and Forty-Hour Week

Peering under the hood of these core practices, you'll find there's not much new to them that we haven't seen in other Agile methods. They may be described a little differently on the surface, but once you understand them you'll agree they are common. Extreme Programming specifically calls for Test-Driven Development, Coding Standards and Pair Programming so we'll add these three to our chart. Even though Test-Driven Development and Pair Programming are Quality Assurance techniques, we'll list them separately because of their association with XP.

Characteristics	RAD	Scrum	Crystal	XP		
Date	1991	1991	1992	1995		
Daily Stand-up		✓		✓		
Team Empowerment	✓	✓	✓	✓		
Iterative	✓	✓	✓	✓		
Dynamic Requirements	✓	✓	✓	✓		
Verification & Validation	✓	✓	✓	✓		
Testable Requirements	✓	✓	✓	✓		
Timeboxing	✓	✓	✓	✓		
Work Prioritization		✓	✓	✓		
Shared Workplace		✓	✓	✓		
Business Delegate		✓		✓		
Test-Driven Dev.				✓		
Coding Standard				✓		
Pair Programming				✓		
Automated Testing			✓	✓		
Prototyping/Modeling	✓	✓	✓	✓		
Customer Collaboration	✓	✓	✓	✓		
Quality Assurance	✓	✓	✓	✓		
Incremental Delivery	✓	✓	✓	✓		
Configuration Mgmt			✓			

Figure 28 - Agile Comparison Table 4

Dynamic Systems Development Model

The Dynamic Systems Development Model (DSDM) began life when the 16 founding members of the DSDM Consortium met for the first time in January 1994. The consortium's sole objective was to create and market an independent RAD framework. By March of the same year, the high level framework was collectively accepted by the growing body of 36 members. While the basic concepts have remained static, the framework has since evolved and been refined. The DSDM Consortium proclaims it to be the "de facto" standard for rapid application development and asserts it is applicable in nearly every technical and business environment where systems are needed quickly. The Consortium was formed in the United Kingdom, but interest in DSDM can be found world-wide.

The first version of the DSDM framework was published in February 1995. A second version was published later that year in December. Almost two years later in October 1997, the third version was published. The first on-line version was published in 2001. Version 4.2 is the latest on-line version of the original DSDM model available on the Consortium's website today.

The DSDM Consortium has now released Atern, the newest DSDM evolution. The latest version of Atern can be found on www.dsdm.org. When DSDM first started, its focus was RAD and IT projects. Atern is a generic DSDM process that can be used for a broad array of projects, not just RAD and IT projects. It is used across a variety of industries as a framework to deliver on time solutions which meet or exceed the expectations of businesses. The DSDM Consortium has made "Project-in-a box" available as a free download on their website. Project-in-a-box is a .NET based software product to manage your DSDM projects. DSDM/Atern is complementary to the PRINCE2 project management method. PRINCE2 is a de facto standard developed and used extensively by the UK government and both UK and international private sectors.

For historical purposes, we'll look at DSDM as it originally evolved as a RAD/Agile method. DSDM has nine underlying principles which are:

1. User involvement: both users and developers share a workplace so decisions can be made quickly and accurately
2. The project team is empowered to make decisions that are important to the progress of the project
3. A focus on frequent delivery of products, with assumption that to deliver something "good enough" earlier is always better than to deliver everything "perfectly" in the end.

4. The main acceptance criterion for any deliverable is that it addresses the current business needs
5. Development is iterative and incremental and driven by users'
6. All changes during development are reversible
7. The high level scope and requirements are baselined before the project starts
8. Testing is carried out throughout the project life cycle
9. Project stakeholders are required to communicate and cooperate for an efficient and effective project

A fundamental assumption of the DSDM approach is that nothing is built perfectly first time. The Pareto principle is then applied to this assumption. If you recall from Chapter 1, the Pareto principle is the 80/20 rule. Applying it to DSDM yields the postulation that 80% of the solution can be produced in 20% of the time that it would take to produce the total solution.

The DSDM framework consists of three sequential phases, the pre-project, project life-cycle and post-project phases. The project phase is the most elaborate and consists of 5 stages that form an iterative step-by-step development approach.

Phase 1 - The Pre-Project phase is an IT Governance activity. Candidate projects are identified, project funding is secured and commitment is gained.

Phase 2 - The Project life-cycle consists of five stages: Feasibility Study and Business Study, Functional Model Iteration, Design and Build iteration and Implementation. The first two studies are sequential complementary steps. For simplicity's sake, Figure 29 depicts the two steps as a single stage called Feasibility. After these phases have been concluded, the system is developed iteratively and incrementally in the Functional Model Iteration, Design & Build Iteration and Implementation stages.

Phase 3 - Post-project ensures the system continues operating effectively and efficiently. Maintenance, enhancements and fixes progress according to DSDM principles. Maintenance is seen as continuing development based on the iterative and incremental nature of DSDM. Instead of finishing the project in one cycle, the project can return to previous phases or stages so that the previous step and the deliverable products can be refined.

DSDM is very much like Scrum in its techniques and roles. One technique that is different is the way in which items are prioritized. DSDM calls for using the MoSCoW method of prioritization. MoSCoW is an acronym that stands for Must Have, Should Have, Could Have, and Would Have. We're going to discuss MoSCoW in greater depth in Chapter 6—Requirements Analysis, Tracing & Inspection. The other techniques are Timeboxing, Prototyping, Testing, Workshop, Modeling and Configuration Management.

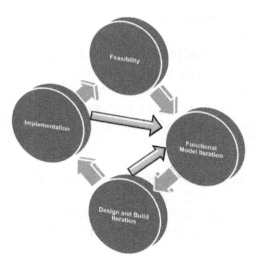

Figure 29 - DSDM Development Process

There are twelve roles in DSDM, Executive Sponsor, Visionary, Ambassador User, Project Manager, Technical Coordinator, Team Leader, Developer, Tester, Scribe, Facilitator and

Specialist Roles. The fact that there is a separate Tester Role leads to the assumption that DSDM's philosophy is more about quality control rather than quality assurance. The tester is also responsible for documenting parts of the system. There is one role that is glaringly absent from DSDM. That's the role of business analyst. DSDM assumes a programmer/analyst elicits the requirements and develops the system. Business analysis and programming require two distinctly different skill sets. While it has been a common practice in the past to use programmers to develop requirements, progressive thought leadership distinguishes and separates the roles.

Characteristics	RAD	Scrum	Crystal	XP	DSDM	
Date	1991	1991	1992	1995	1995	
Daily Stand-up		✓		✓		
Team Empowerment	✓	✓	✓	✓	✓	
Iterative	✓	✓	✓	✓	✓	
Dynamic Requirements	✓	✓	✓	✓	✓	
Verification & Validation	✓	✓	✓	✓	✓	
Testable Requirements	✓	✓	✓	✓	✓	
Timeboxing	✓	✓	✓	✓	✓	
Work Prioritization		✓	✓	✓	✓	
Shared Workplace		✓	✓	✓	✓	
Business Delegate		✓		✓	✓	
Test-Driven Dev.				✓		
Coding Standard				✓	✓	
Pair Programming				✓	✓	
Automated Testing			✓	✓	✓	
Prototyping/Modeling	✓	✓	✓	✓	✓	
Customer Collaboration	✓	✓	✓	✓	✓	
Quality Control					✓	
Quality Assurance	✓	✓	✓	✓		
Incremental Delivery	✓	✓	✓	✓	✓	
Configuration Mgmt			✓		✓	

Figure 30 - Agile Comparison Table 5

Lean Development

Lean is a thought process. It is a way of thinking that can be applied to a broad scope of product development and production activities. Larman and Vodde[39] (2009) liken it to watching the baton in a relay race, not the runners. They said:

"Does your organization measure 'productivity' or 'efficiency' in terms of how busy people are, or time spent—watching the runner? Or, in terms of fast delivery of value to the real customer—watching the baton? What is the value-to-waste ratio in your work? And what are the impediments to the flow of value—and how can people feel inspired to continuously strive to improve that flow? Lean thinking addresses this."

Lean was first identified as such in *"Lean Software Development: An Agile Toolkit"* by Mary Poppendieck and Tom Poppendieck, Addison-Wesley Professional (May 18, 2003). Lean grew out of a generic manufacturing process derived from the Toyota Production System (TPS) now known as "The Toyota Way." TPS helped drive Toyota's steady growth from a small company to the world's largest automobile manufacturer.

The main goal of TPS is to design out "muri (無理), mura (斑) and muda (無駄)" which translates to English as "overburden, unevenness (or inconsistency) and waste." As a thought process, it means keeping development and production practices as simple and flexible as possible without stress or "muri" (overburden) since this contributes to the "muda" (waste) generation. The seven kinds of muda addressed by TPS include:

1. Over-production
2. Motion (of operator or machine)
3. Waiting (of operator or machine)
4. Conveyance
5. Processing itself
6. Inventory (raw material)
7. Correction (rework and scrap)

Toyota experts agree that the management tools are of little importance to the process. Toyota CEO Katsuaki Watanabe said:

---

[39] Craig Larman and Bas Vodde, *"LEAN PRIMER,"* Copyright (c) Craig Larman & Bas Vodde 2009, (http://www.leanprimer.com/downloads/lean_primer.pdf)

The Toyota Way has two main pillars: continuous improvement and respect for people. Respect is necessary to work with people. By 'people' we mean employees, supply partners, and customers.

…We don't mean just the end customer; on the assembly line the person at the next workstation is also your customer. That leads to teamwork. If you adopt that principle, you'll also keep analyzing what you do in order to see if you're doing things perfectly, so you're not troubling your customer. That nurtures your ability to identify problems, and if you closely observe things, it will lead to kaizen—continuous improvement. The root of the Toyota Way is to be dissatisfied with the status quo; you have to ask constantly, "Why are we doing this?"

With these two pillars, Toyota management stresses the order of building people then building products. The two pillars, continuous improvement and respect for people are outlined this way:

- **Continuous Improvement**
    - Challenge (We form a long-term vision, meeting challenges with courage and creativity to realize our dreams.)
    - Kaizen (We improve our business operations continuously, always driving for innovation and evolution.)
    - Genchi Genbutsu (Go to the source to find the facts to make correct decisions.)
- **Respect for People**
    - Respect (We respect others, make every effort to understand each other, take responsibility and do our best to build mutual trust.)
    - Teamwork (We stimulate personal and professional growth, share the opportunities of development and maximize individual and team performance.)

Many becoming familiar with Lean tend to focus on waste reduction as the primary driver for their thought processes probably because waste reduction is the most familiar of the muri, mura, muda trilogy. Nothing could be further from the truth. In reality, practices that focus on reducing muri and mura result in the natural reduction of muda without specifically focusing on its reduction.

Lean is a very powerful approach to improve the quality, productivity and performance of requirements, systems engineering and software engineering. One of the key steps in Lean is the identification of which requirements add value and which do not. Lean principles include:

- Identify the customer defined value stream. Process = "value"
- Continuously eliminate non-value added activities (e.g., waste, rework, defects)

- Align your organization through visual communications (models, use cases, user stories)
- Amplify learning: use short timeboxed iteration cycles—each one coupled with refactoring and integration testing.
- Increase feedback via short feedback sessions with Stakeholders
- Deliver as fast as possible
- Empower the team
- Build integrity in

Lean thinking teaches that everything not adding value to the Customer is considered to be waste. For the SDLC this includes:

- unnecessary code and functionality
- delay in the software development process
- ambiguous requirements
- bureaucracy
- slow internal communication

After becoming a Six Sigma Greenbelt, I was asked to take a look at an IT Governance process that was perceived by the business as overly cumbersome and lengthy. The leaders of this particular IT group put a lot of thought into it and believed they had built the foundation for a solid, well-oiled governance model. They didn't understand the root cause of the business users' criticisms.

I poured over all of the documents related to the process and then laid out a linear timeline showing the process steps from start to finish and the amount of time allotted for every approval step. From the time the business requested a project initiation to the point where all IT reviews and approvals had been secured required a timeline extending from six to nine months! IT leadership was surprised and refused to accept the finding without empirical data to back up the time frames. They felt that their processes were being executed concurrently and the time therefore would be reduced accordingly. "It couldn't possibly be taking 6-9 months," they said.

We went back and began a review of all projects started in the past two years which is the time the governance process had been put in place. Granted some of the approvals may have been handled concurrently, but the actual measured average time to receive project approval turned out to be seven months. No wonder the business complained. IT leadership finally agreed their process was flawed and needed refinement.

Using Lean principles I challenged the process and asked which steps added value for the customer and which steps were for IT only. We continued to refine the steps, moving some of them to post approval project phases. By removing the requirement for wet signatures and applying automation to approval workflows, we reduced the average project approval time down to 30 days. Lean principles worked and it didn't cost the company anything for the process improvement! By eliminating the waste in the process we gained over a 90% improvement in approval times.

The Poppendiecks name several Lean development "tools" which are how they express Lean practices. Examples of such practices include:

- Seeing waste
- Value stream mapping
- Set-based development
- Pull systems (demand-driven)
- Queuing theory
- Motivation
- Measurements

While these tools don't map exactly to Agile development practices, they are parallels. For example a Lean Workcell is the equivalent of an Agile cross-functional team. As a set of principles and thought processes Lean can be applied to any Agile or Waterfall development methodology just as ICM can be applied to any Waterfall variant. Since Lean doesn't call for any specific processes, we're going to label Lean as a philosophical approach having the most common Agile characteristics. We'll also add continuous improvement metrics since they are specifically mentioned as a Lean characteristic.

Labeling Lean as a philosophy and including it on the comparison chart is likely to cause controversy and possible disagreement. But please, before rushing to judgment keep in mind what Toyota experts Yoshihito Wakamatsu and Tetsuo Kondo[40] said about the Toyota Way, "The essence is that each individual employee is given the opportunity to find problems in his own way of working, to solve them and to make improvements." By applying the Lean thought processes to the comparison chart, we can utilize its principles to find the best solution for a best-in-breed SDLC.

Characteristics	Agile Variants					Philosophy
	RAD	Scrum	Crystal	XP	DSDM	Lean
Date	1991	1991	1992	1995	1995	2003
Daily Stand-up		✓		✓		✓
Team Empowerment	✓	✓	✓	✓	✓	✓
Iterative	✓	✓	✓	✓	✓	✓

---

[40] Authors, *"Building People and Products the Toyota Way"* (2001)

Characteristics	Agile Variants					Philosophy
	RAD	Scrum	Crystal	XP	DSDM	Lean
Dynamic Requirements	✓	✓	✓	✓	✓	✓
Verification & Validation	✓	✓	✓	✓	✓	✓
Testable Requirements	✓	✓	✓	✓	✓	✓
Timeboxing	✓	✓	✓	✓	✓	✓
Work Prioritization		✓	✓	✓	✓	✓
Shared Workplace		✓	✓	✓	✓	✓
Business Delegate		✓		✓	✓	✓
Test-Driven Dev.				✓	✓	✓
Coding Standard				✓	✓	✓
Pair Programming				✓	✓	✓
Automated Testing			✓	✓	✓	✓
Prototyping/Modeling	✓	✓	✓	✓	✓	✓
Customer Collaboration	✓	✓	✓	✓	✓	✓
Quality Control					✓	
Quality Assurance	✓	✓	✓	✓		✓
Continuous Improvement						✓
Incremental Delivery	✓	✓	✓	✓	✓	✓
Configuration Mgmt			✓		✓	

Figure 31 - Agile / Lean Comparison Table

Understanding It All

In this chapter we've taken a look at twelve of the most well-known and popular Waterfall and Agile methodologies to progress over a generation starting in the 1930s and ending in 2006. Each comes with its own set of principles, practices, philosophies and thought processes. We've charted primary characteristics from each of the methodologies to look for commonalities across them. Let's be cautious however, as a comparison study this is only a beginning. It is beyond the scope of this book to penetrate any deeper than a surface analysis. To perform a more in-depth scientifically protocoled study examining all of the nuances and minutia of the various methodologies at a cellular level requires significant time and resources and would no doubt result in a book of its own.

The philosophies behind Waterfall and Agile differ greatly, yet maybe not as much as we once thought. The data shows the two families, as they continue to evolve, are beginning to merge into a common collection of best practices. Waterfall methods grew out of the aerospace, science and defense domains. They are used to manage super-large, high risk projects costing many millions and in some cases billions of dollars. Some projects were successful, some abysmal failures and some were cancelled before having a chance to demonstrate success or failure. Agile methods grew out of the IT industry. Some of the greatest and most renowned industry thought leaders are behind the principles of Agile. Agile methods are light-weight, intended for smaller projects run by self-empowered teams.

Many consider Waterfall to be "plan-driven" and Agile to be "feedback-driven." Agile methodologies are feedback-driven. Major importance is placed on continuous learning throughout the iterations. As components are developed, customers collaborate and provide feedback to the developers assuring the product is meeting their needs. Feedback-driven development is a pull approach to just-in-time engineering. Engineering and refactoring take place as the customers demand is more fully comprehended.

I do not like the term "plan-driven" when referring to Waterfall, preferring to think of Waterfall as *"forecast-driven"* because these models tend to be driven by forecasts of the future. One of the commonalities of the Waterfall variants is that business requirements must be known up front. With the introduction of the Spiral Model this changed a little and there was some accommodation for limited requirements iterations. Still, gathering business requirements upfront necessitates making certain assumptions, sometimes even guessing. When variances occur to schedule, cost or the requirements themselves due to changing business need, it can often be attributed to faulty execution or faulty assumptions.

Forecast-driven approaches are push approaches because the product is created and then pushed on the users whether their needs change over time or not. Since systems development is the business of manufacturing a specific product to be delivered to end users, we can learn from the manufacturing industry. In manufacturing, pull approaches always bring better results than push approaches. If a company wants to use forecast-driven models for their SDLC, they need to shorten the "development to delivery" cycle times which equates to significant gains in the "concept to business value" equation.

Of all of the approaches we looked at, only two mention any specifics about their compatibility with project management methodologies. The DSDM Consortium talks about DSDM/Atern's compatibility with PRINCE2 and the German V-Modell includes an integrated project management methodology. Other than in Ambler's definition of what an Agile method is, not one of the models themselves express anything about touch points with IT Governance. Is this an oversight? Is this because IT Governance isn't important to systems development? Is it because the scientists creating the methodologies are so focused on single outcomes that they are missing the big picture? Or could it be because the methodologies were created outside of a corporate governance model?

I don't know the answers to these questions. Only the creators of the methodologies can reply to them and explain their omission, but I don't believe it's because the framers think IT Governance is unimportant. It's been my experience that many a systems developer knows very little about IT Governance until they are called onto the carpet to explain some point of their project. Then it hits them right in the face. In the next chapter we will begin to remove some of the mystery and identify some of the details about how IT Governance, Project Management and the SDLC are inextricably linked into one holistic approach to systems development.

To understand best practices and what we need to include in a best-in-breed SDLC, our next step is to merge the Waterfall and Agile methods into a single chart to see which, if any, commonalities emerge across the two families. The result is in the table below.

Characteristics	Waterfall Variants					Hybrid	Agile Variants					Philosophy
	Linear Waterfall	Modified Waterfall	Spiral	Vee-Model	Dual Vee	ICM	RAD	Scrum	Crystal	XP	DSDM	Lean
Date	1930s	1970	1986	1991	2005	2006	1991	1991	1992	1995	1995	2003
Linear	✓											
Daily Stand-up								✓		✓		✓
Team Empowerment							✓	✓	✓	✓	✓	✓
Iterative		✓†	✓	✓	✓	✓	✓	✓	✓	✓	✓	✓
Manages Risk		✓	✓	✓	✓	✓						✓
Dynamic Requirements			✓†	✓†	✓†	✓	✓	✓	✓	✓	✓	✓
Verification & Validation				✓	✓	✓	✓	✓	✓	✓	✓	✓
Testable Requirements				✓	✓	✓	✓	✓	✓	✓	✓	✓
Concurrent Engineering				✓††	✓	✓						✓
Timeboxing						✓	✓	✓	✓	✓	✓	✓
Reusable Components			✓			✓						✓
Work Prioritization								✓	✓	✓	✓	✓
Shared Workplace							✓	✓		✓	✓	✓
Business Delegate								✓		✓	✓	✓
Test-Driven Dev.								✓		✓		✓
Coding Standard								✓		✓		✓
Pair Programming								✓		✓		✓
Automated Testing									✓	✓	✓	✓
Prototyping/Modeling			✓	✓	✓	✓	✓	✓	✓	✓	✓	✓
Customer Collaboration		✓†	✓	✓	✓	✓	✓	✓	✓	✓		✓
Quality Control	✓	✓	✓	✓	✓					✓		
Quality Assurance						✓	✓	✓	✓	✓		✓
Continuous Improvement												✓
Incremental Delivery			✓	✓	✓	✓	✓	✓	✓	✓	✓	✓
Configuration Mgmt									✓		✓	
Big Bang Delivery	✓	✓										

†Limited capability   ††off-core activity

Figure 32 - Waterfall / Agile / Lean Comparison Table

We can definitely see there are commonalities across the families. For a slightly different view of the data, let's sort the characteristics by their popularity with popularity being defined as a count of the number of methodologies that calls out the specific characteristic as one of their primary best practices.

Characteristic / Popularity		Characteristic / Popularity		Characteristic / Popularity	
Customer Collaboration	11	Quality Assurance	6	Daily Stand-up	3
Iterative	11	Team Empowerment	6	Pair Programming	3
Dynamic Requirements	10	Quality Control	6	Reusable Components	3
Incremental Delivery	10	Shared Workplace	5	Test-Driven Dev.	3
Prototyping/Modeling	10	Work Prioritization	5	Big Bang Delivery	2
Testable Requirements	9	Automated Testing	4	Configuration Mgmt	2
Verification & Validation	9	Business Delegate	4	Continuous Improvement	1
Timeboxing	7	Concurrent Engineering	4	Linear	1
Manages Risk	6	Coding Standard	3		

Figure 33 - Best Practices by Popularity

Just because a specific practice is not labeled a primary activity of a particular methodology doesn't mean the practice isn't conducted in the methodology. There is a lot of overlap and as we can see above, many shared common practices. It's not surprising that Customer Collaboration, Iterative Development, Dynamic Requirements, Incremental Delivery and Prototyping/Modeling are the top five in the standings followed closely by testable Requirements and Verification and Validation. These are all very important characteristics of any methodology. They won't guarantee a project's success, but they'll sure get you on the right path.

Our first surprise is Risk Management. The Waterfall methods specify risk management as a major activity, the Agile varieties don't. Does this mean that Agile doesn't consider risk management to be important? No, not at all! Risk management is not unimportant to Agile methods. It is handled differently in Agile methods.

Risk management is about the identification, assessment and prioritization of risks. Risks are identified in part by requirements elicitation processes. Once the business requirements are understood, risks can defined, categorized and work planned to address them. In Waterfall, requirements are gathered at the beginning of the project cycle. It makes sense to include risk management as an early project activity. In Agile, requirements are refined at the beginning of each cycle. Therefore, risk is handled within the just-in-time engineering activities. Risk management is always important regardless of the chosen method. It's a matter of whether the process is formalized by the method or not.

There a few other surprises as well. For example, ICM specifies timeboxing but not work prioritization. You can't schedule timeboxes correctly without prioritizing the work. While ICM doesn't specifically highlight prioritization, it is implied by specifying timeboxing. The biggest surprise is how low reusable components and continuous improvement are on the popularity scale. With a Six Sigma background, I rate continuous improvement highly. The only philosophy mentioning continuous improvement is Lean which is often associated with Six Sigma. Reusable components are a best practice regardless of their standing on this chart. It is most likely low on the chart because reusable components find a ready home in the Service Oriented Architecture (SOA) world and none of these methodologies discuss SOA. But the absence of mention of reusable components does not mean these methodologies are averse to reusable components.

The last surprise we'll chat about in this chapter is Configuration Management (CM). Both Crystal and DSDM consider CM a major activity. Configuration management was first developed as a technical management discipline in the 1950s by the Department of Defense and has since been widely adopted and refined by many technical management models including the majors such as Capability Maturity Model Integration (CMMI), ISO 9000, PRINCE2, COBIT and Information Technology Infrastructure Library (ITIL).

While some practitioners view software configuration management as the best method for managing change to software environments, holistically CM goes way beyond software management. It extends to the entire infrastructure. Configuration management is creating and maintaining an up-to-date record of all the components of the production infrastructure, including software and related documentation. CM's purpose is to illustrate the components (configuration items) that make up the infrastructure and to show the physical locations and links between each configuration item. This information is stored in the configuration management database (CMDB) which in addition is often used as an asset tracking system.

There's no argument that CM is an important aspect of managing an IT infrastructure. As CM is defined today, the inclusion of CM as a major activity of an Agile development methodology is disputable. Perhaps the definition of CM was different and appropriate in the day when Crystal and DSDM were developed. There are SDLC touch points for sure, but CM as it has evolved belongs with the group handling change management, release management, or infrastructure management, not the product development team. CM is an integration point for the product development team into the IT infrastructure. A product's configuration management specifications are apt details for SDLC production turnover artifacts.

Requirements Maturity, IT Governance & Planning

Have you ever endured the experience of working day and night for months on a project only to hear your end users say when they see the product for the first time, "That's not what we wanted?" These haunting words immediately have the effect of metamorphosing our pride of accomplishment into disappointment. The disappointment quickly turns to dread as we realize that we need to go back to the drawing board and maybe start over if we can't easily repair the perceived damage. It's disheartening.

If you live in a corporate world, these words mean an increased budget and timeline if the project doesn't get canceled outright. You may have to bring in additional help which automagically invokes Brooks' Law,[41] blowing the schedule. If you are a consultant working on a fixed bid project, this could mean absorbing the cost of repairs yourself, eating away at your hard earned profits. Whether you can or can't fix the problem may not be the question. As a consultant, it could mean that you'll be calling upon an in-law you don't particularly like who works as a litigation attorney because you'll soon need a good one to defend you in a failure to perform law suit. And if your customers tell you that time and money are of no consequence, then enjoy yourself and have fun. Take as long as you need to fix the problem and charge as much as you can because you've just stumbled across the Lost Dutchman's Gold Mine![42]

System development breakdowns and rework are nothing new and something we've all experienced at one time or another. They've been with us since the advent of the "castle clock," the earliest programmable analog computer invented by Al-Jazari[43] in 1206. The root cause of many modern day systems development project overruns, failures and rework are directly attributable to poor requirements. Look at these study conclusions published over a 13 year period beginning in 1995:

"Requirements problems have been proven to contribute to 20-25% of all project failures. The average project overran its budget 189% and its schedule by 222%"—Chaos Report/The Standish Group 1995

---

[41] Brooks' law is a principle in software development which says that "adding manpower to a late software project makes it later." –Fred Brooks, *"The Mythical Man-Month."*

[42] A very rich gold mine reportedly hidden in the Superstition Mountains, near Apache Junction, east of Phoenix, Arizona in the United States

[43] Abū al-'Iz Ibn Ismā'īl ibn al-Razāz al-Jazarī (1136-1206) (Arabic: الجزري الرّزاز بْنُ إِسْماعِيلِ بْنُ اَلْعِزِ أَبُو) was a prominent Arab polymath: an Islamic scholar, inventor, mechanical engineer, craftsman, artist, mathematician and astronomer from Al-Jazira, Mesopotamia.

"Requirements Errors account for 70% to 85% of rework" —Liffingwell, 1997

"Poor requirements account for 71% of project failures" —Grady, 1999

"Between 40 and 60 per cent of all software defects can be attributed to bad requirements" —Abbott, 2001

"Only 34% of projects expected to finish on time; 52% had proposed functionality; 82% had time overruns; 43% had budget overruns" —The Chaos Chronicles/ The Standish Group 2004

"Flawed Requirements Trigger 70% of Project Failures" —Infotech Research, 2005

"Gaps in the Technical Requirements accounted for more than 70% of program problems" —United States Government Accountability Office, 2008

In addition to these startling conclusions about how poor requirements contribute to project rework and failures, the 1995 Chaos Report added that 94 out of every 100 projects require restarts, sometimes multiple restarts, citing a California Department of Motor Vehicles case study to illustrate the claim. The Standish Group reports, "Only 9% of projects in large companies were successful." Medium size companies demonstrated a 16.2% success rate and small companies showed 28% successes. The most successful case study highlighted in the report is the Hyatt hotel reservation system. The report stated, "Hyatt had all the right ingredients for success: user involvement, executive management support, a clear statement of requirements, proper planning, and small project milestones." Hyatt finished their project early and under budget.

You would think the statistics would reveal an improving trend line considering the advances made in system development methodologies. Instead, we observe the opposite with the best statistics in 1995 and a worsening trend over time leveling off at a 70% failure/rework rate since 2005. And this is only with the projects that have been surveyed. How many more are out there we don't know about? The cost of these project failures and cancellations run into the high billions. The Chaos Report estimated American companies and government would spend $81 billion dollars (USD) on failed or canceled projects in 1995. How much more would that be in today's dollars in light of the worsening failure rate?

A February 2009 article by Jeff Roster,[44] a member of the Gartner Blog Network, revealed 2008 worldwide spending statistics broken out by industry segment. The industries and how much they spent in 2008 for IT projects are listed below. The figures are read as billions in US Dollars.

- Financial Services: $558.4
- Retail: $153.3
- Transportation: $105.9
- Utilities: $128.1

- Communications: $368.3
- Manufacturing: $482.7
- Healthcare: $ 88.0

The article predicted the growth rates through 2012 in IT spend for these industries which range from a low of 2.8% for manufacturing to 5.2% for Utilities. In 2008, total IT investment was just under $1.9 trillion dollars in these market segments which do not take into account government spending. If we apply the conservative 1995 Chaos Report metric of 25% for project failures to the 2008 spending statistic, it means that we can estimate that in 2008 $475 billion dollars was spent on failed or canceled projects worldwide.

You have to admit there's something definitely going on here. As we saw in Chapter 2, as new development methods were introduced to the world, they each brought new best practices, greater accountability and process efficiencies with them. Why have project failures, rework and defects increased in light of the introduction of more robust development practices? The answer cannot be provided simply in a few words without offending someone's sensibilities. But if requirements are genuinely a root cause as the studies concluded, the reality is that many people in the role of eliciting and documenting requirements are not sufficiently trained in the competencies required to adequately perform the job. As a result, they function out of instinct or from following examples of someone or something they observed in the past which may not have been the right way to go about things.

As an operational definition, good requirements are cohesive, complete, consistent, correct, feasible, modifiable, necessary, prioritized, reusable, testable, traceable, verifiable and unambiguous. If requirements aren't captured to this high standard, rework or project failure is the natural consequence. No one will ever get good requirements that meet this standard by walking into a room and asking the customers "What are your requirements?" This is not a disciplined enough approach. Yet, it's what many companies do. Good requirements are elicited. The word "elicit" means to "draw out" which means the competency of requirements elicitation necessitates a great degree of interaction, organization and customer involvement to draw good requirements out of the users.

---

[44] Source: http://blogs.gartner.com/jeff_roster/2009/02/11/it-spend-by-industry-worldwide/; Accessed February 22, 2010

To punctuate the need for training, let's examine another case study from a small company. After a number of failed projects or significant project rework, senior management sought to understand the competency level of everyone in their application development group with the job title of business analyst. They tested 32 people, 24 Business Analysts and 8 managers. The test they chose is from Kenexa®. Kenexa[45] is a company that provides business solutions for human resources that support the entire employee lifecycle from pre-hire to exit.

The Kenexa product mix includes pre-hire tests known as "Prove-It" exams. Prove-It exams are generally used during the pre-interview screening process to verify the genuineness of a candidate's skill set claims. Kenexa does not have a Prove-it exam specifically tailored for Business Analysts, so the company selected the next best thing, the Business Systems Analyst (BSA) exam. You may be asking yourself, "What is the difference between a Business Analyst and a Business Systems Analyst?" An individual with the title of "Business Analyst" may be a broadly accomplished generalist where a "Business Systems Analyst" may specialize in system design and the technical aspects of the solution.

The BSA exam consists of 49 questions in basic, intermediate and advanced categories designed to test the knowledge of a broadly accomplished IT Generalist. That's why it's suitable to offer the test to Business Analysts despite the title of the exam. Each of the 49 questions pertains to a specific competency or knowledge area which should be familiar to most anyone in a systems development domain. The exam is comprehensive and the topics balanced to test for a broad scope of IT knowledge.

Eight of the business analysts (33%) failed the test with scores less than 70%. One of them scored 51% and another 43%. Five scored in the 70s. Ten scored in the 80s and the remaining one scored above 90%. Of the eight managers, one scored above 90%, the others were all in the 80%s. As senior management conferred to flush out the root cause for the not so stellar performance, they examined the actual job duties of the business analysts and compared them against the written job descriptions. They realized that 18 of the 24 business analysts actually perform the duties of Tier 2 or Tier 3 support analysts and are not acting in the capacity of true business analysts. Of the six people who were identified by their job descriptions as true business analysts, two failed with scores less than 70 and the others achieved scores in the 70s and 80s. The need for focused training is evident.

Perhaps you've seen the system development life cycle cartoon depicted as the steps required for developing a tire swing? (Figure 34) The cartoon hung on many an office wall in the UK during the 60s and in the US in the 70s and 80s. Variations of the cartoon have appeared in many publications over the years including the University of London Computer Centre Newsletter No.

---

[45] North American Headquarters, 650 East Swedesford Road, 2nd Floor, Wayne, Pennsylvania 19087; http://www.kenexa.com/

53, March 1973,[46] the San Francisco Examiner on Sunday, October 12, 1975, John Oakland's book Total Quality Management, first published in 1989 and Guide to Good Programming Practice, Editors: B L Meek and P M Heath. The author and origin of the cartoon are unknown.

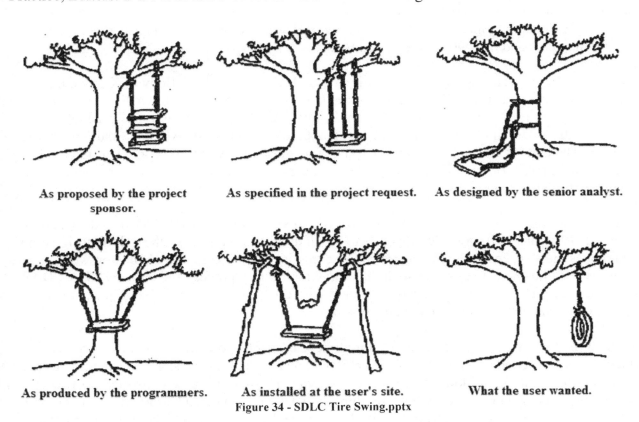

As proposed by the project sponsor.

As specified in the project request.

As designed by the senior analyst.

As produced by the programmers.

As installed at the user's site.

What the user wanted.

Figure 34 - SDLC Tire Swing.pptx

While the cartoon is designed to produce a "LOL"[47] type of response from the observer, it portrays a tautology that should be all too obvious to everyone by now. If the requirements aren't right from the beginning of the project or iteration, the work product suffers. Requirements are the foundation of any systems development project and its resulting work product. Getting requirements right is the domain of the Business Analyst. The cost for correcting mistakes because of poor requirements increases exponentially as a project evolves. If you haven't experienced a speed bump in a project yet due to blown requirements, just wait. You probably will. It's like being a motorcycle rider. There are two types of motorcycle riders, those who have laid their bikes down and those who *will* lay their bikes down.

---

[46] Source: http://www.businessballs.com/treeswing.htm; (accessed February 19, 2010)
[47] Laugh out loud

To be fair to Business Analysts, business analysis as a profession has just moved past its toddler years. Business analysis as an organized profession began to gain ground with the formation of the International Institute of Business Analysis™ (IIBA®). The IIBA is an independent non-profit professional association for Business Analysis Professionals. It was formed in October 2003 with 28 founding members from eight countries and as of May 2010 boasts more than 12,000 members and over 90 chapters worldwide.

The IIBA is most well-known for the creation of the Business Analysis Body of Knowledge (BABOK®), the collection of knowledge within the BA profession reflecting current generally accepted best practices. Draft versions 1.0 and 1.4 of BABOK were released to the general public in 2005. The first formal release, Version 1.6, followed in 2006 with the final 1.6 version in 2008. The current edition, Version 2.0, is a major revision of Version 1.6 and was released in March, 2009. BABOK is defined and updated by the professionals who use it every day and is under continual active review.

The IIBA has also created the Certified Business Analysis Professional™ (CBAP®) designation, and as of February 2010, awarded this title to 847 individuals. To receive the CBAP designation, candidates must successfully demonstrate their expertise by itemizing their hands-on work experience in business analysis through the CBAP application process and pass the IIBA CBAP examination.[48] The IIBA is to the business analysis profession what the Project Management Institute is to the project management profession.

Well-formed requirements are necessary for all development efforts including new systems, upgrades, support and maintenance. And as Figure clearly demonstrates, good requirements are necessary for building our kids' backyard jungle gyms. If you start out to construct an office building and leave gaps in the foundation, think of what would happen by the time you get to the roof. Don't let anyone deceive you. We need to change the way we think about requirements. Build a strong foundation and the edifice stands erect.

Requirements are a process, not an exercise in filling out a template. It is not a one-time or minimally iterative activity as in the Waterfall variants or an activity that is performed only at the beginning of Agile-styled sprints. It is an on-going process of elicitation, baselining, refinement, change management, communication, feedback and tracing, ideally performed by Business Analysts who possess a right balance of competencies and domain expertise. One of its main focus points is on the people and relationship building aspect of systems development as opposed to technical execution, although technical expertise is a major part of it. As the BA collaborates with customers, mistakes are caught earlier in the process which helps get the requirements right rather than to discover problems later due to poor elicitation technique or faulty assumptions. Every BA I've ever had an opportunity to lead has heard me say, "It's all about the relationship."

---

[48] Source: http://www.theiiba.org/AM/Template.cfm?Section=About

We can easily fix problems with technical execution. It's much more difficult to fix people issues especially in the politically charged corporate office environment.

The inauguration of the requirements process is variably dependent on the kind of business you are in and the type of project you are on. For example, if you are a consultant for hire, the requirements process begins at a high level during the investigative phase when a client initially contacts you with some of the particulars of the project. After a contract is secured, you may begin an earnest requirements discovery process. If you work for the government, there are many rules for project inception and the procurement of resources. Follow the respective agency's governance policy. If you work in a corporate environment, the requirements process for new systems or upgrades required to support strategic organizational goals begins with early IT Governance activities provided there is a corporate IT Governance structure in place. If your organization doesn't have an IT Governance structure, you are probably functioning as an internal consultancy where the convention for a hire-on-demand contracting organization may apply. Whatever the situation, the goal is to get the requirements right at the beginning of the life cycle.

In Chapter 1 we touched briefly on IT Governance and the SDLC. We're going to build upon that discussion in the next section. However, IT Governance and how it meshes with the requirements process may not be of interest to you at this time or not applicable to your particular business area. If you are working someplace where there is no IT Governance structure in place or don't want to learn about it now, skip to the following section of the chapter where we begin to decompose requirements elicitation competencies, otherwise keep reading. If you work in a corporate environment, this is definitely a section for you. If you do decide to skip ahead now, please make sure to come back later and read this. You will learn something new.

IT Governance and the Requirements Process

Corporate IT Governance primarily focuses on the financial aspects of Information technology. It's about IT investments and providing maximum return to the business. One facet of optimizing the value chain is controlling the work intake process. As senior managers decide to invest in high value projects, it becomes difficult to calculate resource costs and schedules if the resources are distracted to work on lower priority maintenance and support issues. Ideally, resources should be dedicated to major projects whether it means FTEs[49] or contingent workforce. But in the age of tight budgets and recessionary cuts, that's not always realistic. IT personnel often wear many hats and dedicating resources to a specific project comes with its own risks. For example, if FTEs are dedicated to a project, who takes care of the day-to-day support for the customer?

---

[49] Full time employee or full time equivalent

FTEs could be backfilled with contingent workers but that increases project costs and delays things as the temp staff trains. If the project is staffed with contingent workers, how efficiently is the transfer of knowledge at the end of the project going to be handled as the support and maintenance duties are turned back over to the FTEs?

Another more serious and potentially costly issue related to contingent workers is relative to how a company manages them. It cost Microsoft a reported $97 million in payouts to contingent workers after running afoul of the Internal Revenue Service's 20-point employee classification test.[50] After the IRS reclassified the contractors as employees, statutes from the Employee Retirement Income Security Act of 1974 (ERISA) applied to anyone working more than 1,000 hours per year. Microsoft settled the case before the United States Court of Appeals for the Ninth Circuit could issue its final ruling. The problems Microsoft faced stemmed from their engagement of "'freelancers' on specific projects where they performed a number of different functions, such as production editing, proofreading, formatting, indexing, and testing. Microsoft 'fully integrated' them into its regular workforce. They often worked on teams along with the 'regular employees,' sharing the same supervisors, performing identical functions, and working the same core hours. Microsoft required that they work on-site and, thus, they were given admittance key cards, office equipment and supplies by Microsoft. Instead of being paid by the Payroll Department, however, they submitted 'invoices' to and were paid by the Accounts Payable Department."[51] The laws governing contractor vs. employee are complex and companies should consult with legal experts to help determine compliance.

The companies I've worked for all used different approaches to project staffing. One company staffed every project with contractors. Money was no object at the time. The only full time IT staff at that company consisted of business analysts and project managers. Another company had such tight budgets and staff shortages that every work request, regardless of how short the estimate to complete or the perceived urgency, needed to be logged into a PVCS tracking system and went through a weekly demand planning review. Sometimes it took weeks to get a one-hour cosmetic fix completed because of waiting through the approval process. The only thing we were allowed to work on without permission was a production system down scenario, but not before notifying half a dozen managers. Then a third company provided a more balanced approach to work intake, creating thresholds below which either the responsible IT Director or a business unit steering committee could decide to move forward. IT Governance reviewed requests only if they exceeded 500 hours. For the purpose of this study, we'll inspect this balanced approach to understand the linkage between IT Governance and the requirements process.

---

[50] For more information, visit: http://www.irs.gov/businesses/small/article/0,,id=99921,00.html
[51] Source: *Employee or Independent Contractor? The Implications of Microsoft III* By Dennis D. Grant of Arter & Hadden LLP, February 2000 (http://library.findlaw.com/2000/Feb/1/127759.html)

Be mindful of the fact that the IT Governance model presented here is representative of a generic IT Governance process. Job titles, hierarchies, roles and responsibilities are unique and specific to every organization. How IT Governance functions in your company may be completely different from this representation, but principles learned still apply. Much of how IT Governance operates is based on the company's IT funding model. For example, are your IT projects funded through a centralized capital budget or through business unit budgets or even some third level source as in a chargeback model? This model assumes a corporate capital budget and functional IT groups that are aligned to the business units they support, a very popular way of doing things. It is not intended to model shared services support organizations or funding that comes from any source other than the central budget. The model calls for the following roles: IT Governance Committee (or Council), Business Unit Steering Committee and IT Director. These roles are defined as follows:

IT Governance Council (ITGC): The ITGC is composed of the senior most leaders in an organization. The facilitator and committee chair is the Chief Information Officer. The committee includes the Chief Executive Officer and/or Chief Operating Officer and the heads of the business units with the greatest vested interest in information systems. Composition varies from company to company. The ITGC reviews all new strategic IT projects, determines their business value and approves the funding. They review enhancement and maintenance requests requiring more than a specified threshold per hours of estimated effort. They review progress reports and change orders for all ITGC approved projects. The ITGC approval threshold is >=500 hours of estimated effort.

Business Unit Steering Committee: For each business unit the steering committee consists of the senior most leader of the business unit and the directors of the different departments operating within the business unit. For example, a Human Resources steering committee may include the Senior Vice-President of HR and the Directors of HR, Compensation, Payroll and Benefits. Steering committee meetings are facilitated and chaired by the IT Directors supporting the business unit. Steering committees review all work requiring an estimated effort falling within a threshold range of hours. They are responsible for providing business justification for larger projects requiring ITGC approval. The senior-most manager on the steering committee is responsible for making any presentation to the ITGC for large projects requiring their approval. The Steering Committee approval threshold range is >120 and <500 hours of estimated effort.

IT Directors are the department heads of the IT functional support teams aligned to the business units. The IT Director is the primary liaison between the business unit and IT. The IT Director manages the day-to-day operations of their team, manages communications with the business, develops the business case for ITGC presentations, helps align business and IT strategies and facilitates the business unit steering committee functions. The IT Director is the first point of contact for enhancement or change requests originating in the business. IT Directors are empowered to schedule work if the level of estimated effort is less than a specified threshold of hours. The IT Director approval threshold is <=120 hours.

Regardless of whether you work for a large company or a small company, the lessons learned at the micro level still apply to the macro. Large companies with bigger budgets and greater headcount often have higher thresholds and greater responsibilities. At one company I worked for, as an IT Director I had an authorized signature level of $5,000 with very little decision making scope. In another, as an IT Director I had an authorized signature level of $75,000 and broad decision making authority which was equivalent to a Senior Vice-President position at the first company. It all depends on the company and its policies.

Figure 35 depicts the representative IT Governance hierarchy.

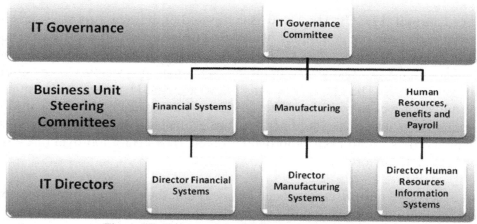

Figure 35 - Representative IT Governance Hierarchy

Work Intake

How do you acquire the work you perform? What is your work intake process? In a corporate environment, the work commonly comes from:

- Strategic organizational goals
- Enhancement/change request from the business
- Regulatory changes/updates
- Help desk problem resolution

- Routine maintenance tasks
- Defect repairs
- IT projects for IT's sake

Strategic organizational goals generally lead to new projects or major upgrades to older systems. The goals drive a company's target profitability. IT systems developed in response to an organizational goal are major investments and deemed strategic enablers that provide a company with a competitive advantage. These types of projects originate with the company's Executive team and ITGC and are funded with capital dollars. Capital dollars are a finite, annually renewable resource reliant on the company's prosperity. Bad financial times mean less capital dollars. Fewer capital dollars means a reduction in new IT projects and possibly headcount. With reductions in projects and headcount, IT has to work smarter and not harder to create their work product faster, better and cheaper.

Business users often ask for enhancements and change requests to their systems. They can be as simple as creating a new report or adding additional input fields to a screen. Sometimes, requests are a little more complicated like adding a new screen for additional functionality or tweaking the underlying database or SQL to improve system performance. Every request that originates from the business must be evaluated to determine additional business benefit, level of effort, cost, impacted systems and teams, priority against other work in the pipeline, resource availability, assumptions and constraints.

Regulatory changes and updates are always going to be with us. In the United States, the Sarbanes-Oxley Act of 2002 (SOX) is probably one of the most widely known pieces of legislation that led to widespread system enhancements to ensure compliance with its stringent financial accountability mandates. If you've ever worked in the pharmaceutical industry, you understand the Food and Drug Administration's system validation directives. If your company has assets in Europe, you appreciate Safe Harbor compliance. If you run a payroll system, you regularly have to deal with tax updates. And if you have a business in California, you know how difficult it is to configure time and attendance systems to comply with the work-break laws.

Perhaps your company is large enough to have a Tier 1 support structure in the form of a help desk or customer support center. Whenever a customer has a problem they first call the help desk so trained personnel can triage the event. If the Tier 1 resource cannot conclude a first call resolution to the customer's problem, the call ticket is escalated to Tier 2 or Tier 3 resources depending on the severity of the issue and perceived priority. Sometimes the caller may have uncovered an unknown defect for which there is no known workaround or may be requesting an enhancement. The secondary, tertiary and/or quaternary resources evaluate the issue and form their response. If the issue cannot be fixed in the amount of time governed by the service level agreement, the need is transferred to the work pipeline for resolution where it follows the standard governance rules.

Routine maintenance encompasses all the tasks required to keep systems functioning at their maximum operational efficiency. This includes firmware upgrades, service pack applications, OS updates, minor software and hardware configurations/upgrades or swapping out a faulty component. Many routine maintenance tasks can be performed in a few hours and require nothing more than a Director's approval. More extensive maintenance operations may require system down time during normal business hours and require the permission of the business to proceed. Sometimes service pack applications require a full-scale project to complete. For example, Oracle regularly releases family packs for their enterprise products. Family packs can require a 6-8 week project to fully apply and test the family pack before releasing to production.

Defect repairs can be a way of life for some systems. The sad truth is that systems are often rolled into production with way too many known defects. There are many reasons for this, cutting corners to meet schedules or budget, poor quality assurance practices, poor defect tracking, no requirements traceability, poor development practices and sometimes purposeful reasons as when defects are considered a lower priority rather than show stoppers. The response to defects can be to do nothing, offer a workaround, fix them right away or fix them and release them as part of a regularly scheduled service pack. The way to get relief from the vicious cycle of defect discovery and repair is to reduce defects to a minimum before production deployment by observing sound SDLC practices.

IT projects for IT's sake often fly under the radar. IT groups can be so focused on delivering value to their organizations that projects necessary for the health and welfare to IT itself can often be overlooked or delayed indefinitely. Take the SDLC for example. It may literally take years before an IT organization has any documented processes to make up their SDLC. This is especially true of small, rapidly growing IT departments. People are too busy working on projects to support their customers' needs to focus on their own foundational essentials. Even if a courageous CIO brings IT focused projects to his/her governors, the chances of having the project shot down are high. Senior business leaders often don't understand the importance or value of foundational IT projects.

Figure 36 is a generic process flow demonstrating the linkage between IT Governance work intake and the requirements process. Before explaining the process steps, let's remind ourselves of SDLC Principle #2 defined in Chapter 1.

Principle #2: "Investment opportunities cannot be estimated accurately until the requirements are known."

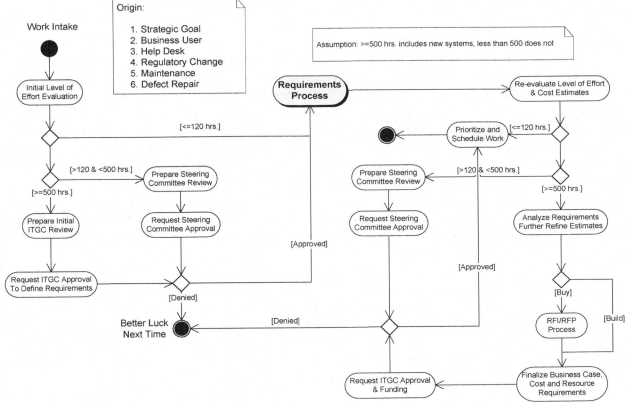

Figure 36 - Generic Work Intake/Governance Process Showing Requirements Link

The initial level of effort estimate is performed by technical resources and/or architects familiar with the system and technologies under discussion. Initial estimates are based on a combination of system intimacy, experience with similar changes or sometimes a best guesstimation. This initial evaluation is to provide a "ball park" estimate so the work request can be categorized to determine next steps. Often times the answer is evident considering the nature of the requested work.

For small projects, flushing out the requirements is the next step. If the ball park estimate is large enough, the work request is conveyed to the appropriate governance team for deliberation. The IT Director prepares the business case, supporting documentation, frames an initial cost based on the ball park estimate and either reviews with the steering committee or supports the business as they present to the ITGC. The goal of the first review is to seek approval to move forward with the requirements process to determine the details more accurately. The requirements process for medium or large projects requires dedicated business analysts for a period of time. The cost associated with dedicating BA resources to investigative activities is measurable in both hard currency and lost time to other prioritized work because they have to be redirected from something they're working on to focus on the new priority. The governance teams must agree to the requisite concessions.

The requirements process during governance activities has the goal of eliciting the business requirements in sufficient quantity and of high enough quality to allow the analysis to more accurately determine the project's feasibility, cost, resource requirements and value proposition. These metrics are then utilized to strengthen the business case brought before the governing committee. The resulting Business Requirements Definition (BRD) artifact is baselined and managed going forward under the project management change control process. A baseline does not mean the requirements are finalized at this point. Before any development begins the requirements are reviewed to determine if they still meet the current needs of the business and are modified if necessary using project change control to adjust the baseline. For small projects, a line or two to a paragraph from a business user may be all that's needed as the BRD. The larger the project however, the elicitation process and its work product requires the commensurate rigor.

Once the requirements are sufficiently complete, there is a re-evaluation of the original guesstimation (but not the last one). The ability to accurately estimate the time and/or cost for a project to reach its successful outcome is a serious challenge for systems engineers. Single point estimates such as the outcome of this governance step are proven to be dubiously accurate. Depending on a single point estimate results in movement of the schedule's baseline to adjust for variances. Accuracy improves over time as data is collected and a project progresses.

The problem we have here is that when we present our proposal to the governing body, the project hasn't even been commissioned. All we've been permitted to do is gather the major business requirements. Yet we must include a timeline which may frequently be a prognostication. Senior leaders hold us accountable for what we promise to deliver when we say we will deliver it. Nothing is more awkward than to return to a governing body and ask for more time or money because of blown estimates. The use of a repeatable, clearly defined and well understood SDLC has been shown in recent years to be the most effective method for gaining useful historical data that can be used for statistical assessment.

It is beyond the scope of this book to endorse or teach any specific estimation method. However, as a practical matter, wise organizations master multiple estimation techniques that correspond to the various scenarios they encounter. Sometimes, you'll achieve greater results by combining techniques. The method you choose depends on several factors. For example:

- What is the nature of the project? Is this new development, an embedded system, hardware, telecom, etc.?
- Is this a small, medium or large project?

- What type of project is this? Is this a system upgrade, service pack release or something else, like a Greenfield perhaps if you are in retail and launching a new brick and mortar location?

There are many methods available for project estimation that run the gamut of historical analysis, counting or work decomposition. Many books have been written about project estimation and there are many training sources available. Be encouraged to do your own research or consult with experts to learn the techniques that are a best fit for your environment and culture. Some popular methods include:

- Analysis Effort method
- COCOMO
- Evidence-based Scheduling Refinement
- Function Point Analysis
- Parametric Estimating
- Program Evaluation and Review Technique (PERT)
- Proxy-based estimating (PROBE)

- SEER-SEM Parametric Estimation
- SLIM
- The Planning Game (from Extreme Programming)
- TruePlanning Software Model Parametric
- Use Case Points Analysis
- Wideband Delphi

After the re-evaluation, determine if the project still belongs to the same governance "bucket" as first assessed. If not, prepare the appropriate documents and move forward. If the project is large, there may be a build vs. buy or buy with customization decision to consider. In which case, a Request for Information (RFI) or Request for Proposal (RFP) process should be followed. It's important for this step to be included now because the total cost of ownership of a buy decision must be incorporated into the overall project estimate. Some governance models require an interim step to request permission from the convening body to move forward with the RFI/RFP if the decision looks like it is headed in the direction of buy.

The final analysis and evaluation takes place when all of the details have been assembled. Sometimes a project is approved but the funding isn't available until a subsequent budget cycle which for some companies can mean several budget cycles over the course of many years. If the project and funding is approved…great! The project kicks-off and everything goes perfectly according to the vision, right? If the project isn't approved and/or funded then better luck next time! That is IT Governance in a nutshell.

Requirements Maturity

The Gartner Group states, "A proven, effective, real world approach to Business Requirements Analysis is one of the most significant factors in ensuring the success of any system development project. A defined and consistent method that is easily learned and easily applied leads directly to increased IS productivity and reduced systems development and maintenance costs."

The single most difficult aspect of any project is getting the business requirements right. You've seen the statistics. If the requirements were right in the surveyed projects, there would never have been as many reported failures, cancellations, rework or restarts. We've discussed how we have to change the way we think about requirements and begin to understand that requirements and their maturity are a process and not an isolated deliverable. It is a process that consists of the steps of Generation, Analysis, Inspection, Approval and Baselining. After baselining, the process continues through the end of the project life cycle with pre-development iteration activities, tracing the requirements to their realization and the strategies for managing changes and scope creep. Fortunately, this is not as onerous as it sounds and the competencies required for successful requirements maturity and management can be readily acquired and mastered.

The Information Architecture Group (IAG Consulting) located in New Castle, Delaware, is one of the 28 founding members of the IIBA, a heavy contributor to BABOK[52] and a thought leader in requirements maturity best practices. In 2008, IAG conducted a survey of over 100 larger companies with development projects in excess of $250,000 where significant new functionality was delivered to the organization. The average project size was $3 million. The survey resulted in the publication and distribution of their first *"Business Analysis Benchmark: The Impact of Business Requirements on the Success of Technology Projects,"*[53] written by Keith Ellis, Vice President Marketing & Strategic Alliances, IAG Consulting. In Q2 of 2009, just under 550 companies chose to participate in a second survey, the *"Business Analysis Benchmark 2009: Path to Success,"* leading to 437 qualifying responses. The intent of this survey is to "assess the link between an organization's maturity in requirements definition and management and project outcomes." The full text of the *"Business Analysis Benchmark 2009"* may be found on the accompanying CD courtesy of Keith Ellis and IAG Consulting.

According to IAG's 2009 findings, "Requirements maturity may be more important than any other single factor in the determination of overall development effectiveness. The graph below [Figure 37] illustrates that low requirements maturity organizations underperform high requirements maturity organizations on <u>EVERY</u> measure of development efficiency. Not only are high requirements maturity organizations noticeably better at servicing the needs of the business, they perform nearly twice as well on every measure of development productivity:

- On time delivery
- On budget delivery
- Percentage of projects delivering the required functionality

[52] Business Analysis Body of Knowledge
[53] Available for free download by registering at http://www.iag.biz

- Percentage of projects deemed successful"

One set of conclusions in the 2009 benchmark is particularly edifying because of its concord with one of the messages in Chapter 1:

IAG believes if an IT organization:

- is continuously late in delivery,
- is continuously well over budget,
- continues to deliver only one third of projects successfully; and,
- consumes unnecessarily large amounts of its resources in maintenance rather than delivering substantially new functionality to the business,

a crisis of confidence in the leadership of this IT organization will eventually occur.

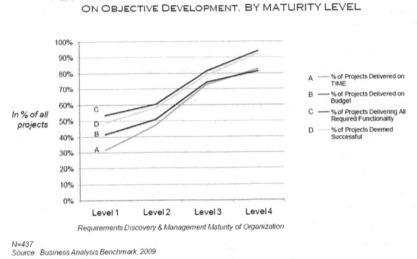

PERFORMANCE CHANGES TO ON TIME, ON BUDGET, ON FUNCTION, ON OBJECTIVE DEVELOPMENT, BY MATURITY LEVEL

N=437
Source: Business Analysis Benchmark, 2009

Figure 37 - Graph from IAG's Business Analysis Benchmark 2009

In the 2008 benchmark, IAG said, "In absolute terms, the quality of requirements will dictate the time and cost of the solution." The quality of requirements is directly related to the competency of the Business Analyst or BA team managing the requirements process along with the robustness of the requirements oversight practices of the Quality Assurance team. Figure 38 is a graph from the 2008 Benchmark survey that demonstrates an increasing project success rate as the Business Analysis competencies in requirements elicitation increase. Companies that have achieved "Excellence across 5 categories of elicitation competency" realize the greatest success rates. IAG said, "Simply put, a project manager increases their chance of getting an 'unqualified success' by over 400% by using elite analysts with specific competencies at the start of requirements discovery."

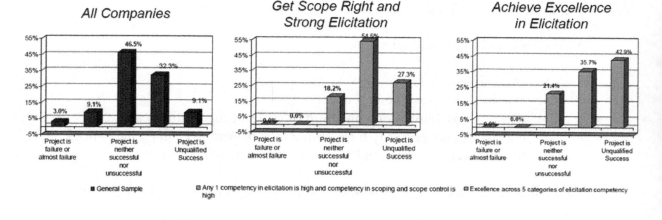

Source: IAG Business Analysis Benchmark, 2008

Figure 38 - Image from IAG's 2008 Benchmark Analysis

Since the release of the BABOK by the IIBA, Business Analysts have a definitive fundamental resource to turn to from which they may learn of the competencies required to develop an elite skill set. The definition of a competency is the knowledge, skills and ability (or behaviors) to perform a given task. Knowledge is defined[54] as (i) the fact or condition of knowing something with familiarity gained through experience or association; (ii) the range of one's information or understanding; or (iii) the fact or condition of having information or of being learned. Knowledge is what we gain from the educational process whether from school or hands-on experience. Skills are the ability to use knowledge effectively and readily in execution or performance. Ability is a natural aptitude or acquired proficiency. In the case of a BA, ability is the capacity to navigate an organization's cultural, physical, hierarchical and political boundaries to build strong relationships and influence outcomes.

The BABOK describes six rudimentary Business Analysis areas of knowledge along with the associated activities, tasks, required skills and underlying competencies necessary to be effective in their execution. The six areas of knowledge are:

---

[54] Merriam-Webster Collegiate Dictionary (11th Edition)

- Business Analysis Planning and Monitoring
- Elicitation
- Requirements Management and Communication
- Enterprise Analysis
- Requirements Analysis
- Solution Assessment and Validation

BABOK Ver. 1.6 documented 76 tasks the BA should be capable of performing. Version 2.0 condenses this number to 32. In February 2010, the IIBA released their first Business Analysis Competency Model. This is a tool for assessing the ability of business analysts to properly perform their role. The tool details 53 performance competencies and the associated competency indicators, underlying competencies, associated techniques and associated tasks. The Competency Model tool and BABOK are available to IIBA members free of charge. All others pay a nominal fee to download them for their individual personal, professional or educational use.

BABOK defines business analysis as:

"…Business analysis is the set of tasks and techniques used to work as a liaison among stakeholders in order to understand the structure, policies, and operations of an organization, and recommend solutions that enable organizations to achieve its goals…"

By and large, a Business Analyst then is any person who performs these activities, no matter what their job title or organizational role may be. BA practitioners include:

- Business Architects
- Business Systems Analysts
- Data Analyst
- Enterprise Analysts
- Management Consultants
- Process Analysts
- Product Managers
- Product Owners
- Requirements Engineers
- Systems Analysts
- Usability/UX Analyst
- Any other person performing BA tasks

In a universal sense, BAs are responsible for eliciting and analyzing new business requirements and assessing them against existing systems, components and processes. They design and document the solution in textual format accompanied by diagrams and graphical models that express system interactions, data flows, business rules and logical operations. Finally, they present and review the artifacts with the business and once approved, work with system architects and developers to build and implement the system. Different job titles indicate a specialty in a specific competency.

The role of Business Analyst has become crucial to the life-blood of many organizations. The BA is the link between IT and the stakeholders to elicit, generate, analyze, communicate, verify and validate business requirements for information systems, business processes, policies and procedures. But the role of the business analyst should not merely be confined to business or IT solutions. A forefront mission of the BA is to define solutions which help the organization execute its planned strategy to achieve its goals and realize a profit whereby increasing shareholder value. Seasoned BAs comprehend and may perhaps foresee problems and discover opportunities in the context of business requirements and strategic goals. BAs are involved at all levels of an organization in identifying challenges, needs and process improvement prospects.

What is expected of an analyst varies widely from organization to organization and from project to project. So much so, it's neither likely nor realistic to define a one-size-fits-all job description. Looking over the practitioner list we see that BAs may be asked to wear many hats and hold any one of many titles. BAs may work closely with projects managers and assist with project planning. If the organization doesn't have the role of project manager or a project is too small to assign one, the BA might even assume the PM role in addition to their regular BA duties. The BA coordinates with Quality Assurance to assure test cases really do test the requirements and test results meet or exceed the expected outcomes. The BA facilitates the User Acceptance Test.

Someone once asked, "How do you know when a BA is effective in their role?" Aside from analyzing the performance metrics, you'll know a BA is effective in their role when the business customers consider the BA to be one of their own; that is, a valuable member of the business team rather than an IT resource assigned to work with the business team. There's a huge contrast between those two perceptions. Building relationships to this high level of confidence and trust implies the BA has to be competent in soft skills such as conflict resolution, communication and leadership as well as having business know-how and possessing strong domain and technology proficiency. Some of the more advanced areas in which a BA should possess some level of expertise are:

- Communication Skills
- Conflict Resolution
- Cultural Awareness
- Decision-making
- Escalation Skills

- Facilitation Skills
- Interviewing Skills
- Leadership
- Logic
- Meeting Management

- Negotiation Skills
- Presentation Skills
- Relationship Skills
- Self-awareness
- Systems Thinking

Requirements Planning

As straightforward as the term "requirements planning" sounds on the surface, there probably isn't a more controversial knowledge area in BABOK because of the perceived overlap and/or conflict of duties with those presented in PMBOK. Many clashes between BAs and PMs are observed as they struggle within an organization to determine who is responsible for planning project requirements activities. In organizations with a well-defined and closely followed project management method, the answer is the project manager is responsible for planning all project activities. BAs respond that they are responsible for choosing stakeholders and planning and scheduling the requirements activities because BABOK says so. They say, "Stay out of our area PMs!" In 2009 the leadership of the IIBA and PMI agreed that overlap and conflict exists in a number of areas between the two bodies of knowledge and they embarked on a multi-year cooperative effort to harmonize the guides. We can now look forward to the future when the two complementary guides are released.

BABOK defines the eight tasks required for requirements planning as:

- Identifying Stakeholders
- Defining Stakeholders Roles and Responsibilities in the BA Effort
- Estimating Business Analysis Tasks
- Planning the Stakeholder Communication Approach
- Determine How Requirements will be Approached, Traced, and Prioritized
- Determine the Artifacts to be Produced
- Define and Determine Business Analysis Processes
- Determine BA Monitoring Metrics

Seven of these eight tasks are practices defined in the SDLC, Project Management Method or Organizational Change Management Plan. The only task requiring a free thinking approach on behalf of the BA is Estimating Business Analysis Tasks. This is a collaborative effort between the BA and PM because scheduling of resources and the determination of the BA milestones are the outcomes. Normally, estimates are developed utilizing standard organizational templates and methods. In early project phases like this one, methods such as function point or use case analysis don't work at all because the requirements haven't been captured yet. Estimating the BA tasks can be difficult to pin down because they are of a personal nature subject to the assigned BA's experience, past history and competency level. The best approach for estimating the BA tasks is to ballpark the time and add a percentage for contingency. It's better to produce the results early and give time back to the project than to run over schedule. The outcomes of this task are reported in project progress reports. If an organization has well documented practices and procedures, there is no question at all over who is responsible for the other seven tasks because they have been defined through organizational governance constructs.

Major Stakeholders are identified by senior leaders when the project is conceived. These stakeholders decide who participates in the business analysis process, not the BA or PM. The BA and PM may suggest certain stakeholders participate based on their domain knowledge and organizational savvy, but they do not make the final decision, the stakeholders do. Participation is driven by the severity of the business problem to be solved, known risks, resource availability and complexity of the project. It is not possible to completely identify all of the stakeholders required for the requirements process during the planning stages. Additional stakeholders are often identified during discovery workshops as hidden or derived requirements become known and the people present realize that someone else not in the room is the subject matter expert for that particular area.

The roles and responsibilities in business analysis tasks are finite. There may be many participants but their roles can be reduced to a generic list. There are sponsors, users, technical resources, and subject matter experts (SME). The following non-inclusive list suggests some of the generic roles you may want to define in your SDLC or Project Management Method:

- Executive Sponsor
- Project Sponsor
- Project Manager
- Business Analyst / BA Team
- Business Liaison
- Architects

- Business Users
- Compliance Regulator
- Customers
- Developers
- Domain SMEs
- End Users

- Implementation SME
- Infrastructure Support
- Operational Support
- Quality Assurance
- Suppliers / Vendors
- Training Resources

The one role to highlight on this list is that of Business Liaison or Product Owner. The role is identified in Chapter 2 as a best practice first documented by Schwaber and Southerland in their presentation of the Scrum methodology in 1991. Experientially, this is a best practice role critical to a project's success and the one that is most overlooked, forgotten or ignored largely due to the business's reluctance to dedicate a full or part time resource to an IT project. The Business Liaison must work as an integrated project team member, ideally sitting proximally to the team. The Business Liaison must be empowered to make design decisions and to speak on behalf of the business.

How communications plans are constructed and executed are dictated either by a company's organizational change management plan or a central communications group if the company has one. In their absence, the project management method may have a communications plan associated with it. Larger companies often prohibit email blasting or sending communications to remote managers if they have brick and mortar or virtual sales locations dealing directly with the public as the case may be for retail businesses, wholesale distribution or field sales positions.

RACI Charts

The first artifact produced as the outcome of the communications planning step is the RACI chart, known alternately as the RACI Assignment Matrix, RACI Matrix or Linear Responsibility Chart. The RACI chart is a list identifying the project stakeholders and their corresponding RACI category. RACI is an acronym for Responsible, Accountable, Consulted and Informed.

Responsible categorizes those resources responsible for achieving the work. Accountable (also Approver or Final Approving Authority) is the person who signs off on the work completed by the Responsibles. This is usually the Executive Sponsor, Project Sponsor or Business Liaison. The Consulted are those whose opinions are sought and with whom there is frequent two-way communications. The Informed are those stakeholders who are kept up-to-date on a project's progress. There is only one category per stakeholder per project task if the chart is broken down to the task level.

There are a number of variations of the RACI chart that have been used by different project teams which include:

- DACI (Driver, Approver, Contributors, Informed): A version that centralizes decision making and clarifies who has the responsibility for reopening discussions
- PACE (Process Owner or Process Leader, Approver, Consulted and Executors): A "speed-to-decision" making matrix designed to reduce stakeholder debate time.
- PARIS: Variation with the categories of Primary, Assigned, Review Required, Input Required and Signature Required.
- RACIO (CAIRO): An expanded version of the standard RACI with one additional category, Out-of-the-Loop (or Omitted) which specifies which stakeholders do not participate in a task.
- RACI-VS (VARISC): An expanded version of the standard RACI with two additional categories, Verifier and Signatory. Verifiers are QA resources who check that product meets the acceptance criteria. The Signatories approve the work of the Verifiers and authorize product hand-off to the implementers.
- RASCI (RASIC): An expanded version of the standard RACI dividing the Responsible category into two categories of Responsible and Support, the resources allocated to assist the Responsibles in completing the task.
- RSI (Responsible, Sponsor, Informed): Version used by the Project Management Institute

The following three tables are examples of RACI charts of increasing complexity. The first two are suitable for small to medium size projects. The third one is suitable for more robust medium and large size projects.

Role	RACI
Executive Sponsor	I
Project Sponsor	A
Project Manager	R
Technical Architect	C
Developers	R
Subject Matter Experts	C

End Users	I

Figure 39 - RACI Chart Example #1

Role	R	A	C	I
Executive Sponsor				✓
Project Sponsor		✓		
Project Manager	✓			
Technical Architect			✓	
Developers	✓			
Subject Matter Experts			✓	
End Users				✓

Figure 40 - RACI Chart Example #2

ID	Name	Executive Sponsor	Project Sponsor	Project Manager	Technical Architect	Developers	SMEs	End Users
Phase 1	Requirements							
Phase 2	Analysis							
Phase 3	Development							
3-04	User Interface	I	C	A	R	R	C	C
3-10	Interfaces	I	I	R	A	R	C	I
3-22	Reports	I	C	A	R	R	C	C
Phase 4								

Figure 41 - RACI Chart Example #3

Communications Plan

The second artifact to be delivered out of the requirements communications planning activity is the communications plan itself. The manner in which and when stakeholders receive formal communications and progress updates from the project team is documented. This does not include the informal day-to-day ad hoc communications that take place between project team members and stakeholders. The scope of this activity in the SDLC is limited to the business analysis activities and may form a subset of the overall project communications plan. The communications plan addresses five questions:

- Who is the intended audience?
- What needs to be communicated?
- When should the communication take place? (actual date or before, during or after planned activity date TBD)
- Where should meetings occur? (e.g., small, medium, or large conference room, video conference, auditorium, classroom, etc.)
- How will the communication be disseminated (the vehicle to be used)?

Effective communications planning requires some basic understanding of organizational change management practices. To help with understanding these practices, the following chart[55] lists common communications vehicles and the generally accepted impact rating for their primary characteristics of Commitment, Durability, Frame of Reference, Information and Trust. The impact scale is 1 = High, 2 = Medium and 3 = Low or none. High impact characteristics are highlighted.

Communication Vehicle	Characteristics				
	Commitment	Durability	Frame of Reference	Information	Trust
E-Mail	3	3	3	2	3
Memo	3	3	3	1	3
Newsletter / Corporate Communications	3	3	2	1	3
Online Forum	3	3	3	1	3
Personal (Face-to-Face)	1	1	1	1	1
Small Group	1	1	1	1	1
Town Hall	2	3	2	2	2
Video	3	3	3	1	3
V-Mail	3	3	1	1	2
Web Page / Wiki	3	2	3	1	2

Figure 42 - Characteristics of Change Management Communications

Modern technology adds texting, instant messaging, social networking and internet and video conferencing which are variants of several of the vehicles listed above. The most important thing to remember about the communication plan is the message itself. Communicate progress and always be honest about remaining problems and those not anticipated. Identify lessons learned, check for understanding and communicate the next changes or milestone event. Repeat the message often if the communications are to support the transition state of a significant change.

Complex projects require formal documentation. There are many communication plan templates available on the internet for download for your personal or non-commercial professional use. Google "Communications Plan" and you are sure to find one that can be tailored for your specific needs. This is an example of a very simple communications plan which should suffice for most small and medium projects:

---

[55] Source: © 2003 IMA. AIM Change Management Methodology 2003 Training Guide

Who?	What?	How?	Where?	When?	Budget
All Stakeholders	Survey	Zoomerang	N/A	Pre-JAD (date TBD)	N/A
JAD Invite	Invitation to selected stakeholders to attend 3-day requirements workshop	Email	Lrg Conf. Room	1 week post project kick-off	$600 for JAD food / snacks
JAD follow-up	Status of JAD session	Email	N/A	Post JAD	N/A

Figure 43 - Sample Communications Plan (Simple)

Four of the five remaining requirements planning tasks, Determine How Requirements will be Approached, Traced, and Prioritized, Determine the Artifacts to be Produced, Define and Determine Business Analysis Processes and Determine BA Monitoring Metrics are addressed in Chapter 4, 5, 6 and 10. It is appropriate to define these tasks once and incorporate them within the SDLC to allow flexibility in the artifacts for different sized projects.

Requirements Elicitation

One of the worst things that can happen is if a development team jumps into development and commits to delivery before users have made all of the requirements known because the team assumes they understand their users' objectives. Habit #5 in Stephen Covey's famous self-help book, *"Seven Habits of Highly Effective People,"* is "Seek First to Understand, Then to be Understood." This is one habit that should always be made a high priority in systems development, particularly in the requirements process. All too often, users request features that a development team considers scope creep because the development team has made assumptions about the extent of the users' requirements. If the team has committed to development before the user requirements are completely known, trouble ensues, particularly if users' perceive some disadvantage from the failure to implement requirements. Systems may be left incomplete or implemented without all of the required functionality in order to meet delivery deadlines and avoid the cost of rework.

For the BA, elicitation is where the rubber meets the road. There aren't any skills more important for the BA to master. Every gifted artist uses an ample supply of colorful paints and brushes to unfold a fantastic story on canvas for the world to admire and adore. Aptitude in an assortment of elicitation techniques is the BA's artist toolkit. Instead of telling a story on canvas, the BA spins a fascinating trail of user stories into good business requirements and system designs with which equally talented programmers and developers use to sculpt a creation that meets or exceeds their customers' vision.

Early versions of BABOK defined ten requirements elicitation competencies:

- Brainstorming
- Document Analysis
- Focus Group
- Interface Analysis
- Interview
- Observation
- Prototyping
- Requirements Workshop
- ~~Reverse Engineering~~
- Survey

Version 2.0 dropped Reverse Engineering from the mix to leave nine elicitation competencies for the BA to master.

IAG's 2008 Business Analysis Benchmark concluded that companies achieving excellence across five areas of elicitation competencies reported the highest project success ratios. Looking at the revised list of 9 elicitation competencies (don't include reverse engineering), which five do you think would provide the greatest value if you could execute them with excellence? Most people who are asked this question bet their money on Document Analysis, Interface Analysis, Interview, Prototyping and Requirements Workshops, although many flip a coin between Brainstorming and Interface Analysis.

A project manager once offered her opinion about Brainstorming and said she saw little value to the competency because Business Analysts "don't have the skill to execute it effectively." Before you start screaming, please don't let the misguided opinion one misinformed PM flame a war between BA and PM professionals. The comment so pushed my hot buttons though, that now whenever I teach a BA skills class, it always starts with a Brainstorming demonstration and the creation of a mindmap to show how easy it is and how much fun it can be.

We're going to look at the elicitation competencies in more detail and discuss the processes for their execution. Each competency has activities for planning, execution and wrap-up. The SDLC's UML activity diagrams presented in this chapter are generic and adaptable to an organization's needs. Use the algorithms as checklists to ensure all steps are complete. The diagrams are created in either Visio Professional 2007 or 2010. The Visio files are on the accompanying CD. We shall not be covering Reverse Engineering and we're going to hold off with Document Analysis and Interface Analysis until Chapter 6—Requirements Analysis, Tracing & Inspection.

Brainstorming

Brainstorming, also known as Mindmapping, is a technique used to generate a large number of ideas to solve a specific problem in less time. Brainstorming was popularized by the 1953 book *"Applied Imagination"* by Alex Faickney Osborn (1888-1966), advertising executive and founding partner of Batten, Barton, Durstine & Osborn (BBDO), a worldwide advertising agency. He later established the Creative Education Foundation.

Osborn proposed that groups could double their creative output through brainstorming. Research published in 1991 and 2003[56] refutes Osborn's claim. Researchers have not found any evidence of brainstorming's effectiveness for enhancing either quantity or quality of generated ideas, although there may be benefits provided, such as boosting morale, improving team work and making work more fun. At least seven variations of the brainstorming technique exist:

---

[56] (1) Nijstad, B. A., Stroebe, W., Lodewijkx, H. F. M. (2003). Production blocking and idea generation: Does blocking interfere with cognitive processes? *Journal of Experimental Social Psychology*, 39, 531-548.;
(2) Diehl, M., & Stroebe, W. (1991). Productivity loss in idea-generating groups: tracking down the blocking effect. *Journal of Personality and Social Psychology*, 61, 392-403;
(3) Mullen, B., Johnson, C., & Salas, E. (1991). Productivity loss in brainstorming groups: a meta-analytic integration. *Basic and Applied Social Psychology*. 12, 3-23

- Directed Brainstorming
- Electronic Brainstorming
- Group Passing Technique
- Individual Brainstorming
- Nominal Group Technique
- Question Brainstorming
- Team Idea Mapping Method

Brainstorming promotes diversion thinking. Diversion thinking inspires a broad or diverse set of options. The technique can be applied effectively in attempting to determine root-cause when troubleshooting high severity issues. Brainstorms help answer specific questions such as:

- What options are available?
- What have we done so far?
- What factors constrain us?
- What causes problem 'X'?
- How do we solve problem 'Z'?
- Where do we go from here?

The planning phase begins with the problem definition. The problem must be clear and capable of being captured in a single question like "What is causing the CPU utilization on the database server to spike every day at 3:00pm giving our customers the perception of poor performance?" If the issue can't be addressed in a single question, it's probably too big and needs to be broken out into its component parts. Each component part is the focus of one brainstorming session until all the answers are in and a complete picture of the resolution can be drawn. Sessions can run sequentially, concurrently or one sessions each day over the course of several days as resources allow.

After the problem and question are defined, the facilitator runs through the usual list of checklist items for setting up and managing a meeting such as selecting the participants, reserving a meeting room, drafting an invitation that states the defined question and logistical details. The invitation should be sent far enough in advance of the meeting to allow participants time to think through the problem and begin to generate ideas. In a firefighting situation, where a root cause analysis for a production down situation has to be conducted forthwith, the luxury of time doesn't exist.

The final prep step is to construct a list of "lead questions" and design a warm-up exercise if novice users will be in attendance. Lead questions help the facilitator stimulate creativity. Examples of lead questions are:

- Can we combine those two ideas?
- Where do you see that idea taking us?
- May we explore that thought further?

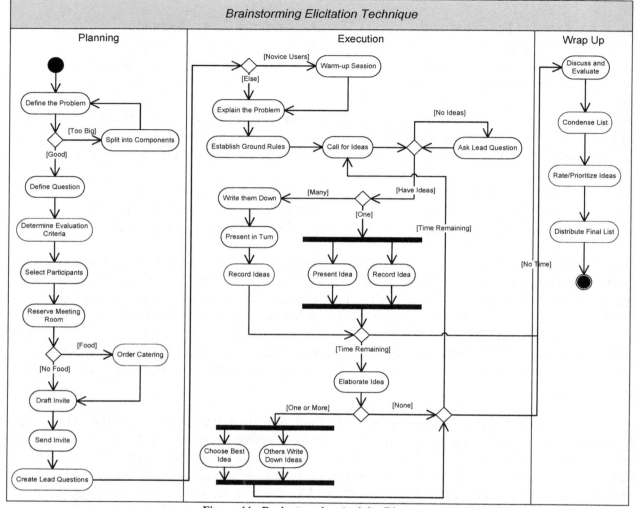

Figure 44 - Brainstorming Activity Diagram

The warm-up exercise is to introduce the new participants to the brainstorming technique. It can be as simple as brainstorming a vacation wish list. The output of a brainstorming session can be a mindmap like that shown in Figure 45 or an Ishikawa diagram like the one shown in Figure 46.

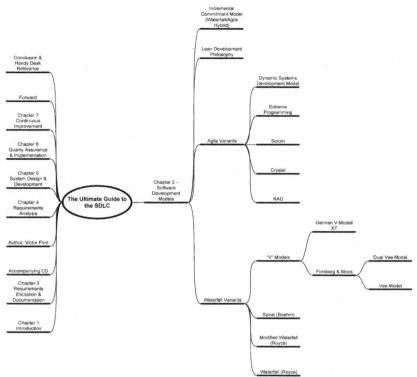

Figure 45 - Example Mindmap Diagram

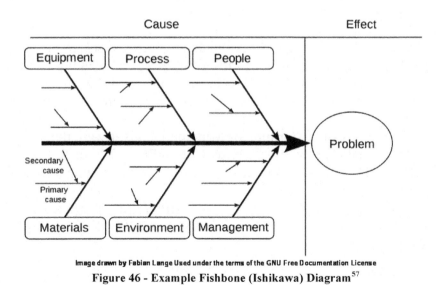

Image drawn by Fabian Lange Used under the terms of the GNU Free Documentation License

Figure 46 - Example Fishbone (Ishikawa) Diagram[57]

---

[57] Image drawn by Fabian Lange. Used under the terms of the GNU Free Documentation License

Brainstorming works best when the group is kept relatively small. Six to eight participants is optimal and there should never be more than 10. One participant important to every brainstorming session is the scribe or idea collector. This person is responsible for numbering the ideas, sorting them to the specified categories or documenting the mindmap while projecting it for all to see.

Make sure the meeting room is set up with the tools you need to conduct an effective session. You may need a white board and markers, flip chart paper, post-it notes and perhaps colored stickers to facilitate multi-voting if that is part of your process. Strictly enforce time constraints. If the meeting is scheduled for one hour, make sure it begins and ends on time. Leave ample room after the idea generation for the evaluation and selection of the best options. Come to the meeting with basic ground rules ready, but allow the meeting participants to suggest their own or modify the ones you suggest. Rules that work well are:

- Focus on quantity. Don't get hung up on a single idea until all have been presented that can be heard in the allotted time.
- Challenge ideas, not people. Be civil and withhold criticism. If someone's idea is criticized, that person will stop participating. Foster an environment where everyone feels safe to express themselves.
- Welcome all ideas, especially the unusual ones that come from out-of-the-box thinking. An unusual idea may represent a new way of looking at the question.
- Condense and improve ideas. Individual ideas may form the building blocks for a better idea. Encourage participants in associative thinking.

Wrap up the meeting by leading the group to evaluate the ideas and select one to pursue as the proposed solution to the presented problem. Multi-voting is a good technique to use for the selection process. Post-meeting, send all participants a summary of the meeting, its outcome and next steps with the condensed list of ideas and/or brainstorming diagram or mindmap attached.

Plenty of vendors have created Brainstorming or Mindmapping software that is either licensed for free under the Educational Community License, EPL, GPL, LGPL or Ruby License or available at nominal cost. The free software products available at the time of this writing are:

- Compendium
- FreeMind
- Freeplane
- Pimki
- SciPlore Mindmapping
- WikkaWiki
- VUE
- XMind

The choices for nominally priced Mindmapping software products include:

- 3D Topicscape
- Buzan's iMindMap
- Creately
- Inspiration
- MAPMYself (Mapul)
- MindGenius

- Microsoft Visio
- MindManager
- MindMapper
- Mindomo
- MindView
- NovaMind

- OmniGraffle
- PersonalBrain
- Solution Language Tool
- Visual Mind
- XMind Pro

Focus Group

Qualitative and Quantitative research methods are employed by researchers in certain academic disciplines, such as the social sciences, as well as market research professionals. The chosen research method depends on the researcher's objectives and the properties of the subject matter. Qualitative researchers look to gain a thorough understanding of human behavior and the underlying motives that govern behavior. The qualitative method probes the why and how of decision making, not just the what, where and when. The objective of quantitative research is to develop and employ mathematical models, theories and/or hypotheses pertaining to measurable attributes, observable events and their relationships. Empirical data collected through quantitative methods is often used to verify the truthfulness of qualitative hypotheses. In qualitative studies, small focused data points are desired rather than large samples. The Focus Group is one method for accumulating qualitative research.

Focus groups were created at the Bureau of Applied Social Research by Robert K. Merton (1910-2003). Merton was a distinguished sociologist perhaps best known for coining the phrase "self-fulfilling prophecy." The term "focus-group" was made up by Ernest Dichter (1907 - 1991), a psychologist and marketing expert often considered to be the "father of motivational research." The focus group is a means to elicit ideas and observe behaviors as a group of people are asked about their perceptions, opinions, beliefs and attitudes toward a product, service, concept, advertisement, idea or packaging. Interviews are conducted in an interactive group setting where participants freely talk with other group members. In an IT context, focus groups are an important tool for acquiring feedback regarding new products or user interface designs. The studies may be valuable during any life cycle phase, but especially good for determining the effectiveness of a system's usability features by monitoring the reactions of humans as they interact with and use the product.

Focus groups produce the best results when the participants are limited to 6 to 12 attendees. The topic in the spotlight influences who should be invited. For new systems products it's best to include both novice and veteran users. You may have to invite double the number of intended participants to allow for no-shows and other work priorities. Be thoughtful about the composition of the group or you may obtain unexpected or less than useful results.

Groups are either homogeneous which means they are composed of individuals with similar characteristics or heterogeneous which means the group is composed of individuals with diverse backgrounds and perspectives. Both types of groups come with their respective cautionary disclaimers. Individuals in homogeneous groups will not share differing perspectives and you may find yourself in the situation where you will need to conduct separate sessions for different homogeneous groups. On the other hand, individuals comprising heterogeneous groups may be uncomfortable and inhibited expressing their true feelings in front of others with different backgrounds which results in lower quality data.

Focus groups are not without their critics or perceived problems. The first problem many point out is that the size of the focus group is not a statistically significant sampling to represent a complete population although 6 to 12 users for an IT system, depending on the functionality being reviewed, may comprise an entire user population. A second problem is that it can be easy to lose control of the topic as participants "chase rabbits" and pursue an entirely irrelevant or surprising thought process. The third issue is that data is difficult to analyze because many thoughts are expressed in reaction to another user's comments. Observers and data collectors must be well trained and remain alert.

Douglas Rushkoff[58] is a media theorist, writer, columnist, lecturer, graphic novelist and documentarian best known for his association with the early cyberpunk culture and his advocacy of open source solutions to social problems. Rushkoff argues that focus groups are often useless, and frequently create more difficulties than they are intended to solve, aiming often to please rather than providing frank opinions or evaluations. He contends that cited data often seems to support a particular conclusion, while ignoring a significant portion of related cases or data that might contradict that position.

The moderator of the focus group is an experienced group facilitator with superior people skills. S/he must be able to keep the session focused while ensuring all participants engage in the conversation. The facilitator promotes interaction and discussion among the group, asks open ended questions, is quick thinking and flexible to adapt to unexpected directional shifts and above all, remains neutral. To imagine what a skilled moderator looks like in your mind, think "talk show host," but just not the Jerry Springer variety.

---

[58] Rushkoff, Douglas, *"Get back in the box : innovation from the inside out,"* New York : Collins, 2005

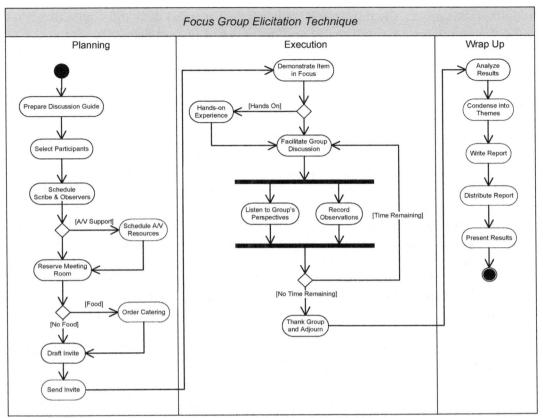

Figure 47 - Focus Group Activity Diagram

To prepare for the focus group, the moderator creates a discussion guide which is a pre-planned script of specific issues to be addressed and an explanation of the activity's goals and objectives. The guide consists of 5 to 6 questions for which the researcher is seeking answers. To complete the preparation, the moderator manages the standard tasks required for meeting management including scheduling a scribe to transcribe the session and ensuring that audio/video support is available to digitally document the event. Observers are assigned to notate the audience's response and expressed perceptions.

When the focus group is conducted, the script may allow time for a presentation of the item in focus and/or a short period of hands on experience for the group, especially if your research is about a new user interface or report. Afterward, the discussion takes place with the moderator leading the group as closely to the script as possible. To the group, the discussion appears natural, authentic, free-flowing and unstructured. Allow 1-2 hours to conclude the focus group. Record all observations and thank the participants for their feedback.

To wrap-up the focus group, the moderator analyzes the captured data and condenses it into themes. S/he then prepares a written report and/or presentation and distributes it to the appropriate parties. A live presentation may be also made to the commissioning authority.

Interview

We're all familiar with the concept of interviewing from having to look for a job, getting accepted into university or some other reason. Some of us have been interviewed in one-on-one situations or have endured the dreaded panel interview. In this day of fiscal restraint, it's not unusual to hear of interviews conducted over webcams, formal video-conference or by teleconference. In its most simplistic terms, if you've ever asked anyone a question and received an answer, you've conducted an interview, informal perhaps, but an interview nonetheless. Interviewing is a key business analysis skill that is commonly performed either in preparation for a requirements workshop or following a workshop to clarify a specific need. Interviews may also be conducted as part of the stakeholder analysis to determine a stakeholder's relationship to and expectations for the project or to analyze change requests to clarify the meaning or business value of the request.

An interview is a conversation between two or more people where questions are asked by the interviewer and the interviewee provides the replies. Interviews may be structured or unstructured. In a structured interview, the BA creates a pre-defined set of questions which need answers. During the interview, the BA sticks to the script posing each question in succession. The BA may also ask follow-up questions to clarify a particular response. Unstructured interviews are free-form. There is no list of pre-defined questions. While the BA might have some target goal in mind, the discussion between the BA and interviewee is open-ended and largely conversational where the answer to one question may lead to additional questions and answers.

Preparing for the interview is the most extensive part of the process. The BA first identifies the potential interviewees and reviews the list with the project sponsor. The sponsor is in the best position to determine who in the business has the most current information on the topic of interest, its relative importance and what the possible interviewee's stake is in the project. The BA and sponsor continue this activity until they are in agreement and the interviewees are chosen.

Designing the interview is next. The BA can construct a single interview for all interviewees or a separate custom interview for each interviewee. The decision depends on several factors including the goal for the interview, the rapport of the BA with the interviewee and the readiness and willingness of the interviewee to impart their knowledge. The design process settles on two questions:

- Will the interview follow a structured or unstructured format?
- Shall I ask closed or open questions?

If using the structured format, start by asking general questions seeking broad answers and as the interview progresses move to questions requiring a precise response. Closed questions are designed for single word or very short answers. Examples of closed questions are "How long does it take to enter an invoice?" or "Do you need 24/7 uptime?" Open questions are used to begin a dialog and elicit answers that take some explanation. For example, "Tell me how you envision the process working?"

The interviewee should be as comfortable as possible in the environment selected for the interview. When the interviewee is relaxed, the discussion is more open and there's a richer exchange of information. It's best to avoid the interviewee's office or workstation because of the tendency for distractions to pop-up and interrupt the discussion. Call the interviewee to discuss the date, time and location for the interview to take place. Ask if you can record the interview or if a scribe would provide greater ease. If the interviewee prefers a scribe, bring someone with you who can document the conversation quietly without interference. If the interviewee is at a remote location and a face-to-face meeting is not possible, schedule a video or teleconference to facilitate the interview, otherwise reserve a local meeting room. Send out a calendar invite and confirm the details with the interviewee and scribe, if there is one, via email.

When you arrive at the designated location or begin the video or teleconference, greet the interviewee warmly and introduce yourself if you've never met before. Thank him/her for making the time to see you. Restate the purpose of the interview and address any initial concerns the interviewee expresses. If you are permitted to use a recorder, tell the interviewee you are going to turn it on and let it run during the meeting. The interviewee may be nervous about this. Many people do not like being recorded. Reassure the person that anything said in confidence will remain confidential. You will not share any information with anyone without the interviewee's consent. Keep your word on this one!

Begin asking your questions and stick to the script if this is a structured interview. Use active listening when the interviewee speaks. The term "active listening" was invented by clinical psychologist Thomas Gordon in his 1977 book, *"Leader Effectiveness Training."* Gordon said, "Active listening is certainly not complex. Listeners need only restate, in their own language, their impression of the expression of the sender. ...Still, learning to do Active Listening well is a rather difficult task..."

Active listening is a structured way of listening and responding to others. It focuses attention on the speaker. It requires a listener to understand, interpret and evaluate what is heard. It is not an automatic response to sounds. It is important to watch the speaker's behavior and body language. Interpreting a person's body language allows the listener to develop a more accurate understanding of the speaker's words.[59] The listener then paraphrases those words. It's important to note that the listener is not necessarily agreeing with the speaker but simply restating what was said.

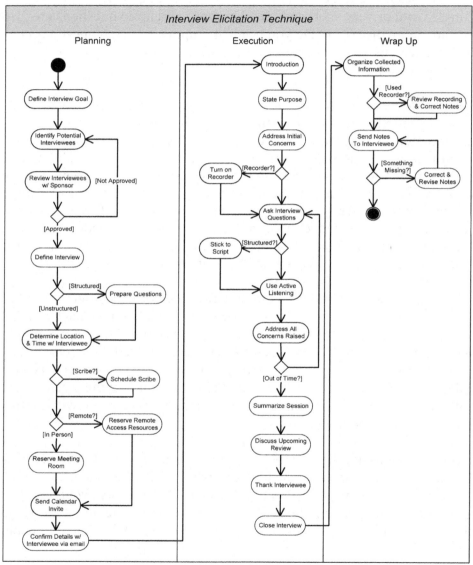

Figure 48 - Interview Activity Diagram

[59] Atwater, Eastwood (1981). "I Hear You." Prentice-Hall. p. 83.

Throughout the interview, continue to address any concerns raised by the interviewee. Before the allotted time runs out, summarize the activity to confirm your mutual understanding of what has just taken place. Set expectations for the interviewee and discuss the upcoming review process. The review is not to confirm the validity of any elicited requirements nor should there be any promises made that the requirements will make it into the final deliverables. Explain the next steps and once again reassure that confidential information will remain in confidence. Thank the speaker and close the interview.

As soon as possible after the interview, while it is still fresh in your mind, organize the notes and listen to the recording provided you made one. Revise any incorrect notes and send them to the interviewee for review and approval. Ask if either you or the scribe missed anything, is everything documented correctly and does the interviewee have anything they'd like to amend or add. Update the team with the details when the reviews are complete.

Observation

The observation elicitation technique is also called "job shadowing" or "following people around." It has its origin in high school and college programs. In its most traditional sense, job shadowing is a high school program where students follow someone around on their job to find out what it's like to be employed in a specific profession. The program is designed to help students become interested in a profession in order to guide their choices in higher education opportunities. On a collegiate level, job shadowing is often included as a condition of an internship. Non-student adults are also known to job shadow if they want to experience a particular career opportunity. As a BA elicitation technique, job shadowing assists in gaining a greater understanding of a stakeholder's work processes. Sometimes people are so habitual in their routines that it is difficult for them to explain what they do or why they do it. The BA may need to observe the workers as they perform their daily tasks so they can understand the work flow. For many projects understanding "as-is" processes is as noteworthy as process improvement.

There are two basic approaches to observation: active/visible or passive/invisible. In both approaches the BA observes the subject matter expert at work and takes detailed notes. In the active/visible method, the BA may dialog with the SME as work is taking place and may even assume the role for a brief time to gain hands-on experience with the job. In the passive/invisible approach, the BA remains quiet and observes. There is no conversation until the observation period is over, then the BA may ask clarifying questions. The passive/invisible method may require several observational sessions before requirements are fully elicited. At the extreme end of the spectrum, the BA may even work as an apprentice to gain a full appreciation of the work flow.

It is absolutely critical the BA makes the shadowed individual feel comfortable and offers the reassurance that their work is not being questioned but that the observation and resulting documentation serves as input to the requirements. Allow the worker to stop the observation at any time if they feel pressured or distracted. Suggest that the user "think aloud" as they perform their job duties so the BA understands the worker's challenges, objectives and apprehensions. Quite often a shadowed worker will express an idea of how the job could be done more efficiently. Be alert for these ideas and explore them. This could lead to the next big system process improvement. At all costs, refrain from discussing future solutions. Nothing will make a person become more uneasy than the thought of a future system that may reduce or eliminate their job responsibilities.

Preparing for an observation session is not unlike preparing for an interview. If you think things through, observation really is a type of interview because of the relationship that exists between the observer and the person being watched. The observer asks questions about what is seen and the one being observed provides the answers. Preparation begins by working with the sponsor to select the target user population. After the target shadowees are identified, draft a list of questions to serve as a guide. More often than not, new questions will arise as the BA observes the work. Arrange the date and time with the worker and send out a calendar invite and confirmation email if the worker has access to those resources.

On the day of the observation, introduce yourself and make the worker feel comfortable. State the purpose of the observation and address any initial concerns. If this is a passive observation, make yourself comfortable and situate yourself in a position convenient to observe everything the person does without being intrusive. Remain quiet until the end of the observation period. Ask clarifying questions when the observation is over. If an active session, ask probing questions throughout. Whenever questions are asked, make certain to use active listening and address all concerns raised. Complete the session by thanking the worker and explaining the next steps.

The next steps required to wrap up the observation are to collect answers to any open questions, review the notes with the shadowed worker, correct and revise the notes as needed, identify the commonalities and differences among all the jobs shadowed and prepare the final report. Once the final report is complete, review it with all shadowed workers. The final review may take place either in person or by email with follow-up phones calls if necessary. If you are conducting an in person review, follow the standard procedures for reserving a meeting room, preparing the agenda, inviting participants, etc.

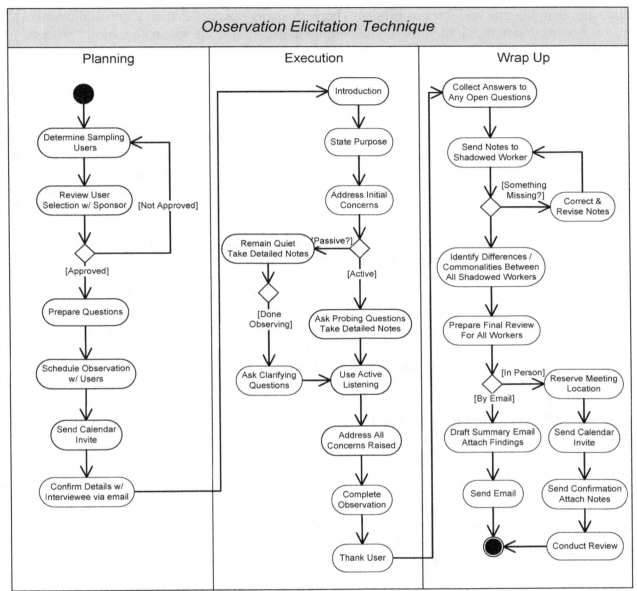

Figure 49 - Observation Activity Diagram

There is no recommended number for the amount of people to shadow for requirements elicitation to be effective. This is something that BAs have to decide for themselves. The important thing to remember is that the sampling has to be large enough to completely understand the underlying business processes. Looking for commonalities and differences from among the sampled population helps synthesize the underlying processes. The nature of a person's work is…well…*personal*. Not everyone approaches work in the same way even if they have the same job title and responsibilities. There are many nuances that an individual interjects into a process that makes it their own. The commonalities define the true nature of the process, not the differences.

Prototyping

Prototyping/Modeling scored very high on the scale of the common best practices we reviewed in Chapter 2 as we looked at a dozen of the more well-known and popular software development methods. In fact, it was listed as a best practice in every development method beginning with Boehm's Spiral Model in 1986. Prototyping is a development activity isn't it? Why then is it included as a BA elicitation competency? What does it have to do with requirements elicitation?

The answers to these questions can be understood in the context of how humans learn and comprehend ideas, concepts, data and other information. There are three basic learning styles: Auditory, Kinesthetic and Visual. Auditory learning is where people learn through listening. Auditory learners ascertain the meaning of words by listening to audible signals like changes in tone. They are good at responding to lectures and oral exams. Kinesthetic or "tactile" learning takes place by carrying out a physical hands-on activity rather than listening to a lecture, reading or watching a demonstration. For tactile learners, performing the task provides more benefit than any other means. Visual learners are people who learn best when information is presented visually. When visual learners see or visualize something, they are able to retain and recall it better. They have an easier time conceptualizing difficult ideas within the context of visual models, graphs, concept and idea maps, plots, and illustrations. An estimated 60% of all people claim that they learn best using visual aids.[60]

A prototype is defined[61] as:

1. : an original model on which something is patterned : ARCHETYPE
2. : an individual that exhibits the essential features of a later type
3. : a standard or typical example
4. : a first full-scale and usually functional form of a new type or design of a construction

Roget's Thesaurus of Synonyms & Antonyms (1972) lists the word "model" as one of many synonyms for the word "prototype." Other synonyms include: pattern, example, guide and template. A model therefore is as much a pattern, example, guide or template for something to be built, as is the prototype. It's important to note the similarity in the definitions for the words "prototype" and "model" because there is at least one IT school of thinking that believes a

---

[60] Source: *What is the Visual Learning Style?*; VisualLearningStyles.com (accessed March 1, 2010)
[61] Merriam-Webster Collegiate Dictionary, Eleventh Edition

prototype must be fully functional to be considered a prototype at all. The generally accepted definitions of the two words refute that idea. For clarity's sake, the words prototype and model and their various forms are used interchangeably in this book.

Modeling business requirements, processes and activities leads to greater comprehension and accuracy for all involved in a project rather than simply providing written textual requirements. It improves the quality of the requirements and of the specifications provided to the developers. Since it is proven that late changes to requirements cost exponentially more to implement, determining what users really want early, before development begins, results in faster development and less expensive systems. Modeling begins with the business analyst in the creation of the BRD and continues through the elicitation, analysis, development and deployment life cycle phases.

Modeling Standards

One purpose of the SDLC is to define standards to use within an organization. When it comes to the business analyst and modeling business requirements, there are two standards that are already defined by the industry: the Unified Modeling Language (UML)[62] and Business Process Modeling Notation (BPMN).[63] UML is a standardized general-purpose modeling language used in the field of systems engineering. BPMN is a standard for business process modeling. UML was created and is managed by the Object Management Group (OMG).[64] BPMN was developed by the Business Process Management Initiative (BPMI) and is also maintained by the OMG since the two organizations merged in 2005.

The OMG is a consortium originally formed to set standards for distributed object-oriented systems. It is now focused on modeling programs, systems and business processes and model-based standards. According to the OMG, "UML, along with the Meta Object Facility (MOF™), provides a key foundation for OMG's Model-Driven Architecture® which unifies every step of development and integration from business modeling, through architectural and application modeling, to development, deployment, maintenance and evolution."

At the time of this writing, the current working standard for UML is Version 2.2. Version 2.3 Beta 2 is under review by the OMG. Since version 2.0, the UML specification has been divided into two components, Infrastructure and Superstructure with 14 types of diagrams divided between the two categories. Seven diagram types represent structural information and the other

---

[62] Specification: http://www.uml.org
[63] Specification: http://www.bpmn.org
[64] Object Management Group formed: 1989; headquarters: Needham, Massachusetts; website: www.omg.org

seven represent general types of behavior, including four that represent different aspects of interactions. These diagrams can be categorized hierarchically as shown in Figure 50.

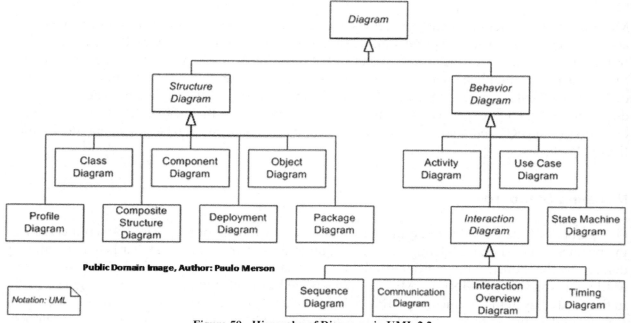

Figure 50 - Hierarchy of Diagrams in UML 2.2

UML does not restrict element types to specific diagram types. In general, every UML element may appear on almost any type of diagram. UML profiles may define additional diagram types or extend existing diagrams with additional notations. In keeping with the tradition of engineering drawings, a comment or note explaining usage, constraint or intent is allowed in a UML diagram.

BPMN provides a graphical notation for specifying business processes in a Business Process Diagram (BPD) based on a flowcharting technique similar to activity diagrams from UML. The objective of BPMN is to support business process management for both technical users and business users by providing a notation that is intuitive to business users yet able to represent complex process semantics. BPMN models are made by simple diagrams with a small set of graphical elements. It is easy for business users as well as technical resources to understand the flow and the process. The four basic categories of elements are as follows:

- Flow Objects
    - Events, Activities, Gateways
- Connecting Objects
    - Sequence Flow, Message Flow, Association

- Swim lanes
  - Pool, Lane
- Artifacts
  - Data Object, Group, Annotation

BPMN is the modeling language of choice for defining Web Services behavior in the Service Oriented Architecture (SOA) environment. A number of commercially available tools provide a detailed mapping of BMPN notation to the Business Process Execution Language (BPEL). BPEL is short for *Web Services Business Process Execution Language* (WS-BPEL), an OASIS standard executable language for specifying interactions with Web Services. Processes in BPEL export and import information by using Web Service interfaces exclusively. As a Web Services orchestration language, BPEL provides for the execution and control of a business process.

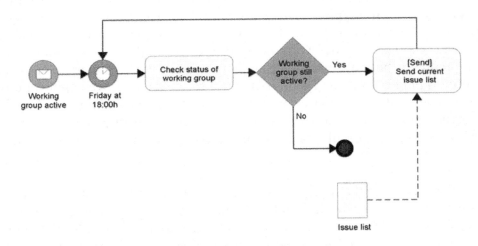

Figure 51 - Example of a BPMN Diagram

BPMN is constrained to support only the concepts of modeling that are applicable to business processes. This means that other types of modeling done for non-business purposes are out of scope for BPMN. For example, the following models are not a part of BPMN:

- Organizational structures
- Functional breakdowns
- Data models

And while BPMN shows the flow of data (messages) and the association of data artifacts to activities, it is not a data flow diagram.

It won't take long to find many books, training classes and web sites that teach UML and BPMN. Some of these resources are free. A good place to start is with the OMG at www.uml.org or www.bpmn.org. The OMG lists many learning resources. While BAs should know all types of UML diagrams, at a minimum they should understand how to read and draw the Use Case, Activity and Sequence behavioral diagrams for requirements artifacts. BAs involved with requirements development activities for web services and SOA must be conversant in BPMN.

Prototype Types

There are many variants to system prototypes, but all are based in some way on two major types: Throw-away Prototypes and Evolutionary Prototypes. Throw-away prototyping, also called close ended prototyping or rapid prototyping, refers to the creation of a model that will eventually be discarded rather than becoming part of the final delivered software. Evolutionary Prototyping, also known as breadboard prototyping, is very different from Throwaway Prototyping. The main goal of Evolutionary Prototyping is to build a very robust prototype in a structured manner and constantly refine it. Another form of Evolutionary Prototyping called Incremental Prototyping is where the final product is built as separate design prototypes which are merged at the end. One more form of prototyping is Extreme Prototyping used for developing web applications. It breaks down web development into three phases, each one based on the preceding one. The first phase is a static prototype that consists mainly of HTML pages. In the second phase, a simulated services layer is used to program fully functional screens. In the third phase the services are implemented.

Adding to the model types are the dimensions of vertical or horizontal prototypes. You're probably familiar with the terms vertical and horizontal as they apply to product marketing. Vertical products are tailored to specific industries such as retail, medical, legal, manufacturing, etc. Horizontal products are built for a broad spectrum of users across any industry. Think of Microsoft Office as an example of a horizontal product. As applied to prototyping, vertical and horizontal have the same meaning as in product marketing. A vertical prototype models very specific system functionality to a well-defined target population. For example, if you are rolling out an ERP system that includes finance, HR and payroll, you wouldn't necessarily demonstrate functional payroll models to accounts payables, nor would you show a model for posting to a G/L account to HR generalists.

Horizontal prototypes offer the "balcony view" of a system and often do not contain working simulations. To understand the balcony view, close your eyes for a moment and dream about that long awaited vacation in some exotic and idyllic paradise. You've entered your upper floor hotel room and stepped out onto the balcony. Your breath is taken away as you get that first glimpse of nature's beauty surrounding you. Okay, you can wake up now. So an IT system isn't exactly nature's bounty, but the balcony view does allow us to see the big picture which is exactly what a horizontal prototype does.

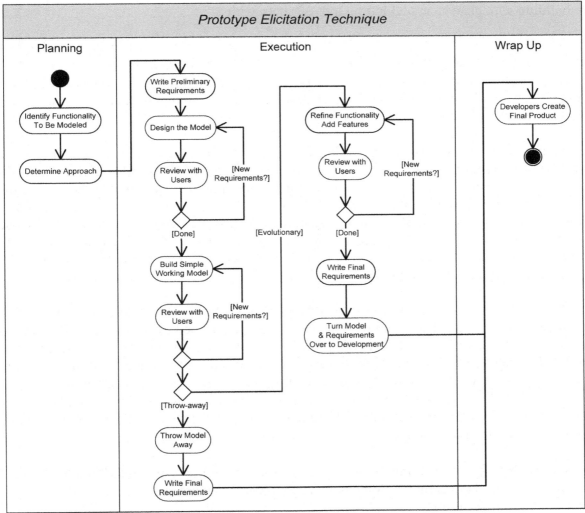

Figure 52 - Prototype Activity Diagram

Prototypes work best for designing systems with human-computer interfaces. User interface or report prototypes are wire frame, mockups or functional simulations. There are many tools on the market that allow the BA to create simulations without any programming knowledge. John Crinnion, author of *"Evolutionary Systems Development, a practical guide to the use of prototyping within a structured systems methodology,"*[65] says, "It has been found that

---

[65] Plenum Press, New York, 1991. Page 18.

prototyping is very effective in the analysis and design of on-line systems, especially for transaction processing, where the use of screen dialogs is much more in evidence. The greater the interaction between the computer and the user, the greater the benefit is that can be obtained from building a quick system and letting the user play with it."

Systems with little user interaction benefit the least from prototyping. Such systems include web services, batch processing, those that provide system input/output functions or those that primarily do calculations. Of these systems, Crinnion said, "Sometimes, the coding needed to perform the system functions may be too intensive and the potential gains that prototyping could provide are too small."

The planning steps for prototyping/modeling are to decide what functionality to model and the approach to follow for that particular functionality. The execution steps differ slightly depending on whether you've chosen a Throw-away or Evolutionary approach, although both start out the same. Both begin with writing the preliminary requirements, designing the model and reviewing it with the users. The preliminary design often consists of wireframes and/or mockups. The users are able to visualize what the BA perceives they are asking for and have the chance to revise the model, add new requirements or amend existing requirements. Next is a simple working model which simulates the interactive features.

Once the users approve the interactions, the two approaches follow alternate paths. For the throw-away approach, the final requirements are written and turned over to the development team to create the real product. The model itself is not literally thrown away in a trash can, but placed under archive to allow for future reference where it remains an integral component of the requirements to aid the development team in creating the real product. In the evolutionary approach, the model continues to be refined adding features and functionality before being turned over to the development team to evolve the model into the final product. The evolutionary approach is a key feature of model driven architecture.

Despite the ubiquity of prototyping in the agile methods, there are researchers[66] that name six disadvantages with the technique. Some have labeled the disadvantages as misuse of the technique. The concerns are:

- Developer attachment to prototype
- Expense of implementing prototyping
- Incomplete documentation

- Insufficient analysis
- Systems may be left unfinished or implemented before being fully ready
- Users expect the performance of the system to be the same as the prototype

---

[66] Adapted from C. Melissa McClendon, Larry Regot, Gerri Akers.

Developers at times can be a prideful bunch, but in a good way. They work very long and hard to create the best product they can. They take pride in their accomplishments. There's absolutely nothing wrong with that. We should feel good about the products we produce. But sometimes, developers may become too attached to the prototypes they have spent a great deal of time and effort producing. This leads to problems like attempting to convert a limited prototype into a final system when it does not have an appropriate underlying architecture.

Startup costs to add prototyping to a development team's tool box may be high if companies have development methodologies in place that do not include prototyping. Changing them can require retraining, retooling or both. Another problem is that many companies that do implement prototyping tend to jump into it under the assumption that their resources already know how to do it well and they don't bother to train their workers adequately. In a 1992 report written for Rome Laboratory at Griffiss Air Force Base, Rome, NY called *Software Prototyping and Requirements Engineering,* Joseph E. Urban of Arizona State University said, "A common problem with adopting prototyping technology is high expectations for productivity with insufficient effort behind the learning curve. In addition to training for the use of a prototyping technique, there is an often overlooked need for developing corporate and project specific underlying structure to support the technology. When this underlying structure is omitted, lower productivity can often result."

Documentation is often victimized because of the desire to rapidly move prototypes into production. Users get excited when they see their vision come to fruition and their needs met which results in implementation corners being cut. System documentation suffers as the development team moves onto something new. As a general rule of thumb, do not claim success for a project until all deliverables are complete. Documentation is as important a deliverable as the product itself.

The development team can easily be distracted from completing a proper systems analysis because their focus shifts to demonstrating limited functionality in a prototype and they lose sight of the big picture. They overlook the fact that there may be better solutions available to solve the business problem. They move so fast that systems specifications are left incomplete and converting the limited prototype into a final product results in a poorly designed system that is difficult to maintain. And since a prototype is limited in functionality, it may not scale well if used as the basis for the final deliverable. The development team may not realize this until too late if they excessively focus on building a prototype.

Users may think that a throw-away prototype is actually the final system under development and that it just needs to be finished. They are often unaware of the effort needed to add features which it may not have such as error-checking, data access, security and logging. System performance with a prototype is usually much better than a production level system because of the controlled data set, lack of disk I/O and background features. This leads users to expect the same level of performance from the final system even though this is not the intent of the prototype. Prototypes often demonstrate features which are removed from the final system specification. Users become attached to those features that were once included only to test their feasibility. For the above reasons, this leads to confusion and conflict.

Users may have just enough development knowledge to be dangerous. A user group once came forward with a prototype they developed in Microsoft Access. They went through all of the company's IT Governance processes using their prototype to demonstrate the functionality they wanted as an enhancement to their production system. Funding for the project was approved and the development team began their interactions with the users. Conflict quickly arose because the users insisted they wanted the production system to have the look, feel and functionality of their Microsoft Access application. They liked what they had built for themselves in Access! The problem is that their production system is an Oracle application. Oracle applications and Microsoft Access applications don't look anything alike. Performance is vastly different as well. The performance they received with Access and 1,000 data rows will never compare to the performance they will get from an Oracle database and 28,000,000 data rows. Fortunately, the end users finally understood the issues with their prototype and happily accepted the final solution in Oracle. They didn't have any choice.

Despite the caveats, prototyping is and will remain a best practice that can result in an improved bottom line and enhanced productivity for your organization, but only if it's accompanied by adequate training of your resources, proper focus, awareness of its limitations and a firm structural foundation. When implemented correctly, its advantages outweigh the criticisms and include:

- Exposes developers to future system enhancements
- Facilitates system implementation
- Quantifiable user feedback
- Reduces development costs

- Reduces development time
- Requires user involvement
- Results in greater user satisfaction
- Users know what to expect

Requirements Workshop

While all of the elicitation techniques are important, the most vital is the Requirements Workshop, known alternately as Requirements Discovery Session, Joint Application Design (JAD), Joint Requirements Planning (JRP), Facilitated Workshop or Elicitation Workshop. To keep it simple, we shall use the term JAD. JAD sessions are a powerful, structured way of obtaining quality requirements and specifications. JAD sessions, when led by highly skilled BAs, are a major step to the path of requirements maturity. JADs have been used in business and systems development for decades.

In 1976, Michael Doyle and David Strauss published[67] *"How to Make Meetings Work."* After reading the book, Chuck Morris, a system engineer with IBM Raleigh, adopted ideas from Doyle and Strauss to gather requirements for the implementation of a software product called "COPICS." Tony Crawford of IBM Toronto worked with Morris to formalize the process which is known today as JAD. They began widely teaching the approach through workshops in the 1980s. JAD is designed to bring system developers and users of varying backgrounds and opinions together in a productive, creative and collaborative environment. For many new systems, the majority of their business requirements are elicited through JAD sessions. Yet, many organizations still don't know how to conduct a JAD effectively and some organizations don't even know what it is.

I wasn't kidding when I mentioned earlier that I have observed an IT Director enter a room and ask a group of business users "What are your requirements?" This is his concept of a JAD session. He even calls it a JAD session. The IT Director never had any formal business analysis training even though he's been in the industry for almost 30 years. When the Director finally allowed a true BA to facilitate one session, he didn't allow the BA to go very far. He dominated the conversation and drew the participants off track. The BA barely got through the ground rules and started on a context diagram for the system under discussion. He never had the opportunity to complete it. The Director asked the BA to sit down and reverted back to "What are your requirements?" To "help" the users, the Director described current processes and had his development manager demonstrate the legacy system through a laptop and projector. The Director asked if the users wanted to continue to do things as they are now or did the business want to change any of their processes to improve them. Using the legacy system as the only frame of reference, the answer from the business is that "We want to continue doing things as they are now. We've never thought about how to improve them." To which the Director responded, "Okay then, we'll take the current processes and view them as the requirements."

Later, with only IT people in the room, I suggested we change the approach and ask about business process and document use cases and user stories to gain a better understanding of what the users need and see if there's a way we could suggest process improvements. People looked at me as if I had just stepped out of the Twilight Zone and gave them their first close encounter of the third kind. A development manager with over 20 years' experience said, "You're scaring me to death. Use cases have no bearing on requirements." Afterward, the Director apologized to me privately and said "I know I don't have the business analysis background you do. But this is the way I've always done things and I don't have time to learn any new ways of doing it now." The

---

[67] Jove Book (January 1, 1976)

project these "requirements sessions" were for was to replace a major legacy system with a new product at an estimated cost in excess of $10 million dollars.

When the so-called JAD sessions were complete, there were more than 600 requirements captured in an Excel spreadsheet that had been maintained by a very expensive consultant from a major international accounting and consulting firm. This consultant should have known better but bowed to the Director's instructions. The spreadsheet was the BRD. While documentation standards are important, they shadow an excellent elicitation technique. When the new product is eventually put into place, the company will no doubt have a project that has overrun its budget and schedule and be nothing more than a repainted version of the legacy system on a new technology platform. Process improvement will not be addressed. Following this approach should scare anyone to death. What a waste!

Eliciting requirements is a practice best jointly owned by business and technology. Nowhere does this come into play more visibly than the JAD session. The JAD process includes approaches for enhancing user participation, expediting development and improving the quality of specifications. The DSDM Consortium is an organization that embraces JAD sessions as a core technique. DSDM Public Version 4.2 lists 42 suggested reasons for conducting JAD sessions that range from the Business Case to User Documentation Requirements and everything in between. Some of the more central purposes are:

- Business case
- Configuration management strategy
- Contingency planning
- Cutover plans

- Escalation procedure definition
- Problem definition
- Problem resolution
- Prototype review

- Requirements change control
- Requirements Prioritization
- Support level definition
- Training needs analysis

The DSDM Consortium claims five benefits from the JAD elicitation technique:

- Rapid, quality decision-making
- Greater user buy-in
- Building team spirit

- Process redesign by the user community
- Clarification of requirements when they are unclear

A JAD is a highly productive and focused event attended by carefully selected key stakeholders and subject matter experts for a short, intensive period, typically from one to five days. There are seven key roles required for running an effective multi-day JAD session:

- Executive Sponsor
- Project Sponsor
- Project Manager
- Business Analyst / Facilitator / Session Leader
- Scribe / Modeler / Recorder / Documentation Expert
- Knowledge Workers / Participants
- Observers

With all the role pseudonyms listed here, it appears as though there might be thirteen roles instead of seven, but it really is just seven; and not all of them are necessary for every JAD session. The most intensive JAD session is the requirements kick-off meeting and draws the greatest number of attendees. As the requirements process progresses, the presence of only those deemed necessary is obligatory. The facilitator and scribe are always necessary.

The Executive Sponsor is the individual who charters the project and is the de facto system owner. Frequently this is a senior level executive and perhaps a member of the company's operating committee or ITGC. The person must be high enough in the organization to be capable of making decisions to guide the necessary vision, strategy, planning and direction for the project.

The Project Sponsor generally reports to the Executive Sponsor and is responsible for day-to-day business decisions in the project's operational domain. The Project Sponsor is usually a Director-level or higher position and perhaps a department head. For example, if the project is for an accounts receivable system, the Project Sponsor is the head of the accounts receivable department. If the company has adopted the concept of a project Business Liaison as a best practice, day-to-day business related and user interface design project decisions are delegated to the Business Liaison who works for the Project Sponsor or Executive Sponsor.

The Project Manager role should be self-explanatory. A project manager is a professional in the field of project management, preferably holding PMP certification. Project managers have the responsibility of planning, scheduling, coordinating, reporting and closing the project. Ideally the project manager and business analyst have a first-class working relationship.

Well-run workshops are one of the most effective ways to deliver high quality requirements quickly. The facilitator is the means to a well-run workshop and the key functionary of the JAD session. This is the person who walks into the room and asks everyone, "What are your requirements?" *(Just kidding!)* The facilitator promotes trust, mutual understanding and strong communication among the participants. The facilitator establishes a professional tone and keeps the meeting discussions on track. Good facilitators are highly skilled and completely impartial. Critical key skills are the ability to build consensus and conflict resolution.

If at all possible, the facilitator should have no stake in the outcome of the workshop and preferably comes from outside the project team, perhaps from a different area of domain expertise, a shared services organization or a third party such as a consultant, contractor or contingent worker. The facilitator must remain neutral and not take sides. S/he establishes the ground rules, enforces them and maintains order in the session. Additional responsibilities are to manage scope creep and referee disputes. If the facilitator is a business analyst, the preference is to use someone who possesses the CBAP designation.

The Scribe records what happens within the workshop and does not contribute information to the meeting, although clarifying questions may be asked. The primary responsibilities are to document requirements in the format decided during the planning activity, publish the meeting minutes and keep track of open issues. The role may be held by a co-facilitator, a business analyst, developer or user as long as the individual has the requisite understanding of the objectives in order to know what to record. For major JAD sessions, there may be two Scribes assigned to the workshop. One of them might use a graphical tool to directly model the system under discussion while the other takes down the discussion notes for later reference and incorporation into the BRD.

Participants are the project stakeholders or their representatives. They are members of both the business and systems development communities. They are the subject matter experts who are knowledgeable in the functions of the domain for the system under discussion. They manage and operate the business and its systems and include business users, customers, managers, supervisors, clerical and IT staff. On the IT side, contributors may be from many roles. Participants could be suppliers, business analysts, data modelers, enterprise and domain architects, auditors or any of a number of specialist roles.

The Observers are generally members of the application development team assigned to the project or support staff gathering useful background. They sit behind the participants and silently observe the proceedings. They do not actively contribute to the output of the workshop. If they need to take part, they should do so as participants. The observer gallery could include people auditing either the workshop process or the facilitator's performance. An observer may also be a trainee or apprentice facilitator who wants to observe group dynamics without actually being part of the group.

Preparing for the JAD begins with identifying the purpose and objectives of the meeting. It is vital to have clear objectives for the workshop. With so many people in attendance, it's easy to get off track. Planning and scoping set the expectations for the workshop with the sponsors and participants. Scoping identifies the business functions that are within range for the JAD. By far, the majority of JADs are conducted for the purpose of determining business requirements for a new system or enhancements to an existing system.

Identifying participants is the same as in other elicitation techniques. The BA confers with the project sponsors until everyone agrees to the participant list. The difference between this participant selection activity and those of other elicitation techniques is what comes next. The BA conducts pre-workshop interviews with the key stakeholders and knowledge experts. These interviews are not meant to elicit requirements in advance of the workshop. Instead, they ensure that the stakeholders understand the purpose of the requirements workshop and that the workshop aligns with each attendee's needs. Additionally, they alert the attendees to make ready with any preparations needed for the session. Interviews should take place 1 to 5 days before the workshop

The facilitator designs JAD activities and exercises to build interim deliverables toward the final output of the workshop. The pre-JAD planning and interviews help determine the design of the workshop exercises. Once the objectives are established and you know where you're going, you can decide on the route you are going to take to get you there. A workshop combines serial and parallel exercises. Serial exercises successively build on one another in a linear fashion. With parallel exercises, each sub-team works on one piece of the puzzle or on the same piece for different functional areas. The facilitator leads the high-intensity activities to energize the group and thrust it forward to a specific goal. Low-intensity exercises allow for detailed consideration before decisions are made. The discussions may involve the entire group or sub-teams may work on specific issues and present a limited number of ideas for group deliberation.

The facilitator integrates the participants either homogenously or heterogeneously. People with similar expertise from different departments are matched up or participants learn from each other by mixing expertise. Workshops function on both the technical and political levels. It's the facilitator's prerogative to mix and match sub-team members to meet organizational and cultural goals while keeping office politics in mind. The facilitator's job is to build consensus, affect communications and force issues out early in the process. Why worry about technical details of a system if underlying business issues are not resolved?

Many organizations use document templates for their requirements. For those organizations with immature requirements practices, creating the BRD is simply an exercise in filling out the template, but this ought not to be the case. Organizations with mature requirements practices approach documentation differently. They plan their approach and determine ahead of time the level of detail needed while adhering to acceptable guidelines. For example:

- To analyze and document a specific Business Process, what is needed?
- Is the process for a web service or user interaction with the system?
- Do we use UML or BPMN?
- Which toolset?

- Do we need a use case diagram or will a textual use case suffice; or both perhaps?
- What about an activity diagram, a sequence diagram or a state machine diagram?
- Do we select all of the above or none of the above?

It is important to define the level of technical diagramming appropriate to the exercise. The most critical success factor of any diagram is its ease of comprehension. It must be understood by the users and comprehensible by anyone viewing it even if they aren't with the project team or familiar with the project domain. Veteran facilitators design exercises into the workshop agenda to have the group develop a variety of high-level diagrams that may include business processes, context diagrams, interface diagrams, activity diagrams, use cases and data flows among others.

Workshop materials consist of documentation, worksheets, diagrams, and even props that aid participants to understand the business function under investigation. The facilitator and project manager may decide to include a straw man or briefing document to send out as part of the workshop materials. The briefing document might be called the Statement of Work, Briefing Guide, Project Scope Definition—or anything else appropriate to your organization. The brief is a document of no more than eight to twelve pages in length and provides a clear definition of the scope of the project for the participants.

The initial JAD for a new system or large maintenance or upgrade project should not be less than three days especially if the JAD is being conducted with a project team whose members have not worked together before. With newly formed teams it is important to view the initial JAD session as more of a team building exercise rather than a requirements elicitation workshop. There will be requirements elicited, but teambuilding is important in any environment. Its focus brings out the best in the team to ensure effective communications and enables team members to collaborate and problem solve.

In any new team environment, participants take most of the first day to get comfortable with their roles, each other and the environment. The second day is spent learning to understand each other and develop a common language with which to communicate issues and concerns. By the third day, real productivity is achieved because everyone is working together on the problem. For veteran teams with much interaction in the day-to-day environment, team assimilation is much faster and the focus on team building can be reduced to a few warm-up exercises or ice breakers. After the initial workshop, shorter more focused sessions can be scheduled for subsequent phases of the project. Figure 54 is an example of a 3-day JAD agenda.

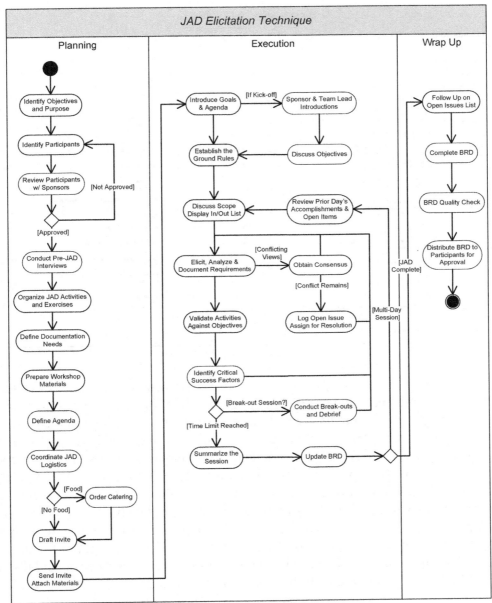

Figure 53 - JAD Activity Diagram

AGENDA

INITIAL JAD SESSION
January 14-16, 2004
9:00 a.m. – 5:00 p.m.

Meeting called by [Name]

Attendees: [Attendee List]
Please read: [List Workshop Materials]
Please bring: [List Prepared Items from Pre-JAD Interviews]

DAY 1

Time	Activity	Room
8:30 a.m. – 9:00 a.m.	Continental Breakfast	Rainier Room
9:00 a.m. – 9:15 a.m.	Introductions and Agenda Facilitator: *Kari Hensien*	Rainier Room
9:15 a.m. – 9:25 a.m.	Project Overview & Kick-off Project Sponsor: *Robert Cosgrove*	Rainier Room
9:25 a.m. – 9:35 a.m.	Project Plan Review Project Manager: *Anna Simpson*	Rainier Room
9:35 a.m. – 10:00 a.m.	JAD Overview, Meeting Objectives, Guidelines and Ground Rules Facilitator: *Kari Hensien*	Rainier Room
10:00 a.m. – 10:30 a.m.	Project and Business Objectives, Scope Discussion (In/Out List) Facilitator: *Kari Hensien*	Rainier Room
10:30 a.m. – 10:45 a.m.	Break Facilitator: *Kari Hensien*	Rainier Room
10:45 a.m. – 11:15 a.m.	Project and Business Objectives, Scope Discussion (In/Out List) Facilitator: *Kari Hensien*	Rainier Room
11:15 a.m. – 11:45 a.m.	Warm-up Exercise / Ice Breaker Facilitator: *Kari Hensien*	Rainier Room
11:45 a.m. – noon	Warm-up Exercise Debrief Facilitator: *Kari Hensien*	Rainier Room
noon – 1:00 p.m.	Lunch	Catered
1:00 p.m. – 3:00 p.m.	Requirements Discovery: Order Entry Facilitator: *Kari Hensien*	Rainier Room
3:00 p.m. – 4:00 p.m.	Break-out Sessions	Snoqualmie Room Red Carpet Room East Conference Room
4:00 p.m. – 5:00 p.m.	Wrap-up Break-out Debrief Summarize Day's Progress Preview-Tomorrow	Rainier Room

DAY 2

Time	Activity	Room
8:30 a.m. – 9:00 a.m.	Continental Breakfast	Rainier Room
9:00 a.m. – 10:00 a.m.	Debrief Day 1/ Review Progress	Rainier Room
10:00 a.m. – noon	Requirements Discovery: Business Area 2 Facilitator: *Kari Hensien*	Rainier Room
1:00 p.m. – 3:30 p.m	Requirements Discovery: Business Area 3 Facilitator: *Kari Hensien*	Rainier Room

DAY 3

Time	Activity	Room
8:30 a.m. – 9:00 a.m.	Continental Breakfast	Rainier Room
9:00 a.m. – 10:00 a.m.	Debrief Day 2/ Review Progress	Rainier Room
10:00 a.m. – noon	Requirements Discovery: Business Area 4 Facilitator: *Kari Hensien*	Rainier Room
1:00 p.m. – 3:30 p.m	Requirements Review: Validation and Prioritization Facilitator: *Kari Hensien*	Rainier Room
3:30 p.m. – 4:30 p.m.	Wrap-up Debrief Day 3 Next Steps Q&A	Rainier Room

Additional Instructions:
Use this section for additional instructions, comments, or directions.

Figure 54 - Sample 3-Day JAD Agenda

To minimize distractions and interruptions, JAD sessions are best held off-site. Logistically, arranging off-site meetings presents more challenges than booking a campus conference room. Budget is a big consideration. You also have to make sure that everything you need to conduct a successful meeting is either available at the remote venue or brought with you. Items that you normally take for granted such as projectors, screens, PCs, tables, markers, masking tape, Post-It notes and any other props have to be considered in advance. If the budget allows, you'll want to order food for breakfast, lunch, coffee breaks and snacks for the convenience and comfort of the participants. Arrive early to the JAD location to assure the layout of the room promotes communication and interaction of the participants. The U-configuration in Figure 55 works well for workshops. Break-out sessions work best with tables and chairs configured for sub-teams of 6-8 people as shown in Figure 56. The final JAD preparation steps are to write and distribute the invite (Figure 57). Don't forget to attach the workshop materials.

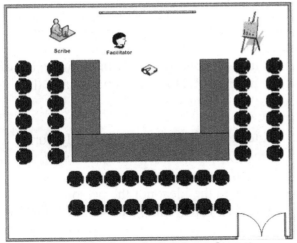

Figure 55 - Example JAD Room Layout

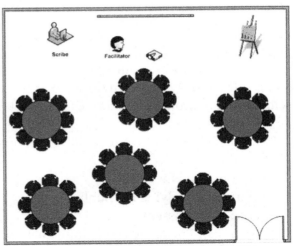

Figure 56 - JAD Break-out Session Layout

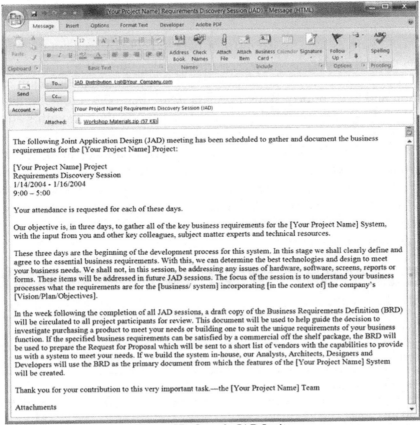

Figure 57 - Sample JAD Invite

For the initial JAD, start with introductions and short addresses by the Executive and Project Sponsors followed by a high-level review of the project plan by the project manager. The facilitator then establishes the ground rules. Seed the ground rule discussion by unveiling a list of ground rules already prepared on a flip chart and ask the participants to add or change any they deem important. Some ground rules that work well in a JAD setting are:

- Everyone participates (except the observers of course)
- Every opinion is welcome
- Disagree privately; agree publically
- Silence means assent
- "Because we've always done it that way" is an unacceptable justification

- Mute cell phones, use laptops only during breaks, and limit side conversations
- Start and end on time
- Challenge the idea, not the person
- There is no such thing as a stupid question

Managing Scope Creep

One of the greatest challenges for anyone in Information Technology is managing scope. Scope creep is a bane to a project's success metrics. Scope creep occurs for a variety of reasons like poor change control practices, not understanding project objectives, poor requirements practices, poor communication and even poorly skilled project team members, project managers and business analysts. In a JAD session, where everyone is offering their thoughts and opinions, scope creep can crawl in almost before anyone realizes a topic has veered off course. In Chapter 3 of the book *"Writing Effective Use Cases,"* Alistair Cockburn talks about an "absurdly simple and remarkably effective" method to control scope that he learned from consultant Rob Thomsett. The method is so simple, yet proven to be so effective, that it personally led to a true "AHA!" moment for me. The method is called the in/out list. It draws a boundary for meeting participants between what is in scope and what is out of scope for the discussion. Figure 58 is an example of a simple in/out list.

Topic : Order Entry	In	Out
Entering standard orders	In	
Forms of payment	In	
Combining multiple orders to reduce customer shipping costs		Out
Partial deliveries, late deliveries, wrong deliverables	In	
Invoicing in any form		Out

Topic : Order Entry	In	Out
Out of stock inventory		Out

Figure 58 - Example In/Out List

Introduce the in/out list right after establishing the ground rules. Write it on the white board or on flip chart paper and post it for all to see. Allow it to remain visible for the entire discussion. Use a new in/out list at the introduction of any new requirements discovery activity since topics in focus are likely to change every few hours. Give details about the points that are in scope for the current topic of discussion and explain that the out of scope items will be discussed at an appropriate time in a future meeting. Give the audience a chance to acquiesce to or contest the in/out list. Allow time for the group to debate any opposition and concede to consensus. During the course of the topic's discussion, someone may bring up an entirely new item for reflection that had not been thought of before. Allow the group to decide if it is in scope for the day's activities or not. If it is, add it to the in/out list and ask what needs to be dropped to make up the time difference. If the group says no, log it as an open issue and make sure to schedule it for another meeting. The in/out list is effective in any kind of meeting, not just JADs.

The JAD continues with cycles of eliciting, analyzing and documenting requirements. The analysis at this stage is preliminary. A much deeper analysis comes later and will be discussed in the Chapter 6. Analyzing requirements is as much about finding ways to improve business processes as it is about satisfying business need. It is okay to challenge requirements that might not make sense in light of the objectives, current technology or implementation cost. Ask probing questions about why debatable business processes are the way they are and do not accept "because we've always done things that way" as the answer. Lead the participants into a process improvement course of action instead of letting them settle for the status quo.

The inclination to cultivate interpersonal conflict is the greatest disadvantage of the JAD. Disagreements between participants may occur in a JAD setting which cannot be settled within the confines of a single session. The scribe logs it as an open issue and the facilitator assigns the disputing parties the task of coming to a single source of truth and reporting the resolution by an agreed upon date. Validate all the activities against the objectives established early in the meeting. Identify the requirements' critical success factors. Good requirements are measurable and testable. For every requirement ask two questions: How will we know that the planned changes have been effective? How will success be measured? If break-out sessions are planned, make sure to debrief when they are over. Close the day's activities by summarizing what happened and what was accomplished. Review any open issues and ensure that each one has an assigned resolver and a resolution date.

When the participants leave, the scribe and BA stay to add the day's requirements to the BRD if the scribe hasn't done this in real time during the session. Yes, it is possible to write most of the draft BRD while the JAD is in session. Multi-day JADs begin subsequent days with a review of the prior day's accomplishments. When the JAD is completely over, follow-up on any remaining open items and complete the BRD. Before sending the BRD out for review by the participants, confirm its readiness through the quality review process described in Chapter 6. If JADs are run effectively and follow-up items resolved quickly, a final BRD can usually be delivered to the participants within 7 to 10 days post JAD, quality check and all.

Survey

The last elicitation technique we'll look at in this chapter is the survey. Surveys are frequently used in quantitative marketing studies and social research to accumulate information from a select target group in a very short time. Depending on its purpose, data collected can be quantitative used for statistical analysis or insights and opinions not easily elicited through other methods. In an IT Context, surveys are most often used for:

- Comprehend Attitudes, Beliefs and Values
- Conduct a Stakeholder Analysis
- Customer Satisfaction
- Employee Satisfaction
- Organizational Change Management Readiness
- Pre-JAD Interview Support
- Product Opinions
- Subsequent Action Planning
- Uncovering Past Behaviors
- Understanding Work Practices

Begin by defining the purpose of the survey and selecting the target respondent population. What objectives do you want to accomplish? Define the survey's project frame of reference including the schedule, budget, manpower and intrusion and privacy concerns. Addressing intrusion and privacy concerns can result in higher quality data and response rates. For example: Is the survey going to be anonymous or does it require a respondent's identification in order to receive an incentive? People are reluctant to answer hard questions honestly if they feel there will be repercussions for their frankness. Work with the sponsors to select the target group and define the survey's topics to fit the respondents' frame of reference. Their background affects their interpretation of the questions. Collaborating with the sponsors ensures the respondents have enough details or expertise to react to the topics truthfully.

Choosing a survey type is very much like selecting an interview type. Survey respondents are asked either closed questions as with the structured interview or open-ended questions as with the unstructured or a semi-structured interview. Questions are standardized to reduce bias and ensure the reliability and validity of the data. Standardized questions are neutral as to intended outcome. Biased questions encourage respondents to answer one way rather than another, but even unbiased questions may leave respondents with unanticipated expectations. Whatever survey type you choose, every respondent is presented with the same questions and in the same order as other respondents.

Based on the survey type and the objectives is it necessary to survey the entire population? Differences in geography, culture, regulatory districts and job function or business process may indicate the survey should be distributed to a subset of the population rather than the entire group. To keep things unbiased statistical sampling methods may need to be employed. Work with the sponsors again to refine the target population into a statistical sampling group.

There are a number of choices for distribution method including snail mail, telephone, personal administration, email or the worldwide web. Each has their own pluses, minuses, costs and response rate expectations. Snail mail can take a very long time to collect data and is not appropriate for SDLC purposes. Telephone surveys are fairly cost efficient depending on local carriers, technology used and whether the target population is internal or external to an organization. Response rates can be very good because of the personal contact. Personally administered surveys are the highest cost, but questions can be more detailed as a rapport develops between the respondents and the researcher. Personally administered surveys result in very high response rates. Electronic surveys administered through email or web sites are low cost and can produce very high response rates and fast results. There are many free survey sites offering services on the internet. Zoomerang and Surveymonkey are two that are very popular in corporate environs. This is a partial list returned from Googling "free survey sites:"

- Esurveyspro.com
- Freeonlinesurveys.com
- Impressity.com
- Kwiksurveys.com
- Polldaddy.com
- Surveymonkey.com
- Surveypopups.com
- Tigersurvey.com
- Zoomerang.com

Decide upon your desired outcomes. What response rate is acceptable for your study? If the response rate is too low, the results of the survey may be meaningless. Depending on your objectives, you may want to offer an incentive for completing the survey in order to improve the projected response rate. For example, give something away or enter respondents into a drawing to win one of the latest hi-tech gadgets or a gift certificate. Another method for increasing response rates is to keep the survey brief at no more than one-page or 10 questions. Keeping it brief deters drop-offs. Drop-offs are people who start a survey but find it too long to finish. They drop the survey somewhere in the middle depending on their patience and tolerance levels. Financial incentives, discount coupons, emotional appeal, the promise of anonymity and legal compulsion all help to improve response rates.

Next you have to plan on whether supplemental interview support is necessary to assist in constructing the survey or post-survey to help in clarifying the responses or emergent themes.

Pre-survey interviews with key stakeholders help determine the questions to ask. Post-survey interviews elicit more details about specific responses.

The most difficult part of any survey is writing the questions. Are you planning an open or closed survey? If you recall from the interview technique, open-ended questions are free-form. The respondent writes out an answer. Answers to open-ended questions are evaluated and codified into themes. Closed-ended questions offer choices from which the respondent selects an answer from a given number of options. The options for closed-ended questions are exhaustive and mutually exclusive. There are four types of response scales for closed-ended questions:

- Dichotomous: question with two options
- Nominal-polytomous: question with more than two unordered options
- Ordinal-polytomous: question with more than two ordered options
- Continuous: questions presented with a continuous scale

The "natural" grouping of questions is relevant. Previous questions may inadvertently bias later questions. Wording is to be kept simple with no technical or specialized words or undefined acronyms. Questions are to be clear. Anyone reading a question should understand the meaning of it. Ambiguous words, vague sentence structures and negatives cause misunderstanding. Reword double negatives as positives. The writing style is conversational, concise, accurate and appropriate for the target sampling group. Questions designed to evoke emotional responses may skew results and are to be avoided. It's always a good idea to test a survey before you distribute it. Allow a few people who are not part of the target sampling group to perform a usability test. You can even run a small usability focus group if you wish. Use the results to fine-tune the survey questions. Distribute the survey and wait for the responses.

In addition to the order of questions, the flow of the questions is important. Make sure questions flow logically from one to the next, from the more general to the more specific, from the least sensitive to the most sensitive and from the factual and behavioral questions to attitude and opinion questions. Place questions that don't require help first and the ones that do require help in the form of pop-ups or additional explanatory text last.

When the survey ends, collate the responses. Evaluate the details of open-ended questions and classify them by theme. If you need to collect further details about any responses, conduct post-survey interviews provided the survey wasn't anonymous and you know who the respondents are. Analyze and summarize the results and distribute them to the sponsors.

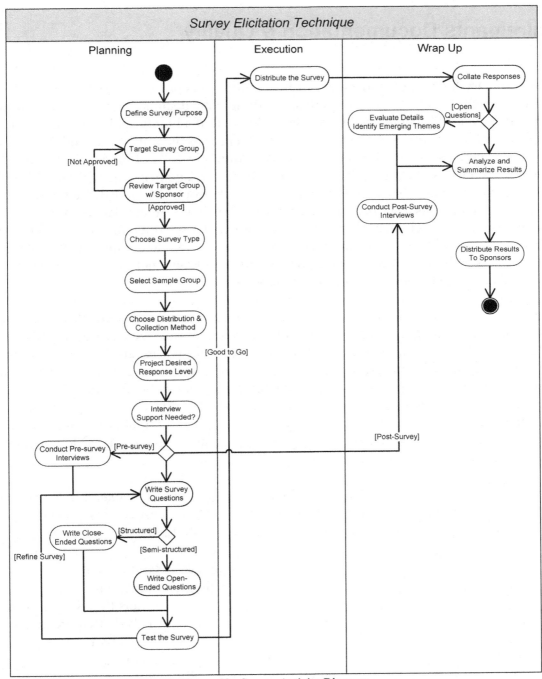

Figure 59 - Survey Activity Diagram

Requirements Documentation & Quality

One of the primary foundational messages of the requirements process chapters is that the requirements process is not simply an exercise in filling out a document template. We know requirements must to be documented somehow and in lieu of a highly sophisticated requirements management tool that captures the requirements and generates the artifacts, a well-constructed BRD template supports the requirements process and minimizes the effort required to build it. Many organizations can't afford the cost of requirements management software and will either create document templates for themselves out of trial and error or download one of the numbers available on the internet as a starting point. They base the choice of template on their understanding of how requirements should be captured, and more often than not, they make the selection because they like the look and feel of the document. While it's important to abide by corporate brand standards, a BRD should reflect best practices and not just look pretty. But really, what does a good requirements template look like?

Let's revisit our operational definition of good requirements. Good requirements are cohesive, complete, consistent, correct, feasible, modifiable, necessary, prioritized, reusable, testable, traceable, verifiable and unambiguous. Requirements reusability is tough to achieve without a requirements repository. Searching and categorizing requirements using standard word processor documents is possible with advanced document management tools, but not easy. The problem with the majority of the templates available on the internet is that they don't support the operational definition of good requirements and are not based on current best practices. But even if you did stumble across a document claiming to be a best practice based BRD template, would you know what elements it should contain?

Before we can know what a good BRD looks like, let's take a look at an example of one that's not so good. If you are not using an excel spreadsheet to capture requirements, you are probably using a document that has a table of contents that looks something like this:

- Author
- Review and Approval
- Scope
- Overview and Objectives
- Business Justification
- Business Requirements
    - o Basic work/Business process
    - o Processes to be automated
- Compliance Requirements
- Functional Requirements
    - o Data Acquisition Requirements
    - o Data Analysis Requirements
    - o Data Output requirements
- Security Requirements
    - o Physical
    - o Logical

- Technical Requirements
  - Hardware
  - Software Configuration
- Usability Requirements

- Operational Requirements
- Data Dictionary
- Test Requirements
- Glossary of Terms

As you review this table of contents, you might be saying to yourself, "This looks like a perfectly good requirements document to me. What are we getting at? How is this not such a good document?" To the untrained eye it is a pretty good requirements document. It appears to have all of the elements needed for designing and building a system; and a team might even successfully deliver a project from it. But a document of this type has some serious issues that could impact a project's success and lead to rework, schedule delays or cost overruns. Let's diagnose what's wrong so we can learn how to recognize a good requirements document when we see one.

First, this document is mixing business purposes. The sections for author and review and approval are necessary components. The next section is scope. What scope does this refer to? Be very clear when writing the scope. Most BRD's contain a scope statement that repeats the scope statement found in the project initiation documents. Project scope has no place in a BRD. The overview and objectives should be here and are required in a BRD. The business justification is an IT Governance concern. It does not belong in a BRD.

Second, the author uses non-standard terms. For example, there is a section for business requirements and another section for functional requirements. Business requirements and functional requirements are the same thing. Argue the point if you'd like, but it won't change the fact that they are one in the same. A business requirement is something the business needs to function. Hence, business requirements are functional requirements. Functional requirements are not about the internal workings of system I/O and data access. Using non-standard terms leads to confusion and makes it difficult to know where to document information. Let's suppose for a minute that this document captures the requirements for an application to manage retail sales. Looking at the table of contents again, ask yourself the following questions:

1. Where do you define "what is a customer?"
2. What are the attributes of a customer?
3. What is the information flow underlying the process?
4. Who or what is interacting with the system?
5. What variations exist for a process?
6. Where are the key success factors of your processes?
7. Where are business rules being captured?
8. What are the system and process interdependencies?

Quality documentation is effective documentation. Well written requirements convey the business need in a clear, concise and verifiable way to the project team and stakeholders. They are unambiguous, accurate and complete. The BRD is useful because it serves its intended purpose and the needs of its intended audience. It is efficient and follows lean principles. It has all of the information needed at a particular point in time and none that is unnecessary. Unnecessary information is waste and of no value to the business.

Every process should be measurable and testable. For a process to be measurable and testable, key performance indicators or success metrics must be defined. Since writing a BRD is a process and by definition all processes are measurable, what success factors can be defined to distinguish a good BRD from a poor one? BRD key success factors ensure that focus is placed on information that affects the outcomes of the project, specifically in three areas:

1. Uncover all interdependencies. There have been many projects deployed to production where something breaks downstream because the system engineers "forgot" that the broken system received information from the production system. Changing the field length of a record should have been a non-event, but because the interdependency between the two systems was overlooked early in the requirements process, there is now a broken production process that the firefighters have to fix.

2. Eliminate unambiguous goals and objectives. For example, what does this requirement mean? "The system shall perform better than the system it replaces." Or this one: "reduction in data input errors." These are actual requirements extracted from documents available on the internet. If you were the business analyst who wrote them or the architects and stakeholders that approved them, what would your expectations be for the developers to deliver them? How would you know when they passed a quality test? What are the acceptance criteria?

3. Ensure that information that supports the process under discussion is documented. This includes business rules, information flows, data definitions, behavioral models, etc.

To envision requirements as a process, think about how an onion grows. The root and core are at the center and layers grow upon layers. The root and core of the requirements process is the requirements scope, the investigation of high level scenarios and the activities within the scenarios where the high level objects are defined. Then as each layer is examined more closely, the BA dives deeper into the details, all the while maintaining control over the process. From the high level scenarios, you move onto the activity scenarios and explore variations that occur within the activities. You define the high level data flow and data definition and discover entity relationships. At the next level, you develop the logical process model and elaborate the variations and conditions at a task level. You construct the logical data model and define the data rules and validations. Proper requirements elicitation must be conducted to the task level of business process, information flow, business rules and interdependencies for scope to be properly assessed.

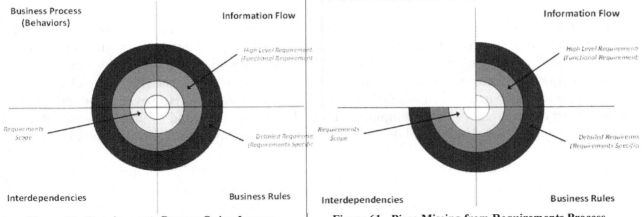

Figure 60 - Requirements Process Onion Layers   **Figure 61 - Piece Missing from Requirements Process**

Figure shows the onion layers for the requirements process and the four critical areas of information that affect project outcomes. If any slice of the pie is missing as shown in Figure 61, the BRD is incomplete and there is a reduced likelihood the project will achieve the status of unqualified success. Even if all the pieces are there, unqualified success is not guaranteed because the project is still dependent on how well the business analyst elicited and documented the requirements and how successfully the rest of the project team executes their respective jobs building quality in from day one.

Now that we understand what a mediocre BRD looks like and why, let's examine a model of a best-practice based BRD. Some of the examples provided in this section are derived from a BRD template courtesy of our friend Keith Ellis at IAG Consulting. IAG Consulting is a resource worthy of your time and examination. IAG offers an extremely practical and flexible approach to requirements planning, elicitation, analysis and management. The approach uses industry best practices and is fully aligned with existing and emerging standards from organizations such as IEEE, Software Engineering Institute (SEI) and IIBA.

Best Practice Business Requirements Definition

A complete example BRD built from an IAG best practice template is on the accompanying CD. The template and its instructional guide are available to you free of charge by registering at the IAG website[68] and downloading them. IAG has a second best practice template for specifying requirements for Business Intelligence and Data Warehouse projects. The IAG templates are a good place to start when considering a best practice based document. However as we look at best practices in more detail, the IAG templates may lack in a few areas and should be modified to suit your organization's individual needs. Let's begin by looking at the table of contents:

- INTRODUCTION
  - Executive Summary
  - Purpose of this Document
  - Business Objectives
  - Summary of Scope
  - Issues
  - Constraints, Assumptions, Risks, Dependencies
  - Project Team
  - Context Diagram
- REQUIREMENTS
  - Functional Requirements List
  - Business Rules List
  - Non-Functional Requirements List
  - Information Requirements List
- PROCESS DEFINITION
- DATA DEFINITION
  - Entity Relationship Diagram
  - Entity-Name
- APPENDIX
  - Appendix 1 – Glossary of Terms and Acronyms

The Executive Summary describes the purpose of the BRD, the intended audience for the document, and a summary of the objectives, scope and description of the requirements collected in the BRD. This example, from the sample BRD, is for a fictitious sales process redesign for ABC Co. It is concise and to the point. It reads:

> The following document is a working document—a definition of the business requirements resulting from an in depth analysis of the sales process. The participants worked together in a facilitated session held in Boston, January 2008.
>
> The project is organized on a multi-generational plan designed to harmonize the 3 legacy systems from companies merged into ABC Co., while also producing a single national sales process. The first generation, Alpha, is aimed at "stopping the bleeding" and led to the development of our harmonized national data registry. The next generation, Beta, is aimed at producing quick and accurate

---

[68] http://www.iag.biz/

quotes. The third generation, Gamma, is aimed at integrating MQS and the Internet into a "once and done" service.

This document represents the output of the efforts during the business requirements phase of Beta—Rapid quoting in support of the "20 seconds to quote" campaign.

It was noted during the kick-off presentation that there are a number of reasons why this project is being undertaken. Included are business reasons (for example, the need to reduce inside acquisition costs) and marketing reasons (for example, the need to reduce the lead generation and inbound new prospect inquiry cost). This new process and infrastructure is also required to deal with a quantum business strategy shift. ABC is now moving away from direct mail to focus on direct television marketing. As a result, ABC does not know as much about a specific customer or prospect when they connect with our call centers. This changes our business process, the support of the process, and requires ABC to develop from a strict "script-based selling" to a more consultative or SPIN-selling approach.

Take note that the Executive Summary does not repeat any details that may have been in the project initiation documents such as cost, schedule or resource requirements. The summary is all about explaining the requirements discovery process, what the document is and where the project is relative to the requirements process. The next section, Purpose of this Document, explains how the document is to be used:

This document is intended to reflect the process that the business will follow in the future with the resulting business requirements that flow from that process description. The document serves as the statement of the business requirements. It also serves as the instructions to the development team to allow them to consider the range of solution options that are available, from off-the-shelf commercial software packages to in-house, self-built solutions. Finally, the Quality Assurance team uses this document as the basis of their focus to make certain that test plans and scripts developed by the Business Analysts ensure that the solution meets the business' needs.

Business objectives are used to measure the success of the project. Objectives are derived from a company's strategic organizational goals and demonstrate how they support those goals. The BRD objectives should note how each one ties back to one or more specific strategic goals. "SMART" is the standard for documenting any objective. "SMART" is an acronym for Specific, Measurable, Attainable, Results-Oriented and Time-Bounded. Example objectives:

Need for Continuously Optimized National Sales Process

- Reduce the variation in time to receive a quote (Level 1 Management Objective)
- Decrease talk time within the customer care center (Level 1 Management Objective)
- Decrease after-call talk time in validating quotation details and resolving the sale (Level 1 Management Objective)
- Lower inside acquisition costs (Level 1 Management Objective)
- Reduce quote time from 10.6 minutes to under 5 seconds (Level 1 Management Objective)
- Reduce system change cycle time for managing new legislative changes, changes to the rating algorithms, or introduction of new products to be quoted (Level 1 Management Objective)
  o Allow the business to update the system wherever possible

The Summary of Scope is just as it sounds…a summary of the scope of the requirements covered in the document. It is not a summary of the project scope. The entire document serves as a definition of scope for elicited requirements for the system under discussion. The scope summary is actually an in/out list exactly like the one we discussed under the JAD Elicitation Technique. It is a list of the in scope and out of scope activities and scenarios uncovered during the requirements discovery sessions that resulted in the creation of the BRD.

In Scope Activities:
- Receive Call from Customer
- Obtain Customer Information
- Obtain Vehicle Detail
- Obtain Customer Driving History
- Obtain Current Carrier Detail
- Obtain Coverage Request and Calculate Quote
- Obtain Payment and Loss Payee Details and Convert to Policy
- Set Follow Up Dates
- Reporting Requirements

In Scope Scenarios:
- Contact from customer by telephone

Out of Scope:
- In person, mail, internet response channels
- Eliminate paper fulfillment – legal and compliance requirements

The issues section is a simple table consolidating all of the issues discovered for each scenario or activity.

Issue	Assigned To	Respond By	Resolution

Figure 62 - Sample BRD Issues Log

Constraints, Assumptions, Risks, Dependencies are factors which limit the project:

- Constraints—factors which inhibit the project's ability to deliver. Constraints may include both business and technical reasons.
- Assumptions—decisions made about scope, functionality, interfaces, etc. which must be confirmed. Assumptions are what the business analyst believes to be true at the time the requirements are elicited.
- Risks—quantifiable losses to the business as a result of not proceeding or as a result of failure of the project
- Dependencies—an external need which the project's completion is contingent upon

These are frequently documented as simple bulleted lists, but as a best practice should include additional details such as date identified, owner, impact, associated risk and other explanatory information. They may be initially written as a bulleted list and reformatted during the analysis phases in a table format with additional selected attributes. The project team is documented in a table format and can be a simple contact list or a combination contact list plus RACI matrix.

When documenting information flow in the BRD, there isn't a more important tool than the context diagram. Context diagrams are so simple to draw that it can easily be done in a JAD session with the stakeholders participating in its construction. The scribe or the BA can build it real time on a laptop while projecting it to the room. A Context Diagram represents the actors outside a system that could interact with that system. The term actor is from UML and specifies a role played by a user or any other system that interacts with the subject under discussion. Context diagrams are used to display how systems interoperate at a very high level or how systems logically operate and interact. Context diagrams are integral to successful interface analysis activities and are an extremely powerful means for uncovering interdependencies.

The BRD contains an overall system context diagram as well as individual context diagrams for every process definition. It's of paramount importance to understand processes in the context of all of their touch points. Figure 63 is an example of a simple context diagram. This diagram can be drawn in Visio as a data flow diagram. Figure 64 is a United States Federal Government public domain image showing an alternate form of context diagram.

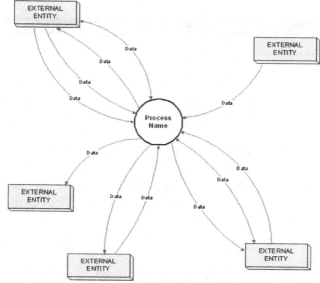

Figure 63 - Context Diagram

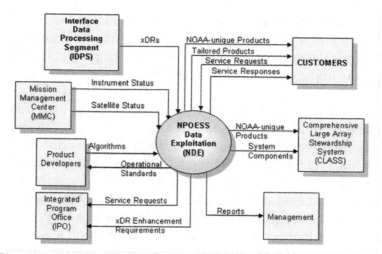

Figure 64 - NDE Context Diagram (US Government Public Domain Image)

Requirements are the lifeblood of the BRD and are categorized in many ways. Some common categorizations are: Customer, Functional, Non-Functional, Performance, Design, Derived,

Allocated or Quality.[69] Regardless of how others may categorize them, on closer inspection they all fall into one of the four areas that affect project outcomes: Business (Functional) Requirements, Business Rules, Information Requirements and Non-Functional Requirements.

Business requirements describe the "whats" of the system not the "hows." They describe what the business system needs so it functions more efficiently, operates more cost effectively and improves processes. Our first focus is functional requirements. Functional requirements are expressed in terms of behaviors or operations the system performs in response to a specific user action or input. Properly written functional requirements describe the capabilities of the system, any conditions necessary for the requirements to be fulfilled and constraints that may prevent the requirements from being executed. They are never written in a manner that restricts the solution design.

ISO 9126 is an international standard for the assessment of software quality. The standard's main objective is to address human biases that adversely affect the perception and delivery of a systems development project. The biases include changing priorities after the start of a project or not having any clear definitions of "success." The first part of the ISO 9126 standard classifies software quality in a structured set of characteristics and sub-characteristics. Each quality sub-characteristic is further divided into attributes. An attribute is an entity which can be verified or measured in the product. Attributes are not defined in the standard, because they vary among different products and are driven by an organization's quality processes.

The SDLC is the vehicle by which an organization defines requirements attributes that help drive systems quality. Think of a requirement as a record in a database with expandable attributes. Attributes are the relative pieces of information attached to each requirement which facilitate the analysis, traceability and quality practices. Attributes are attached to both Functional and Non-Functional requirements. This SDLC discusses some common requirements attributes considered industry best practices. When documenting the BRD, some of the attributes are mandatory, some optional and others derived during later phases of the life cycle as during analysis or prioritization.

Figure 65 is a modified example of a requirements list for the "Obtain Customer Driving History" process definition in our fictitious BRD. The sample BRD requirements have been rewritten from their original form to reflect Lean principles and additional columns for source and acceptance criteria have been added to the table.

The first column (ID#) is an example of a mandatory attribute. The ID# follows the requirement throughout the project life cycle after the BRD is baselined. Prior to baselining, the BRD is a work in progress and the requirement IDs may change as the document is edited. Baselining

---

[69] "Systems Engineering Fundamentals," Defense Acquisition University Press, 2001

renders the ID an immutable absolute reference. The ID is used for tracing the requirements through analysis, development, quality checks, change management, deployment, documentation or anywhere else a requirement may be referenced.

ID#	Requirement	Source	Acceptance Criteria
4.0	**Obtain Customer Driving History**		
4.1	The system shall allow the agent to record the customer's license suspensions history	John Reilly	A license suspension history record for the customer shall be appended to the database
4.1.1	Each suspension history record shall include the suspension date		The suspension date shall appear on the license suspension history record for the customer
4.1.2	Each suspension history record shall include the reinstatement date, if there is one		The reinstatement date shall appear on the license suspension history record for the customer if the license has been reinstated, otherwise the date may be left blank
4.2	The system shall allow the agent to record the customer's history of moving violations including the date and type of each violation.	Level 1 Strategic Goal / Mary Durbin	A moving violation record for the customer shall be appended to the database
4.2.1	Each moving violations record shall include the violation date		The violation date shall appear on the moving violation record for the customer
4.2.2	Each moving violations record shall include the violation type		The violation type shall appear on the moving violation record for the customer

Figure 65 - Example BRD Process Requirements List

The source of the requirement is another mandatory attribute. Every requirement originates from some authoritative source. The authoritative source may not necessarily be a person but may be a strategic goal, project initiation document, scope statement, use case, business rule, legislation or some other origin. The source attribute helps the business analyst follow-up with the appropriate stakeholder if the requirement changes, if more information regarding the requirement is needed or the business goal that drove the requirement obliges further clarification.

Acceptance criteria are mandatory attributes for every requirement without exception. Every requirement must be measurable and testable. Quality assurance test plans are built around the acceptance criteria. They are guides for developing test plans and automation scripts and are the expected outcomes to demonstrate the requirements have been successfully realized. Acceptance criteria are defined by the business customers and expressed in the business domain language. If a requirement is incomplete in any way—vague, ambiguous, inconsistent, incorrect, untestable or not measurable—it is impossible for a solution to be tested to determine whether or not it meets that requirement. It is an invalid requirement.

Notice the use of the word "shall" in these sample requirements. The word "shall" is an imperative. Imperatives are sometimes used to describe the priority of each requirement if the SDLC does not provide for any other method of prioritization. The imperatives "Shall" and "Must" designate a requirement as mandatory. "Should" indicates a requirement is highly desirable, "May" specifies the requirement is optional which is an oxymoron, for if it is a requirement how can it be optional? "Will" means the requirement is outside the scope of the solution. While this is an acceptable practice, using "May" and "Will" do lead to confusion over the priorities. We'll discuss a better way of requirements prioritization, the MoSCoW method, in Chapter 6.

In addition to the attributes above, other attributes you may consider for your requirements are: Assigned-to, Author, Complexity, Cost, Location, Ownership, Priority, Revision #, Stability, Traced-from, Traced-to, or Urgency. With the exception of the author attribute, all others are derived in the analysis or later phases of the life cycle. Author is documented at the time the requirement is captured. In the absence of this attribute, the author of the requirement is presumed to be the author of the BRD.

It should go without saying that any type of requirement is to be written to be understood by anyone reading it. Unfortunately, with the high number of projects that have fallen victim to poor requirements, it's easy to surmise that what may be clear to an author is not always clear to the developers or business users. In fact, allowing someone not familiar with the project to read the document is a great way to test its lucidity. Applying Lean principles to writing requirements works very well and verifying the quality of the writing with a QA inspection stage gate works even better. The inspection stage gate takes place just before the elicitation artifacts are baselined.

Here is a simple guideline that helps to construct good Lean requirements as well as produce a QA inspection passable BRD.

General guidelines for writing good requirements:

- Always write in the active voice
- Lean requirements are 1 sentence long
  - A requirement addresses one and only one thing
  - A requirement is *atomic*, i.e., it does not contain conjunctions. If a requirement contains conjunctions, it should be written as two different requirements.

- Keep sentences relatively short
- Communicate facts with as few words as possible
- Each requirement may have multiple 1 sentence sub-requirements
- Use the process definitions and models to help consolidate requirements into groups such as products, components, use cases and user stories
  - Each group contains 5 to 9 requirements which helps with reusability
- Question every requirement: "Does this add value?"
- Question every requirement attribute: "Does this add value?"
- Question every word of every requirement

When writing paragraphs in the BRD body:

- Create logical paragraphs:
  - A group of sentences all relating to one basic idea
  - First sentence is often a topic sentence that binds all the sentences together
  - Each sentence develops logically from the preceding one
  - Use "connector" words or phrases to clarify the logic to the reader
- Ensure paragraphs are "right sized" and neither too long nor too short
  - Avoid paragraphs with only one sentence
  - Break paragraphs into two if more than half a page in length
- Avoid long, complex sentences.
- Begin most sentences with the subject, rather than with a dependent clause, an adverb or a prepositional phrase
- Avoid repeating words and/or phrases in proximity to one another

Non-Functional Requirements

Non-functional requirements are sometimes named "ilities" after the suffix that many of them share. They are also known as Quality of Service (QoS) requirements, Non-Behavioral Requirements, System Qualities, Constraints, Quality Attributes or Quality Goals. They describe what a system is supposed to be in contrast to functional requirements which describe what a system is supposed to do. Generally, non-functional requirements are divided into two main categories: Execution qualities and Evolution qualities. Execution qualities address qualities which are observable at run time such as security and usability. Evolution qualities refer to those that are embodied in the static structure of the system, such as scalability, testability, maintainability and extensibility. This is a list of some of the common quality attributes. It is not an exhaustive list.

- Accessibility
- Accountability
- Accuracy
- Adaptability
- Administrability
- Affordability
- Auditability
- Availability
- Compatibility
- Composability
- Configurability
- Correctness
- Credibility
- Customizability
- Debugability
- Degradability
- Demonstrability
- Dependability
- Deployability
- Determinism Ability
- Distributability
- Durability
- Effectiveness
- Efficiency
- Evolvability
- Extensibility
- Fidelity
- Flexibility
- Installability
- Integrity
- Interchangeability
- Interoperability
- Learnability
- Maintainability
- Manageability
- Mobility
- Modifiability
- Modularity
- Nomadicity
- Operability
- Orthogonality
- Portability
- Precision
- Predictability
- Process Capabilities
- Recoverability
- Relevance
- Reliability
- Repeatability
- Reproducibility
- Responsiveness
- Reusability
- Robustness
- Safety
- Scalability
- Seamlessness
- Securability
- Serviceability
- Simplicity
- Stability
- Supportability
- Survivability
- Sustainability
- Tailorability
- Testability
- Timeliness
- Traceability
- Ubiquity
- Understandability
- Upgradability
- Usability

In the 1980s, Hewlett-Packard created a model for quality attributes called FURPS. FURPS is an acronym for Functionality, Usability, Reliability, Performance and Supportability. The model was first publically shared by Robert B. Grady and Deborah L. Caswell in their 1987 book, *"Software Metrics: Establishing a Company-wide Program."* HP continued to evolve the model and later added a "+" to the acronym to emphasize the additional attributes of Design, Implementation, Interface and Physical requirements. FURPS+[70] is now widely used in the software industry. The FURPS model categorizes the ilities as:

- Functionality - Feature set, Capabilities, Generality, Security
- Usability - Human factors, Aesthetics, Consistency, Documentation
- Reliability - Frequency/severity of failure, Recoverability, Predictability, Accuracy, Mean time to failure
- Performance - Speed, Efficiency, Resource consumption, Throughput, Response time
- Supportability - Testability, Extensibility, Adaptability, Maintainability, Compatibility, Configurability, Serviceability, Installability, Localizability, Portability

---

[70] An IBM article explaining FURPS+ can be accessed here:
http://www.ibm.com/developerworks/rational/library/4706.html

Which non-functional requirements you choose to document and model is a decision only your organization can make. The important thing to remember is not to overlook them. They are as important as the functional requirements to the success of a project. Even if the project does not require new hardware or impact performance, document the non-functional requirements in the BRD anyway. It shows that you at least considered them if anything goes wrong later.

Process Definitions

Process definitions are in the form of use cases. A use case is a description of a system's behavior as it responds to a request that originates from outside of that system. The use case describes "who" can do "what" with the system under discussion. In the BRD, uses cases are captured first in textual form with perhaps an accompanying UML use case model depicting the actors and their interaction with the process. Use cases are elaborated during the requirements analysis phase to include activity and sequence diagrams and the use case diagram if it wasn't done during elicitation. Process definitions always begin with a context diagram that shows how the current process interacts with its touch points. Here's the example for the Obtain Customer Driving History from the sample BRD.

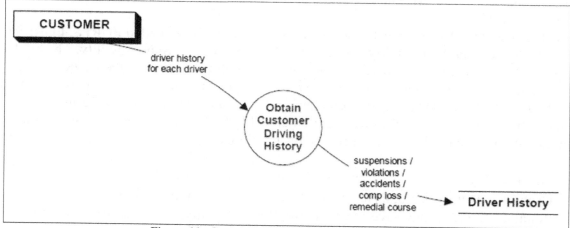

Figure 66 - Context Diagram from IAG Sample BRD

Summary

Usage Narrative

The agent must obtain from the customer the driving history for each driver to be included in the quote.

Triggering Event(s) and Pre-conditions

- The customer is ready to provide driving history details

Outcome(s) and/or Post-conditions

- The details of each customer's license suspensions and reinstatements, driving violations, comprehensive losses, accidents, and remedial courses taken has been recorded

Variations Considered

- None considered

Use Case Action Steps

NOTE: the agent must obtain customer driving history for each driver to be added to the quote

4.1. Determine if license has ever been suspended

- the agent determines if the customer's driver's license has been suspended within the last "X" years (state-specific)
- for each suspension disclosed, the agent determines when it was suspended, the reason for the suspension, and if it has been reinstated, the date of the reinstatement
- Need to determine and document state-specific rules around driver exclusions.

4.2. Determine if any moving violations

- the agent will determine if the customer has had any moving violations within the last "Y" years (state-specific)
- for each violation disclosed, the agent must obtain the date of the violation and the type of the violation

4.3. Determine if any comprehensive losses

- the agent will determine if the customer has had any comprehensive losses within the last "Z" years (excluding theft and vandalism)

- for each loss disclosed, the agent will determine the date of the loss and the amount paid for each loss

4.4. Determine if any accidents

- the agent will determine if the customer has been involved in any accidents
- for each accident disclosed, the agent will determine:
- the date of the accident
- the amount of any bodily injury (BI) payment
- the amount of any personal damage (PD) payment
- who was at fault

4.5. Determine if any remedial courses taken

- if the customer discloses any driving violations, the agent will determine if any remedial courses were taken by the customer (state-specific)

Design Considerations

- System must allow 35 violations and/or accidents

Issues/Assumptions/Risks

- Need to determine the table for accident and violations on a state-specific basis.
- Need to consider adding pre-selection box for obvious DNQ situations
- Need to determine the 'named driver exclusion (NDE)' process - Bill Polk
- Determine state specific rules for all driver history elements.

As you document the use cases, textual requirements and context diagrams, be on the alert for opportunities to document information flow elements. Stakeholders don't always understand the concept of databases and tables, but they do know what they need to run their business. Information flow elements are often expressed as nouns. For example, if the context diagram for the system under discussion indicates an interaction with a customer, when you document the requirement the word "customer" is a noun. Ask how the business defines a customer and capture the details.

Information flow is captured in data definitions and entity diagrams. BAs frequently bristle over the idea of capturing a data definition in a BRD, protesting that a data definition is a design element and not a requirement. That is a narrow-minded view of requirements definition. As potential data elements come out in a requirements session, it's important for the BA to document the customer's expectations as to what data needs to be captured and if there are any business rules demarcating the data. That's why a data definition is indispensable. Design elements such as field length and type are not captured at this phase. We're interested only in what the data is and how the business defines it.

The information flow section begins with a summary list of the business data requirements:

1. The system must have the ability to maintain ACCOUNT data as described in the BRD
2. The system must have the ability to maintain AGENT data as described in the BRD
3. The system must have the ability to maintain CALL data as described in the BRD
4. The system must have the ability to maintain CAMPAIGN data as described in the BRD

The list is followed by a preliminary definition, as the business sees it, for each of the data requirements listed. Business terms are used to describe the data:

Agent

Definition
- Information needed about an agent for paying commissions

Data
- The system shall provide for the following data elements and business rules:

Data Element	Description
Agent-id	Unique identifier
First Name	
Last Name	
Department	
Affiliation Code	
Type	Local or Remote

Figure 67 - Sample BRD Data Definition

The BA continues documenting the information by drawing a simple entity-relationship model. An entity-relationship model (ERM) is an abstract and conceptual representation of data. It is not a final data design. At this stage of the requirements process, it simply documents what the customers' need, how they perceive different data elements are related and business rules.

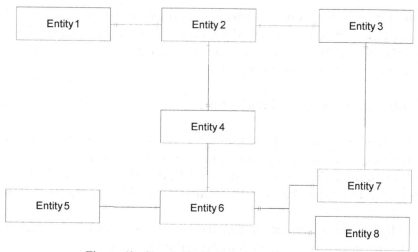

Figure 68 - Simple Entity Relationship Diagram

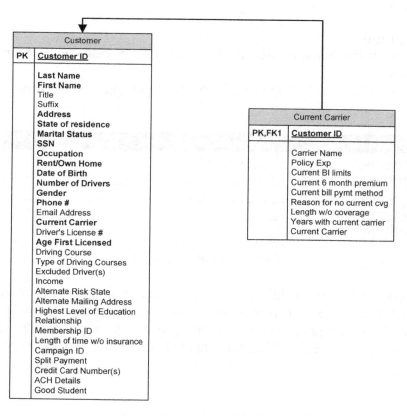

Figure 69 –Detailed Entity Relationship Model

As the design progresses, the entity-relationship model takes on additional features as the developers and architects provide details to the data model definitions such as the primary and foreign keys, field lengths, data types, indexes, triggers, data validation check clauses, capture masks, etc. Eventually, the ERM appears in the preliminary System Design Specification as in Figure 69.

Business rules are captured in any of several places. They may be found intertwined in the use cases, textual requirements or information flow definitions. Make certain business rules clearly articulate which elements of the system they govern.

Good Requirements Quality Checklist

> **Principle #4: "Write requirements that are cohesive, complete, consistent, correct, feasible, modifiable, necessary, prioritized, reusable, testable, traceable, verifiable and unambiguous."**

To prepare a requirements artifact to pass the Quality Assurance inspection stage gate, utilize the same criteria for writing the requirements as the Quality Assurance analysts use for evaluating the requirements once the document is complete. To fully appreciate the quality criteria, we must once again visit the operational definition of good requirements. Good requirements are cohesive, complete, consistent, correct, feasible, modifiable, necessary, prioritized, reusable, testable, traceable, verifiable and unambiguous.

The good requirements quality checklist is a quality guide to ensure requirements meet the operational definition of good requirements. The checklist is based on the Requirements Verification Checklist released to the public domain in May 2008 by the United States of America State of Texas Department of Information Resources as part of Version 1.1 of the Texas Project Delivery Framework.[71] Each characteristic of good requirements applicable to the quality inspection is listed in alphabetical order, defined and reinforced by supporting questions intended to direct a quality review.

I.   **Cohesive**: A set of requirements is cohesive if it relates to only one thing. All requirements in a set or group support the overall purpose and scope of the system or component under discussion, whether that is a business process definition, business rule, information flow, data flow or so forth.

---

[71] The Texas Project Delivery Framework is available from http://www.dir.state.tx.us/pubs/framework/extensions/

1.   Are the requirements consolidated into groups such as products, components, use cases and user stories?
2.   Do the requirements align with their process definitions and models?
3.   Does each group contain 5 to 9 requirements? (Note: This is not a failing criterion if more than nine although, it may indicate the group can be divided.)
4.   Do the grouped requirements flow logically from one to the next, from the more general to the more specific or from the least sensitive to the most sensitive?

II.   **Complete**: To be complete, all known relevant requirements are documented and all conditions under which a requirement applies are stated. A BRD is complete if, and only if, it includes the following elements:

- All significant requirements, whether relating to functionality, performance, design constraints, attributes or external interfaces.
- Definitions of the responses of the system/software to all realizable classes of input data in all realizable classes of situations.
- Descriptive labels for and references to all figures, tables, models and diagrams in the BRD and definition of all business terms, acronyms and units of measure.

1.   Does each requirement contain all the information necessary for the technical team to design, build and test that component of the solution?
2.   Are all the inputs to the system/software specified, including their source, accuracy, range of values and frequency?
3.   Are all the outputs from the system/software specified, including their destination, accuracy, and range of values, frequency and format?
4.   Are all the communication interfaces specified, including handshaking, error checking and communication protocols?
5.   Has analysis been performed to identify missing requirements?
6.   Are the areas of incompleteness specified when information is not available?
7.   Are the requirements complete such that if the product satisfied every requirement it would be acceptable?
8.   Are all figures, tables, models and diagrams labeled in a descriptive manner?
9.   Are all figures, tables, models and diagrams referenced within the document?
10.   Are all business terms, acronyms and units of measure defined appropriately?

III.   **Consistent**: Consistency demands that the requirement can be met without causing conflict or contradiction with any of the other requirements. Requirement should be stated in a way to allow the widest possible selection of implementation options.

1.   Do the requirements avoid prematurely determining a solution?

2. Do the requirements avoid specifying a design?
3. Are the requirements specified at a consistent level of detail?
4. Should any requirements be specified in more detail?
5. Should any requirements be specified in less detail?
6. Are the requirements consistent with the content of other organizational and project documentation?

IV. **Correct**: Requirements must accurately describe the functionality to be built. Only the source of the requirements, the customers, users or stakeholders, can determine their correctness.

1. Do the requirements fulfill the original business need?
2. Has the scope of the system/software been bounded?
3. Have the overall function and behavior of the system/software been defined?
4. Has the required technology infrastructure for the system/software been adequately specified?
5. Are all the tasks to be performed by the system/software specified?
6. Can each requirement be allocated to an element of the solution design where it can be implemented?
7. Does each task specify the data/information content used in the task and the data/information content resulting from the task?
8. Is each requirement associated with a use case or process flow?
9. Have requirements for communication among system/software components been specified?
10. Have appropriate constraints, assumptions, and dependencies been explicitly and unambiguously stated?
11. Are the hardware requirements specified?
12. Are the physical security requirements specified?
13. Are the operational security requirements specified?
14. Is the maintainability of the system/software specified, including the ability to respond to changes in the operating environment, interfaces, accuracy, performance, and additional predicted capabilities?
15. Is the reliability of the system/software specified, including the consequences of failure, vital information protected from failure, error detection, and recovery?
16. Are internal interfaces such as software and hardware defined?
17. Are external interfaces, such as users, software and hardware defined?
18. Is each requirement relevant to the problem and its solution?
19. Is the definition of the requirement's success included? Of failure?

V. **Feasible**: Feasibility means each requirement is implementable within the existing infrastructure, budget, timeline and resources available to the team. The business analyst needs to work with the project team to make these determinations.

1. Are the requirements technically feasible and do they fit within the project funding and timing constraints?
2. If not, is the project able to develop the capability to implement the requirement?
3. Even if a requirement is technically feasible, it may not be attainable due to constraints. Are there any constraints that prevent the requirement from being attained?
4. Is it possible to implement each requirement within the capabilities and limitations of the technical and operational environment?
5. Is it possible to implement each and every requirement?

VI. **Necessary & Prioritized**: Requirements must be ranked for importance and/or stability. A necessary requirement is one that is essential to meet business goals and objectives. A priority is assigned to each functional requirement or feature to indicate how essential it is to a particular solution release. If all requirements are considered equally important, it is difficult for the project team to respond to budget cuts, schedule overruns, staff turnover or new requirements added during development. Ranking requirements for stability is in terms of the number of expected changes to the requirement. Stable requirements are ready to be developed.

1. Do requirements have an associated identifier to indicate either the importance or stability of that particular requirement?
2. Do conflicts exist regarding the importance and/or stability ranking of the requirements?
3. Are all requirements ranked the same?

VII. **Measurable, Testable & Verifiable**: Verifiable means that the requirement states something that can be confirmed by examination, analysis, test or demonstration. A good requirement does not contain words that are not testable and measurable. If it is impossible to ensure that the requirement is met in the solution, it should be removed or revised.

- Testable requirements are designed to demonstrate that the solution satisfies requirements. Tests may include functional, performance, regression, and stress tests.
- The verification method and level (i.e., the location in the solution where the requirement is met) at which the requirement can be verified should be determined explicitly as part

of the development of each requirement. Requirement statements that include words that have relative meaning are not verifiable. For example:

- Adequate
- Better than
- Comparison
- Easy
- Maximum
- Minimum
- More efficient
- Quality product
- Substantial

1. Are the requirements written in a language and vocabulary that anyone can understand? Do the stakeholders concur?
2. Is the expected response time from the user's point of view specified for all necessary operations?
3. Are other timing considerations specified such as processing time, data transfer and throughput?
4. Are acceptable tradeoffs between competing attributes specified? For example, between robustness and correctness?
5. Does each requirement capture a metric by which it can be measured?
6. Is each requirement testable?
7. Will it be possible for independent testing to determine whether each requirement has been satisfied?

VIII. Traceable: Requirements are traceable if their origin is known and the requirement can be referenced or located throughout the solution. The requirement should be traceable to a goal stated in the project charter, vision document, business case or other initiating document. Requirements are traceable backwards and forwards.

- Traceable backwards: each requirement can be traced back to specific customer, user or stakeholder input, such as a use case, a business rule, or some other origin. It can also be traced from any specific point in the life cycle back to an earlier phase, component or document.
- Traceable forward: each requirement should have a unique identifier that assists in identification, maintaining change history and tracing the requirement through the solution components.

1. Are requirements uniquely identified?
2. Can each requirement be traced to its origin or source, such as a scope statement, change request, business objective or compliance regulation?
3. Is each requirement identified such that it facilitates referencing in future development and enhancement efforts?
4. Has each requirement been cross-referenced to previous related project documents?

IX.   **Unambiguous**: Requirements must be clear, concise, simple and free from ambiguity. They must be stated without technical jargon, acronyms (unless defined) or other obscure verbiage. Requirements express objective facts, not subjective opinions. Vague requirements are often misunderstood resulting in rework and corrective actions during the design, development and testing phases. If the requirement can be interpreted in more than one way, it should be removed or clarified.

- All readers of a requirement should arrive at the same interpretation of its meaning.
- All specialized terms and terms that might be subject to confusion should be well defined.

1.   Are the requirements written with simple, short sentences?
2.   Are the requirements specified clearly enough to be turned over to an independent group for implementation and still be understood?
3.   Are functional requirements separated from non-functional?
4.   Are requirements stated in a manner that avoids the likelihood of multiple interpretations?
5.   Do all the requirements avoid conflicts with other requirements?
6.   Do any of the requirements contain undefined acronyms?
7.   Are all requirements stated in one place only?
8.   Have redundant requirements been consolidated?
9.   Has each requirement been specified separately, avoiding compound requirements?
10.   Are the requirements written with proper grammar and correct spelling?
11.   Do any requirements contain vague subjects, adjectives, prepositions, verbs and subjective phrases?
12.   Do any of the requirements express negative statements?

Requirements Analysis, Inspection & Tracing

Now that we're done eliciting and documenting requirements with the techniques learned in the previous chapters, we're ready to move into the analysis phase. Requirements analysis is the first step in the system engineering process and is critical to the success of a systems development project. In a discussion of analysis activities, the *"Guide to the Software Engineering Body of Knowledge"*[72] (SWEBOK) says:

"It is widely acknowledged within the software industry that software engineering projects are critically vulnerable when these activities are performed poorly."

Requirements analysis incorporates all the activities and tasks that go into determining the needs or conditions required to deliver the capabilities in a solution designed to meet the stakeholders' business goals. This differs from the system analysis phase in that requirements analysis produces artifacts that do not extend to the depth of exacting detail. The output of the analysis process is a complete and elaborated BRD and System Requirements Specification (SRS) written to a level of detail sufficient for the development team to produce a System Design Specification (SDS). If you are working under an IT Governance model, both artifacts are necessary to produce accurate cost estimates in order to obtain funding and approval to move the project forward. Depending on the complexity of the project, the BRD may suffice as long as the details needed to elaborate the SRS are appended to the BRD.

The analysis phase is where the BA:

- Accounts for conflicting requirements
- Baselines the produced artifact(s)
- Determines requirements feasibility & risk
- Discovers derived / allocated requirements
- Ensures requirements meet the definition of good requirements
- Makes certain all requirements relate to identified business goals or opportunities
- Models requirements
- Performs the Document and Interface Analysis elicitation techniques
- Prioritizes the requirements
- Submits the requirements to the Quality Assurance inspection process
- Validates the requirements
- Verifies the requirements

The path to successful requirements analysis can be fraught with issues the BA must be capable of circumventing if not entirely preventing. Issues arise from the stakeholders or the technical

---

[72]"Chapter 2: Software Requirements" (2004 ed.); Los Alamitos, CA: IEEE Computer Society Press. http://www.computer.org/portal/web/swebok/html/ch2. Accessed 03-16-2010.

team. The BA is right in the middle of both groups and must be alert to the dangers these issues present to a project. In his book *"Rapid Development: Taming Wild Software Schedules,"*[73] Steve McConnell details a number of ways stakeholders can stall the requirements process:

- Communication with users is slow
- Users are technically unsophisticated
- Users can't express their needs plainly
- Users don't have a clear idea of their requirements
- Users don't know about current technology

- Users don't know what they want
- Users don't understand the development process
- Users insist on new requirements after cost and schedule are fixed
- Users often do not participate in reviews or are incapable of doing so
- Users won't sign off on the requirements

These problems generally lead to the situation where user requirements keep changing even after development has begun. Expert Business Analysts are skillful to guard against this type of scope creep and keep it at bay at all costs. None of these issues are showstoppers if the BA keeps the channel of communication open with all the stakeholders to make certain they always know what's going on and to teach them what they need to know about IT process and technology. Assigning a Business Liaison to the project goes a long way toward preventing these issues as well. When there's a Business Liaison on the team, s/he hopefully works closely enough with the IT team to benefit from osmotic communication. Once the requirements artifacts are baselined, legitimate requirements changes are managed through the project change management process and are assessed for their business value, feasibility, impact and cost to the project.

Problems caused by engineers and developers during requirements analysis are frequently attributable to poor communication where technical personnel and stakeholders use different vocabularies. They may be using the same words but the meaning and understanding behind them is completely different depending on the individual's frame of reference. For example, what does the acronym ASP mean? To the stakeholder it could mean Application Service Provider and to the developer it could mean Active Server Pages. In another example, what does ATM mean? To the stakeholder it could mean Automated Teller Machine and to the systems engineer it could mean Asynchronous Transfer Mode. As a result of these communication difficulties, everyone may wrongly believe they are in perfect agreement until the product is furnished, then the fun beings. This can be especially true when the parties are separated by continents or cultural diversity, in which case it pays to hold training to understand cultural language norms such as high vs. low context dialogue and native colloquialisms before the project begins. Not doing so is an established root-cause for the downfall of many an outsourcing engagement.

---

[73] McConnell, Steve (1996). *"Rapid Development: Taming Wild Software Schedules"* (1st ed.). Redmond, WA: Microsoft Press.

Another problem is that engineers and developers sometimes attempt to make requirements fit an existing architecture, system or model, rather than develop a solution explicit to the needs of the stakeholders. Architecture standards are a best practice. No company wants to support multiple architectures if they can avoid it, but force fitting a solution isn't appropriate either. Sometimes concessions have to be made. To illustrate, suppose a decision is made to buy a COTS application. It's the only product on the market that fits the stakeholders' requirements perfectly, but the vendor says the software only runs on a .NET platform with a SQL Server backend and you run a J2EE and Oracle shop. The vendor adds that an Oracle version is currently in Beta and will be available within the next 6 months. What are your choices?

Lastly, analysis activities may be carried out by people with the wrong skill set. System engineers or programmers may have the right technological skills to develop a solution but may not have the right people skills and domain knowledge to properly evaluate stakeholders' needs.

Overall, the analysis process is generally straightforward and can be completed rapidly by experienced team members. However, there is always a danger that "Analysis Paralysis" can set in. Analysis paralysis often occurs due to the lack of experience on the part of business analysts, project managers or software developers. It may also be due to a rigid and formal organizational culture. It occurs in any life cycle phase and manifests itself through exceedingly long periods of planning, elicitation and analysis, design and modeling. More often than not, there is little or no extra value created by these elongated steps. When extended over too long a timeframe, bureaucracy becomes the emphasis rather than the project's value-creating characteristics. If you subscribe to the Lean philosophy, everything not creating value for the business is waste. Overly bureaucratic processes are waste.

Requirements elicitation and analysis activities cannot continue *ad infinitum*. To prevent analysis paralysis, some companies limit these activities in their SDLC to no more than two iterations which also leads to problems. Two iterations might be too low of a boundary because requirements need to be complete and of sufficient detail to lead to a system design. Can you write requirements of sufficient detail in two iterations? For the most part, yes you can if you understand what "sufficient detail" means. Sufficient means "enough to meet the needs of a situation or a proposed end." In other words, it means all of the information necessary at that particular point in time and none that is superfluous.

Novice BAs often over analyze every potential attribute of a requirement which also leads to waste. Those attributes may not add value to the BRD. They may surface later when writing the detailed system design or test plans, but often aren't important to the BRD. Knowing when enough is enough comes with experience. Agile development methodologies seek to prevent analysis paralysis by promoting iterative work cycles that stress functioning products over product specifications. The problem with Agile methods is that they don't fit well with IT Governance structures where the requirements must be gathered before project approval.

If analysis paralysis occurs within the stakeholder camp, the BA must lead the stakeholders through a decision making process to the final selection of a course of action from among several alternatives. A frequent point of confusion that occurs in decision making is that both the BA and stakeholders begin down a problem analysis path focusing on the wrong things in their attempt to arrive at consensus. Since the two are often confused, it's extremely important to understand the differences between problem analysis and decision making.

Problem analysis is a diagnostic that often serves as a pre-requisite to the decision making process. The primary objective of problem analysis is to determine the root cause of a problem, where the most likely conclusion is generally the one that explains all the facts of the situation. Think of it as when a medical doctor is piecing together evidence in a hospital setting to determine a sick person's diagnosis. The objective is to improve the patient's quality of life. The physician compiles the results of many different tests to decide the best remedy to prescribe for the malady. The tests come first; the decision comes after the tests are concluded. Falling between the tests and decision is the consultation with other physicians and subject matter experts to weigh the advantages and disadvantages of the various courses of treatment. When consensus is reached the prescription is authorized and the patient is hopefully cured.

Decision making on the other hand, is about setting objectives and evaluating alternatives against those objectives. The objectives must be established first, classified and prioritized. Objectives are variable and are determined by the project's goals. The alternatives need to be developed and evaluated against all the objectives. The alternative that satisfies all of the objectives is the tentative decision. The tentative decision is then further discussed to uncover any potential consequences. Once fully vetted, decisive actions are taken including any agreed upon which mitigate predictable adverse circumstances that may arise from the decision.

Decision making is often a JAD activity rather than an analysis phase activity although issues do arise during analyses that require decisions. Perhaps you are familiar with the technique known as the Ben Franklin close? This is a popular sales closing technique where the sales rep lists all of the advantages and disadvantages of a particular solution. The alternative with the greatest advantages usually wins. The same technique is one that can be used for requirements analysis decision making. Multi-voting is another popular and effective method. Sometimes a decision results from just following the advice of a SME and acquiescing to that individual's authority as the expert.

Different people can make decisions about the same objective and seemingly be in agreement with everyone else. Then they introduce cognitive interventions or biases aimed at "improving" the decision making outcomes to meet their personal agenda. Biases regularly creep into the decision making process. Be very careful about not allowing them to establish a foothold when leading a decision making session. Recognize them for what they are and do your best to diminish their influence. Here are some of the more common cognitive biases to be aware of:

- Anchoring and adjustment—decisions are unduly influenced by initial information that shapes our view of subsequent information.
- Choice-supportive bias—we distort our memories of chosen and rejected options to make the chosen options seem more attractive.
- Group think—peer pressure to conform to the opinions held by the group.
- Inertia—unwillingness to change thought patterns that we have used in the past in the face of new circumstances
- Premature termination of search for evidence—we tend to accept the first alternative that looks like it might work
- Recency—we tend to place more attention on more recent information and either ignore or forget more distant information.
- Repetition bias—a willingness to believe what we have been told most often and by the greatest number of different of sources.
- Selective perception—we actively screen-out information that we do not think is important.
- Source credibility bias— we are inclined to accept a statement by someone we like and reject something if we have a prejudice against the person, organization, or group to which the person belongs.
- Wishful thinking or optimism bias —we tend to want to see things in a positive light and this can distort our perception and thinking.

Two types of requirements mentioned earlier that require further explanation are derived and allocated requirements. Derived and allocated requirements are often uncovered through the document and interface analysis techniques. Derived requirements are implied or transformed from higher-level requirements. For example, suppose the project is for a government weapons system and there is a performance requirement for a long range or high speed missile. This may result in a derived design requirement for low-weight components even though weight was not discussed during the elicitation meetings.

Allocated requirements are created by dividing or otherwise allocating a high-level requirement into multiple lower-level requirements. Expectantly, if Lean principles are followed during elicitation, there won't be many allocated requirements since each requirement refers to one thing only. However, let's look at the missile's derived weight requirement again. Suppose the design calls for a go-onto-target (GOT) active homing guidance system that weighs no more than 500 pounds. There are three subsystems to every GOT system: target tracker, missile tracker and guidance computer. The 500 pound weight requirement is allocated amongst the three components. Each component has its own allocated weight requirement, the sum of which is equal to the 500 pounds.

Document Analysis

Document analysis is performed for existing systems or replacing an existing system either in preparation for other elicitation techniques or post elicitation during the analysis phase. It is the study of all available documentation for a system, provided of course there is documentation for the existing system. Documentation includes but is not limited to:

- Business Plans
- Comparative Product Reviews
- Competing Products Literature
- Contracts
- Customer Request Logs
- Emails

- Guidelines
- Market Studies
- Memos
- Problem Reports
- Requests for Information

- Requests for Proposals
- Service Level Agreements
- Standard Operating Procedures
- Statements of Work
- System Specifications
- Training Guides

In reviewing the documentation, the BA identifies all existing relevant information such as business rules, entities and attributes that need to be incorporated into the upgrade or new system. Document analysis details the "as-is" environment and is especially useful in situations where the subject matter experts are either no longer with the company or unable to participate in the elicitation sessions.

The activities required to perform document analysis are simple. First, identify the relevant system and documentation to review. Most likely, the system is identified for you since it is the subject of the project. You need to identify and assemble the documentation. Hopefully, the documentation is stored in a central repository and not scattered around the office on book shelves or in desk drawers and filing cabinets. The next step is to review the documentation and record any pertinent business details discovered. Document them as requirements and jot down questions you have to be followed up with subject matter experts later. Once all the documents are reviewed, follow-up with the SMEs and organize the requirements for cohesiveness. Obtain the answers to all outstanding questions and you are done. Figure is the Document Analysis Activity Diagram.

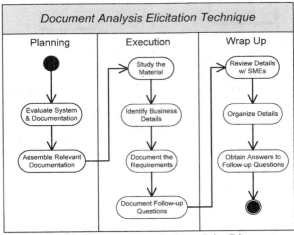

Figure 70 - Document Analysis Activity Diagram

Interface Analysis

Interface analysis begins with the context diagrams drawn during the elicitation sessions. For this example we'll use the Sales Process context diagram from the IAG BRD. The System Under Discussion (SUD) is the Sales Process. Each of the shadowed boxes encircling the SUD is an actor that interacts in some way with the SUD. The curved arrows represent the information exchanged during those interactions. In other words, the arrows represent the system's interfaces.

Begin by assigning the ID # to each interface for traceability and then describe the purpose, interaction type and directional flow of the interface. There may be a large number of interaction types, consider internal, external, system-to-system, application-to-application, hardware device or user as a starting point. Directional flow is in, out or both. If the details of an in and out flow for an entity are different, log them as two separate interfaces. Note whether the interface is synchronous or asynchronous as well. Synchronous means real time data exchange and asynchronous means the data may be exchanged through a scheduled or batch process.

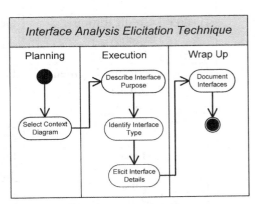

Figure 71 - Interface Analysis Activity Diagram

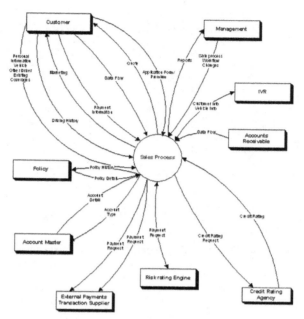

Figure 72 - Example Context Diagram

ID#	Interface	Purpose	Type	Flow
IF-001	Account Master	Customer account details	Internal	In / Out
IF-002	Accounts Receivable	Check payment history	Internal	In
IF-003	Credit Rating Agency	Get customer's credit history	External	In / Out
IF-004	Customer	Customer interactions	User	In
IF-005	External Payments Transaction Supplier	Process credit card payments	External	Out
IF-006	IVR	Accept input via interactive voice response system	User	In / Out
IF-007	Management	Distribute reports and receive direction	User	In / Out
IF-008	Policy	Obtain policy details	Internal	In / Out
IF-009	Risk Rating Engine	Calculate payment risk	Internal	In / Out

Figure 73 – Sample BRD Interface Definition

As the analysis proceeds, document the details of any non-user interfaces in data definitions along with their inputs and outputs, business and data validation rules, trigger events and any other details that may need to be specified. User interfaces are elaborated in Use Cases and prototypes.

Requirements Elaboration

┌───┐
│   *Principle #5: "Model the requirements."*   │
└───┘

Requirements elaboration is the continuation of the modeling exercises begun during elicitation. Conceptual models are a key to effective requirements analysis. If a picture is worth a thousand words, models and prototypes do more to express the precision of the technical team's understanding of stakeholders' business needs than any other means. In the BRD, models help to convey the business problem or process in a clear picture. As design progresses, they crystalize the solution to the problem or process improvement. Models exhibit real world relationships and dependencies between systems components. Let's access the sample BRD again and elaborate the use case for Obtain Coverage Request and Calculate Quote.

Figure 74 - Sample BRD Obtain Coverage Request Activity Diagram

As with the interface analysis technique, elaborating the use case begins with the context diagram supplemented by the textual use case.

Usage Narrative

The agent obtains the coverage request for each vehicle from the customer. The agent considers the customer's current limits and coverage, and factors relating to the vehicle in assisting the customer in determining the appropriate coverage for each vehicle. Once the coverage request has been determined, the system calculates the premium to be quoted to the customer.

Triggering Event(s) and Pre-conditions: The customer is ready to provide his/her coverage request

Outcome(s) and/or Post-conditions

The coverage request has been recorded
The quoted premium has been calculated and the customer has been advised of the quote

Variations Considered: None considered

In this usage narrative, we have two named actors: the customer and the agent. The customer requests coverage information from the agent who then looks up information in the system to determine the quote. The agent relays the quote back to the customer with recommendations for additional savings. Figure 75 is the use case model that results from elaborating the user story

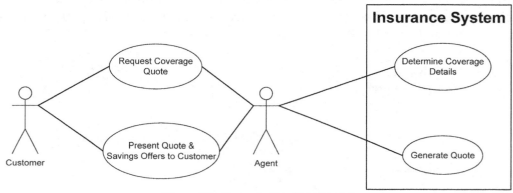

Figure 75 - Example Use Case Model

This is a very simple use case model that depicts the interactions between the customer, agent and system at a very high level, but modeling the requirements for this process isn't complete yet. There's another part to the textual use case that outlines the activities that take place:

Use Case Action Steps

6.1. Display current coverage
   - the system displays the current BI coverage
     - Rule: PD cannot be higher than BI

6.2. Determine if customer wants same coverage
   - The agent determines the customer's current coverage and limits
   - the agent determines if the customer wishes to obtain a quote based on the same coverage

- if the customer wishes to get a quote based on different coverage, the agent will record the requested coverage
- If customer does not know what the current coverage is:
  - Provide the customer with the "default" to national average or state minimum
  - 2,000,000 Per Person / 80,000 per accident
  - obtain BI request

6.3. Identify coverage opportunities
- if the agent determines that there are opportunities to obtain a reduced quote and still meet the customer's needs, the agent will discuss the opportunities with the customer

6.4. Validate coverage selected
- the system verifies that the relationship between coverages requested meets state-specific rules
- if the coverage does not meet the rules, the agent advises the customer and obtains a different coverage request

6.5. Calculate Premium
- once the customer's coverage request has been determined and all other necessary factors have been determined, the system calculates the premium

6.6. Advise Customer
- the agent advises the customer of the quote

6.7. Record quote details
- the system records the details of the quote
- if more than one version is calculated based on different requests, the system records the details of each version

Figure 76 is the elaboration of the textual use case activities:

There is a glaring omission in the activities documented in this use case. Did you catch it? The business rule is specified for "Personal Damage (PD) cannot be higher than Bodily Injury (BI)," but there is no behavior recorded to explain what needs to be done to resolve the error condition. This is something the BA needs to clarify with the stakeholders. What happens in the event that PD is greater than BI? What is the agent supposed to do? How is the system supposed to behave in response to the error condition? Or does it even matter? In any case, this is a hole in the requirements that needs to be flushed out.

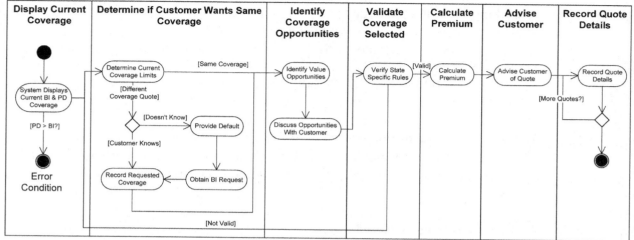

Figure 76 - Use Case Activities Elaborated

This particular use case has some documented design considerations that need to be incorporated into the elaboration models:

Design Considerations

- Should not discuss coverages twice during call
- Easier for customer to read coverages to you and you verify rather than the other way around.
- Capture top 5 reasons that people are not covered properly or ways to save money and consultative sell
- Build logic that suggests that you don't need certain types based on other data (i.e. if retired, don't sell work loss coverage, if older car, don't sell comprehensive coverage)
- Display a state minimum quote and then other package quotes on one screen.
- Predictive modeling – to predict which coverages (limits and deductibles) are likely in place based on the BI coverage
- May be spending more on comp coverage than vehicle is worth.
- Once quote is complete, display rate. If coverages are changed then continue to change the rate as it is affected.

In addition to the design considerations, pay close attention to the textual functional requirements captured during elicitation. Make certain any business rules captured are included in the models. For example, requirement ID 6.1 says the system displays both BI and PD coverage, where the activity for 6.1 says BI is displayed. The activity, textual requirement and model should all reflect the single truth about the requirement. Not only that, but according to the SDLC guidelines for writing good requirements, what's wrong with requirement ID 6.1?[74]

ID#	Requirement	Source	Acceptance Criteria
6.0	Obtain Coverage Request and Calculate Quote		
6.1	The system shall be capable of displaying the current BI and current PD coverage.		
6.2	The system shall be capable of allowing the agent to record the customer's coverage request.		
6.3	The system shall be capable of verifying that the coverage requested meets state specific minimums/rules.		
6.4	The system shall be capable of displaying a default standard coverage for a state.		
6.5	The system shall be capable of calculating the premium based on the coverage requested by the customer.		
6.6	The system shall be capable of recording multiple versions of quotes calculated as a result of changes in the customer's coverage request.		

Figure 77 - Sample Textual Requirements Definition

As the modeling activities move further into the design phase, the use case is further elaborated to include a sequence diagram. A sequence diagram in UML is a type of interaction diagram that shows how processes operate with one another and in what order. The diagram shows different processes or objects that live simultaneously on lifelines (parallel vertical lines). It also captures messages exchanged between the objects as horizontal arrows in the order in which they occur. Messages are synchronous or asynchronous. The sequence diagram specifies simple runtime scenarios in a graphical manner. It is one of the prototypes which developers use as a basis for their system design.

Another type of diagram that can be drawn during requirements elaboration activities is the UML State Machine Diagram, although in many cases they are components of design documents. Many systems are event-driven, which means they continuously wait for the occurrence of some external or internal event such as a mouse click, a button press, a time tick, or the arrival of a data packet. Systems recognize the event and react by performing an appropriate response that may include a computation, hardware manipulation or the generation of "soft" events that trigger other internal software components. Once event handling is complete, the system returns to a

---

[74] Requirement 6.1 is a compound requirement using the word "and." Compound requirements can lead to ambiguity. It's quite possibly the reason the display of PD was missed during the documentation of the activity.

wait state until reacting to the next event. Figure 79 is a diagram representing a computer keyboard state machine.

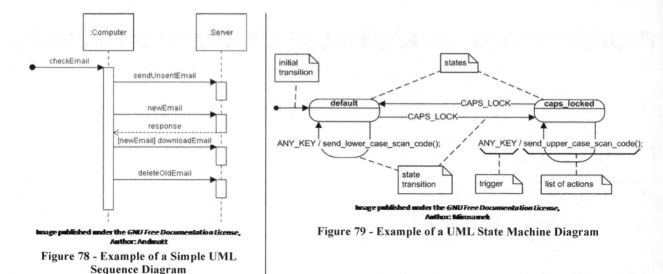

Image published under the GNU Free Documentation License, Author: Andmatt

Figure 78 - Example of a Simple UML Sequence Diagram

Image published under the GNU Free Documentation License, Author: Mirosamek

Figure 79 - Example of a UML State Machine Diagram

Behavioral requirements are not the only type of requirements elaborated through models. All types of requirements can and should be modeled. User interfaces are elaborated through simulations and prototypes and information flows through context diagrams, data definitions and entity relationship diagrams. As we move into system design, class models, component diagrams, object diagrams and composite structure diagrams are appropriate. Models even apply to implementation activities in the form of deployment and package diagrams.

Requirements Prioritization

Requirements prioritization determines which requirements are to be addressed by each build cycle to minimize risk during development. It is a decision making process used to weigh the relative importance of requirements and reach a common understanding with stakeholders on their significance so that the most important or high risk requirements are implemented first. The concept of prioritizing requirements is sometimes difficult for stakeholders to grasp because if they didn't think they needed a particular feature it wouldn't have been named as a requirement. For the stakeholder, every requirement is important. The SDLC defines the criteria to assess requirement priorities fairly and objectively. There are a number of popular methods for prioritizing requirements including:

- 100-Point Method (100P)
- Binary Search Tree (BST)
- Planning Game (PG)
- Planning Game with Analytic Hierarchy Process (PGcAHP)
- Quality Function Deployment (QFD)

One approach developed by Focal Point is the Cost-Benefit method. Focal Point was acquired by Telelogic in 2005. The basic idea is to determine the cost of implementation versus the business value for each individual requirement. The assessment of values and costs is accomplished using the Analytic Hierarchy Process (AHP). AHP is a structured technique for dealing with complex decisions. AHP decomposes the decision problem into a hierarchy of more easily comprehended sub-problems, each of which can be analyzed independently. Numerical priorities representing the alternatives' relative ability to achieve the goal are calculated and considered for the various courses of actions. So for all pairs of requirements an analyst assesses a value or a cost comparing the one requirement of a pair with the other. For example, a value of 3 for the Req1, Req2 pair indicates that requirement 1 is valued three times as high as requirement 2.

Even though the Cost-Value method is considered to be a simple way to prioritize requirements, both BABOK and PMBOK recommend a much simpler prioritization technique that is easy for stakeholders to comprehend. It is called the **MoSCoW** method. The capital letters in the term MoSCoW mean:

- **M—MUST** have this
- **S—SHOULD** have this if at all possible
- **C—COULD** have this if it does not affect anything else
- **W—WON'T** have this time but WOULD like in the future

The o's in the word have no meaning and are added to make the term readable, pronounceable and easy to remember. The MoSCoW method was developed by Dai Clegg of Oracle UK Consulting in his book *"CASE Method Fast-Track: A RAD Approach."*[75] Clegg subsequently donated the intellectual property rights for the MoSCoW method to the DSDM Consortium. As a best practice, MoSCoW is often used in conjunction with timeboxing. Timeboxing is a best practice found in the ICM Waterfall Hybrid and every Agile method we examined in Chapter 2 starting with RAD.

All requirements are important, but the first importance is to deliver the highest value and most immediate business benefit as early as possible in the project life cycle. The MoSCoW method

---

[75] Clegg, Dai; Barker, Richard (Nov. 9, 2004). *Case Method Fast-Track: A RAD Approach*. Addison-Wesley.

when combined with timeboxing allows the project team to meet that vital goal. However, it's not possible to guarantee that all agreed upon requirements can be delivered within the boundaries of a specified timebox. Requirements prioritization sets the stakeholders' expectations and confidence in what is reasonable to anticipate from a development cycle.

Initially, all of the requirements are prioritized against each other. This is an activity facilitated by the BA in collaboration with the stakeholders and key members of the technical and architectural teams. The strategy for evaluating requirements includes assessing business value, regulatory compliance and the feasibility of implementing each requirement. For each requirement, the following criteria are considered:

Regulatory Compliance:

1. Is this a regulatory requirement or in compliance to some policy?
   a. Regulatory or policy requirements take precedence over other stakeholder interests.

Business Value:

1. What is the business value of this requirement?
   a. Perform a cost-benefit analysis for each requirement. High value requirements are developed first.
2. Do all stakeholders agree upon this requirement's business value?
   a. If the stakeholders reach consensus on a requirement's usefulness or business value, take their word on it. They probably know what they're talking about.
3. What is the urgency for implementing this requirement?
   a. If the requirement is time sensitive, schedule it for early implementation.
4. Is this requirement related to or in support of another requirement?
   a. Low value requirements are candidates for early implementation if they support other high-priority requirements.

Feasibility:

1. What is the business or technical risk for implementing this requirement?
   a. High risk requirements present the chief risks for project failure. Implement high risk requirements first to ensure as little has been spent as possible should the project fail.
2. What difficulties are there to implementing this requirement?
   a. If piloting a new development process or tools or implementing a COTS solution, take the easiest, lower-risk requirements first to gain familiarity with the new products.

3. What is the likelihood of our success in implementing this requirement?
    a. If the project is a proof of concept or controversial in nature or requires early successes to gain support, focus on the low hanging fruit and implement the requirements that are likely to produce quick wins.

Once all of the requirements have been corporately prioritized as Must Have, Should Have, Could Have or Won't Have, they are pigeonholed into timeboxes. Timeboxing in one form or another has been adopted as a best practice by virtually all Agile development frameworks. It is a best practice for the SDLC as well. Timeboxing is the process whereby the project team collaborates with the stakeholders to determine the objectives for each development cycle or iteration. Timeboxing is a negotiation with the stakeholders because it is the stakeholders who determine the important deliverables, not the development team. The facilitating BA must be capable of applying strong negotiation skills.

Someone may be thinking, "Why don't we just do all of the Must Haves first, then focus on the Shoulds and Coulds? We're not going to do the Won'ts anyway, at least not now." It doesn't work like that because of the nature of good requirements. Good requirements are cohesive, aren't they? They've been captured and documented in unified chunks based on the functionality they represent. Functionality is prioritized as is each individual requirement within the functional areas. It makes no sense whatsoever to work to chunk requirements for analysis and then fracture their cohesiveness for development.

Since we can't run off and build all of the Must Have requirements first, the negotiation with the stakeholders is to determine what percentage of the total estimated effort of each timebox is to be assigned to Must Have requirements. Historically,[76] what typically works is to limit the level of effort dedicated to the Must Haves to 50-65% of the timebox depending upon the experience level of the development team. The more experienced the team, the higher the percentage of Must Haves. In doing so, 50-70% of the Shoulds and Coulds can be delivered as well.

Timeboxes are generally scheduled in two to six week increments although some timeboxes are known to have been as short as 48 hours. Each timebox has its own objectives, deliverables, deadline and budget. The idea is to never exceed the boundaries of a timebox to deliver the Must Haves. As soon as the team realizes all of the Must Haves will not be deliverable within the boundaries, the timebox ends and renegotiation with the stakeholders begins.

The biggest problem with timeboxing is the apparent tendency to compromise coding standards in order to achieve the Should Have and Could Have deliverables. According to the *"MoSCoW Prioritisation Briefing Paper"* published by the DSDM Consortium:

---

[76] Sources: DSDM Consortium, *"MoSCoW Prioritisation Briefing Paper"* and *"Timeboxing Briefing Paper"*

"Source code; within a given time period it could be specified that:

    a. Must Have – the code must 'work'
    b. Should Have – the code should be fully commented to agreed standards
    c. Could Have – the code should be fully formatted to agreed standards"

The SDLC defines an organization's coding standards and provides guidelines for achieving them. If the goal is to deliver a high quality product that meets or exceeds stakeholders' expectations, coding standards are never compromised for the sake of a timebox. The quality of code must be consistent regardless of the priority of the requirement. Negotiate timebox schedules with the stakeholders to allow the time to apply the same quality rigor to the Should Haves and Could Haves as is applied to the Must Haves. All code must work and be fully commented and documented according to the standards established by the management team.

Referring to the IT Governance model, the requirements process frequently happens before the project has been approved. The requirements process is necessary to determine the overall cost, schedule, and resource requirements. MoSCoW prioritization and timeboxing allow us to get a fairly accurate estimate to the Governance Board. Once the project is approved and development begins, requirements prioritization and timeboxing are reviewed and renegotiated if necessary at the start of each development cycle with zero to minimal impact to the cost and schedule.

System Requirements Specification

In addition to the BRD, many organizations require a second artifact known as the Systems Requirements Specification (SRS) as a deliverable of the analysis phase. The SRS is also a BABOK recommendation. The SRS covers high-level details of the project that are not explicitly documented in the BRD but that are necessary to explain the full course of the project. The artifact is generally required by an architecture or quality review board. If the organization doesn't have an architecture or quality review board, it's still a good idea to document the SRS topics as addenda to the BRD. At least it demonstrates to the project sponsors that you thought about them.

- High Level Architecture
- High Level Development Plan
- List of Impacted Systems
- Reusability
- SOA Governance
- Methodology to follow
- System Environments
- Test Strategy

The SRS depicts the high level architecture for the system under discussion. The BRD documents and models the behavioral characteristics of the system as well as pertinent non-functional requirements. There is the overall context diagram that shows the system under discussion in the context of its touch points. But thus far, there hasn't been any formal description of the system's architecture, how it fits into the current infrastructure and meets existing standards. The high-level architecture maps the proposed functionality onto the existing infrastructure's hardware and software components; and the software architecture onto the hardware architecture. Also, there hasn't been any discussion of the environments required for the project. The environments need to be specified so any additional hardware and/or virtual assets can be identified and the costs calculated into the budget.

Traditional development environment design suggests a minimum of four different environments to complete a project lifecycle. The traditional environments are development, integration, staging and production. Ironically, some consider the development environment to be optional. The development environment is the working environment for individual developers or small teams in which radical changes may be attempted without adversely affecting the rest of the project team. The integration environment is a common environment where all changes are committed and tested before promotion to the staging environment. The staging environment is a clone of the production environment. The staging environment may be used for user acceptance testing, demonstrations and/or training. Final code is migrated from the staging environment to production. The production environment is the environment used for real business transactions.

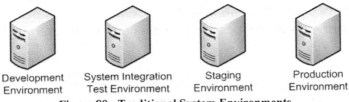

| Development Environment | System Integration Test Environment | Staging Environment | Production Environment |

Figure 80 - Traditional System Environments

The SDLC focuses on quality-centric practices and four environments are not enough to support a quality-centric systems approach. There should actually be a minimum of six environments. A quality-centric approach to systems environments adds a user acceptance test environment and a fail over or disaster recovery environment. The development environment is not considered optional either. It is the primary working environment. If someone wants to try radical changes for a proof of concept or some other reason, an optional sandbox and/or project environment may be stood up alongside the six working environments for a total of up to eight. Sometimes there is also a ninth environment for quality assurance purposes only. With the arrival of relatively low-cost virtual environments, the investment required to set up additional environments can be minimal.

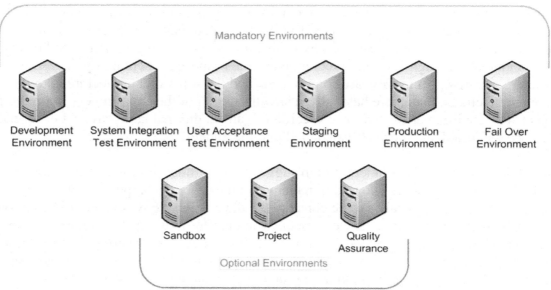

Figure 81 - Quality-Centric System Environment

With the media's coverage of major corporate financial scandals, global regulatory compliance has changed the way in which companies manage their internal controls for IT systems which necessitates quality-centric systems environments. International Organization for Standards standard # ISO 17799 provides guidelines for implementing such controls. ISO 17799 is based on the British Standard 7799.

To ensure the prevention or detection of fraud and misconduct in financial reporting, an internal control recommended for today is to lock developers out of the production environment for anything other than a well-monitored process to troubleshoot severity 1 defects that cause the system to fail. This is also called separation or segregation of duties. In many organizations, developers are only permitted access to development, system integration and sandbox or project environments.

The staging and fail over environments are clones of production in terms of hardware, configuration, and data. The failover environment must be a real time clone of the data. The data for staging needs to be as close to production as possible. Frequent data refreshes may be necessary to keep the staging environment relevant. All other environments should be a limited subset of data that is useful for testing "boundary conditions" in the application. Securing the limited subset of data by masking sensitive pieces of information such as salary or national id is extremely important.

The high-level development plan elaborates the development approach by explaining the timeboxes in more detail. The list of impacted systems considers any system not specifically designated in the context diagram. For example, an Apache web server or Cisco router may be impacted by the implementation of a new system and would not appear on a context diagram but may show on an architecture diagram. What is the anticipated impact to these supporting systems? Is there an impact to performance, load, sizing, etc.?

Reusability explains whether any existing components in a code library are reusable for the new system or whether any proposed functionality of the new system is foreseen as being reusable for other systems in the future. Code reuse has been practiced from the earliest days of programming. Developers have always reused sections of code, templates, functions and procedures when building new systems. A partial or complete program written at one time can be, should be or is used in another program written later. Code reuse is classified as opportunistic or planned. Opportunistic reuse is when the team can take advantage of library components to save time and cost during development. Planned reuse is when the team designs components so they can be reused by the organization at a later time.

Many common operations, such as format conversions, i/o operations, external interfaces or manipulating numbers, words, names, locations, dates, etc. in common ways are needed almost universally. Instead of "re-inventing the wheel," code reuse provides the benefit of using well tested and approved code. One disadvantage to code reuse is the inability to tweak details which may affect performance or desired output without creating an abstraction. Another is the time and cost of acquiring, learning and configuring the library.

If you are building or subscribing to web services, document the rationale for addressing Service Oriented Architecture (SOA) Governance. SOA Governance is for managing SOA metadata. SOA-based environments can include many services that exchange messages to perform tasks. Depending on the design, a single application may generate millions of messages. Managing and providing information on how services interact can be complex. It is even more complicated when these services are delivered by different organizations within the company or even different companies such as partners, suppliers, etc. Navigating the intricacy of an SOA environment often leads to trust issues across teams. The SOA Governance team mitigates the risks.

If the SDLC empowers your project teams to choose from one of several approved development methods, document your reasons for choosing one particular method over another one. If the organization allows for diverting from an approved development methodology, document why the diversion is necessary and which method you've chosen. For example, let's say you have a small project that falls beneath the IT Governance threshold and you want to test the efficacy of a new Agile method. Explain why you've made the choice and include a synopsis of the expected benefits for doing so.

Test Strategy

The last item to include is the test strategy. The business analyst is usually the individual responsible for constructing the test strategy and working with quality control analysts to write the test cases. The test strategy is an outline that describes which tests are to be included in the battery of quality assurance tests and any applicable entry and exit criteria. Its purpose is to inform project team members and stakeholders of the key issues of the testing process. It includes testing objectives, methods, time and resources required. It describes the testing environment and how certain requirements risks are mitigated by testing. The test strategy is high level at this point and will be subject to modification as the system design progresses and the project enters the development phase. The test strategy does not include documented test cases. The test strategy outlines the following points:

- Test Levels: There are primarily three levels of testing: unit testing, integration testing and system testing
- Roles and Responsibilities: The roles and responsibilities of testing resources are to be clearly defined
- Environment Requirements:
  - What operating systems are used for testing
  - What OS patch levels
  - What security updates are required
- Testing Tools: Is this manual and automated testing?
- Risks and Mitigation: Risks that affect the testing process must be listed along with the mitigation
- Test Schedule: Estimate how long it will take to complete the testing phase
- Regression Test Approach: Make sure that a fix does not create some other problems in that program or in any other interface
- Test Groups: Cohesive requirements identify related test groups areas, where features that are functionally similar may be tested together
- Test Priorities: As with the requirements, tests needs to be prioritized as well
- Test Status Collections and Reporting: how often test statuses are collected and method by which they are reported must be clearly defined
- Test Records Maintenance: How are test records going to be stored? Will they be stored in a central repository like HP Quality Center or will they be stored in a specific directory on a central server? The test strategy must clearly indicate the locations and the directories of the test results. The naming convention for the documents and files must also be defined if not defined in the SDLC.

Requirements Inspection

> ### Principle #6: "Quality Assurance begins at project inception"

Up to this point, everything that's been discussed in the previous chapters leads to one singular purpose: to produce mature, quality requirements to reduce the likelihood of cost and schedule overruns, rework and project failures. The Requirements Inspection is the first and only quality stage gate defined in the SDLC for the initial requirements process. A quality stage gate is a special milestone in a project life cycle. Quality gates are situated between phases of a project that strongly depend on the outcomes of the previous phase. Building a quality system depends on getting the requirements right. The requirements inspection stage gate consists of three perfunctory steps: document inspection, requirements validation and requirements verification.

Document inspection is the easiest step to perform. The inspection evaluates a document for ambiguity, clarity and readability. Document inspection is all about driving out ambiguity. An unambiguous document means it is understandable and leaves no questions unanswered in the mind of the reader. Everyone reading the document should arrive at the same understanding of its meaning. If that doesn't happen or the reader is left questioning something, the document is faulty and needs to be reworked. It's much easier and less costly to rework a document early in the project life cycle than to get pretty far down the road and rework a product because vague requirements led to a faulty design.

Have one or more people not involved with the project read the artifacts (BRD and SRS) and when they agree that they understand everything that's been written and the diagrams that have been drawn have them sign off that the inspection is complete. If you have access to a technical communications team, take advantage of their expertise. Ask the technical writers to review the document for ambiguity, grammar and writing format. The actual content is not pertinent to the writing style review and tech writers should refrain from commenting on the content. The tech writer review is for writing style only. Using technical writers requires advanced planning to schedule their time since they are usually kept pretty busy.

The second step is requirements validation. Requirements validation is designed to protect the stakeholders' interests and seeks to answer the questions, "Are the requirements complete and have we captured them correctly?" and "Is this what the stakeholders want?" There are a couple of approaches that can be used to complete the requirements validation. The first is to send the completed documents to the stakeholders to read. Give them a time limit to return either an electronic signature or wet signature to confirm their agreement that the requirements are complete and correctly understood. When you send the cover letter, put a deadline in place for the stakeholder response and you may also want to specify that silence means assent.

One issue with the email approach is that there is no guarantee the stakeholders are actually going to read the final version of the documents. They will probably sign the documents unread, not sign the documents at all or send an email agreeing to the requirements only to deny their agreement later when something goes wrong. If company policy dictates wet signatures, the validation process can become a prolonged exercise in chasing down the stakeholders. For the majority of purposes, electronic signatures are the best method to obtain stakeholder consent. But if you fall under the jurisdiction of the United States Food and Drug Administration (FDA), you are subject to Title 21 CFR Part 11 of the Code of Federal Regulations which deals with the guidelines on electronic records and electronic signatures. Part 11, as it is commonly called, defines the criteria under which electronic records and electronic signatures are considered to be trustworthy, reliable and equivalent to paper records. Make sure you obtain counsel from experts in the law before accepting electronic signatures.

A second approach to accomplishing the requirements validation is to conduct the review in one or more facilitated sessions similar to JAD sessions. Treat the review with the same attention to detail as a JAD session. Send the documents to the invited stakeholders a week or so in advance of the review. Ask them to review the documents and prepare any questions, clarifications or corrections they want to address during the meeting. Conduct the meeting as you normally would any JAD, walking the group through the requirements, models and simulations. Since you have a captive audience, collect wet signatures on the hard copy document before dismissing the stakeholders.

Stakeholders can be a resolute group and it's not uncommon for someone to try to add a new requirement to the BRD during the validation review. Don't allow this to happen. And in the same vein, don't allow the stakeholders to edit the documents. They've been known to sneak new requirements into a project that way as well. Tell the group that the BRD is to be treated as a baselined document. New requirements not previously specified are to be handled through the project change management process. Explain the change management process if you have to, but stress that the requirements validation is for confirming the correctness and completeness of the requirements.

The final step of the requirements inspection stage gate is the verification review. Requirements verification is designed to protect IT's interests and seeks to answer the questions, "Do we have enough information to allow the systems design and development process to begin?" and "Do all of the requirements fall within the capability of our current technology?" SMEs from all IT areas participate in the requirements verification process if the system under discussion has any touch points with their specific domain. Key inspectors include QA analysts and domain and enterprise architects.

QA analysts are responsible for verifying that all of the requirements meet the definition of good requirements. That is, the requirements are cohesive, complete, consistent, correct, feasible, modifiable, necessary, prioritized, reusable, testable, traceable, verifiable and unambiguous. They use the same Good Requirements Quality Checklist from Chapter 5 for the verification that the business analysts used while penning the document. They also ensure that there are no overlapping or duplicate requirements, that all requirements have been stated in one place only and that all business terms and acronyms are defined in the glossary.

The architects and other SMEs confirm the feasibility of the requirements relative to the current technology and infrastructure and ensure that the requirements do not presuppose a solution. If any of the requirements cannot be implemented in the current infrastructure due to a technological constraint, the project team may have to address the build vs. buy decision which at this point in the process leads the team to prepare for the RFI/RFP procedure.

At any point during the inspection stage gate, if any of the requirements are found to be invalid which means they are incomplete in some way—vague, ambiguous, inconsistent, incorrect, untestable or not measurable—the defects are recorded and the documents are returned to the BA for correction. Any comments captured during the review are considered defects and are used to feed the requirements continuous improvement metrics defined in Chapter 10. Invalid requirements make it impossible for a solution to be tested to determine whether or not it meets those requirements. If the documentation defects are minor, the artifacts may pass inspection conditionally pending their correction before baselining. Significant defects in the documentation may mean repeating the entire inspection stage gate again after the corrections are made. In any case, once the documents fully pass inspection, they are baselined.

Requirements Baselining

Requirements baselining is the practice of placing the requirements artifacts under change management control. Change management is an IT Service Management discipline and is generally defined apart from the SDLC. It is most often associated with the Information Technology Infrastructure Library (ITIL), but as a management practice can be traced back to the early 1980s when IBM published their four-volume "yellow-book" series called *"A Management System for Information Systems."* Along with education and expertise provided by IBM, this series of books were key inputs to the original set of ITIL books. ITIL defines the change management process this way:

"The goal of the Change Management process is to ensure that standardized methods and procedures are used for efficient and prompt handling of all changes, in order to minimize the

impact of change-related incidents upon service quality, and consequently improve the day-to-day operations of the organization."

Change management is a formal process to provide the means by which any changes to the project, its deliverables or for system maintenance, requested from any source, go through a review by a Change Advisory Board (CAB). Preparing a change request typically comprises assessing the impact, cost, benefit and risk of proposed changes, developing business justification and obtaining the CAB's approval. IT Governance may be warranted if a change request results in a significant alteration to a project's scope, cost or schedule. Other aspects of the change management process include managing and coordinating the change's implementation, monitoring and reporting on the implementation, and reviewing and closing change requests.

Approved changes are added to the baselined documents and a new baseline is established. Using a tool to manage document versioning is a great assist to managing baseline changes. New versions can be annotated with the explanation of the change and new document version numbers assigned. Versioning can be accomplished by any number of the widely available document management suites or source code control products.

Tracing Requirements

Requirements traceability is a best practice sub-discipline of requirements management. It is documenting the progression of a requirement's lifeline from its origin to the end of the project. Gotel and Finkelstein define requirements traceability as: "…the ability to describe and follow the life of a requirement, in both a forwards and backwards direction (i.e., from its origins, through its development and specification, to its subsequent deployment and use, and through all periods of on-going refinement and iteration in any of these phases)."[77]

The relationships between requirements, people and user groups associated with requirements, all kinds of artifacts, models, analysis results, test cases, test procedures and test results are documented. Its purpose is to help understand a product under development and its artifacts and to manage change. For change management, it helps to assess the impact of a change to a requirement relative to all of its relationships. It enables users to trace the origin of each requirement and track every change which was made to this requirement.

Forward traceability ensures the requirement is satisfied in the evolving product. It demonstrates that the right product is being built and is an indication of the completeness of the product. Take

---

[77] Source: Orlena C. Z. Gotel and Anthony C. W. Finkelstein (1993), *"An Analysis of the Requirements Traceability Problem,"* Technical Report TR-93-41, Department of Computing, Imperial College.

a business rule for example; if it can't be traced forward to a design specification, the specification is incomplete. If a design specification can't be traced forward to an actual build component, the product is incomplete. If a requirement's tracing is well managed, any impact of change to that requirement can be readily understood and managed.

Backwards traceability ensures the project elements can be traced back to a business goal or original requirement. The objective of backwards traceability is to make certain the scope of the requirement is not being expanded. If a design element cannot be traced back to a requirement, there are two possible things going on. A requirement is either missing or the team is engaging in the practice of "gold-plating." Gold-plating is adding something to a design that should not be part of the product. Gold-plating leads to a lack of testing for the design element and adds the high-risk of moving a severe defect to production. Another benefit of backwards tracing is the enablement of root-cause analysis support. If a defect is found in a component, it can be traced back to its source requirement, design element or previous test case to determine where the defect was introduced.

Tracing requirements is one of the most difficult tasks for the BA or PM to administer during a project life cycle. Yet, if managed correctly, it is one of the most rewarding in terms of the value contributed to a project's success. This is because every requirement is traced through its structural evolution. In other words, for every requirement it is known:

- From whence it is derived
- How it is realized or satisfied
- How it is tested
- What impact results if it is changed

The reason tracing requirements is difficult is because requirements are most often traced in a labor intensive artifact known as the traceability matrix. Large projects have hundreds of requirements that come from different sources and tracing them can be a huge task. It's not an insurmountable task, but it does take diligence on the part of the responsible parties to assure the matrix is maintained. If your organization can afford a modern requirements management tool, traceability mechanisms are a feature of their functionality set.

Creating the traceability matrix begins as soon as the BRD is baselined. The process discussed here assumes the absence of a modern requirements management tool and explains the elements needed for traceability to be accomplished successfully using less automated methods.

1. To facilitate backwards traceability, transfer the requirements from the BRD into a spreadsheet, maintaining the same columns and attributes you documented in the textual format. Using the example requirements from the sample BRD, the traceability begins as:

Req ID#	Category/ Functional Activity	Requirement Description	Date Entered	Originator Name/Source	Priority (M, S, C, W)	Risk (H, M, L)
1.0	Receive Call From Customer	Receive Call From Customer				
1.1	Receive Call From Customer	The system shall be capable of determining the number dialed on an incoming call.				

Figure 82 - Beginning the Traceability Matrix

2. To enable forward traceability, add columns for documenting artifact references:

BRD	Use Case/ Process Flow Reference	Model	SRS	SDS	Code Module/ Reference

Figure 83 - Document Artifact References

The artifact references include the name and location of the document and the section header or paragraph number where the requirement can be found. Another column you may want to consider is whether the requirement is related to or supportive of any other requirement.

3. Finish the matrix with additional columns for tracing code modules and test cases:

Test Case Reference(s)	User Acceptance Validation	Status	Release Number	Comments

Figure 84 – Trace Code Modules, Test Cases and Releases

Test cases reference the test case number or name. You may consider another column for test results. The status can be in progress, complete, tested, approved, etc. Status can be designated any way you deem appropriate. Release number is the release or development cycle in which the component is implemented. Comments are used for documenting any additional information about the requirement that can be helpful for the tracing process. If you use any test management suites like Hewlett-Packard Quality Center, the requirements can be mapped and uploaded into the testing tool from the traceability matrix. Requirements Management tools like Blueprint Systems' Requirements Center integrate with Quality Center and provide 2-way communication. If the requirement is changed in either of the two products, the update is automatically reflected in the other product.

IT Governance Next Steps

After the requirements are baselined and the traceability matrix is created, the waiting game begins if working under an IT Governance structure. At this point in the process, the project is probably not yet approved for development. The project team needs to go through the estimation exercise to determine the cost and duration of the project and report back to governance. If it seems that the requirements cannot be satisfied without buying a product or technology, the RFI/RFP process needs to be performed. IT Governance practices may require you to seek permission before taking any further actions including the RFI/RFP.

Even with all the due diligence required by a governance process, sometimes the waiting game can result in delays of months or years before funding is available for a project. Capital funding is a finite resource and competition is fierce to fund business initiatives. What may be a high value, high priority project to one business unit may in fact be designated very low when taking the entire corporate picture into consideration.

A case in point is one project in which I managed a team to verify and validate requirements that were elicited for a potential project four years earlier. The project was for a comprehensive workforce management system with an estimated cost of approximately $5 million dollars. The project appeared on the list of projects for IT Governance budget consideration every year for four years, but funding was never approved because of higher business priorities. During the fifth year, we were asked to verify and validate the earlier requirements, perform an RFI and estimate the cost for the next year's budget cycle. The business unit requesting the system was very hopeful of getting the project funded this time around, but economic reality prevailed. Waiting so long for the project to be approved drove up the estimated cost and the project was denied once again for the lack of capital funding even though everyone from the CEO on down agreed it was important and necessary to the future of the business. The IT Governance council asked that the project be put on hold and revisited in two more years.

Requirements Artifacts

The artifacts required by the SDLC in the Requirements Process are:

Artifact	Artifact Type	Description	Phase
RACI Chart	Deliverable	Responsible, Accountable, Consulted and Informed Stakeholder Matrix	Requirements Planning
Communications Plan	Deliverable	Requirements process communications plan	Requirements Planning
Preliminary Elicitation	Deliverable	Requirements activity	Requirements

Artifact	Artifact Type	Description	Phase
Schedule and Work Breakdown Structure		schedule and resource assignments developed by the BA and PM and incorporated into the overall project plan	Planning
Business Requirements Definition (BRD)	Deliverable	Full Business Requirements Definition which includes both Business and Non-Functional Requirements.	Requirements Elicitation & Analysis
BRD Users Guide	Supporting Document	Users guide to learn how to use the BRD template.	Requirements Elicitation
Business Intelligence and Data Warehouse BRD	Deliverable	For BI and DW purposes only.	Requirements Elicitation & Analysis
Elicitation Technique Process Checklists	Supporting Documents	There is one process checklist available for each of the nine elicitation techniques.	Requirements Elicitation
Requirements Checklist	• Supporting Document (development stage) • Deliverable (inspection stage)	Checklist used by anyone writing, reviewing or testing the requirements document.	Requirements Elicitation & Inspection
Non-functional requirements Checklist	• Supporting Document (development stage) • Deliverable (inspection stage)	Checklist used by anyone writing, reviewing or testing the non-functional requirements document	Requirements Elicitation & Inspection
System Requirements Specification (SRS)	Deliverable	• High level architecture • High Level Development Plan • System Environments • List of impacted systems • Reusability • Service Oriented Architecture Governance • Methodology to follow • Test Strategy	Requirements Analysis
Traceability Matrix	Deliverable	Trace the requirements through all life cycle phases	Requirements Baselining

Figure 85 - Requirements Process Artifacts

SDLC Requirements Phase Activity Diagram

To close Chapter 6, let's begin mapping our best in breed SDLC into an activity diagram for the requirements process as discussed in Chapters 3, 4 and 5. A complete SDLC activity diagram that includes all phases may be found on the accompanying CD.

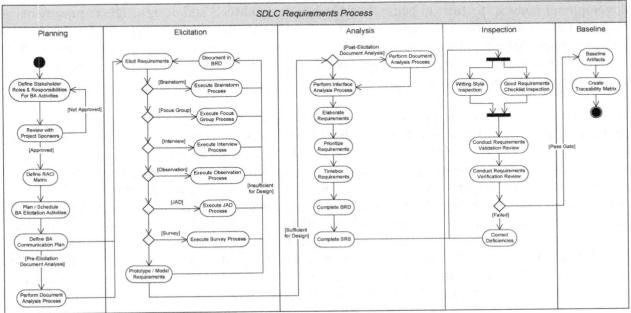

Figure 86 - SDLC Requirements Phase Activity Diagram

Design & Development

Assuming the project has received governance approval to move into the design and development phases, it's time to begin the actual system analysis and design. The requirements analysis performed in the last chapter is vastly different from the analysis required for design. Requirements analysis got us to the point where we could estimate the project's resource needs with a fair degree of accuracy. System analysis methods are a deeper investigation where the hows of the system are defined at an operational level.

If a significant gap in time has passed since the baselining of the requirements artifacts and the approval to begin development is received, hold a requirements validation meeting to reengage the stakeholders, ensure business priorities haven't changed and that the business goals addressed by the requirements are still valid. If business priorities have changed and the requirements are no longer valid, it's back to the requirements process to address only those areas needing reconsideration. New or changed requirements are then submitted to requirements inspection once again and the baseline shifts to reflect the updates. This is the only occasion and circumstance in the SDLC where it may be appropriate to change requirements without submitting to the formal change management process, provided of course the new requirements do not entail an increase in the approved budget or timeline. Adding to the budget and timeline always demands an appropriate level approval without exception.

Much has been written about software design principles and practices. The SDLC is not meant to teach resources how to design and construct systems although formal training is frequently required for the SDLC's successful assimilation into an organization. If you need a design and development reference for software projects, the SWEBOK is one of many excellent commercially available sources.

The SDLC establishes organizational guidelines and standards that are to be observed during the system development process regardless of whether the project is for hardware or software. Some developers almost religiously practice their favorite development methods picked up in school or elsewhere. It is nearly impossible to change deeply embedded habits to implement best practices without hearing complaints that the SDLC infringes upon a developer's creativity and ingenuity. A best in breed SDLC does not intrude upon the creative process, but provides boundaries within which innovation is expressively articulated during design and development.

Fundamental to system analysis and design is for project teams to understand basic system design concepts. A thorough understanding of foundational design concepts leads to a better execution of the more sophisticated system analysis and design methods. There are nine broadly accepted system design concepts:

- **Abstraction**: the process or result of generalization by reducing the information content of a concept or an observable phenomenon, typically in order to retain only the information for a particular purpose
- **Architecture:** the overall structure of a system and the ways in which that structure provides conceptual integrity for a system
- **Control Hierarchy**: structure that represents the organization of a system's components and implies a hierarchy of control
- **Data Structure**: a representation of the logical relationship among individual elements of data
- **Encapsulation**: modules are specified and designed so that information contained within a module is inaccessible to other modules that have no need for the information
- **Modularity:** architecture is divided into well defined, independent components called modules
- **Refinement**: the process of elaboration. A functional decomposition hierarchy is successively developed into more detailed instructions. Abstraction and Refinement are complementary concepts
- **Structural Partitioning**: The system's structure divided both horizontally and vertically. Horizontal partitions define separate modular hierarchies for each major system function. Vertical partitioning distributes control and work from the top down in the system structure
- **System Procedure**: focuses on the processing of each module individually

In addition to the foundational design concepts, there are other considerations when designing a system. The importance of each reflects the goals the system is trying to achieve. Some of these essential considerations are:

- **Compatibility**: the system is able to interoperate with other products and systems
- **Extensibility**: new capabilities can be added to the system without major changes to the underlying architecture
- **Fault-tolerance**: the system is resistant to and able to recover from component failure
- **Maintainability**: the system is sustained at a specified operational capability and can be restored within the time limit contracted in the service level agreement
- **Reliability**: the system is able to perform under the conditions and time periods stated in the service level agreement
- **Reusability**: the components realize their expected functionality and are reusable wherever there are similar needs in other designs

- **Robustness**: the system can operate under stress and respond to unpredictable or invalid input
- **Security**: the system is able to withstand hostile acts and influences
- **Usability**: the system's user interface meets the expectations of its target user/audience. Default values are chosen for the majority of the users. Online help is included and carefully designed.

The deliverable for the design phase is the System Design Specification (SDS). IEEE 610.12-90 defines design as both *"the process of defining the architecture, components, interfaces, and other characteristics of a system or component"* and *"the result of [that] process."* The SDS describes the system's functions and operations in detail, including screen layouts, business rules, process diagrams and other documentation. The output of this stage is a version of the new system modeled on paper and expounded as a collection of classes, modules or subsystems.

The SDS builds upon the requirements artifacts by allocating each requirement to a detail level design element of architecture, components, modules, interfaces and data objects. Design elements describe the desired system features in their entirety and generally include functional hierarchy diagrams, screen layout diagrams, tables of business rules, business process diagrams, pseudo code, and a complete entity-relationship diagram with a full data dictionary. The result is a design that satisfies the specified requirements and describes the system in sufficient detail that skilled developers may build the solution with minimal additional input. All requirements must be allocated to some design element otherwise the design is incomplete. There are four broadly accepted methods to solution design and analysis that include:

- Business Process Analysis & Design
- Object-oriented Analysis & Design
- Service Oriented Analysis & Design
- Structured Analysis & Design

Business Process Analysis & Design

Business Process Analysis and Design is all about helping the enterprise achieve its mission, objectives and priorities by focusing on Business Process Improvement (BPI). BPI is also known as business transformation which is covered in detail in Chapter 10—Continuous Improvement. Virtually all projects can benefit from some level of business process analysis and design. BPI is an on-going activity that focuses on "doing things right" more than it does on "doing the right thing." Effective BPI reduces process variation and/or waste so that desired outcomes are attained with better resource utilization.

On a macro scale, BPI is often associated with organizational restructuring or reengineering which can lead to internal resistance because of fears of layoffs and structure changes. Even at the project or micro level, fear of job loss can become a forefront water cooler conversation with those impacted by proposed process improvements. It is crucial to guard against this fear otherwise a project can be stalled by resistance to change indefinitely. BPI activities are generally spearheaded by the business analyst, but the entire project team remains alert for BPI opportunities throughout the project's life cycle. As an opportunity presents itself, the team convenes with the stakeholders to explore the alternatives.

The industry or project type has no impact on the techniques used to execute BPI. The core principles of BPI and how they apply to business improvement are portable across industries and functions. BPI works by aligning business processes to achieve organizational goals. In systems design, it is a modeling exercise to describe both current and recommended future processes. There are a number of different diagram types and conventions that support Business Process Analysis, such as Activity Diagrams, Flowcharts and Workflow Models. The first step is to define the as-is structure and process. Then the process owners determine what outcomes add value to the business goals and how best to align the to-be processes to achieve those outcomes. BPI requires stakeholder collaboration at all levels otherwise it will not be successful. To achieve the greatest success when executing a BPI initiative, keep these five rules in mind:

- Start with a small process that can be completed in a short time frame.
- Set and communicate clear timelines
- Do not over commit resources
- Focus on the short term payoff (low hanging fruit)
- Collaboration between management and the primary stakeholders is paramount or else even a limited implementation will fail

Object-oriented Analysis & Design

Many of the modern programming languages in use since the early 1990s are based on an Object-oriented Programming (OOP) paradigm that uses "objects" consisting of attributes known as properties and operations known as methods together with their interactions. OOP techniques include features such as data abstraction, encapsulation, modularity, polymorphism and inheritance. Object-oriented analysis and design (OOAD) models a system as a group of interacting objects or classes. The system is viewed as a collection of classes (the objects) that pass messages to one another. Each class represents some entity in the system and is characterized by its data elements (state) and its behavior.

Various UML models are used to illustrate the static structure, dynamic behavior and run-time deployment of the collaborating objects. A variety of UML models are captured in the requirements artifacts that demonstrate what the system is supposed to do, in other words, they are models of the system's behavior. Modeling behavior in this fashion is the result of Object Oriented Analysis (OOA). We started with the Use Cases and moved to Activity Diagrams and Sequence Diagrams to elaborate the Use Cases and textual requirements.

Object-oriented design (OOD) abstracts the OOA models into class and interface models to produce implementation specifications. OOD transforms the conceptual models produced in OOA to account for the constraints imposed by the chosen architecture and any non-functional—technological or environmental—constraints, such as transaction throughput, response time, run-time platform, development environment or programming language. OOA focuses on what the system does, OOD on how the system does it. The result is a domain solution model comprising a detailed description of how the system is to be built.

While OOD today is the mainstream programming design paradigm, it wasn't very long ago that object-oriented technology was the new kid on the block. OOD represented a very different way of thinking about computer systems from the traditional procedural methods. In their 1989 paper *"A Laboratory for Teaching Object-Oriented Thinking,"* Ward Cunningham and Kent Beck proposed the use of Class Responsibility Collaboration (CRC) cards. They said,

"It is difficult to introduce both novice and experienced procedural programmers to the anthropomorphic perspective necessary for object-oriented design. We introduce CRC cards, which characterize objects by class name, responsibilities, and collaborators, as a way of giving learners a direct experience of objects."

CRC Cards are still used today in the object-oriented design process when first determining which classes are needed and how they will interact. CRC cards are usually created from index cards on which are written:

1. The class name
2. Its Super and Sub classes (if applicable)
3. The responsibilities of the class
4. The names of collaboration classes
5. Author

Using small cards keeps the complexity of the design to a minimum. It focuses the designer on the essentials of the class and prevents getting lost in its details and inner workings at a time when such detail is probably counter-productive. It also forces the designer to refrain from giving the class too many responsibilities. Because the cards are portable, they can be easily laid out on a table and re-arranged while discussing a design with the project team.

One common method to determine what cards are to be created is to look for nouns and verbs in the requirements specification. Consider if each noun should be a class and if each verb should be a responsibility or operation of the noun or class to which it belongs. As you would expect, the mere existence of a noun or verb doesn't mean it must be a class or responsibility in the design, but it is considered a good starting point. Figure is an example of a simple class model.

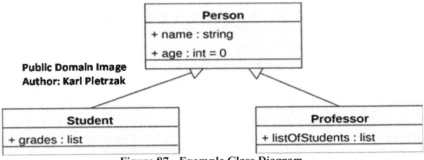

Figure 87 - Example Class Diagram

Service-Oriented Analysis & Design

Service-Oriented Analysis and Design (SOAD) extends traditional object-oriented and component-based analysis and design methods to include elements relevant to and supporting Service Oriented Architecture (SOA). In 2004, IBM announced Service-Oriented Modeling and Architecture (SOMA) as the first publicly announced SOA-related methodology. SOMA implements SOAD through the identification, specification and realization of services, service components that realize those services and flows that can be used to compose services. SOMA builds on current techniques in areas such as domain analysis, functional areas grouping, variability-oriented analysis (VOA) process modeling, component-based development, object-oriented analysis and design and use case modeling. SOMA also introduces new techniques such as goal-service modeling, service model creation and a service litmus test to help determine the granularity of a service.

BPMN is currently the notation language of choice for SOA modeling and the standard for this SDLC. However there is an emerging notation language worth watching that may eventually trump BPMN as the notation language of choice for SOA. In 2008, Michael Bell authored the Service-oriented Modeling Framework (SOMF) and proposed it as a service-oriented modeling holistic language. "Holistic language" means it can be used to design any application, business and technological environment, either local as in a SOA landscape or distributed as in cloud computing. There is at least one modeling tool on the market that has adopted the SOMF language and its notation. The tool is Enterprise Architect by Sparx Systems. Enterprise Architect is a modeling platform that enables development teams to pursue the chief SOMF life cycle disciplines.

SOMF is a life cycle of five major modeling activities to drive a service evolution during design-time and run-time. At the design-time phase a service originates as a conceptual entity (conceptual service), later it transforms into a unit of analysis (analysis service); next it transitions into a contractual and logical entity (design service) and finally is established as a concrete service (solution service). The SOMF modeling activities are:

- Service-oriented discovery & analysis modeling:
  - Discover, identify and analyze services for granularity, reusability, interoperability, loose-coupling and consolidation opportunities
- Service-oriented business integration modeling:
  - Identify service integration and alignment opportunities with business domain processes
- Service-oriented logical design modeling:
  - Establish service relationships and message exchange paths
  - Address service visibility.
  - Craft service logical compositions
  - Model service transactions
- Service-oriented conceptual architecture modeling:
  - Establish an SOA architectural direction
  - Depict an SOA technological environment
  - Craft an SOA technological stack
  - Identify business ownership
- Service-oriented logical architecture modeling:
  - Integrate SOA software assets
  - Establish SOA logical environment dependencies
  - Foster service reuse, loose coupling and consolidation.

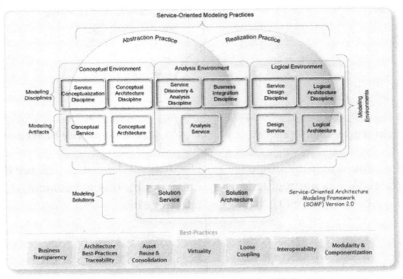

Public Domain Image Created by Angela Martin

Figure 88 - Service-Oriented Architecture Framework[78]

Figure 88 is a model of SOMF Version 2.0. Figure 89 is the SOMF notation. Figures 88-91 are public domain images created by Maria C. Mosak depicting four service analysis modeling examples using the SOMF notation.

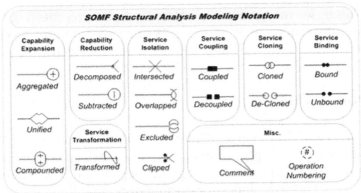

Public Domain Image Created by Angela Martin

Figure 89 - SOMF Notation

---

[78] Based on Michael Bell's book *"Service-Oriented Modeling: Analysis, Design, and Architecture,"* Wiley, 2008

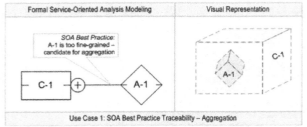

Figure 90 - Service Aggregation Example

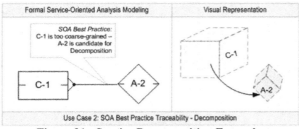

Figure 91 - Service Decomposition Example

Use Case 1 depicts a simple aggregation case, in which atomic service A-1 is aggregated in composite service C-1 because of SOA best practice reasons.

Use Case 2 describes service decomposition. Once again, this is because of an SOA best practice rule.

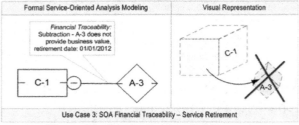

Figure 92 - Service Subtraction Example

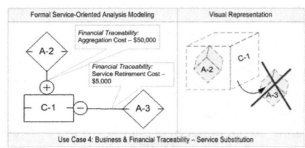

Figure 93 - Service Substitution Example

Use Case 3 illustrates a service retirement (elimination) employing the "subtracted" analysis operation.

Use Case 4 represents a common business substitution operation. Atomic service A-3 was retired and replaced with atomic service A-2.

Structured Analysis & Design

Formal structured analysis and design methods began to appear in the late 1960s when most of the world's commercial programming was being done in BASIC, C, COBOL and FORTRAN. Back in those days there was little guidance on "good" design and programming techniques. Neither were there any standard techniques for documenting requirements and designs. Structured methods evolved as a collection of analysis, design, and programming techniques developed in response to the problems facing the software development world from the 1960s to the 1980s. Figure 94 is a table depicting the evolution of structured analysis and design methods.

When	What	Who	When	What	Who
1967	Structured programming	Edsger Dijkstra	1979	Structured Analysis and System Specification	Tom DeMarco
1969 to 1973	Structured Analysis and Design Technique	Douglas T. Ross	1983	Structured Systems Analysis and Design Method	UK Office of Government Commerce
1975	Structured Design	Larry Constantine, Ed Yourdon, Wayne Stevens	1985	IDEF0	Douglas T. Ross
1975	Jackson Structured Programming	Michael A. Jackson	Late 1980s	Yourdon Structured Method	Ed Yourdon
1978	Structured Analysis	Tom DeMarco, Ed Yourdon, Gane & Sarson, McMenamin & Palmer	1990	Information Engineering	James Martin

Figure 94 - The Evolution of Structured Analysis and Design Methods

Structured Analysis (SA) primarily views a system as a collection of executable processes with inputs and outputs. The analysis is process-centric and focuses on the exchange of data flowing through the processes. Structured analysis uncovers information through successive top down functional decomposition. Decomposition places the attention on important details and omits the irrelevant. The result of SA is a set of related graphical diagrams, process descriptions and data definitions that describe the transformations needing to take place and the data required to meet a system's functional requirements.

Functional decomposition is also known as factoring. It is the process by which a complex problem or system is broken down into parts that are easier to conceive, understand, program and maintain. There are basically two types of functional decomposition. In structured analysis, *algorithmic decomposition* breaks a process down into well-defined steps. In object-oriented analysis, decomposition breaks a large system down into progressively smaller classes or objects that are responsible for some part of the problem domain. Decomposition diagrams show a high-level function, process, organization, data subject area, or other type of object broken down into lower level, more detailed components. Figures 95 and 96 are examples of decomposition diagrams.

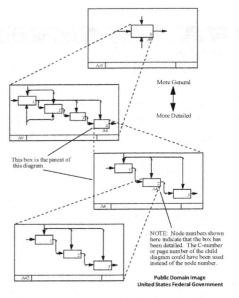

Public Domain Image
United States Federal Government

Figure 95 - Decomposition Structure

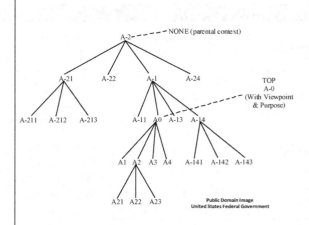

Public Domain Image
United States Federal Government

Figure 96 - Negative Node-Numbered Context

Structured Design (SD) is the creation of modules and organizing them into a "module hierarchy." Structured design is appropriate for procedural development languages. Two principles are critical to design an optimal module structure and interfaces:

- Cohesion: the grouping of functionally related processes into a particular module
- Coupling: the flow of information or parameters passed between modules
    o Optimal coupling reduces the module interfaces and system complexity

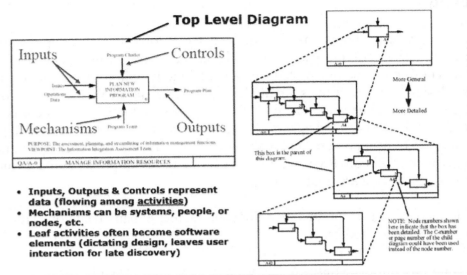

Top Level Diagram

- **Inputs, Outputs & Controls represent data (flowing among <u>activities</u>)**
- **Mechanisms can be systems, people, or nodes, etc.**
- **Leaf activities often become software elements (dictating design, leaves user interaction for late discovery)**

Public Domain Image Courtesy of the United States Federal Government

Figure 97 - Structured Analysis and Design Approach

Despite the significant progress in structured methods, no standards bodies have ever codified the models used for structured analysis and design. Modeling techniques commonly used to support structured analysis include Context Diagrams, Flowcharts, Data Flow Diagrams, Functional Decomposition Diagrams and Entity Relationship Diagrams.

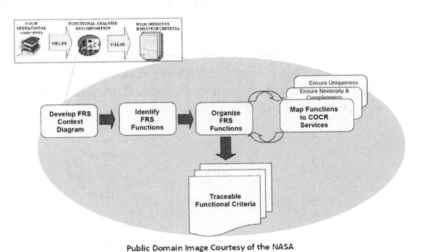

Public Domain Image Courtesy of the NASA

Figure 98 - NASA Example of Structured Analysis Approach

Data Modeling

After designing the system components, its operations and flows, the next step is to finish the data design started during requirements elicitation and elaboration. During elicitation we captured the data definition and elaborated a conceptual model with Entity Relationship Diagrams. The design phase continues the modeling exercise and explicitly defines the physical data model and expands the definition of the data, whether structured or unstructured, by expounding additional elements and attributes. The data model is a means to enable project team members from different backgrounds and with different levels of experience to communicate with one another with precision. Precision means that the terms and rules of a data model can be interpreted only one way and are unambiguous.

There are no defined standards for data modeling and there are many techniques for creating models. Models are categorized as:

- Data Structure Diagrams
- Database Models
- Entity Relationship Models
- Generic Data Models
- Geographic Data Models
- Semantic Data Models

The topics addressed by these models include data architecture, data modeling, data properties, data organization, data structure, data model theory and patterns. In addition to these models, there are related models, some of which have already been discussed. The related models include data flow diagrams (context diagrams), information models, object models, object role models and a variety of UML models. Some of these models have multiple variants as well. For example, the database models can be flat, hierarchical, network, relational, object-relational, snowflake schema or star schema. Another example is data structure which can include arrays, hash tables, linked lists or stacks. This is why the position of dedicated data architect evolved. Data modeling can be very complex, but without an accurate data model, the system design is incomplete. Figure 99 is a model of the data modeling process.

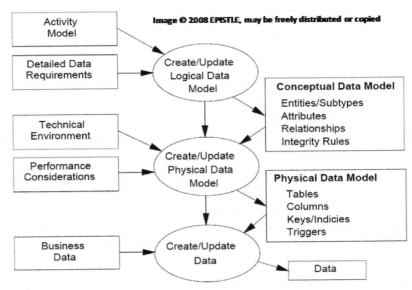

Image © 2008 EPISTLE, may be freely distributed or copied

Figure 99 - Data Modeling Process

Since there are no standards for data modeling, as you deploy your SDLC, you'll have to decide which models and techniques are appropriate for your organization. As a general rule, provide enough detail for the developers to create the target system's schema, its tables, indexes and triggers to satisfy the requirements. As a starting point, consider the following list of common data attributes and elements as part of the data design:

- **ID Number**: A number associated with the data element name for use in technical documents and traceability
- **Data Business Rules**:
  - Rules that define how data is managed within an information system (e.g., colors could be coded (1=Red, 2=Blue, 3=Green)
  - Codes are included in the data dictionary for use by developers and users
  - Rights to the four basic functions of persistent storage, create, read, update or delete records (CRUD Matrix), are assigned if necessary
- **Data Type**: The type of data e.g. character, numeric, alpha-numeric, date, list, floating point, blob, Boolean, etc.
- **Default Value**: A value that is predetermined. It may be fixed or a variable, like current date and time of the day
- **Definition**: Meaning of the data element
- **Edit Mask**: An example of the actual data layout required, (e.g., yyyy/mm/dd)
- **Field Constraints**:
  - Data Element is a required field:

- ▪ Required fields must be populated
- o Conditional Field:
  - ▪ Conditional fields must be populated when another related field is populated
- o "Null" field
  - ▪ "Not null" describes fields that must contain data
  - ▪ "Null" means the data type is undefined
- **Field Name**: The name used for this data element in computer programs and database schemas
- **Indexes**: Data structure that improves the speed of data retrieval operations at the cost of slower writes and increased storage space
- **Name**: Commonly agreed, unique data element name
  - o There are likely to be multiple data element names for a particular domain
- **Precision**: The level to which the data will be reported (e.g., 1 mile plus or minus .001 mile)
- **Size and Decimal Places**: The maximum field length that will be accepted by the database together with any decimal points (e.g. 30(2)) refers to a field length of 30 with 2 decimal points)
- **Triggers**: Procedures that are automatically executed in response to certain events on a particular database table, field or view
- **Value**: The data
- **Views**: A stored query accessible as a virtual table composed of the result set of a query

The more precise you are in defining the data objects, the greater the chances of first build success. Keep in mind that if the data you are defining is to be used in an interface to another system, the other system must be capable of accepting the data as defined or transforming it into the format it requires. That is, the receiving table on the other end should match the type and length of the data that you are sending in the interface. The goal is to minimize altering the other system if at all possible. If interfaces aren't matched up, the cost of modifications can severely impact a project. You design an interface one way for your project and don't tell the receiving system's team about the design. The first time you run a test and it fails could mean emergency rework on both sides of the interface equation. The costs could be prohibitive. Make certain all interface specifications are well defined and equate for both sides of the data transfer. Figures 100 and 101 are public domain examples of different types of data modeling diagrams.

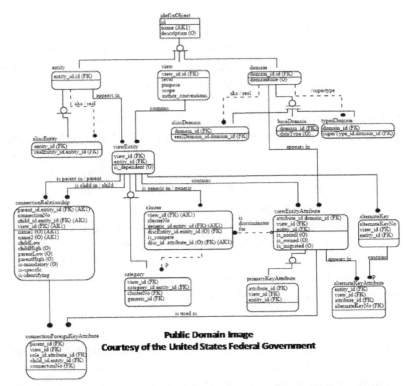

Public Domain Image
Courtesy of the United States Federal Government

Figure 100 - Integration Definition for Information Modeling (IDEFIX)

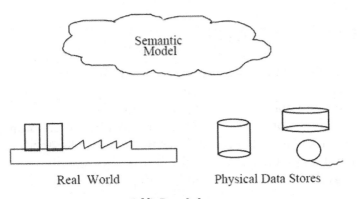

Real World   Physical Data Stores

Public Domain Image
Courtesy of the United States Federal Government

Figure 101 - Example of Semantic Data Models

No matter what kind of system you are building, these four system analysis and design methods address the gamut of what you may encounter in your projects. Note however, that they are not the only analysis and design methods out there. Systems and software engineers have developed many methods over the years including those dependent on Computer Aided Software Engineering (CASE) tools, workbenches and environments designed to result in high-quality, defect-averse and maintainable software products. Even so, these other methods still fall under one of the four categories. Regardless of the methods you have chosen for your organization, make sure the SDLC empowers teams to decide the right approach for their projects.

To finalize the SDS, refine the timeboxes proposed during requirements analysis in preparation for the development cycles. During requirements analysis the stakeholders prioritized the most important deliverables using MoSCoW prioritization. But at the time, the project team lacked detailed specifications and the knowledge of what solution would be the end result of addressing all of the requirements. It is impossible to analyze and define all specifications before the start of the realization phase. The realization phase begins with system design. Now that the system is designed, it is easier to gain a grasp on the resources required to deliver the solution. In the earlier timeboxing activity, the timeboxes are generally over estimated to account for contingencies. In this timeboxing activity, more accurate estimates are forwarded and if it appears that all of the functionality promised for a specific timebox cannot be delivered within the agreed period, a negotiation with the stakeholders takes place at the beginning of that particular iteration during the kick-off review.

Review the overall design with the entire team to make sure nothing was missed or over or under stated. Skilled developers are certain to let you know if the design contains sufficient detail for them to build the solution with minimal additional input. Complete the SDS, update the traceability matrix and submit it to the Design Quality Review stage gate.

Design Quality Review Stage Gate

The Design Quality Review is the second formal SDLC defined stage gate. It is not too unlike the Requirements Inspection Stage Gate. The SDS is reviewed for writing style and comprehensibility in the same manner as the requirements artifacts. The SDS can be given to people, preferably developers, not involved with the project or project domain to read and comment on the document's clarity. If they all have the same understanding of what the document conveys, then it's good to go, otherwise it needs rework. If a technical writing team is available, they can assess the document for good writing style and grammar.

Quality Assurance's role is somewhat different for this review. During the Requirements Inspection, QA uses checklists to ensure the requirements meet the definition of good requirements. QA's role during this inspection is to ensure that every good requirement is allocated and traceable to a design element. If any requirement is not addressed in the design, QA rejects the artifacts and sends them back to the author for editing. How exactly does QA accomplish this task? The task is accomplished by examining the completeness of the traceability matrix, that's how.

The last hurdle to pass in this stage gate is the System Design Review Board. Some organizations call this an Architecture Review Board, but in practice the review is a walkthrough of the system design with subject matter experts from every area the design touches upon. The composition of this review board is going to change based on the nature and scope of the project. Architects are a part of the review board, but the board may also include experts from any IT area including senior developers or managers, systems administrators, data base administrators, system security, infrastructure, network, telecomm, etc. The purpose of the review is to ensure the design is sufficient to move forward and achievable within the current or proposed architectural and technological boundaries. In other words, it's the last opportunity for IT to say "yes we can or no we can't do this" before committing to the build.

If the design passes muster, the SDS is baselined and the traceability matrix is versioned. The system build begins for the development team(s) and in a concurrent set of activities, the business analysts and documentation resources are kept busy with development monitoring tasks and creating pre-implementation artifacts. The pre-implementation artifacts include defining the detailed QA test battery and implementation plans and preparing the end user training and production turnover materials. If the SDS does not pass inspection, it is returned to the author(s) for correction and reinspection.

Development Cycles

From our comparison study of the twelve system development methods in Chapter 2, it is safe to conclude that waterfall models don't work well for the majority of system development projects. All of the Agile methods and the ICM hybrid model proposed by Boehm and Lane in 2006 consider iterative and incremental development to be a best practice. The basic idea behind iterative development is to build a system incrementally, allowing the development team to take advantage of the lessons learned from earlier increments and system deliverables. Stakeholder collaboration is a major success factor for the learning process which comes from both the development and use of the system.

Key steps in the process are to start with a simple implementation of a subset of the system requirements and iteratively enhance the evolving deliverables until the full system is implemented. Design modifications are made and functional capabilities added within every cycle. The best in breed SDLC focuses on iterative and incremental development methods as its best practice model. The development best practices adopted in the SDLC extend primarily from DSDM, Extreme Programming and Scrum.

Iteration Kick-off Meeting

> **Principle #7: Keep the stakeholders engaged in the development process.**

Since MoSCoW prioritization and timeboxing are DSDM best practices, each development iteration starts with another DSDM best practice related to MoSCoW prioritization and timeboxing—the kick-off meeting. The goal of the kick-off meeting is to validate the MoSCoW prioritization for the particular timebox. It also reengages the stakeholders in a meaningful way. Other than the business liaison,[79] the stakeholders may not have been involved in the design due to the activity's highly technical nature. The kick-off meeting provides the stakeholders with the opportunity to review the timebox deliverables from an input and output perspective and understand the project teams' expectations for them during development. The stakeholders must remain engaged throughout the iteration.

Because of its similarity to a requirements workshop, you could follow the same process as a JAD session for scheduling the kick-off meeting with the exception of the pre-meeting stakeholder interviews and the catering. Nevertheless, for your convenience Figure 102 is a kick-off meeting activity diagram. The kick-off is scheduled as close as possible to the beginning of actual development, but no earlier than a week before. The kick-off meeting is designed to finalize the iteration's timebox plan and address the following questions:

1. Are the levels of effort estimates achievable?
2. Do we agree with the acceptance criteria for the timebox deliverables?
3. Does the project team have a high degree of certainty that they will build and test the Must Haves to the highest quality standards in the available time?
4. Do all key stakeholders agree to the review dates?
5. Will the team commit to delivering, at a minimum, the Must Haves by the end of the timebox?
6. Have lessons learned in previous timeboxes been considered for this timebox?

During requirements analysis, the stakeholders decide the priority of the Requirements based on business value. The requirements are then roughly assigned to timeboxes in order to estimate resource needs. As system design progresses, the timeboxes become more refined as development activities and deliverables are scheduled in the order of greatest to least business value. For a particular timebox, Must Have requirements are guaranteed to be delivered in the

---

[79] another best practice from the Scrum Agile Method

available time. Sometimes, a Must Have requirement may actually have a lower priority than a Should Have or Could Have depending on how it integrates into the overall design. And even though a lower priority Must Have could be delivered in this timebox, it may be designated for the next one. It's all part of the negotiation process with the stakeholders.

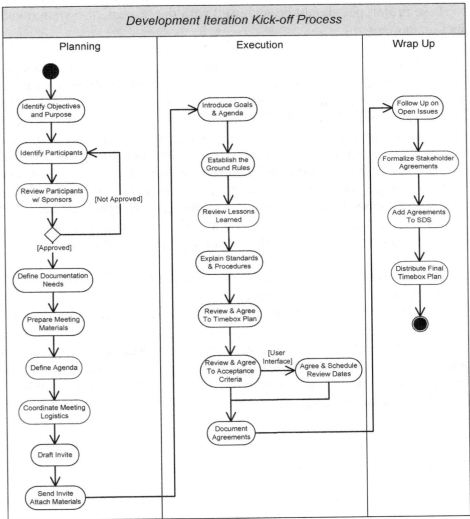

Figure 102 - Development Iteration Kick-off Meeting Activity Diagram

Acceptance criteria are collected during the requirements elicitation. For deliverables to be considered complete, they must satisfy the acceptance criteria. During the kick-off meeting, review the acceptance criteria with the stakeholders to verify their expectations. If building components for a user interface, schedule key review dates with the stakeholders to evaluate the working prototypes and accept their feedback. If you are familiar with Oracle's AIM project management methodology, these review meetings are known as conference room pilots. The purpose is to conduct a hands-on demonstration of the functionality stakeholders interact with while it is early enough to easily correct design flaws. There is little to no value in reviewing functionality with stakeholders if the components are internal to the system or only interact with other systems. These prototypes should be reviewed with the respective system owners or technical subject matter experts.

The iteration kick-off meeting is facilitated by the Business Analyst, Project Manager, Development Manager or project Team Lead. All stakeholders and project team members participating in the timebox are required since their agreement to the timeframe and acceptance criteria is essential. The Project Manager must be present to ensure that any changes to the timebox do not adversely impact other current and planned activities. It's a good idea to have a scribe available to take meeting minutes and document any agreements between the stakeholders and project team. Agreements are formalized after the meeting and added as addenda to the SDS. Remember to follow change management principles, appropriately comment and version the SDS. The Development Manager and/or Domain Architect are necessary to make certain any system-level issues are considered and to agree to any technical aspects of the acceptance criteria. These individuals are also responsible for making certain the team members understand:

1. The architecture and design decisions relevant to the timebox
2. What standards and procedures to follow
3. Any non-functional requirements that extend across timeboxes

The kick-off meeting is a one-time event that takes place at the start of every development cycle without exception. Don't forget to review lessons learned from previous timeboxes. During the course of the cycle, there is another administrative meeting that helps keep the timebox on track. This is called the Daily Stand-up Meeting.

Daily Stand-up Meeting

The Daily Stand-up meeting is a best practice based on the Daily Scrum from the Scrum Agile method. The biggest difference between the Daily Scrum and the SDLC's Daily Stand-up Meeting is that you won't see a pig or chicken in sight unless you're playing Farmville on the office computer. The work environment is and should be fun, but nowadays in corporate venues calling meeting participants chickens or pigs can result in complaints lodged with Human Resources for creating a hostile work environment. This is especially true if the terms are offensive to someone's personal belief system or faith-based practices. It's best to avoid any potentially offensive terms even if they are only meant in jest.

The daily stand up is not a typical status meeting nor is it a problem-solving or issue resolution meeting. As with the Daily Scrum, the meeting never exceeds 15 minutes in length and is held in the same place and at the same time every day. It focuses on what each team member accomplished yesterday and plans to achieve today. Hold the meeting early at the start of the day before the team becomes absorbed in their daily routine. All development team members are required to attend daily stand-up meetings. Business users may attend as observers. The business liaison, as an integral member of the project team, may actively participate. The overarching goal of the meeting is process transparency. Transparency leads to greater trust, open communication, better interpersonal engagement and increased satisfaction between the stakeholders and project team. Each active participant answers the following three questions which are the only questions to be discussed at a Daily Stand-up:

1. What did you do yesterday?
2. What will you do today?
3. Are there any obstacles that are preventing you from accomplishing your goal?

Through these meetings, the team gains an excellent understanding of the work that has been done and what remains to be completed. By discussing what is to be done today, the team members are making commitments and are accountable to each other to deliver on their promises. If there are any obstacles revealed, the issues are taken offline and dealt with by the development manager, project manager, business analyst or other responsible party after the daily stand up concludes. The parties responsible for resolving any issues are determined by the nature of the problems. Daily stand up meetings are easily adaptable to maintenance activities or as a general project/program management approach.

Test-Driven or Test-First Development

Principle #8: "Build systems with minimal defects."

Traditionally, developers write code or build a component, class or module and test and debug it repeatedly during the writing or build process or immediately thereafter. This type of testing is called unit testing. A unit is the smallest testable part of a system. A unit test verifies if the unit is fit for the purpose for which it is intended and meets the expected acceptance criteria for the requirements it addresses. Test-Driven Development (TDD), also known as Test First Development (TFD), is a unit testing best practice from Kent Beck's Extreme Programming Agile method. Beck is attributed with having developed or "rediscovered" the technique in his 2003 book *"Test-Driven Development by Example."* Beck's concept of test-driven development centers on two essential rules:

- Never write a single line of code unless you have first written a failing automated test
- Eliminate duplication

Test design takes place before any part of a unit is built by a developer. It relies on repeating very short development cycles in which the developer:

- Writes a failing automated test case to address a desired improvement or function
- Produces code to pass the test
- Refactors the code to acceptable standards

In his book, Beck states that TDD encourages simple designs and inspires confidence. Noel Llopis, in his 2005 article *"Stepping Through the Looking Glass: Test-Driven Game Development (Part 1),"* says, "TDD gives you the courage and the tools to dive in head first into any part of the code, even the scary parts, make any necessary changes, and walk away like a hero."

TDD critics complain that it takes more lines of code to write automated tests than it does to actually code a function. In reality, writing automated tests first reduces the volume of debugging required. Reducing the volume of debugging is proven to result in greater productivity gains. In a 2005 study that resulted in a paper titled *"On the Effectiveness of Test-first Approach to Programming,"* Hakan Erdogmus and Torchiano Morisio concluded, "We found that test-first students on average wrote more tests and, in turn, students who wrote more tests tended to be more productive."

Mike Clark, founder of Clarkware Consulting, developed a course called "The Test-Driven Development with JUnit Workshop." JUnit[80] is a simple open-source framework to write repeatable tests based on the xUnit architecture for unit testing frameworks. Primarily built for Java, JUnit has been ported to other languages including:

- Ada (AUnit)
- C# (NUnit)
- C++ (CPPUnit)
- Fortran (fUnit)

- Delphi (DUnit)
- Free Pascal (FPCUnit)
- JavaScript (JSUnit)
- Objective-C (OCUnit)

- Perl (Test::Class and Test::Unit)
- PHP (PHPUnit)
- Python (PyUnit)
- R (RUnit)

Clark says, "In fact, test-driven development actually helps you meet your deadlines by eliminating debugging time, minimizing design speculation and re-work, and reducing the cost and fear of changing working code."

Test-driven development requires developers to create automated unit tests immediately before writing the code itself. The test case defines a set of conditions or variables which determine whether a unit is working correctly or not. The conditions and variables must trace back to a prioritized business or technical requirement. The differentiating feature of test-driven development versus writing unit tests after the code is written is that the developer focuses on the requirements before writing the code. This may seem like a backwards approach, but it is a subtle but important difference.

Principle #9: "Make changes in the smallest steps possible"

What this all means is that the developer writes a single test for a very small piece of functionality, then writes a small piece of code and tests it. The size of the development steps should always be small—as few as 1 to 10 edits between each test run. The smaller the changes made the more effective the TDD. If new code does not rapidly satisfy a new test, or other tests fail unexpectedly, the programmer should undo the changes or revert to a previous version in preference to excessive debugging.

There are no doubts that TDD brings benefits to the SDLC as long as it is implemented correctly. According to Steve Loughran[81] of HP Laboratories, one of the greatest obstacles to implementing TDD is politics and the resistance to change. TDD represents a significant change to the most traditional development methods. As with any organizational change, top down

---

[80] Project hosted on Sourceforge.net
[81] Source: *"Testing,"* HP Laboratories November 6th, 2006. http://people.apache.org/~stevel/slides/testing.pdf. Accessed April 5, 2010

management support is essential because if the entire organization does not believe and embrace that test-driven development is going to improve the final product, the time spent writing tests is wasted. As an added benefit, TDD concepts may be applied to improving and debugging legacy systems developed with older techniques.

The topic of effective unit testing is very personal to me. For most of my professional life I worked as a developer. Over the years I've written hundreds of thousands of lines of source code in both procedural based and object-oriented languages. I have always taken great pride in turning over minimally defective working code to those who have contracted with me. Nothing is more irksome than a developer who sits down to write code and programs for hours without testing the code even once. Nobody is that good! These developers literally write hundreds of lines of code and then suffer through hours, days or weeks of debugging, never finding all of the mistakes they've made while writing. And then they're surprised when their code fails in system integration testing or worse yet, when it gets to production. Writing code in this manner is one of the poorest and worst habits a developer can nurture.

To illustrate what can result from these bad habits, I once worked with a contractor who wrote code as described. The system we were working on was for an application to support a corporate compensation cycle. We both sat in the same office at adjacent desks. He would code for days at a time without ever executing a single unit test. I never understood how he thought he could write good code with his approach. In contrast, if I change even a single character in a line of code that I've already tested and debugged, I rerun my tests and debug again.

After the system rolled into production, a nasty defect surfaced in a module he had authored which brought the production system to a grinding halt. The development manager asked him to debug the problem and apply a fix. We were all amazed when he fixed the problem and had the system back up and running in about 30 minutes. Later, I asked him about the problem, how he found it and fixed it so quickly. He said, "I don't know what's wrong with the code. I fixed the problem by changing the data so the bug's not there anymore." To fix his defect, he literally changed a critical data element on over 47,000 compensation records. It took the rest of the team almost two days to restore the system, fix the bug and undo his mess. Believe it or not, the manager didn't fire him. She slapped his wrist and said "don't do that anymore." In fact, she was angrier with me because I used harsh words to publically criticize his stupid move. Now do you see why there's a need for segregation of duty controls?

TDD offers more than simple correctness validation. It also drives the final design of the system. It may surprise you to learn that components built under TDD often look entirely different than those that are built first and then tested. This is because by focusing on test cases first, the developers think through the process of how the functionality is used by the stakeholders. The frequent nature of the tests helps to catch defects early in the development cycle. The unit is more thoroughly tested than can be achieved by other means. This results in a higher quality unit that is maintainable. Eliminating defects early in the process avoids lengthy and tedious debugging and rework and averts the defects from becoming endemic and inflating costs later in the project. One last advantage off TDD is that, when used properly, it ensures that all system units are covered by tests. This gives the development team and stakeholders a greater level of confidence in the system. Figure 103 is a model of the classic TDD approach.

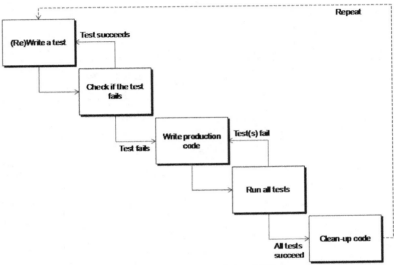

Figure 103 - Extreme Programming TDD Approach

The end goal for manufacturing any system and implementing an effective SDLC is to create products that meet or exceed our customers' expectations. Effective unit testing is the first wave assault in the development process toward achieving that objective. Unit testing is not expected to catch every error in a system. It is impossible to evaluate every execution path in all but the most trivial systems. By definition, unit testing only tests the functionality of the units themselves. It will not catch integration errors or broader system-level errors such as functions performed across multiple units or non-functional test areas such as performance or load balancing. Unit testing must be the first of many steps in the overall testing suite. Like all forms of system testing, unit tests only unearth the presence of defects; they cannot show the absence of errors or errors of omission.

The Development Cycle

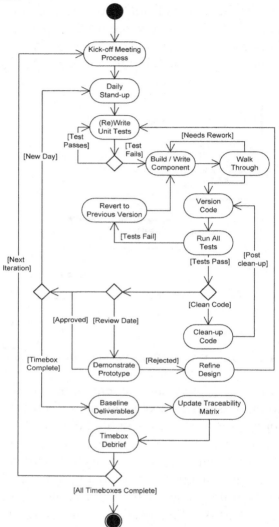

Figure 104 - SDLC Development Iteration

Even as the SDLC incorporates TDD principles into its development cycle, the SDLC approach is somewhat different than the classic TDD approach. Figure 104 is the SDLC's development iteration activity diagram. We've already discussed the importance of the kick-off meeting and its process as well as the daily stand-up. As we discuss the balance of the development iteration, please refer to the diagram as often as necessary to visualize how the various steps integrate in context.

To set the scenario for our deep dive into the development cycle, let's assume for this discussion that we have just started a brand new iteration. The kick-off meeting took place last Tuesday. All of the activities needing to be accomplished in follow-up to the kick-off are complete. Today is Monday of the new week and we are starting development. After the daily stand-up, the first day in the life of a development iteration proceeds with the developers writing failed automated tests against the specifications and requirements for the functionality that is assigned to them. We understand TDD requires writing tests first, but why a failed test? This might not make a whole lot of sense, but when you think it through, the test must inevitably fail the first time because it is written before the feature has been implemented, correct?

To write the tests, the developers must clearly understand the features that are to be implemented. This is where all the hard work invested in the modeling exercises during requirements elaboration and system analysis and design comes into play. The developer studies the use cases, user stories, textual requirements and models that cover the requirements, exception conditions and acceptance criteria. As the tests are written, the design may imply that variances, alternate paths or modifications to existing tests may need to be considered. Once these first tests are written, run them through the automated test harness. If the test fails, then development starts. If the test passes, something is wrong and the developer needs to determine just what that is and fix it so the test fails. The code is now written for the functionality being tested.

All of the methods we looked at in Chapter 2 follow a traditional approach to systems development except one, Extreme Programming. The traditional approach is assigning functionality to a single developer to work on those features, unit test them and migrate them to the next step when they are done. Extreme Programming is non-traditional in the sense that it incorporates a quality concept known as pair programming. There are varying opinions as to whether two developers can be as productive when working together as when working separately. Pair programming is where one developer actually sits and watches a second developer write code to make sure it is being written according to specification. The two programmers work on the same piece of functionality at the same workstation and swap roles throughout the day. In these days of tight corporate budgets, you may think that it doesn't make sense to keep two programmers tied up on a single piece of functionality, but pair programming advocates believe it results in a large number of benefits:

- Shorter programs, better designs, fewer bugs
    - To check in program code, it must be readable to both partners, not just the driver
    - Pairs typically consider more design alternatives than programmers working solo
    - Pairs arrive at simpler, more-maintainable designs
    - Pairs catch design defects very early
- Results in a large decrease in the defect rate and reduces software development costs

- Knowledge passes easily between pair programmers:
    - They share knowledge of the system specifics
    - They pick up programming techniques from each other as they work
    - New hires quickly pick up the practices of the team through pairing
- Collaborating pairs find that seemingly "impossible" problems become easy, quick or possible to solve
- Programmers report greater satisfaction and confidence that their work is correct
- There is less risk to management if one programmer leaves the team
- When working with a partner, developers are less likely to:
    - Skip writing unit tests
    - Spend time web-surfing or on personal email
    - Violating company computer use policies
- Paired partners "keep each other honest."
- Interruptions are less likely to occur when working in pairs than when working alone

Critics argue that pair programming doesn't work well for several reasons:

- Some developers prefer to work alone
- A less experienced or confident developer is intimidated when pairing with a more experienced developer and participates less as a result
- Experienced developers find it tedious to tutor a less experienced developer
- Experienced developers working alone are capable of producing clean and accurate code at the outset
- The benefits of paired programming are not worth the cost of an additional developer in some situations
- Personality conflicts can result in one or both developers feeling awkward or uncomfortable
- Differences in coding style may result in conflict.

There are a number of studies which seem to support either side of the argument. A Sept. 2001 article in *The Economist* called Agility Counts says, "Laurie Williams of the University of Utah in Salt Lake City has shown that paired programmers are only 15% slower than two independent individual programmers, but produce 15% fewer bugs. (N.B.: The original study showed that 'error-free' code went from 70% to 85%; it may be more intuitive to call this a 50% decrease of errors, from 30% to 15%) Since testing and debugging are often many times more costly than initial programming, this is an impressive result." The 2000 Williams study showed an improvement in correctness of around 15% and 20 to 40% decrease in time, but between a 15 and 60% increase in effort. The study also cites a 1998 study by Nosek which also had a 40% decrease in time for a 60% increase in effort."

A Lui 2006 study[82] presents a rigorous scientific experiment in which novice–novice pairs against novice solos experience significantly greater productivity gains than expert–expert pairs against expert solos. A larger 2007 study by Arisholm[83] et al. had a 48% increase in correctness for complex systems, but no significant difference in time, while simple systems had 20% decrease in time, but no significant difference in correctness. Overall there was no general reduction in time or increase in correctness, but an overall 84% increase in effort.

The conclusion of these studies is that pair programming seems to reduce the time to write code and produces fewer defects. Fewer defects in the coding process means less debugging time later and hopefully fewer defects in subsequent test suite steps. This results in a lower cost to produce the product. On the other hand, the studies also conclude an increased effort in development even though the time is shorter and Arisholm had mixed results for time and correctness, but a significant across the board increase in effort.

For these reasons, the SDLC is neutral on guidance as to whether to use paired programming or not. That's a decision each individual organization needs to make. However, the underlying principle for pair programming is quality. Quality practices are must have requirements throughout the entire SDLC. If there is no pair programming practices at your location to drive quality, there must be some type of peer review regardless. Peer reviews also help to enforce development and coding standards in a uniform manner. Whether working on hardware or software it is an important quality principle to check and double check the work being created through peer review. The SDLC process includes a walk though step immediately following the code/build step. How you conduct the peer review is up to you, just make certain someone double checks the work.

Before making any further changes and running all tests, check the source code into a version control system. If you don't have a version control system, consider it a priority to implement one. There are many version control systems on the market, and some very good ones are free. Every change made to source code should be versioned no matter how small or how large the change. Make it a firm habit in your development practices to check your code in and out regularly as you make changes. If a defect is introduced by any change it is much easier and cheaper to revert to the previous version and start the change again than to spend a lot of time and cost debugging a system. This is another reason why Principle # 9 is so important, "Make changes in the smallest steps possible."

[82] Lui, Kim Man; Keith C. C. Chan (September 2006). *"Pair programming productivity: Novice-novice vs. expert-expert."* International Journal of Human-Computer Studies
[83] Arisholm, Erik; Hans Gallis, Tore Dybå, Dag I.K. Sjøberg (February 2007). *"Evaluating Pair Programming with Respect to System Complexity and Programmer Expertise."* IEEE Transactions on Software Engineering

After versioning, run all of the tests and see if they succeed. If all test cases now pass, you can be confident that the code meets all the tested requirements. If the tests don't pass, you can either spend the time debugging the code or revert to the previous version saved under source control and begin writing the functionality again. The choice is yours but make your choice wisely based on the time needed for either task. The task with the shorter time to correction is the logical choice.

If the tests did pass, refactor the code. Refactoring code simply means cleaning it up. Make sure that any constants or magic numbers used to set up the tests are removed. Be certain to check that all of your comments and headers are updated and that all of your variables and constants meet the coding standards established by the SDLC. After refactoring is complete, version the refactored code and rerun all the tests to be confident that refactoring has not damaged any existing functionality.

If you are working on a prototype that needs to be reviewed by the stakeholders, schedule the meeting for the review date agreed upon during the kick-off meeting. If the prototype is for a user interface, assure that the stakeholders have a hands-on experience. If the stakeholders don't approve of the work that's been completed to this point, the design may need to be refined somewhat and the build process revisited. Be very careful to guard against scope creep at this juncture. If the stakeholders disapprove of the prototype because they want to add new functionality that has never been discussed or agreed to, accept the new requirement as a change management request and walk it through the process. Never add new functionality to a design without conducting the appropriate due diligence and receiving approval, otherwise it's gold-plating. If the stakeholders approve, move onto the next set of requirements for the timebox.

When the timebox is complete, and by complete it means that all agreed to timebox functionality has been finished, passed all tests, and the prototypes have been approved by the stakeholders or technical SMEs, baseline the timebox deliverables in the version control system and label them as ready for integration testing or with a predetermined release number. Update the traceability matrix and conduct the timebox debrief to capture lessons learned. The lessons learned are discussed in the next timebox kick-off. The participants for the timebox debrief include both stakeholders and the project team. Start the next timebox and continue to repeat the cycles until all promised functionality is complete. Integration testing may take place in iterations also. Whenever enough timeboxes have been completed to deliver sufficient functionality where an integration test makes sense, conduct an integration test. After all functionality is complete, a system test for all functionality is appropriate before moving to the next step in the testing suite.

Development and Coding Standards

No SDLC is complete without defining development and coding standards to provide a reference for a common vernacular and practices for systems development. A comprehensive development and coding standard encompasses all aspects of the system lifecycle. Standards are followed from inception to completion. Adhere to the standards whenever possible and thoroughly document why if you can't. Imposing standards after a project has been started is not realistic. Standards are applied to hardware or software projects. But since a major focus of the SDLC is application development, the standards presented in this SDLC are for software, but any principles learned can also be applied to the hardware environment.

Regardless of the number of developers on a project, standards help build solid coding techniques and good programming practices. Final source code reflects a harmonized style, as if a single developer wrote it all in one session. The purpose of good standards is to yield high-quality, well-performing code that is easy to maintain. Consistently applying well-defined coding standards and proper coding techniques to the development process and holding regular code reviews is going to produce a system that is easy to comprehend and maintain.

According to Microsoft's MSDN Library,[84] "The readability of source code has a direct impact on how well a developer comprehends a software system. Code maintainability refers to how easily that software system can be changed to add new features, modify existing features, fix bugs, or improve performance. Although readability and maintainability are the result of many factors, one particular facet of software development upon which all developers have an influence is coding technique."

The SDLC establishes the coding standard to ensure that all developers on the project are working synchronously. Sometimes, the platform in which you are working dictates the standards to follow. For example, if you are working on a customizable COTS application, the software vendor may provide standards to be followed when modifying their application. If developing in Java, Sun has a good coding standards document available. If working with Oracle, the standards may be completely different than for C#, Ruby or Python. And when the software project requires modifying existing source code or performing maintenance on an existing software system, the coding standard should provide direction on how to deal with the existing code base. For example, do you continue to version the base code or create a new branch in the version control system and leave the trunk branch intact? Or, do you go back and fix something that wasn't coded to standards the first time?

If you search the internet for coding standards and practices, you can find any number of well written documents related to the topic than can be adopted for your own internal purposes. One

---

[84] Source: http://msdn.microsoft.com/en-us/library/aa291591(VS.71).aspx, retrieved April 5, 2010

particularly excellent, well written document is *"General Style and Coding Standards for Software Projects"* authored by Michael Buckley, Department of Computer Science and Engineering, University at Buffalo, The State University of New York, Buffalo, NY 14260-2000. Thanks to Dr. Buckley you can benefit from this fine standards artifact because he has graciously granted his permission to include his paper on the accompanying CD. In doing so, Professor Buckley said, "You may use the document and distribute it with your book. I wouldn't mind attribution so the world knows that the University of Buffalo teaches and takes this seriously."

Pre-Implementation Activities and Artifacts

Are you wondering what the rest of the project team is doing while all this development work is taking place? One thing is for certain, they aren't sitting on idle hands. There are quite a few parallel work streams in the pipeline to ready the project for the quality assurance test battery, implementation and production turnover. There are monitoring and reporting activities to keep stakeholders apprised of the progress the team is making. There may also be project spotlight reports to an IT Governance group which tracks progress against budgets and schedules. Since the monitoring and reporting activities are generally defined by the project management method, the SDLC is concerned with the preparations for implementation, the test battery and production turnover. There are a lot of questions to be resolved and work to be performed before the next major stage gate, the Implementation Readiness Review. Many of the non-development SDLC activities initiated during the development phase spill over into the quality assurance test battery and complete just prior to the implementation phase.

Implementation Plan

The Implementation Plan describes how a system is to be deployed, installed and transitioned to a state of operational readiness. It provides the details necessary to perform the steps required to deploy the system into an operational environment and prepare the system for operational use. A key differentiator between the SDLC's Implementation Phase and all other lifecycle phases is that all project activities prior to implementation are performed in isolated, protected, safe and secure environments. Issues and mistakes that appear in these environments have little or no impact on day-to-day business operations. Once system deployment begins, this is no longer the case. Slip-ups during implementation almost certainly translate into direct operational and/or financial impacts to the organization. Only careful planning, execution and management can minimize the likelihood of these events. Plan suitable contingency tactics should it become necessary to invoke them.

The Implementation Plan is started during the Design Phase as system details emerge and is updated during the Development Phase. The artifact continues to be modified with the final version provided sometime during the QA Test Battery. It guides the activities of the Implementation Phase. Among other topics, most implementation plans address:

- System Overview
- Description of the Major Implementation Tasks
- Staffing Resource Needed
- Site-specific Requirements

- Contingency Plan
- Data Conversion Plan
- Detailed Test Plan
- Maintenance Manual
- Release Plan

- Operating Procedures
- System Security Plan
- Training Plan
- User Manual
- Version Description Document

These are not the only topics that may be addressed in the implementation plan. Topics vary based on your organization's needs and sometimes by where you live and the regulatory authorities you must follow. At a minimum, the first four topics are part of every Implementation Plan. A typical Implementation Plan outline includes:

- **System Overview**: comprised of the System Description and System Organization sections.
  - o **Description**: an overview of the processes the system is intended to support
    - ▪ For a database or an information system, a general description of the type of data maintained and the operational sources and uses of the data
  - o **Organization**: describes the system structure and the major system components essential to the implementation
    - ▪ Describes both hardware and software, as appropriate
    - ▪ Implementation models, charts, deployment diagrams, network maps and other graphics are captured in this section
- **Major Tasks**: a list of the major tasks required for the implementation of the system shown in chronological order with beginning and end dates
  - o Not site-specific, but generic or overall project tasks to install hardware and software, prepare data, and verify the system
  - o For every task, answer the following four questions in your narrative:
    - ▪ What does this task accomplish?
    - ▪ What resources do we need to accomplish the task?
    - ▪ Who are the key people responsible for the task?
    - ▪ What are the success criteria for the completion of the task?
  - o Examples of major tasks include:
    - ▪ Acquire any special hardware or software
    - ▪ Conduct Training
    - ▪ Ensure all artifacts applicable to the implementation are complete and available
    - ▪ Ensure all prerequisites are fulfilled before the implementation date, such as OS patching and testing, firmware upgrades, etc.
    - ▪ Overall planning and coordination for the implementation
    - ▪ Perform data conversion before loading it into the system
    - ▪ Perform pre-implementation site surveys

- Prepare site facilities for implementation
- Provide all necessary technical assistance
- Schedule any special pre-implementation computer processing
- Schedule implementation resources

- **Implementation Schedule**: schedule of activities to be accomplished during implementation
- **Security**: if not creating a separate System Security Plan, briefly describe the security features and requirements for the implementation
  - Include the primary security features associated with the system hardware and software
  - Discuss protection of sensitive data and information
  - Address how security is provided to prevent the compromise or theft of preloaded sensitive data during shipping, transport and installation of hardware
- **Implementation Support**: describe the support software, materials, equipment, facilities and personnel requirements for the implementation
  - **Hardware**: list of support hardware and equipment used for testing the implementation. For example, a network monitor or "sniffer" might be used with test programs to determine system performance at high-utilization rates
  - **Software**: list of software and databases required to support the implementation
  - **Facilities**: identify the physical facilities and accommodations required during implementation
    - Examples include physical workspace for assembling and testing hardware components, desk space for software installers and classroom space for training and/or rehearsing the implementation staff
    - Specify the hours per day needed, number of days and anticipated dates
  - **Material/Media**: list of required support materials, such as magnetic tapes and disk packs, supplies, etc.
- **Performance Monitoring**: describes the performance monitoring tools and techniques and how they help determine if the implementation is successful
- **Configuration Management Interface**: if your organization has matured to the point where you have deployed configuration management, describes the interactions required with the Configuration Management Database (CMDB) and CM Manager. Examples:
  - When software listings will be distributed
  - How to confirm that libraries have been moved from the development to the production environment
- **Site Specific Requirements**: describes site-specific implementation requirements if they differ from the overall project implementation requirements and procedures
  - If deploying to multiple sites and the requirements and procedures differ by site, repeat this section for each site

- **Site Implementation Details**: address the specifics of the implementation for a remote site. Include a description of the implementation team, schedule, procedures, database and data updates if they differ from the overall project details
- **Roll Back Plan**: specify when to make the go/no go decision and the factors to be included in making the decision. Provide a detailed list of steps and actions required to restore the site to the original, pre-conversion condition
- **Post-Implementation Verification**: describe the process for reviewing the implementation and deciding if it was successful.
  - Plan an action item list to rectify any noted discrepancies
  - Reference the Roll Back Plan for instructions on how to back-out the installation, if a no-go decision results due to the post-implementation verification

The rest of the topics addressed by the Implementation Plan are usually separate documents attached as addenda and started as early as the project's planning phase. Not every project is going to require all of the artifacts. Unless required for regulatory purposes, the SDLC empowers the project team to create only those artifacts deemed vital for the size and type of project they are developing. If the team chooses not to create a particular artifact, the rationale for why it is excluded should be mentioned in the Implementation Plan. Separate documents include:

- **Contingency Plan**: describes the strategy for ensuring system recovery in accordance with agreed to recovery times and recovery point objectives
- **Data Conversion Plan**: describes the strategies involved in converting data from an existing system/application to another hardware and/or software environment. It includes an inventory and cross reference of source and target data elements, schema, metadata and all self-describing files; process for data extraction, transformation and loading for each data source; tools needed to execute the conversion; and strategy for data quality assurance and control.
- **Maintenance Manual**: describes the sources of software components and other assets, how the architecture was implemented, the use of the architecture and assets and how it is to be maintained. Maintenance includes instructions and schedules for patch management.
- **System Security Plan**: describes the actual managerial, technical and operational controls, documenting the current level of security implemented within the system. The System Security Plan is initiated in the Requirements Analysis Phase and is continually refined during the Design Phase, Development Phase, and Test Phase. The SSP is finalized during the Implementation Phase. United States Government entities are required by the Federal Information Security Management Act (FISMA) of 2002 to create a System Security Plan for all information systems that store or process sensitive information.

- **Standard Operating Procedures**: documented procedures for performing tasks associated with equipment administration, network administration, application administration, system administration, data administration and database administration
- **Release Plan**: describes what portions of the system functionality are to be implemented in which releases and the rationale for each release, provided that is that the project is utilizing a phased release approach in its development and implementation. Iterative and incremental approaches should always include a Release Plan. The artifact is started in the Planning Phase, expanded during Requirements Analysis and finalized in the Design Phase.
- **Version Description Document**: the primary configuration control document used to track and control versions of software being released to testing, implementation or the final operational environment.

Detailed Test Plan

The detailed test plan builds on the test strategy artifact created during requirements analysis. System testing is the process of validating and verifying that a program, application, or systems product meets the business and technical requirements that guided its design and development and that it works as expected. Validation asks, "Have we built the right system?" Verification asks, "Have we built the system right?" According to the IEEE Standard Glossary of Software Engineering Terminology:

- Validation is the process of evaluating a system or component during or at the end of the development process to determine whether it satisfies specified requirements.
- Verification is the process of evaluating a system or component to determine whether the products of a given development phase satisfy the conditions imposed at the start of that phase.

The primary purpose for testing is to uncover system defects so they may be corrected. System testing can be implemented at any time in the development process. Unit testing and some integration testing are completed during the iterative and incremental development process. However, most test efforts occur after the development process has been concluded. Testing answers the question as to whether the system does what it is supposed to and needs to do. It is impossible for testing to establish that a product functions properly under all conceivable conditions. In addition to providing the guide to fixing defective systems, the results of system testing may be used to correct the processes by which the system is developed. Capturing metrics to drive a continuous improvement practice are an important aspect of system testing.

Testing is conducted against both the functional and non-functional requirements. Functional testing verifies a specific behavior or operation of the system. The behaviors are documented in the BRD. Functional tests answer the questions: "can the user do this" and "does this particular feature work." Non-functional testing refers to the system aspects that are not related to specific behaviors or user actions. Non-functional testing answers such questions as "how many people can log in at once" or "how easy is it to penetrate the system."

Not all system defects are caused by development errors. Gaps in the requirements are one common source of costly defects, but if the elicitation, requirements analysis and change management processes are followed diligently, these gaps are kept to a minimum if not completely eliminated. When system faults are the result of a development error, the most common cause is that a developer made a mistake which results in a defect. The mistake could be in the automated test harness or the system code. If the defect is executed, it produces incorrect results under certain circumstances causing a failure. Not all defects necessarily result in failures. For example, defects in dead code never result in failures. Defects can become failures when the operating environment is changed. Changes in the operating environment include a new hardware platform, alterations in source data or interacting with different external systems. A single defect may produce a wide array of symptoms.

Software testing methods are traditionally divided into black box and white box testing. These two approaches are used to describe the point of view that a test writer takes when designing test cases. Black box testing treats the software as a "black box"—the test designer is without any knowledge of internal structures of the component being tested. White box testing is when the tester has access to the internal data structures and algorithms, including the source code that implements them. There is a third testing method known as gray box testing (or "grey" if you prefer the U.K. spelling) that requires having access to internal data structures and algorithms for purposes of designing the test cases, but testing is conducted at the user or black-box level.

Black box testing methods include:

- **All-Pairs Testing or Pairwise Testing**: testing method that, for each pair of input parameters, tests all possible discrete combinations of those parameters
- **Equivalence Partitioning**: technique that divides the input data of a system unit into partitions from which test cases can be derived. Partitions represent valid or invalid ranges. For example, let's say you are testing a feature that accepts a numerical month as a parameter. The valid range for months is 1 to 12 which represent January to December. This valid range is called a partition. There are also two additional partitions of invalid ranges. The first invalid partition is <= 0 and the second invalid partition is >= 13.
- **Boundary Value Analysis**: testing technique for the range of a component's input or output boundary values on the edge of its equivalence partition or the smallest value on

either side of an edge. If the boundary tests pass, valid values falling between the boundaries also pass. This reduces the number of test cases required.

- **Exploratory Testing**: approach to system testing described as simultaneous learning, test design and test execution. Cem Kaner[85] coined the term in 1983 and defines exploratory testing as "a style of software testing that emphasizes the personal freedom and responsibility of the individual tester to continually optimize the quality of his/her work by treating test-related learning, test design, test execution, and test result interpretation as mutually supportive activities that run in parallel throughout the project."[86]
- **Fuzz Testing**: technique that provides invalid, unexpected or random data to the inputs of a component. If the component fails by crashing or failing built-in code assertions, the defects are documented
- **Model-Based Testing**: a model that describes all aspects of the testing data, test cases and test execution environment. The testing model is derived in whole or in part from the requirements and design models built during elicitation and elaboration activities
- **Specification-Based Testing**: tests the functionality of software according to the applicable requirements.[87] This testing requires thorough test cases to be provided to the tester. The tester inputs a given value and verifies the expected output value or behavior. Specification-based testing is necessary, but it is insufficient to guard against certain risks.
- **Traceability Matrix**: ensures that every requirement is traceable to the high-level design, detailed design, test plan, and test cases

White box testing methods include:

- **Application Programming Interface (API) Testing**: testing of the application using Public and Private APIs. APIs are interfaces implemented by system components to enable interaction with other components, similar to the way a user interface facilitates interaction between humans and computers.
- **Code Coverage**: quality metric that indicates the degree to which source code is tested. For example, the test designer creates tests to cause all statements in the program to be executed at least once There are a number of coverage criteria, the main ones are:[88]
  - **Branch Coverage**: Has every edge in the program been executed?
  - **Condition or Predicate Coverage**: Has each Boolean sub-expression evaluated both to true and false?

---

[85] Professor of Software Engineering, Florida Institute of Technology
[86] Cem Kaner, *"A Tutorial in Exploratory Testing,"* p. 36. (http://www.kaner.com/pdfs/QAIExploring.pdf) Accessed April 6, 2010.
[87] Laycock, G. T. (1993) *"The Theory and Practice of Specification Based Software Testing."* Department of Computer Science, Sheffield University, UK.
[88] Glenford J. Myers (2004). *"The Art of Software Testing,"* 2nd edition. Wiley

- o **Decision Coverage**: Has every control structure (such as an IF statement) evaluated both to true and false?
- o **Condition/Decision Coverage**: Both decision and condition coverage should be satisfied.
- o **Function Coverage**: Has every function or subroutine in the program been called?
- o **Statement Coverage**: Has every node in the program been executed?
- **Fault Injection Methods**: technique for improving the coverage of a test by introducing faults to test code paths, in particular error handling code paths, that might otherwise rarely be followed
- **Mutation Testing**: testing method which involves modifying source code or byte code in small ways.[89] Tests which pass after code has been mutated are considered defective.
- **Static Testing**: checks the sanity of the code, algorithm or document through syntax checking, code reviews, inspections, walkthroughs and manually reviewing the code or document to find errors.

White box testing methods are also used to evaluate the completeness of a test suite created with black box testing methods. This allows the software team to examine parts of a system that are rarely tested and ensures that the most important function points have been tested. Tests are grouped by where they are conducted in the system development process or by the level of specificity of the test, for example, unit and integration testing. Unit testing is discussed in detail earlier in the chapter. Tests to be addressed in the Detail Test Plan are:

Functional Testing

- **Integration Testing**: seeks to verify the interfaces between components against a system design. System components are integrated in an iterative way or all at once in a "big bang." The former is a best practice since it allows issues to be localized more quickly and fixed.
- **System Testing**: tests a completely integrated system to verify that it meets its requirements
- **System Integration Testing**: verifies that a system is correctly integrated to any external or third party systems defined in the system requirements
- **Regression Testing**: focuses on uncovering software regressions after a major system change has occurred. A software regression is a system defect which makes a feature stop functioning as intended after a certain event such as a system upgrade, system patching or a change to daylight saving time.
- **Acceptance Testing**: can mean one of two things:

---

[89] Source: *"A Practical System for Mutation Testing: Help for the Common Programmer"* by A. Jefferson Offutt (http://cs.gmu.edu/~offutt/rsrch/papers/practical.pdf). Accessed April 6, 2010

- o **Smoke Test**: used as an acceptance test prior to introducing a new build to the main testing process, i.e. before integration or regression
- o **User Acceptance Testing (UAT)**: testing performed by the customer, often in a lab environment, as part of the hand-off process between any two phases of development.
- **Alpha Testing**: simulated or actual operational testing by potential users/customers or an independent test team at the developers' site. Often employed for off-the-shelf software as a form of internal acceptance test before the software goes to beta testing
- **Beta Testing**: candidate versions of the software are released to a limited audience outside of the programming team so that further testing can ensure the product has few defects

Non-Functional Testing

Non-functional testing establishes the correct operation of the system environment and verifies that the software functions properly even when it receives invalid or unexpected inputs. Non-functional tests include:

- **System Performance Testing**: determines how fast a system or sub-system performs under a particular workload. Serve to validate and verify other system quality attributes such as:
  - o Scalability
  - o Reliability
  - o Resource Usage
- **Load Testing**: Tests that a system can continue to operate under a specific load, whether large quantities of data or a large number of users. Variations include:
  - o **Volume Testing**: method to test functionality
  - o **Stress Testing**: method to test reliability
  - o **Endurance Testing**: method to test performance
- **Stability Testing**: checks to see if the system can continuously function well in or above an acceptable period
- **Usability Testing**: checks if the user interface is easy to use and understand.
- **Security Testing**: essential for systems that processes confidential data to prevent system intrusion by hackers. This may also be called attack and penetration testing.
- **Internationalization and Localization**: verifies that an application still works after it has been translated into a new language or adapted for a new culture (such as different currencies or time zones)
- **Destructive Testing**: attempts to cause the software or a sub-system to fail in order to test its robustness, fail over or disaster recovery capabilities

For each of the tests documented in the test plan, there are seven particulars that encompass every detail needed to successfully conduct the testing process:

1. **Formal Entry and Exit Criteria**: every test has a precise entry and exit criteria. The criteria allow for the careful progression of the system development process. Fulfillment of the criteria triggers the movement from one testing stage to another. Entry criteria usually require all development to be complete, unit tested, integration tested, and the test environment setup and initialized. Exit criteria usually state the acceptable test coverage percent, that all tested requirements must pass the required acceptance criteria, ensure all test documentation is updated and complete, and the disposition of defects based on their severity level (e.g., Severity 1 & 2 defects 100% corrected, Severity 3 & 4 may be deferred to routine maintenance, etc.).
2. **Test Case**: a set of conditions or variables under which a tester determines whether system component is working correctly or not. Consists of a unique identifier, requirement references from the design specification, preconditions, events, the series of steps known as actions to follow, inputs, outputs, expected results and actual results. Actual results are captured as the test is run.
3. **Test Datasets**: multiple sets of values, data or changeable environmental components used to test the functionality of a particular feature
4. **Test Groups and Participants**: Who is conducting each test in the test battery? What are their roles?
5. **Test Procedures**: instructional artifact that teaches testers how to execute a suite of test cases
6. **Test Scenarios**: a scenario is a hypothetical story to help a person think through a complex problem or system for a testing environment
7. **Test Scripts**: a set of instructions that are performed on the system to test that it functions as expected

These details are thorough and ensure that every acceptance criterion captured during elicitation and subsequent phases are addressed. Writing a detailed test plan is a lot of work, but on the bright side, once tests are written to this level of detail, they are, as are requirements and components, reusable. Using a test repository tool, such as HP's Quality Center, makes the reusability part easy. After the tests are written, update the traceability matrix with the test details (test number or name) so that each requirement is traceable to one or more tests.

Now that we understand what goes into a detailed test plan, the question is, "Who writes the plan and test cases?" The answer is "it depends on your organizational structure and preferences." The SDLC clearly defines the roles and responsibilities of the test planning and documentation process, but as every organization is different, you'll need to decide who is responsible for what. In many cases, the business analyst is responsible for planning, documenting and guiding the testing. If your organization has a Quality Control or Quality Assurance Team, they may be responsible for either writing or supervising the construction of the tests. You may have a dedicated testing engineer as part of the project team on whose shoulders the responsibility falls. One popular emerging trend is to have a BA coordinate writing test cases for the User Acceptance Test with the end users who actually author the tests. There are many possibilities that need to be considered, but ultimately only you can decide the right fit for your culture.

Training Artifacts

For any project, the primary focus is on the development and delivery of a product that satisfies the business requirements and keeps the stakeholders happy. But what so frequently happens after the product is delivered to the intended audience is that the users realize they haven't developed the skills to use the new system properly. A few minutes of hands-on experimentation with a prototype is no substitute for a concentrated training experience. As a result, customer engagement and satisfaction decline, users express frustration with the new-fangled system and IT takes one on the chin because the project team is blamed for not delivering what they promised.

Skilled IT people are generally indifferent to user manuals and prefer to figure things out as they go along, referring to the manual only if completely stymied. They often forget that end users are not as tech savvy as they are. There are many end users who not only lack confidence in their own computer skills, but fear the machines as well. Some who do possess a confident attitude toward using computers have never graduated beyond the basics of Microsoft Office. These people need training to grow and prosper in their respective jobs. You won't see the envisioned bottom line benefits of a new system unless the end-users can successfully make the transition to using it. Training gives them the confidence and know-how to succeed. There's an old adage that goes something like this, "People might forget what you say and what you do, but they'll never forget how you made them feel." Proper training makes end users feel good about their jobs and the project team's performance.

Training is often one of the last priorities addressed by project teams as they scurry to meet the deadlines they've promised to senior managers. Yet, suitable training is one of the most important aspects of the project to drive user acceptance and commitment. A scalable end-user training program makes your new system deployment a more cost effective and pleasant experience for everyone involved. Training needs to be addressed long before the implementation takes place. It is partially addressed during the early stakeholder analysis phase and elaborated during the development phase. There are six steps necessary to build an effective training strategy:

- Assessing End User Needs
- Develop the Training Materials

- Setting Training Goals
- Determine the Training Delivery Methods
- Scale the Program
- Tailor the Training Program

Assessing End User Needs

The early stakeholder analysis should have included an evaluation of the technical skill level(s) of those who will actually use the new system on a daily basis. If this evaluation was omitted from the stakeholder analysis, plan and execute such an evaluation now. The survey method is an effective means for conducting the evaluation. As mentioned earlier, end-users are not particularly tech savvy, but may have different technical skill levels within a specific group. If that's the case, it's important to provide different levels of training. Novices need more focused, step-by-step instruction in the basics. Skilled computer users may quickly pick up the basics or skip over them entirely and benefit from additional training that shows them how to use the more difficult to understand or advanced features of the system. Attempting to train the two groups at once results in the novices being overwhelmed and confused and the more skilled users feeling that they are wasting their time and would be more productive if they would just be allowed to do their work.

Setting Training Goals

The primary objective in providing training is to minimize productivity losses associated with the transition to a new system. This means the end users have to get up to speed as fast as possible and acquire the skill level required for them to adequately perform their jobs. At the very least, they must be able to carry out their duties as quickly and accurately as they did before with the old system or manual methods. Once basic training is complete, the focus shifts to process improvements to help users do their jobs more rapidly, precisely, securely and at a lower cost than before. From the governance perspective, it's vital to be realistic about the timeframes in which you expect to accomplish these objectives. The timeframes are dependent on the complexity of the new system as well as the number of users who need training and their skill levels.

Determine the Training Delivery Methods

How will you deliver the training? Again, the answer depends on the number of users requiring training, their skill levels and your implementation strategy. For example, are you rolling the system out to everyone at once or are you planning alpha or beta phases or a limited pilot program and subsequent staged rollout? Depending on your implementation goals, there are a number of methods for delivering training. All vary in their levels of complexity and effectiveness.

- **Book-based, Self-paced Training**: A series of workbook lessons on how to perform common tasks illustrated with screenshots. Unless the completed workbooks are returned to a central training unit for evaluation, it is not possible to produce training metrics or track training progress using this method. People can receive the books and leave them sitting on their desks.
- **Computer Based Training (CBT)**: Self-paced training accessible via a computer or handheld device in which end-users complete interactive lessons that walk them through the processes of performing common tasks. The software tests and grades them on their performance and understanding. Often delivered through a Learning Management System (LMS). A LMS is software for delivering, tracking and managing training and education. It can distribute courses over the Internet and offers features for online collaboration. With an LMS, training can be assigned at individual and group levels and an administrator can track when the user takes the training and the score s/he receives. Metrics for this type of training can be tracked and evaluated for progress against organizational and personal goals. This is particularly effective in regulated environments where Standard Operating Procedures (SOP) must be mastered before operating manufacturing systems such as in the pharmaceutical industry. In fact, it is possible to integrate smart card technology with the LMS to assure operators are compliant with SOP training before a manufacturing machine can even be powered up.
- **Hands-on Classroom Style Instructor-led Training**: An instructor teaches users how the system works and how to perform common tasks with the students performing the tasks themselves in a classroom/lab setting. If at all possible, it's best to hold classroom training off-site to minimize distractions. When a class is held on the corporate campus, the temptation exists for users to sign the attendance sheet, stay in class for an hour or two, then leave to take care of work issues.
- **Individual Hands-on Instructor**: An instructor tutors each user individually through the process of performing common tasks and answers questions. This may be effective for small groups of users, but is cost prohibitive for large scale deployments unless you create a train the trainer program and ensure there are ample coaches to provide the education.
- **Seminar Style Group Demonstration**: An instructor shows a large group of users how the system works and how to perform common tasks in a live demonstration. Modern technology can effectively allow an individual to address a large number of students in a virtual classroom setting.

Of all the training methods available to you, the "tossing the kid into the water" method is the least effective of all. As a child, you may have learned how to swim when one of your parents picked you up and threw you into a swimming pool, lake, ocean or other body of water. Faced with the prospect of drowning, you figure things out pretty quickly to get yourself to safety. For an IT system, getting tossed into the water is where a system is deployed through automated means and it suddenly shows up on a user's desktop, maybe with a copy of the manual if you are lucky. The only paybacks you reap from this method are user frustration and an increase in help desk calls. But no matter which delivery method(s) you choose, conduct a pilot training program first for a small, select group of users that best represents your overall customer base. This helps identify issues with the various training methods before committing to them.

Develop the Training Materials

An important component of the training materials is the lesson plan. A lesson plan is a detailed description of the course and instructions for each individual lesson. Planning the material is much more difficult than creating and delivering the lessons. While there are many formats for a lesson plan, most lesson plans contain some or all of these elements, typically in this order:

- **Title of the Lesson**
- **The Purpose of the System and the Organizational Goals it Addresses**
- **How it differs from previous versions or the products it's replacing (if applicable)**
- **Time required to complete the lesson**
- **List of required materials**
- **List of Behavioral and Knowledge Objectives**:
    - What the student can do at lesson completion
    - What the student knows at lesson completion
- **Set, Lead-in or Bridge-in**: focuses students on the lesson's skills or concepts—these include:
    - Pictures or models
    - Leading questions
    - Reviewing previously lessons
- **Instructional Component**: describes the sequence of events that make up the lesson which includes:
    - The teacher's instructional input
    - Guided practice the students use to try new skills or work with new ideas
- **Independent Practice**: allows students to extend skills or knowledge on their own
- **Summary**: instructor wraps up the discussion, answers questions and discusses:
    - Common problems users may encounter
    - Security issues related to the system
- **Evaluation Component**: tests for mastery of the instructed skills or concepts

- **Analysis Component**: reflects on the lesson itself—such as what worked, what needs improving
- **Continuity Component**: reviews and reflects on content from the previous lesson

Developing the training materials takes the most time and may be the most costly part of the process depending on how you've decided to deliver the training. Many organizations have internal instructional design resources working in a Learning and Organizational Development Department or Company-owned University. These resources may be available to help develop training materials. If you have access to technical writers, they may be available to help create training documentation and manuals. Even with internal resources, you may find costs difficult to contain during this phase because of a company's accounting practices and internal charge back policies. Paying charge backs for fully loaded FTEs may exceed the cost of contracting with external service providers. If the costs exceed your budget, you may have to cut back on the quality of the training materials. Plan the training material development activities carefully.

CBT programs can be very costly to develop. CBT developers are specialists in their field and are experts with technologies such as Adobe Flash and standards such as SCORM. SCORM is a specification of the Advanced Distributed Learning (ADL) Initiative from the Office of the United States Secretary of Defense. The word "SCORM" is an acronym for Sharable Content Object Reference Model which is a collection of standards and specifications for web-based e-learning. It defines communications between client side content and a host system called the run-time environment, usually the LMS. SCORM also defines how content is packaged into a transferable ZIP file which it calls its "Package Interchange Format."[90] As of March 2009, SCORM 2004 (4th Edition) is the most recently published version of the standard.

As you develop the training materials, keep the following questions in mind as they all impact cost:

- Are user's guides and training materials going to be in color or gray scale?
- Will they be offset printed and bound or produced in-house?
- Do we use internal or external resources to write them?
- Are we producing CBT?
- Will the CBT be internally or externally hosted?
- Where will we get the instructors from?
- Will we conduct a train the trainer program?
- Are we going to use internal or external training facilities?
- Do we have to translate the materials into multiple languages?
- Is a single training approach adequate or do we have to consider multiple avenues?

---

[90] Source: http://www.scorm.com/scorm-explained/technical-scorm/, Accessed April 12, 2010.

Scale the Program

A training program has to be scalable to accommodate both small and large numbers of users. Small numbers may participate in pilot programs or the UAT, which also requires instruction in the test procedures. Large numbers occur when a system is deployed company-wide. The program also needs to be flexible enough to allow users to train on an ad hoc basis after the deployment training run is complete. For example, system training is usually required when a new employee joins the company. A combination of computer-based training and seminar-style training provides many of the benefits of individualized training without the high cost. CBT scales up or down depending on the number of users you train. Users proceed at their own pace rather than having to stay in sync with the rest of a class which frequently leads to its own frustrations. Seminar-style training can be recorded on video for later playback through the web which further reduces costs but provides high quality instruction although the interactive part is absent.

Tailor the Training Program

If you are developing training for a large, multi-divisional, multi-national company or other conglomerate, tailor the materials to each business unit's brand standards if there is no corporate brand standard. Use divisional or business unit logos, preferred type-fonts and business unit specific examples if appropriate. Doing so renders the end-user experience more enjoyable, memorable and effective.

Operational Turnover Artifacts

There are two main areas of concern when considering operational turnover matters: on-going support and maintenance. The end goal for building a new system or upgrading an existing system is to consign it to production with a minimal amount of disruption to the business. Ideally there should be no interruption at all. Production turnover should be a non-event from a business user perspective. The customers want the system to function as promised. Every once in a while, something may happen to cause the system to record data incorrectly, halt operations or raise questions from the users that require someone to provide further guidance and instruction in the system's operation. Many times these issues arise through user error or an embedded defect that remained either undiscovered or unaddressed during the quality assurance test suite. On-going support operations are intended to address these and other issues.

User error is generally the easiest problem to fix. The customer calls a technical support resource, whether a help desk support analyst or development team member, and receives guidance over the phone to correct their problem. If a problem is related to a defect and the customer discovers it through their normal day to day operations of the system, the initial process is similar to the user error problem. The customer calls a technical support resource to report the issue. The technical support resource triages the call to determine the nature of the problem by following a troubleshooting algorithm designed by the development team. If the problem is determined to be a defect or some other problem the technical resource cannot solve during the first call from the customer, the issue is escalated to higher levels of the tech support hierarchy.

To better serve a business or customer base, tech support is often divided into tiers or levels. The number of levels in a tech support group depends on what a business needs, wants or desires to satisfactorily sustain their customers or users. A multi-tiered support structure is proven to provide the best service in the most efficient manner possible. Technical support success is reliant on three facets of technician understanding:[91]

1. Their level of responsibility and commitments
2. Their customer response time commitments
3. When to appropriately escalate an issue and to which level

The most common technical support structure is the three-tiered system:

- **Tier 1, Level 1 or L1** is the initial support level responsible for basic customer issues. A Tier 1 support analyst collects the customer's information and attempts to determine the customer's issue by analyzing the symptoms and diagnosing the underlying problem. A goal for Tier 1 support is to close up to 80% of the problem calls before escalating the issue to a higher level.[92]

- **Tier 2, Level 2 or L2** provides more in-depth technical support than Tier 1. Tier 2 analysts possess experience and knowledge in a particular product or service. If a problem has never been encountered before or Tier 2 analysts cannot determine a solution, the issue is escalated to the Tier 3 support group.

- **Tier 3, Level 3 or L3** is the highest level of support responsible for handling the most difficult or advanced problems. Tier 3 analysts are experts in their field and are responsible for assisting Tier 1 and Tier 2 analysts and researching and developing solutions to new or unknown issues.

---

[91] Source: Walker, Gary (2001). *"IT Problem Management"* Prentice Hall
[92] Source: Kajko-Mattsson, Mira (July-October 2004). *"Problems within front-end support"*—*Journal of Software Maintenance and Evolution: Research and Practice*

Some organizations extend the three-tier support model to include a Tier 4 escalation route. Tier 4 is an escalation that moves outside of organizational boundaries to a third party provider or support organization. Tier 4 resources often include the hardware or software vendor. Tier 4 is invoked after all internal support paths have been exhausted and a problem remains without a root cause and resolution.

System maintenance is the second area of concern for operational turnover and gaining an understanding into the factors that impact system maintenance help reduce its costs. Meir "Manny" Lehman was a Professor and Head of the Computing Department at Imperial College London from 1972 to 2002. Over a twenty-year period beginning in 1974, Lehman and his colleague Laszlo Belady conducted research which led to the formulation of the eight "Laws of Software Evolution" which are also known as "Lehman's Laws." Software evolution is the process of initially developing a product and then repeatedly updating it for various reasons. As with other areas in this SDLC, the principles discussed here relative to software can be applied to all areas of system maintenance. Lehman's eight Laws[93] are:

1. Continuing Change—systems must be continually adapted or they become progressively unsatisfactory
2. Increasing Complexity—as a system evolves, it becomes more complex unless work is performed to maintain or reduce it
3. Self-Regulation—the system evolution process is self-regulating with distribution of product and process measures close to normal
4. Conservation of Organizational Stability—the average effective global activity rate in an evolving system is invariant over the product's lifetime
5. Conservation of Familiarity—as a system evolves, everything associated with it, (i.e., developers, sales personnel, users), must maintain mastery of its content and behavior. Excessive growth diminishes mastery.
6. Continuing Growth—the functional behavior of systems must be continually improved to maintain user satisfaction over their lifetime
7. Declining Quality—systems quality will appear to be declining unless rigorously maintained and adapted to operational environment changes
8. Feedback System—evolution processes constitute multi-level, multi-loop, multi-agent feedback systems and must be treated as such to achieve significant improvement over any reasonable base

For ease of understanding, Lehman's eight laws can be condensed into two:

---

[93] Source: *"On Understanding Laws, Evolution, and Conservation in the Large-Program Life Cycle"* —*Journal of Systems and Software*, Volume 1, Pages 213-221. 1980

- The Law of Continuing Change: a system undergoes continuing change or degrades in effectiveness
- The Law of Increasing Complexity: systems that are changed become less and less structured. Changes de-evolve the system from order to disorder and increase the complexity of the program

Based on what we've learned from Lehman, maintenance is an on-going series of activities to provide both corrective and non-corrective actions to a system. Many studies and surveys conducted over the years have shown that more than 80% of the total cost of system maintenance is spent on non-corrective activities over the lifetime of a product.[94] A robust maintenance organization is needed to make sure a system continues to operate at a level of efficiency to continue to satisfy or exceed the customers' expectations and demands. Routine maintenance activities include:

- Adapt System to Changing Environments
- Change Requests and Enhancements
- Improve System Design
- Improve Performance and Maintainability
- Latent and Effective Fault Correction
- Migrate Legacy Systems to New Platforms
- New Interfaces to Other Systems
- Sun-setting Obsolete Systems

When a product goes live, most project management methods include a short warranty period of perhaps 30-90 days where the development team supports and maintains the system to shake out any buried defects that may not have been uncovered during the quality assurance test suite. In addition to taking corrective actions, the development team functions as Tier 2 and Tier 3 support analysts until the warranty period expires. Once the warranty period expires, support and maintenance may fall under the responsibility of different teams.

The one common factor affecting all of the support and maintenance personnel is that they may not have gained any familiarity at all with the new system or process improvements during the project's lifecycle. This is especially true if the company has opted to outsource its support operations to remote vendors. Thus, operational support resources need as much training as the end users do, just in different topics. The project team is responsible for creating the operational turnover documents to support any training that must be supplied. Additional to the operational turnover documents included with the Implementation Plan, other artifacts include, but are not limited to, help desk scripts and service level agreements.

---

[94] Sources: A. Abran and H. Nguyenkim, *"Measurement of the Maintenance Process from a Demand-Based Perspective,"* Journal of Software Maintenance: Research and Practice, vol. 5, issue 2, 1993, pp. 63-90 and T.M. Pigoski, *"Practical Software Maintenance: Best Practices for Managing your Software Investment"*, first ed., John Wiley & Sons, 1997

Service Level Agreements

A Service Level Agreement (SLA) is part of a formally defined service level contract. A SLA is a negotiated agreement between two parties where one is the customer and the other is the service provider. In the case of the SDLC, the customers are your stakeholders and you are the service provider. The SLA is a record of the common understanding about services, priorities, responsibilities, guarantees, and warranties and may specify levels of availability, serviceability, performance, operation or other attributes, such as billing if used with external customers. SLAs are executed with internal or external customers, call centers or service desks, outsourcers or to control the use and receipt of cloud computing resources from and by third parties. SLAs commonly include sections to discuss:

- Definition of Services
- Performance Measurement
- Problem Management
- Customer Duties

- Warranties
- Disaster Recovery
- Termination of Agreement

Change Request

Change requests are the lifeblood of a project change management practice. When change management practices are in place in an organization, nothing can be moved into production without an approved change request. All too often, development teams wait until the last possible moment to file a change request. This can result in delays in the implementation. A good change management policy imposes a waiting period between when the change request is filed and when it can be executed. It needs to be reviewed by the CAB and the availability of the resources required for the change confirmed. A typical waiting/review time is five business days. In other words, the change request needs to be filed with the CAB at least five days before the change is scheduled to take place. This means it takes planning on the part of the project team to properly schedule the change request.

Change policies include provisions for emergency and exception changes. Emergency changes are for production down situations, like when an implementation fails and the roll back plan doesn't get executed properly. Exception changes are non-emergent changes that require implementation in less than the five day waiting period. Exception changes often occur in HR or Financial systems when there is a mandatory tax update or other regulatory update. There is no excuse for a project team to ever file an exception change request if they've planned their project properly.

Keep in mind that change requests apply to changes to all baselined artifacts as well as system changes. The outline of a good change request includes:

- **Header Details**
  - Change Request Title
  - Change Request Number (assigned by the CAB)
  - Requestor's Name
  - Requestor's Organization
  - Requestor's Phone
  - Requestor's Email
  - Date Submitted
  - Target Resolution Date/Event
- **Change Type**
  - New/Add Requirement
  - Modify Requirement
  - Delete Requirement
  - Documentation, Design
  - Hardware
  - Software
  - Firmware
  - Other (Specify)
- **Change Reason**
  - Legal/Legislation
  - Policy
  - Business-Better Understanding
  - Business-Improve Operations
  - Performance Tuning
  - Defect
  - Other (Specify)
- **Priority**
  - High (Emergency/ Mission Critical)
  - Medium (Urgent/Needed but not mission critical, Exception)
  - Low (Routine, Standard)
- **Version/Release, Requirement, and/or Problem Report Reference(s)**
- **Description**: include supporting documentation as appropriate
- **Impact Analysis**
  - Business/User Impact
  - Software/Module(s) Impact
  - External System(s)/Interface(s) Impact
  - Operations/Site(s) Impact

- o Hardware Impact
- o Data Impact
- o Documentation Impact
  - Include document name, configuration item control number, issuance date, section/paragraph number, page number, etc., as applicable
- o Training Impact
- o Security Impact
- o Schedule Impact
  - High (More than xx weeks)
  - Medium (xx to xx weeks)
  - Low (Less than xx weeks)
  - None (No Impact)
- o Cost Impact
  - High (More than $xx)
  - Medium (Between $xx and $xx)
  - Low (Less than $xx)
  - None (No Impact)
- o Budget Impact
- o Level of Effort: include impact on applicable SDLC phases
- o Basis of Estimate: rationale for impact assessment
- o Alternate Changes
- o Related Changes
- o Technical Recommendation
- o Miscellaneous Notes/Comments
- **Final Disposition**
  - o Decision
    - Approve
    - Disapprove
    - Defer
    - Request Additional Information
    - Escalated to <organization/committee/senior manager name>
  - o Decision Date
  - o Implementation Priority
    - High (Emergency/ Mission Critical)
    - Medium (Urgent/Needed but not mission critical, Exception)
    - Low (Routine, Standard)
  - o Planned Release
    - Schedule
    - Future/Current Release
    - Implementation/Deployment Date

- o Miscellaneous Notes/Comments
- **Submitting Organization's Approving Authority**
  - o Signature, Printed Name, Date, Phone Number, Position Title
- **CAB Approving Authority**
  - o Signature, Printed Name, Date, Phone Number, Position Title

Design & Development Phase Artifacts

There are 34 potential artifacts that can be delivered during the Design & Development Phase. Fortunately, they aren't all necessary for every project. This is another area where the SDLC grants project teams the discretion to choose from among the artifacts they deem necessary for the size and type of the project they plan to deliver. Large, major projects need all of them. Medium size projects need many of them but the size of the content will be reduced compared to a large project. For example, applying a major patch set to an ERP system may not require hardware performance testing or a data conversion plan. Small projects such as minor enhancement requests need minimal artifact content.

Artifact	Artifact Type	Description	Phase(s)
System Design Specification	Deliverable	The detailed system design	System Design, Development, Maintenance
Development and Coding Standards	Supporting Document	Organization and/or platform dependent standards for development and coding	Development
Unit Tests	Deliverable	Quality assurance tests design to test specific functionality of the components being created	Development
Implementation Plan	Deliverable	Describes how a system is to be deployed, installed and transitioned to a state of operational readiness	System Design through Implementation
Contingency Plan	Deliverable	Describes the strategy for ensuring system recovery in accordance with agreed to recovery times and recovery point objectives	Implementation, Production
Data Conversion Plan	Deliverable	Describes the strategies involved in converting data from an existing system/application to another hardware and/or software environment	Implementation
Maintenance Manual	Deliverable	Describes the sources of software components and other assets, how the architecture was implemented, the use of the architecture and assets and how it is to be maintained	Production Support

Artifact	Artifact Type	Description	Phase(s)
System Security Plan	Deliverable	Describes the actual managerial, technical and operational controls, documenting the current level of security implemented within the system	Requirements Analysis, System Design, Development, Test
Standard Operating Procedures	Deliverable	Documented procedures for performing tasks associated with equipment administration, network administration, application administration, system administration, data administration and database administration	Production Support
Release Plan	Deliverable	Describes what portions of the system functionality are to be implemented in which releases and the rationale for each release	Planning, Requirements Analysis, System Design, Implementation
Version Description Document	Deliverable	The primary configuration control document used to track and control versions of software being released to testing, implementation or the final operational environment	Implementation
Detailed Test Plan	Deliverable	Plan for conducting testing against both the functional and non-functional requirements	Test
Integration Test Plan	Deliverable	Test cases, datasets, procedures, scenarios and scripts for integration testing	Development, Test
System Test Plan	Deliverable	Test cases, datasets, procedures, scenarios and scripts for system testing	Test
System Integration Test Plan	Deliverable	Test cases, datasets, procedures, scenarios and scripts for system integration testing	Test
Regression Test Plan	Deliverable	Test cases, datasets, procedures, scenarios and scripts for regression testing	Test
Smoke Test Acceptance test Plan	Deliverable	Test cases, datasets, procedures, scenarios and scripts for smoke testing	Test
User Acceptance Test Plan	Deliverable	Test cases, datasets, procedures, scenarios and scripts for user acceptance testing	Test
Alpha Test Plan	Deliverable	Test cases, datasets, procedures, scenarios and scripts for Alpha testing	Test
Beta Test Plan	Deliverable	Test cases, datasets, procedures, scenarios and scripts for Beta testing	Test
System Performance Test Plan	Deliverable	Test cases, datasets, procedures, scenarios and scripts for system performance testing	Test

Artifact	Artifact Type	Description	Phase(s)
Load Testing Plan	Deliverable	Test cases, datasets, procedures, scenarios and scripts for load testing	Test
Stability Testing Plan	Deliverable	Test cases, datasets, procedures, scenarios and scripts for stability testing	Test
Usability Testing Plan	Deliverable	Test cases, datasets, procedures, scenarios and scripts for usability testing	Test
Security Test Plan	Deliverable	Test cases, datasets, procedures, scenarios and scripts for security or attack and penetration testing	Test
Localization Test Plan	Deliverable	Test cases, datasets, procedures, scenarios and scripts for internationalization and localization testing	Test
Destructive Test Plan	Deliverable	Test cases, datasets, procedures, scenarios and scripts for destructive testing	Test
Training Strategy	Deliverable	Plan for assessing end user needs, training goals, delivery methods, training materials, scaling and tailoring the program	Implementation
Lesson Plan	Deliverable	Details the target audience, by what means the training will be delivered and the schedule for training delivery.	Implementation and Production
End User Documentation	Deliverable	Any documentation required by the training strategy and lesson plan	Implementation and Production
End User Training	Deliverable	The materials, books, or CBT to be used for training users	Implementation and Production
Help Desk Scripts	Deliverable	Provides Tier 1 resources with details about how to troubleshoot potential issues to drive first call closure. Explains the escalation process if Tier 2 or higher support is required.	Implementation and Production
Service Level Agreements (SLA)	Deliverable	Formally defined service level contract between the stakeholders and project team.	Implementation and Production
Change Request (CR)	Deliverable	Change request to be authorized by CAB	All project phases including artifacts
Traceability Matrix	Deliverable	Updated to trace requirements to design elements, tests and documentation	All lifecycle phases after requirements are baselined
Quality Assurance Process Manual	Supporting Document	Comprehensive guide to all QA processes	All project phases
Change Process Manual	Supporting Document	Guide to the change management process	All project phases

Figure 105 - Development and Pre-Implementation Artifacts

Design & Development Phase Activity Diagram

Let's close this chapter with our best in breed SDLC activity diagram for the Design & Development Phase.

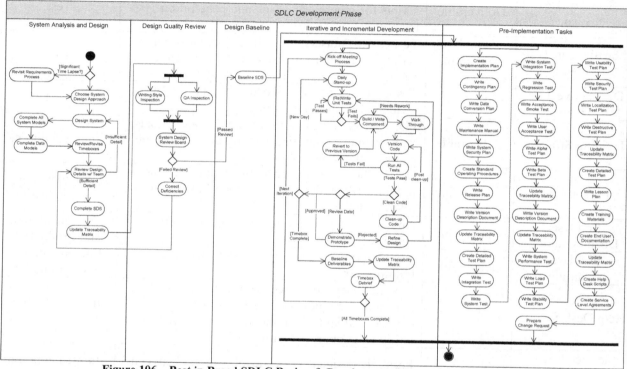

Figure 106 – Best in Breed SDLC Design & Development Phase Activity Diagram

Quality Assurance & Implementation

Principle #6: "Quality Assurance begins at project inception"

There are quite a few topics in IT that can be viewed from varying perspectives, some of which can easily lead to controversy and dispute. For example, a question posted[95] on LinkedIn's IIBA Group resulted in 54 responses that took on the tone of a hotly contested debate. The question is, "Why does there seem to be a 'rivalry' between Project Managers and Business Analysts?" The poster doesn't appear as though she intended to start a debate, but seems to be seeking a real answer to the question. When she posed her question, she said it was for research in preparation to present at the annual Symposium of the Project Management Institute in Detroit and is looking to inject a little humor into her speech. It is clear from the respondents' answers that diversity of opinion, not humor, is the order of the day. And while diversity of opinion can sometimes be humorous in a debate, it does not plot a rational course for the SDLC. The SDLC must be based on recognized best practice, not opinion.

In this chapter, we're going to begin by discussing a set of fundamental questions that often lead to differences of opinion. They are related to Principle #6 that was introduced in Chapter 6 when we discussed Requirements Inspection, "Quality Assurance begins at project inception." Most everyone agrees that the standard of applying quality assurance practices from the start of a project is a sound principle. You probably agree as well. Everyone wants to succeed in their jobs and deliver products that meet or exceed customers' expectations. If we don't believe that, then we have no business being in IT.

The problem that arises is that the approaches organizations take to achieve quality practices vary as much as the opinions posted in response to the LinkedIn question. A root cause is that there are differences in opinion about what the term "Quality Assurance" exactly means. It is often confused with Quality Control which is an entirely different genus altogether. So the questions we're going to discuss are:

- What is quality?
- How does the SDLC help manage quality?
- Who owns quality?
- What are the differences between Quality Control and Quality Assurance?

---
[95] Question posted on March 28, 2010 by Michele Wilke.

- What are three common misconceptions about quality?

If you want to have a little fun, before reading any further and moving onto the answers, frame your own answers to the five questions above, then compare your answers to the ones provided below to see just how well you agree or disagree with them. We're working on the honor system here so promise you won't read ahead until you finish answering the questions for yourself.

What is Quality?

Merriam-Webster's Collegiate Dictionary (Eleventh Edition) defines quality as:

- degree of excellence : GRADE
- superiority in kind

When applied to the SDLC, quality is the characteristic identified by:

- Outputs that satisfy or exceed an agreed upon set of requirements
- Assessed using agreed upon metrics and acceptance criteria
- Produced using an agreed upon process

How Does the SDLC Help Manage Quality?

The SDLC is the process by which a development team builds a quality system product. The system product is an aggregate of many artifacts including:

- Deployed artifacts:
  - o Executable application code, hardware system, etc.
  - o Non-executable artifacts such as user manuals and course materials
- Non-deployed artifacts:
  - o Executables such as automated test scripts and tools used to support development and implementation
  - o Non-executable artifacts such as the implementation plan, test plans and models

The SDLC manages quality in every one of its workflows:

- **Requirements**:
  - o Consistency: Inspection of the requirements artifacts for consistency between artifact standards and other artifacts

- o Clarity: clearly communicates good, lean requirements to all stakeholders and project team members
  - o Precision: appropriate level of detail and accuracy
- **System Analysis and Design**:
  - o Consistency: assessment of the design artifact(s) including the design models
  - o Completeness:
    - Its translation from the requirements artifacts
    - Its translation into the implementation artifacts
- **Development**:
  - o Test-Driven Development:
    - Write unit tests first
    - Test every change regardless of how small or seemingly insignificant
  - o Incremental Changes: make the smallest possible changes one at a time
  - o Peer Reviews: use a second pair of eyes to validate the development work with either pair programming or code reviews
- **Test Battery**: highly focused suite of tests to manage quality
- **Implementation**:
  - o Confirm implementation readiness
  - o Rehearse deployments
  - o Confirm Production Readiness

Who Owns Quality?

Quality is everyone's responsibility. Everyone means all stakeholders and project team members. Quality is *not* the responsibility of or owned by a single group or department. Everyone means everyone! Every person in an organization contributes to the achievement of quality in the following ways:

- **Process Quality**: the achievement of quality in the activities in which any person is involved
- **Product Quality**: the contribution to the overall achievement of quality in each artifact being produced

What are the Differences between Quality Control and Quality Assurance?

Quality Control focuses on the product or deliverable, is reactive and emphasizes testing of products to uncover defects after the fact, in other words, after the product is built. Quality Assurance focuses on the process, is proactive, attempts to improve and stabilize production and associated processes to avoid or at least minimize issues that lead to defects in the first place.

- **Quality Control** is checking a final product or deliverable to ensure that it is defect or error free and meets specifications.
    - Focuses on the end product or deliverables
    - Occurs after the development process is complete
    - Verifies that the product or deliverable meets specifications
    - Detects errors and defects in the final product before deployment to the customer

- **Quality Assurance** is the proactive method of establishing a program to ensure that standards of quality are being met for the systematic monitoring and evaluation of the various aspects of a project, service or facility to produce a product or deliverable that is error or defect free
    - Establishes a sound and capable process
    - Upfront planning and designing of a repeatable, measurable process that produces high quality products or deliverables
    - If the process is properly followed, gives a high degree of confidence that the final product or deliverable meets or exceeds specifications
    - Ensures products are suitable for their intended purpose ("fit for purpose")
    - Reduces and prevents defects or errors in the final product or deliverable by building the product right the first time

What are Three Common Misconceptions about Quality?

The first common misconception about quality is that it can be tested into a product. It cannot. Testing is the evaluation of a product or process to determine if it meets specifications. Specifications begin with the requirements and flow through every aspect of the system development lifecycle. Quality must be built into the process starting with the requirements, applied throughout the construction of the deliverables and evaluated at every stage of their development from requirements to implementation.

If you've ever enjoyed the privilege of building a home, you can think of a systems development project in a similar fashion. Every phase in building a home is reviewed by municipal inspectors to certify the proper materials are used and the home's components meet the local building code. If any phase or component fails to pass a quality inspection, forward construction is halted until the builders or subcontractors redress the violation (defect) by reworking the component and/or providing the proper materials. Only when all inspections are satisfactorily achieved, does the owner receive the certificate of occupancy for their new home, the equivalent of moving the system into production.

But what if the on-going inspection process didn't exist? What if the municipal authorities only performed a final quality control check after the house is complete? They look for defects, but the only details they can thoroughly examine are on the surface. They can test to see if the lights work, the toilets flush and the water runs, but they can never peer inside the walls, ceilings and floors to examine if materials were used for the plumbing and electrical wiring that meet the specifications. If faulty materials are used and not discovered, the home owner may experience the consequences of the hidden defects…a fire or flood which results in a significant impact to their finances and quality of life. All the testing in the world does not build quality into a new home after it has been constructed. Nothing short of stripping the walls down to the studs will allow for the proper materials to be retro fitted or reworked. In a systems sense, if the defects aren't caught early, the rework can bring astronomical economic consequences to the business.

A second misconception is that quality is a single dimension. It is not. Quality is multi-dimensional and measurable in terms of:

- Function: the artifacts implement and execute the requirements and use-cases as intended
- Performance: the artifacts execute and respond according to specification
- Progress: such as demonstrated use-cases or milestones completed
- Reliability: resistance to failure such as crashing, hanging, memory leakages, etc.
- Variance: differences between planned and actual schedules, budgets, staffing requirements, etc.

A third misconception is that Quality Assurance and Quality Control are mutually exclusive; if you have a Quality Assurance process, there is no need for Quality Control and vice versa. This is a fallacious notion. Quality Assurance does not eliminate the need for Quality Control. Quality Control activities are one of the many facets of an overall Quality Assurance program. Therefore, Quality Control practices are a subset of Quality Assurance practices.

Quality Models and Standards

There are many quality models and standards that can be applied to an organizational quality assurance program. No discussion of quality assurance programs is complete without at least a brief mention of two of the most well-known and ubiquitous methodologies: Total Quality Management and Six Sigma.

Modern quality techniques came into being after World War II when General Douglas MacArthur brought W. Edwards Deming and management consultant Joseph M. Juran[96] with

---

[96] Source: Juran, Joseph M. (2004), *"Architect of Quality: The Autobiography of Dr. Joseph M. Juran (1 ed.),"* New York City: McGraw-Hill

him to Japan to assist in the rebuilding of the country and the redevelopment of the Japanese economy. Deming is most well-known for conceptualizing the much-favored quality methodology, Total Quality Management (TQM). In an article titled "Six Sigma vs. Total Quality Management," [97] Tony Jacowski explains TQM this way:

> Total Quality Management is often associated with the development, deployment, and maintenance of organizational systems that are required for various business processes. It is based on a strategic approach that focuses on maintaining existing quality standards as well as making incremental quality improvements. It can also be described as a cultural initiative as the focus is on establishing a culture of collaboration among various functional departments within an organization for improving overall quality.

TQM's primary goals are:

- Aim for the modernization of equipment
- Ensure workers have the highest level of training
- Increase customer satisfaction
- Limit errors to 1 per 1 million units produced
- Reduce the errors produced during the manufacturing or service process
- Streamline supply chain management

TQM contributes greatly to a newer business management strategy known as the Six Sigma quality approach developed by Bill Smith of Motorola. It's not clear when Bill Smith actually formulated Six Sigma for Motorola. Sources place the date as anywhere from 1981 to 1987 with at least one reference stating Bill Smith didn't begin working for Motorola until 1987. No matter what the date, Bill Smith is "The Father of Six Sigma."

Since its inception, Six Sigma has evolved into an all-encompassing management tool for change and customer quality. Early adopters of Six Sigma such as Honeywell and General Electric achieved well-publicized success.[98] By the late 1990s, approximately two-thirds of the Fortune 500 companies had started Six Sigma initiatives to reduce costs and improve quality.[99] Most recently, some Six Sigma practitioners have combined the principles of lean manufacturing to form a hybrid methodology called Lean Six Sigma.

---

[97] Source: http://www.pmhut.com/six-sigma-vs-total-quality-management, Accessed April 20, 2010

[98] Source: *"Six Sigma: Where is it now?"* http://scm.ncsu.edu/public/facts/facs030624.html. Accessed April 20, 2010

[99] Source: De Feo, Joseph A.; Barnard, William (2005). *"JURAN Institute's Six Sigma Breakthrough and Beyond - Quality Performance Breakthrough Methods."* Tata McGraw-Hill Publishing Company Limited

Geoff Tennant[100] says Six Sigma can be seen as:

- A Vision
- A Philosophy
- A Symbol
- A Metric
- A Goal
- A Methodology

Jiju Antony[101] explains, "Six Sigma seeks to improve the quality of process outputs by identifying and removing the causes of defects (errors) and minimizing variability in manufacturing and business processes. It uses a set of quality management methods, including statistical methods, and creates a special infrastructure of people within the organization ('Black Belts,' 'Green Belts,' etc.) who are experts in these methods."

The term "Six Sigma" originates from terminology associated with the statistical modeling of manufacturing processes. The maturity of a manufacturing process is described by a sigma rating indicating its yield or the percentage of defect free products it creates. A six sigma process is one in which there are 3.4 defects per million opportunities. Stated differently, 99.99966% of the manufactured products are defect free. Wouldn't it be great to produce IT systems with comparable metrics for every single project we encounter?

The ISO 9000 series defined by the International Standards Organization provides specifications for quality systems. ISO 9126-1 establishes a software quality model. The first part of the standard classifies software quality in a structured set of characteristics and sub-characteristics as follows:

- **Efficiency**: attributes describing the relationship between the level of performance of the system and the resources amount of used under specified conditions
  - Resource Behavior
  - Time Behavior
- **Functionality**: attributes of functions that satisfy stated or implied needs. Examples:
  - Accuracy
  - Compliance
  - Interoperability
  - Security
  - Suitability
- **Maintainability**: attributes describing the effort needed to make specified modifications
  - Analyzability
  - Changeability

---

[100] Source: Tennant, Geoff (2001). *"SIX SIGMA: SPC and TQM in Manufacturing and Services."* Gower Publishing, Ltd. p. 7
[101] Source: Antony, Jiju. *"Pros and cons of Six Sigma: an academic perspective."* Accessed April 20, 2010 at http://www.onesixsigma.com/node/7630

- o Stability
- o Testability
- **Portability**: the ability of software to be transferred from one environment to another
  - o Adaptability
  - o Conformability (e.g. conformance to a particular database standard)
  - o Installability
  - o Replaceability
- **Reliability**: the capability of a system to maintain its level of performance under stated conditions for an agreed upon period of time.
  - o Fault Tolerance
  - o Maturity
  - o Recoverability
- **Usability**: the effort needed for use and the individual assessment of such use by a stated or implied set of users
  - o Learnability
  - o Operability
  - o Understandability

The ISO 9126-1 standard provides organizations with a framework to define a quality model for a systems product. In addition to the ISO 9126-1 standard, other models that specify quality assurance practices, procedures and specialized activities include:

- Advance Product Quality Planning (APQP)
- Capability Maturity Model Integration (CMMI)
- Failure Mode and Effects Analysis (FMEA)
- Measurement Systems Analysis (MSA)
- Quality Function Deployment (QFD)
- U.S. Department of Defense (DOD) standards

The weakness with most, if not all, quality models is that they leave the task of specifying details of the model up to each individual organization. They define the "whats" that need to be done, but not the "hows" for getting there. They tell you where your final destination is but leave the GPS navigation up to you without any direction for plotting the route. Most organizations reach their destination by defining acceptable target values for quality metrics which evaluate the degree of compliance to the company's specified quality attributes.

In practice, it is important to realize that quality measurements are determined by the intended users, clients or customers in conjunction with IT leadership. They are not defined by the IT society in general. Quality metrics are defined as the acceptance criteria during requirements elicitation.

Quality models are generally documented apart from the SDLC, usually by a QA or enterprise architecture group. While the model can be delegated to the SDLC, the SDLC functions as a process guideline to ensure the development of a quality product. It serves as a constant reminder of this thought attributed to William Adlebert Foster:[102]

> Quality is never an accident; it is always the result of high intention, sincere effort, intelligent direction and skillful execution; it represents the wise choice of many alternatives.

There are many books on the market related to Quality Assurance and its processes and practices. One good reference source is the *"Handbook of Software Quality Assurance (Fourth Edition)"* edited by G. Gordon Schulmeyer and published by Artech House (2008). Another one is the *"Handbook of Software Reliability Engineering"* Michael R. Lyu, Editor; IEEE Computer Society Press/McGraw-Hill.

The Pareto Principle and Quality Assurance

If you recall from the Pareto principle discussion in Chapter 1, the Pareto principle roughly says 80% of the effects come from 20% of the causes. The principle is also known as the 80-20 rule, the law of the vital few or the principle of factor sparsity.

Barry Boehm (Spiral and ICM development models) provides information that systems phenomena follow a Pareto distribution:[103]

- 20% of the modules consume 80% of the resources;
- 20% of the modules contribute 80% of the errors;
- 20% of the errors consume 80% of repair costs;
- 20% of the enhancements consume 80% of the adaptive maintenance costs;
- 20% of the modules consume 80% of the execution time;
- 20% of the tools experience 80% of the tool usage.

According to Thomas J. McCabe and G. Gordon Schulmeyer:[104]

---

[102] William Adlebert Foster is a United States Marine who earned the Congressional Medal of Honor in 1945 during the World War II Battle of Okinawa for "conspicuous gallantry and intrepidity at the risk of his life above and beyond the call of duty"
[103] Source: Boehm, B., *"Industrial Software Metrics Top 10 List,"* IEEE Software, © IEEE September 1987, pp. 84–85.
[104] Source: *"Handbook of Software Quality Assurance (Fourth Edition)"* page 121

The Natural Law of Software Quality says that Pareto's rule holds true, especially in software systems: 20% of the code has 80% of the defects—Find them! Fix them! Remember from Fred Brooks' analysis of the development of OS/360 for IBM Corporation: 4% of OS/360 had more than 60% of the errors. Similarly, on a reusable software library, two of the first 11 modules (20%) had all of the errors.

Juran applied the Pareto Principle to quality management in 1941 and proposed to "concentrate on the vital few, not the trivial many." In later years Juran amended his view to "the vital few and the useful many," signaling that the remaining 80% of the causes should not be totally ignored. Following Juran's line of thinking, defects should never be ignored. Every requirement must be tested to ensure it meets its acceptance criteria, but 20% will result in the most severe defects.

The reality is that there can be so many defects in a system product that it is virtually impossible to eliminate them all, even with the most stringent quality assurance program. It is not possible to conceive a test for every potential conditional variation and environment change. Therefore it is important to have a system of classification for defects that prioritize them according to their severity. The most serious defects receive the highest priority and are the ones that are addressed first.

Defect Classification

ISO 9000 defines a defect as a non-fulfillment of a requirement related to an intended or specified use. Over the years there have been many attempts to classify defects in a standardized way. Unfortunately, defect classification is not as clear cut as the MoSCoW method is for prioritizing requirements. This is because defect classification is a subjective human process prone to human errors, confusion and lack of understanding of the data. What one person considers a severe or critical defect may be a minor or moderate defect to someone else. And when building a defect classification system for a growing IT organization, it'll usually start out as a very simplistic quality control approach using perhaps a two dimensional matrix of severity and priority. For example:

Defect Classification	Description	Defect Priority	Description
Critical	Show stopper, system down (think Microsoft Blue Screen of Death)	Immediate, Severity 1	Fix immediately, all hands on deck
Major	System not working according to specification or variability in functionality—no work around available	As Soon as Possible, Severity 2	Schedule as soon as resources are available. Deploy to production as soon as the fix is complete
Minor	System not working according to specification or variability in functionality—work around available	Normal, Severity 3	Resolve the defect within the course of normal business operations and deploy in a future routine maintenance procedure
Cosmetic	Error detected in the user interface or navigation controls	Schedule, Severity 4	Low priority, no system functionality impact, can be resolved when resources are available and no higher priority defects exist. Deployed in routine maintenance procedure

Figure 107 - Simple Approach to Defect Classification

While this two dimensional system is fine for driving change management decisions and for prioritizing and scheduling defect repair work, it is not a true defect classification system. As organizations achieve process maturity and quality control practices progress into a quality assurance program, the defect classification system also needs to evolve to include in-process measurement for the system development processes. Remember, quality assurance is about defect prevention. The Software Engineering Institute defines defect prevention as a process with the purpose to:

- Identify the common causes of defects, and
- Change the relevant process(es) to prevent that type of defect from recurring

A defect in a system means there is also a defect in the injection and/or detection processes. For defect prevention to work, system defects have to be turned into actionable process defects. During the 1990s, Ram Chillarege of the IBM T. J. Watson Research Center in Yorktown Heights, New York developed the Orthogonal Defect Classification (ODC) system. ODC is a methodology to capture the semantics of in-process and field system defects quickly, characterize them and translate them into actionable process defects. Using ODC, skilled practitioners can classify defects in two minutes or less as compared to the hour or more per defect required for causal analysis; and ODC is less susceptible to human error. In response to the human error concerns mentioned above, Chillarege says:

…each of these concerns can be handled if the classification process is simple, with little room for confusion or possibility of mistakes, and if the data can be easily interpreted. If the number of classes is small, there is a greater chance that the human mind can accurately resolve between them. Having a small set to choose from makes classification easier and less error prone. When orthogonal, the choices should also be uniquely identified and easily classified.

If you recall from your math classes, the term "orthogonal" means either "intersecting or lying at right angles" or "having perpendicular slopes or tangents at the point of intersection." ODC essentially means that we categorize a defect into classes that collectively point to the part of the process which needs attention, much like characterizing a point in a Cartesian system of orthogonal axes by its (x, y, z) coordinates.[105]

In ODC, the orthogonal axes are defect, type and trigger. A goal of ODC is to gather the right data to relate cause attributes with their effect to provide knowledge to the organization for on-going learning. The learning is accomplished through two types of defect analysis: causal analysis and trigger analysis. Causal analysis characterizes process issues that lead to the injection of defects. Trigger analysis characterizes process issues that allow defects to leak through to later phases of the system development life cycle. To prevent system defects means the process that permits their introduction needs to be repaired.

Defect causal analysis is performed in a series of six steps:[106]

1. Identify a set of defects
2. Identify Defect Types with a team of subject matter experts
3. Plot the distribution of Defect Types
4. Map Defect Types back to development activity
5. Develop an action plan to address process deficiencies
6. Monitor processes to ensure changes are effective

In explaining defect types, Chillarege says, "The ideas on Orthogonal Defect Classification become much clearer when we discuss the **defect type** attribute. A programmer making the correction usually chooses the defect type. The selection of defect type is implied by the eventual correction. These types are simple, in that they should be obvious to a programmer, without

---

[105] Source: "ODC for Process Measurement, Analysis and Control," Ram Chillarege Accessed April 20, 2010, http://www.chillarege.com/odc/articles/asqc/asqc.html

[106] Source for analysis steps: *"Software Defect Prevention Using Orthogonal Defect Classification"* presented by Megan Graham, Twin Cities Software Process Improvement Network, January 6, 2005. http://twin-spin.cs.umn.edu/files/ODC_TwinSPIN_010605.ppt, Accessed April 20, 2010

much room for confusion. In each case a distinction is made between something *missing* or something *incorrect*."

Defect Trigger Analysis is also performed in a series of six steps:

1. Identify a set of defects
2. Identify the Defect Trigger with a team of subject matter experts
3. Plot distributions:
   a. Defect Trigger by Family
   b. Review Triggers
   c. Function Test Triggers
   d. System Test Triggers
4. Map the Defect Trigger family back to detection activities
5. Develop an action plan to increase missed Defect Triggers
6. Monitor processes to ensure changes were effective

A defect trigger is a condition that allows a defect to surface. Of triggers, Chillarege says, "The concept of the trigger provides insight not on the development process directly, but on the verification process. Ideally, the defect trigger distribution for field defects should be similar to the defect trigger distribution found during system test. If there is a significant discrepancy between the two distributions, it identifies potential holes in the system test environment."

Since the initial release of ODC, the IBM Center for Software Engineering has expanded the scope of the categories that capture the semantics of a defect from the two perspectives of defect opener and defect closer. ODC Version 5.11 website says,[107] "When a defect is opened, the circumstances leading to the exposure of a defect and the likely impact to the user are typically known. When a defect is closed after the fix is applied, the exact nature of the defect and the scope of the fix are known." The expanded defect classification attributes are now captured in opener and closer sections[108] as depicted in the Figure 108 model.

[107] Source: http://www.research.ibm.com/softeng/ODC/ODC.HTM, Accessed April 20, 2010
[108] Source: http://www.research.ibm.com/softeng/ODC/ODC.HTM, Accessed April 21, 2010

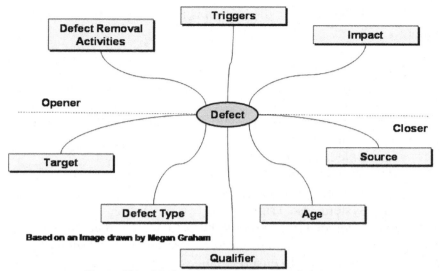

Based on an image drawn by Megan Graham

Figure 108 - ODC v5.11 Defect Classification Scheme

Under ODC Ver. 5.11, the openers include:

Defect Removal Activities	
• Design Review	• Function Test
• Code Inspection	• System Test
• Unit Test	

Figure 109 - ODC v5.11 Opener Defect Removal Activities

Triggers		
• Design Conformance	• Side Effect	• Interaction
• Logic/ Flow	• Rare Situations	• Workload/Stress
• Backward Compatibility	• Simple Path	• Recovery/Exception
• Lateral Compatibility	• Complex Path	• Startup/Restart
• Concurrency	• Coverage	• Hardware Configuration
• Internal Document	• Variation	• Software Configuration
• Language Dependency	• Sequencing	• Blocked Test (Normal Mode)

Figure 110 - ODC v5.11 Opener Triggers

Impacts		
• Installability	• Migration	• Maintenance
• Serviceability	• Reliability	• Usability
• Standards	• Performance	• Accessibility
• Integrity/Security	• Documentation	• Capability
	• Requirements	

Figure 111 - ODC v5.11 Opener Impacts

The ODC Ver. 5.11 closers include:

Target	Defect Type	Qualifier	Age	Source
• Design • Code	• Assign/Initialization • Checking • Algorithm/Method • Function/Class/Object • Timing/Serialization • Interface/OOP Messages • Relationship	• Missing • Incorrect • Extraneous	• Base • New • Rewritten • ReFixed	• Developed In-House • Reused From Library • Outsourced • Ported

Figure 112 - ODC v5.11 Closer Target, Defect Type, Qualifier, Age and Source

In addition to defect classifications already discussed, IBM has further extended ODC v5.11 to classify defects in user documentation or information development, Graphical User Interface, Build / Package / Merge and National Language Support. Overall, ODC is an excellent defect classification system that helps to improve system quality by using readily available data to decrease defect injection and increase defect detection. If you are using a simple quality control approach as shown in Figure 107, deploying an ODC-like system is accomplished in small steps. Remember, organizational change management takes time and you want the process to be successful. Start with field defects then move to in-process analysis as your skill set and comfort level improves. Practice with in-process defect profiling to predict quality outcomes. ODC can easily be tailored to your organization's needs. You can create your own type attributes and define triggers to suit your organizational and cultural norms, even in real time as the process executes. Because ODC takes advantage of defect data you've probably already collected, it is cost-effective to implement.

Much has been written about ODC and ODC is supported by some of the industry's top academicians such as Barry Boehm; John DeVale, ECE Department, Carnegie Mellon University; Professor Lori Clarke, Department of Computer Science, University of Massachusetts at Amherst; and Professor Phil Koopman, ECE Department, Carnegie Mellon University. Regrettably, there isn't enough space or time to dive deeper into the ODC concepts in a guide book to the SDLC. It's highly encouraged that you research ODC to learn more of its details. A good place to start is the IBM Center for Software Engineering ODC website.

If ODC doesn't fit the vision for your organization, please reconsider it. Its principles for defect classification are sound for both hardware and software systems. Please note that ODC does not preclude the use of the simpler classification system in Figure 107. It supplements and extends it. ODC's statistical analysis processes help to prevent defects, but defect repairs still need to be prioritized, scheduled and executed.

The SDLC Test Battery

The SDLC Test Battery is the system level verification review. This is the execution of the tests defined in the detailed test plan. In Chapter 5 we learned there are at least sixteen different quality assurance tests that can be included in a detailed test plan. Depending on the size and nature of the project, the detailed test plan may omit several of the recommended tests where a very large, complex project would include most, if not all, of them. For example, by definition system integration testing verifies that a system is correctly integrated to any external or third party systems defined in the system requirements. If there are no external or third party systems defined in the system requirements, why would you include a system integration test in the detailed test plan? The answer is you wouldn't. Tests are chosen to satisfy the project's requirements.

In the last chapter we also stated the IEEE Standard Glossary of Software Engineering Terminology defines validation and verification as:

- Validation is the process of evaluating a system or component during or at the end of the development process to determine whether it satisfies specified requirements.
- Verification is the process of evaluating a system or component to determine whether the products of a given development phase satisfy the conditions imposed at the start of that phase.

Validation asks, "Have we built the right system?" If the iterative and incremental development cycles are conducted with the appropriate rigor and attention to detail, this question is answered by the consistent execution of unit tests, code reviews and prototype reviews.

Verification asks, "Have we built the system right?" The answer to this question is determined through the SDLC test battery. Prior to conducting any test cycle we ensure the project is ready to move into the verification phase. This is accomplished by the Verification Readiness Review (VRR) stage gate. It is conducted by the Quality Assurance group to substantiate that the system entering verification testing has completed thorough development testing and is ready for turnover to the formal, controlled test environment. The scope of the VRR is to inspect the development test artifacts, test results and traceability matrix for completeness and accuracy. It also verifies that test plans, test cases, test datasets, scenarios and scripts provide adequate coverage of the acceptance criteria defined in the system requirements. The third goal of VRR is to review the test environment, test setup and test data to ensure they are adequately prepared for verification testing.

No matter what tests are defined, the process for executing them is pretty much the same and delineated in the following eight steps:

1. **Setup the Test Environment**: Before running any test, the test environment needs to be setup. Setting up the environment means that all the required elements, i.e., hardware, software, tools, data, etc., are implemented and available to the testing team.

2. **Initialize the Test Environment**: The next step is to initialize the test environment. Initializing the test environment ensures all components are in their proper initial state for the start of testing. Initializing the environment can be a fairly time consuming task, especially if you have to wait for a large database refresh or a project requires different operating systems and versions to support code that runs on multiple platforms or internationalization and localization testing. Experientially, initializing test environments can take a week or longer depending on the availability of technical resources and the level of sophistication of the technical tool box. If at all possible, a best practice goal of the organization should be to implement automated environment generators. Tools that automatically set up environments, run the test cases, record the results, capture the issues and automatically reconfigure to a new environment are high value assets.

3. **Execute the Test Procedures**: 'nuff said.

4. **Evaluate Test Execution**: Each executed test procedure will produce one of two possible outcomes. Either the test will end normally with all the test procedures or scripts execute as intended or the test will ABEND which means to end abnormally or prematurely. The test procedures or scripts did not execute completely or as intended. If the test ended normally, the next step is to review the test results. If the testing ends abnormally, you need to determine why. The root cause of the ABEND needs to be identified and corrected. Since the halted test results are probably unreliable, re-execute the tests before moving on to subsequent testing activities. As a process step, abnormal terminations are followed by Recover from Halted Tests.

5. **Verify Test Results**: When all tests are complete, the test results are reviewed to ensure they are reliable and meet the expected acceptance criteria. Reported failures, warnings, or unexpected results not caused by external influences, such as improper initialization or data, may be due to errors in the test artifacts or problems with the test environment. If such a case, the appropriate corrective action is taken and testing re-executed for further evaluation.

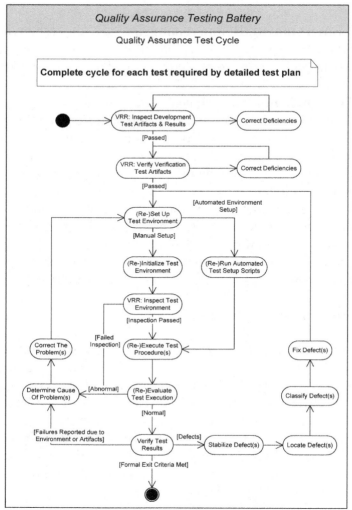

Figure 113 - Quality Assurance Testing Battery Activity Diagram

6. **Recover from Halted Tests**: Tests generally ABEND for two major reasons, either fatal errors or test script command failures. With fatal errors, the system fails due to programming errors, network failures, hardware crashes, or any number of other serious system problems. Test script command failures are specific to automated testing. When a test script cannot execute a command or line of code, it produces an error.
   a. Both types of abnormal terminations may exhibit the same symptoms:
      i. Unexpected actions, windows, or events occur while the test script is running

      ii. The test environment appears unresponsive or in an undesirable state such as hung, crashed or BSOD (if on MS platform)
- b. To recover from halted tests, do the following:
  - i. Determine the actual cause of the problem
  - ii. Correct the problem
  - iii. Re-setup the test environment
  - iv. Re-initialize the test environment
  - v. Re-execute the test procedures

7. **Fix Defects**: Fixing defects is a process of four steps:
   a. Stabilize the fault: The first step is to stabilize the fault or symptom to make it trigger reliably on demand. If you can't make the symptom trigger reliably, it is almost impossible to locate it
   b. Locate the Defect: Execute the test cases that cause the symptom to appear and identify the source of the defect in the code or script
   c. Classify the Defect: If using ODC, classify the defect in accordance with your organizational practices
   d. Fix the Defect: follow good coding practice and guidelines to fix the defect

8. **Repeat Until Done**: Go back to Step 1 and repeat until all tests are executed, defects found, classified, fixed or deferred as defined in the formal exit criteria

Acceptance Testing

> **Principle #10: "Always conduct acceptance testing"**

Acceptance testing is a black-box quality assurance method performed on a system prior to its implementation and delivery to a customer or prior to accepting transfer of ownership if the system is a COTS application or a system provided by an external vendor. Acceptance testing is also known as release testing, final testing, user acceptance testing, end-user testing or site or field acceptance testing. Smoke tests are used as acceptance tests before introducing a new build to the primary testing process.

User Acceptance Testing (UAT) is a formal process to obtain confirmation from the stakeholders that the system meets all agreed to requirements and contains all expected deliverables. These tests are usually performed by the clients or end-users. Traditionally, the tests are written by the development team, but an emerging trend is to have the users write the tests under the guidance of the development team. The tests are designed to cover a range of detail levels under normal use conditions. If the system works as intended and without issue under normal conditions, the sensible conclusion is that an equivalent level of stability can be expected after the system is deployed to production.

The formal UAT is a highly managed process and usually employs the same artifacts and comprises the same activities as the standard QA test battery. The tests are planned and designed as carefully for the UAT as with the comprehensive testing suite, but only a subset of the system tests are utilized. The benefits of the UAT are:

- The functions and features to be tested are known
- The details of the tests are known and can be measured
- Some of the tests can be automated which allows for regression testing
- The progress of the tests can be measured and monitored
- The acceptance criteria are known

For the most part, in a corporate environment the UAT is the final verification the system functions according to the requirements and specifications. It's important to note that the main focus of the UAT is _not_ the identification of minor system faults such as spelling errors and cosmetic defects. Nor should it produce major faults such as show-stopper defects like system crashes or BSODs. It's not meant to duplicate fault finding efforts exerted during the comprehensive system testing. If the Quality Assurance Testing Battery is acceptably conducted, then the testers and developers have already identified all known faults during earlier testing and fixed them before UAT. The goal of the UAT is to build confidence in the system. As a rule, UAT is only conducted on a system in which the development team is self-assured of its production readiness. A successful UAT injects the stakeholders with the confidence to anticipate how the system will perform in production.

Quantified User Acceptance Testing

Quantified User Acceptance Testing (Q-UAT), or the Quantified Approach, is an emerging faster and smarter variation of the traditional UAT that is coupled with TDD. Its development is highly influenced by the "Guerilla Acceptance Testing" methods. Guerilla testing came about because traditional acceptance testing proved to be too costly for some companies to be sustainable for small/medium-scale projects. Guerilla testing is completely unstructured. It involves setting a series of tasks the end-users are to perform and then note any problems they encounter. There are no scripts or procedures to follow. The users just receive a task list and go to work.

The Q-UAT is conducted very much in the same way as a Guerilla test except that periodic in-depth testing is performed against business requirements at explicit prearranged points. Q-UAT is an acceptable alternative to traditional acceptance testing methods only when effective TDD is exercised during the development cycle. Q-UAT relies entirely on the assumption that the highest quality code possible is delivered out of the Development Phase.

Contract and Regulation Acceptance Testing

Two other types of acceptance testing are Contract and Regulation Acceptance Testing. Contract Acceptance Testing is performed against acceptance criteria documented in a contract. A contract is an agreement between two or more parties in which there is an exchange of promises with specific remedies for breaches. It's interesting to note that Chapter 2 of Cockburn's *"Writing Effective Use Cases"* defines use cases as a contract for behavior with the stakeholder. Under contract law, agreement is reached when an offer capable of immediate acceptance is met with a "mirror image" acceptance (i.e., an unqualified acceptance). The most important thing to remember about a contract is that one party or parties makes an offer and another party or parties accepts the offer. In a systems contract, contract acceptance testing is performed to ensure all conditions of the contract are satisfied before a system is accepted by the receiving organization.

Regulatory Acceptance Testing ensures a system complies with government, legal and safety standards. Compliance means conforming to a rule, such as a specification, policy, standard or law. Corporations or public agencies fall under a host of international, national or local regulatory requirements. Such entities generally hire a Chief Compliance Officer to drive efforts to ensure that personnel are aware of and take steps to comply with relevant laws and regulations. To illustrate, in the United States the Sarbanes-Oxley Act of 2002 is perhaps the most well-known of the recently effected compliance measures. In the US there are other regulatory measures such as the Gramm-Leach-Bliley Act (GLBA) also known as the Financial Services Modernization Act of 1999, the Federal Information Security Management Act of 2002 (FISMA) and the Health Insurance Portability and Accountability Act (HIPAA) of 1996.

To help businesses comply with government regulations, the U.S. Small Business Administration launched the Business.gov website in 2006 which provides a single point of access to government services and information. Other compliance frameworks such as the Control Objectives for Information and related Technology (COBIT) or standards such as the National Institute of Standards and Technology (NIST) help organizations to comply with regulations.

In Australia, you can contact the Australian Securities and Investment Commission and the Australian Prudential Regulation Authority (APRA) for more information on regulatory compliance. In the United Kingdom, which is highly regulated, regulatory authorities include the Financial Services Authority (FSA), Environment Agency and Scottish Environment Protection Agency, Information Commissioner's Office and others. U.K. IT organization must understand the implications of the Data Protection Act 1998 and for the public sector, the Freedom of

Information Act 2000. The U.K. equivalent to the Sarbanes-Oxley Act in the U.S. is the Combined Code issued by the London Stock Exchange.

Alpha and Beta Testing

Alpha and Beta tests may be defined in the detailed test plan but they do not fall under the standard SDLC testing battery process steps. Both of these tests are a type of informal user acceptance test except there are no specific test cases defined, no scripts to follow, no test datasets, no test scenarios and no test procedures. The customers and end-users are the testers. The difference in the two tests is that with Alpha testing, the business processes that are to be tested are identified and documented but without any specificity on how to test them. The advantages of an Alpha test are that functions and features to be tested are known, progress is measured and monitored and acceptance criteria are defined. There are disadvantages as well and include:

- Acceptance testing is not under the control of the project
  - Testing resources may be time constricted
- Ample testing, planning and management resources are required
- End users may conform to the way the system works and not uncover defects
- End users may focus on comparing the new system and processes to their legacy system, rather than looking for defects
- There is no control over test procedures being utilized

Beta testing is the least controlled of any user acceptance test. In a Beta test, each user is responsible for creating their own environment, selecting their data and determining what functions, features or tasks to explore. In essence, they do whatever they want to do to test the system. The benefits to Beta testing are that testing is implemented by end users and end users may represent a large volume of potential test resources; by having end users participate, there is increased customer satisfaction with the experience; and the development team uncovers more subjective defects than with formal or informal acceptance testing. As with Alpha testing, Beta testing also has its list of disadvantages:

- Acceptance criteria are not known
- Acceptance testing is not under the control of the project
  - Testing resources may be time constricted
- End users may conform to the way the system works and not uncover or report defects
- Not all functions and/or features may be tested
- Test progress is difficult to measure

Alpha and Beta testing is conducted differently depending on whether in a corporate or commercial environment. In a corporate setting, if Alpha and Beta testing is conducted at all, there is generally one cycle for each the Alpha and Beta phase. The testers are all carefully selected internal, tech-savvy resources. In testing a commercial product, one that is to be sold to the public at large, the Alpha and Beta test phases have different characteristics than the corporate model. First there may be several cycles of Alpha tests, designated by a superscripted differentiator as in $Alpha^1$, $Alpha^2$ and so on. The first one or two Alpha tests are conducted by the company's internal resources. As the product stabilizes, an $Alpha^3$ test may be commissioned and conducted by carefully screened end-users who sign up for the fun and privilege of being Alpha testers.

In Beta testing there are exceptions with as with anything else, but commercial Beta tests are almost always public and conducted for a prolonged period of time. For example, the public Beta for Microsoft Office 2010 began in November of 2009. The product was released to manufacturing in April of 2010, after a Beta testing period of almost six months. Microsoft boasted that they had more than 7.5 million people download the beta version. Typically, software vendors solicit individuals to sign-up for the privilege of being a Beta tester. Figures 114 and 115 depict some of the differences between the corporate and commercial Alpha and Beta testing models. A third diagram, Alpha Cyclic and Beta Testing / Commercial Model, is included on the CD as Figure 116 but not shown in the book.

An emerging trend is to include an Alpha and Beta test at the end of every development cycle to test ideas, processes and the market as well as find defects. Keep an eye out for this idea in case it catches on and becomes a best practice. In a corporate setting, Alpha and Beta tests are often conducted in a parallel production environment by the more sophisticated and tech savvy end users. An environment is established that contains an exact image of the production data. The Alpha or Beta software is deployed to that shadow environment. As individuals go about their daily tasks, they perform whatever activities are required in their legacy systems and then perform the same activities with the new processes in the Alpha or Beta test environment. The results of the two environments are compared for consistency and accuracy.

Alpha and Beta tests are also a popular method for commercial software vendors to test their products before releasing them to manufacturing. Alpha tests are generally conducted by internal teams not affiliated with the project. For Beta tests, vendors publically solicit users to sign up and be part of the testing base. If you've ever been a member of Microsoft MSDN or TechNet, you may have participated in Beta testing one or more Microsoft products.

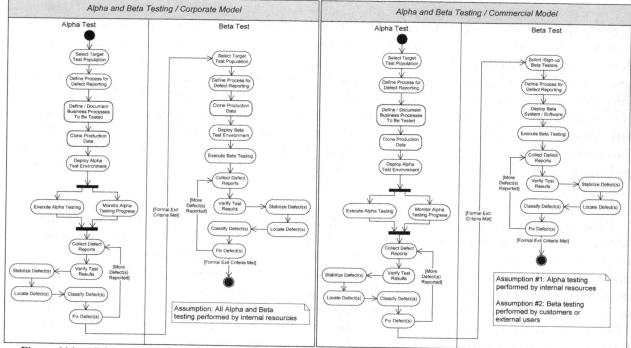

Figure 114 - Alpha and Beta Testing Corporate Model Activity Diagram

Figure 115 - Alpha and Beta Testing Commercial Model Activity Diagram

Additional Testing Best Practices

Quality Assurance testing is a well-studied science and its best practices extend far beyond anything that can be contained in a guide to the System Development Life Cycle. In terms of best practices, there are many more than can be implemented in an organization. The SDLC presents the vital few. But to give you an idea of other testing best practices, here is a sampling of some you may want to consider for your culture and environment. Keep in mind, we haven't even gotten to continuous improvement metrics yet, but we will in the next chapter.

Automated Testing upon Code Check-in

The practice of an automated code check-in test couples an automatic test program like JUnit to a version control system to perform regression tests triggered by the check-in event. This ensures an automatic test runs on all recently changed code so the chances of the new code breaking the next build are minimal. Such a system can be set up in such a way that new code does not get promoted to the next build unless it passes the automated regression test.

Benchmarking

Benchmarking is the process of comparing one's business processes and performance metrics to industry bests and/or best practices from other industries. Benchmarking is a broad concept that applies to many disciplines in different areas. The typically measured dimensions of cost, quality and time lead to lessons learned which drive process improvements to do things cheaper, better and faster. In the SDLC's QA parlance, this means the techniques and performance of system testing methods as experienced by our competitors and customers.

Defect Discovery Incentives

Incentives are great motivators. Both Microsoft and IBM have used an incentive known as defect discovery incentives or "bug bounties" in their system development life cycles to motivate their project teams to focus on detecting system faults. Incentives can take the form of monetary or product awards or even a contest with the winner receiving the latest high tech gadget as a reward for finding the greatest number of defects. Experience with defect bounties proves that such efforts tend to identify a larger than usual number of system defects. With a larger number of defects to fix, additional resources may be necessary to address them, but the bottom line result is a higher quality product.

Memory Resource Failure Simulation

Modern day development languages have largely taken away the onus of memory management from system developers. However, if you are developing UNIX applications in C, a common and particularly nasty defect known as a memory leak which causes the gradual loss of system memory due to the lack of garbage collection or poor heap management. This can bring a system to a grinding halt. The problem isn't isolated to only UNIX and C; it can also exist on other platforms and languages. A best practice to address this situation is to implement commercial tools available to help simulate memory failure and check for memory leaks. For the SDLC, the practice needs to be generic and usable across a broad array of development methods and techniques and capable of determining defects on different platforms and language environments.

Reduce the Number of Regression Test Cases

It's not unusual to find a huge number of regression test cases in organizations with a long history and rich legacy of systems product development. As the organization grew, development practices matured over many releases, as a result a lot of regression tests were written. The greatest negative consequence of owning such a large regression test base is that it takes a long time to execute them if you were to run every single permutation. If the organization has been in business long enough, there has no doubt been a shift from a procedural to an object-oriented development paradigm as well. This often leaves an unclear impression as to which test cases provide little added value due to redundancy. There are several methods to reduce the number of regression tests that need to be executed. Methods include code based test coverage and specification based test coverage (discussed in Chapter 5). Using either or both of these methods allows the testing team to condense the number of regression test cases to a minimum.

Implementation & Maintenance

System implementation is the process of deploying the fully tested artifacts and all project deliverables to their final destination—production. Implementation includes activities for systems deployments and integrations, issuing user policies and standard operating procedures and training and delivery. Post-implementation activities are for maintaining and ensuring the integrity of the products throughout their life cycle. Maintenance is all of the activities necessary to correct post-delivery faults, improve performance or other attributes, adapt the product to a modified environment and manage the patching process.

Implementation and post-implementation knowledge areas include Release Management, Configuration Management, Subcontractor/Vendor Management and Patch Management. Some may debate whether post-implementation topics belong in a SDLC guide book rather than in a book about project management best practices. But since the planning for post-implementation activities is done during the SDLC, it's best to discuss the knowledge areas in both types of books since there are so many touch points to both system development and project management.

Release Management

If you ask most any IT resource, "What is Release Management?" They invariably answer that it is the process for releasing software to production. Ask some resources, "What is a Release Manager?" and the responses range from shoulder shrugs to blank stares and an occasional "I'm not sure" to "That's the person responsible for releasing software to production."

Release Management (RM) is a complex discipline defined by the current ITIL implementation. People who only associate RM to software are making a dreadful mistake. RM's scope extends far beyond software and includes everything that can be released to a production environment in an IT context. For RM to be successful, its processes are incorporated into many aspects of the entire IT Success Trilogy. If you recall from Chapter 1, the IT Success Trilogy is IT Governance, the SDLC and the Program/Project Management Method employed in a given organization. RM's practices are relevant to Patch Management, the SDLC, Quality Assurance, Change Management, Configuration Management and even the sun setting of legacy systems.

Many students walk away from ITIL training programs with the notion that RM might be just a little too advanced and arcane a concept for them to consider deploying it to an entire enterprise. The fact is they are completely surprised when upon further analysis they realize that many of RM's practices are already in place and being observed in their organizations. But instead of being managed by s single individual or group, they are spread across multiple departments or teams. This means that instead of attempting to build an RM practice from the ground up, learn what it really is, take advantage of what you are already doing and leverage the processes and procedures that work for your organization. To illustrate how this can be so simple, take a look at the high-level RM activity diagram in Figure 117.

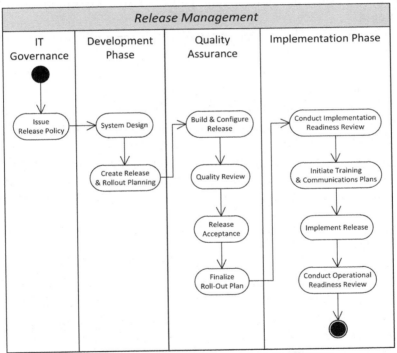

Figure 117 - Release Management Activity Diagram

Examining RM activities from the balcony view reveals that, other than an IT authority issuing a release policy, there isn't anything else new to RM activity-wise that isn't covered in the SDLC, QA practices or project management method. What is new about RM is the concept of having a dedicated Release Manager coordinate and either supervise or participate in all of these activities. Since many organizations don't have a position for a dedicated Release Manager, if considering one for your organization, it's important to understand that a Release Manager may wear many hats. Therefore a Release Manager must possess the competencies to effectively execute any or all of the following roles:

- **Architect**: The Release Manager helps to identify, create and/or implement processes or products to efficiently manage the release of code
- **Coordinator**: The Release Manager coordinates different source trees, projects, teams and components; works with the PM and/or IT Directors to assist with scheduling resources for project or maintenance implementations
- **Facilitator**: The Release Manager facilitates communication between varying business units or departments to warrant the smooth and timely delivery of systems products or updates
- **Production Gatekeeper**: The Release Manager "holds the keys" to all production systems and applications and is responsible for any implementation in the production environment
- **Support Engineer**: The Release Manager helps troubleshoot problems with systems and applications, but not at a source code level

When an organization staffs the position of Release Manager to oversee these activities, the role is proven to reduce the time for implementations and decrease the number of problems that arise from faulty deployments. If you are new to RM and intend to implement a RM practice in your organization, take your time. Implement RM in small increments until you nail the process, then rollout to the entire organization. When reporting to your sponsor and management, always highlight the achievements and process improvements gained by the Release Manager. If implemented right, an organization can reap enormous quality benefits from RM.

Configuration Management

We touched briefly on Configuration Management (CM) at the end of Chapter 2—Software development Models. CM got its start as a technical management discipline in the 1950s with the United States Department of Defense. As originally defined, CM's end goal is to establish and maintain the stability of a system's performance attributes throughout its lifetime, consistent with its functional and physical physiognomies; and its requirements, design and expected operational characteristics. Since then, CM concepts have been widely adopted by quite a few technical management models. Some of these models have transformed CM ideas from their traditional all-inclusive technical management approach into librarian activities. Some also isolate change control and change management as separate disciplines. The models include:

- Application Lifecycle Mgmt
- CMMI
- COBIT
- Integrated Logistics Support
- ISO 9000
- ITIL
- Prince2
- Product Lifecycle Mgmt
- Systems Engineering

In the United States, the National Information Assurance (IA) Glossary defines CM as "Management of security features and assurances through control of changes made to hardware, software, firmware, documentation, test, test fixtures and test documentation throughout the life cycle of an IS [information system]." The National Information Assurance Glossary is a publication of the Committee on National Security Systems[109] (CNSS) which is chaired by the Assistant Secretary of Defense for Network and Information Integration / Department of Defense Chief Information Officer (ASD/NII DOD CIO). The Director of the National Security Agency (NSA) is the National Manager and reports into the Executive Agent for the Federal Government for National Security Systems (NSS) who is the Secretary of Defense.

Regardless of how CM is defined or which model an organization uses, CM works symbiotically with change management. In its purest sense, CM's practices apply to hardware and software configurations and predictive and preventive maintenance activities. CM practices result in the creation and maintenance of up-to-date records for software and hardware components in the production environment and infrastructure, including related documentation. CM is widely used by military organizations world-wide to help manage complex systems, such as weapon systems, vehicles and information systems. Figure 118 is a high level CM activity model from the U.S. Army. Apart from the military, CM practices are appropriate for a wide range of fields and industries in the commercial and government sectors.

---

[109] Source: http://www.cnss.gov; Accessed April 26, 2010

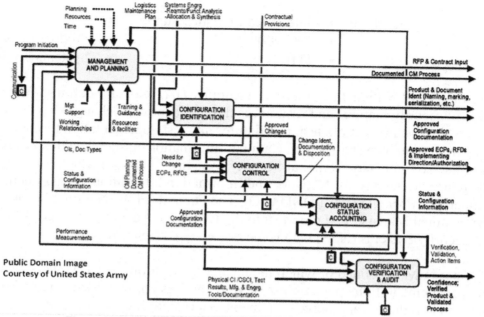

Figure 118 - Top Level Configuration Management Activity Model

Software Configuration Management

During the progression of the SDLC, the one artifact that consistently courses through all of its veins beginning immediately after the requirements are baselined is the traceability matrix. Software Configuration Management (SCM) defines the need to trace changes and verify enhancements to maintain system integrity all the way through an application's lifecycle. SCM is the perpetuation of the traceability matrix after a system has been deployed to production. A comprehensive SCM practice relies on defining four key procedures to manage configuration items. A configuration item is a hardware and/or software product that serves end-users. The four processes are:

- **Identification**: identify the attributes that define every aspect of a configuration item
    - Record attributes in configuration documentation and baseline
- **Control**: formal configuration change control and approval processes to manage changes to a configuration item's attributes and re-baseline them
- **Status Accounting**: record and report on configuration baselines associated with each configuration item at any moment in time
- **Verification**: verification is accomplished through two types of delivery or moment in time configuration audits:

- Functional Audit: ensures that functional and performance attributes of a configuration item are realized
- Physical Audits: ensures that a configuration item is installed in accordance with its detailed design artifact

System Hardware Configuration Management

System Hardware Configuration Management is the process of creating and maintaining an up-to-date record of all the components of the infrastructure and related artifacts and registering them in a Configuration Management Database (CMDB). It provides direct control over IT assets used in the provision of operational services. The CMDB is a rich source of information for support resources. It shows everything there is to know about configuration items that comprise the infrastructure and their physical locations. Some organizations take advantage of the CMDB to manage asset information, even though it's not its primary function. The four processes of Identification, Control, Status Accounting and Verification that are used with SCM also form the basis of the system hardware configuration management practices as well.

Configuration Management and Maintenance

There isn't an IT organization that can be found anywhere in the world that doesn't want to maintain the highest level of serviceability of their systems at the lowest possible cost. CM helps mature and improve both predictive and preventive maintenance practices by ensuring that continuous operations are not interrupted because IT assets or their component parts exceed their anticipated lifespan or their performance characteristics fall below acceptable ranges. Preventive maintenance depends upon knowing the "as-is" state of assets and their component parts in real-time. Predictive maintenance relies upon real-time condition monitoring to assess an asset's live performance and forecast potential future failures based on an algorithmic comparison to historical samples collected through field capability and modeling. If CM is "done right," it provides great added value to these activities because of its readily available accurate and timely data.

Subcontractor Management

In the days leading up to the 2004 United States Presidential election, the impact of outsourcing on the U.S. workforce became a popular political issue largely due to the viewpoint of John Kerry, the Democratic candidate. Kerry vehemently criticized U.S. firms that outsourced jobs abroad and called them "Benedict Arnold Corporations." Benedict Arnold was an American Revolutionary War general who defected to the British Army. He is one of the most well-known traitors in U.S. history, perhaps even in the world. What drove Kerry to this extreme is his perception that companies that outsource are doing so to avoid paying their fair share of U.S. taxes. Today Kerry's decries have faded into the footnotes of history with no value other than to someone trying to win a game of Trivial Pursuit. Outsourcing and managing subcontractors is essential to modern day business operations, especially in IT. It has nothing to do with tax evasion and everything to do with working smarter and increasing shareholder value.

Outsourcing

Outsourcing is contracting out business functions to external third parties known as subcontractors or vendors. If you mention outsourcing to someone, their most immediate thought is about sending work out of the home country to a foreign destination, usually India, China, the Philippines, Russia or Brazil. While that is certainly a valid perspective of outsourcing, it's not the complete picture. Outsourcing is a strategy used to fulfill both strategic and tactical needs. Anytime an organization hires a subcontractor, vendor, consultant, contingent worker or supplemental temporary staff, it's outsourcing.

There are many reasons a company may outsource:

- Access to Talent
- Capacity Management
- Catalyst for Change
- Commodification
- Contract
- Cost Restructuring

- Cost Savings
- Enhance Capacity for Innovation
- Focus on Core Business
- Improve Quality
- Knowledge
- Operational Expertise

- Opportunity Bubbles
- Reduce Time to Market
- Risk Management
- Tax Benefit[110]
- Venture Capital
- Work/Life Balance

Within IT, it's very difficult to find a company that doesn't bring in at a least a few contractors to help with new development projects. Actually, for most it has become the normal course of doing business. After products are deployed to production, it's not unusual to employ offshore resources to provide continuous monitoring or help desktop support. Many companies outsource their datacenter services today to vendors that guarantee 24/7 uptime, monitoring and support. In many cases outsourcing a datacenter is much less costly than building and staffing one. Regardless of the reason for outsourcing, if a company is to achieve any level of success with it, there must be a process in place to effectively manage subcontractors. Taking this one step further, with the tendency to utilize offshore or near shore resources to supply outsourcing services, multi-cultural training is a much overlooked, but highly important success factor for a subcontractor management program.

---

[110] Note: Tax benefit is not tax evasion

Outsourcing carries a number of risks which include:

- **Failure to Deliver Tangible Benefits**: The promise of business transformation often accompanies a request to senior management to engage outsourced services. Typically, outsourcing fails to deliver tangible benefits for two reasons:
    - Providers frequently overstate their capabilities when bidding on an opportunity.
    - Senior management is sometimes unwilling to invest in transformation once an outsourcing contract executed.
- **Labor Issues**: Outsourcing is often regarded as an unwanted change in the workplace by company employees. It is considered a threat, contributes to worker insecurity, labor unrest and resistance.
- **Language Skills**: Have you ever called a vendor's help line and not be able to understand the support analyst who answered the call or realize the responses given to anything you say is being read from a canned script? The call center end-user-experience is perceived to be of lower quality when a service is outsourced.
- **Outsourcer Qualification**: The outsourcer may replace staff with less qualified people or with people with different non-equivalent qualifications.[111]
- **Product Quality**: Outsourcers may deliver defective products or services because of operations-related issues :
    - Asset Specificity: the extent to which investments made to support a particular transaction have a higher value to that transaction than if they were redeployed for any other purpose
    - Capability: lack of supplier capabilities, resources or capacity
    - Communication: poor buyer-supplier communication and lack of common understanding
    - Contract Issues: buyer-supplier contract enforceability
    - Information Asymmetry: transactions in which one party has more or better information than the other
    - Opportunism: the conscious policy and practice of taking selfish advantage of circumstances with little regard for principles
    - Switching Barriers or Switching Costs: the costs and impediments associated with switching supplier
- **Productivity**: less productive facilities offshore appear to be more productive simply because the workers are paid less
- **Public Opinion**: there is strong public opinion that outsourcing when combined with offshoring leads to job displacement and this results in the labor issues described above

---

[111] Source: Stein, R (2005) Hospital Services Performed Overseas. www.washingtonpost.com; Accessed April 27, 2010; http://www.washingtonpost.com/wp-dyn/articles/A12392-2005Apr23.html

- **Quality of Service**: outsourcing contracts may be poorly defined and have no measure of quality or SLA specified. Even if defined in a contract, the SLA may not fulfill expected quality levels due to lack of supplier capability
- **Security**: legal, security and compliance issues need to be addressed through the client and the supplier contract. A company has to be diligent to prevent fraud and the loss of key intellectual property to outsourcers
- **Staff Turnover**: Turnover is shown to be higher under an outsourcer. In call centers, it is not unusual for outsourcers to replace their entire workforce every year[112]
- **Transfer of Knowledge**: language and cultural differences, differences in communications systems and time zones often lead to problems in the transfer of knowledge

Figure 119 illustrates activities necessary to successfully manage subcontractors. Whenever an organization intends to outsource work guided by their SDLC, it's important to understand that the client or prime contractor, not the subcontractor, is responsible for ensuring the high quality standards their customers and stakeholders have come to expect. It is critically important to clearly define and monitor every aspect of the process. There can be no ambiguity. Every process step must be documented in such a way that its purpose, roles/responsibilities, entry criteria, control objectives, inputs, activities, outputs and exit criteria are abundantly clear to anyone reading the artifact.

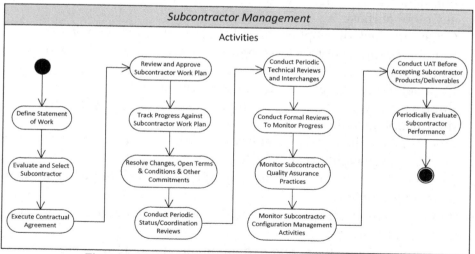

Figure 119 - Subcontractor Management Activity Diagram

The activity diagram shows thirteen activities which govern:

---

[112] Source: Kobayashi-Hillary, M. (2007) India faces battle for outsourcing news.bbc.co.uk; Accessed April 27, 2010; http://news.bbc.co.uk/2/hi/business/6944583.stm

1. The work to be subcontracted is defined and planned according to a documented procedure. This is also known as creating the Statement of Work
2. The subcontractor is selected based on an evaluation of the subcontract bidder's ability to perform the work according to specification
3. The contractual agreement between the client or prime contractor and the subcontractor is used as the basis for managing the subcontract
4. The subcontractor's documented system development plan is reviewed and approved by the client or prime contractor
5. The subcontractor's documented and approved system development plan (a.k.a. project plan) is used for tracking the system activities and communicating status
6. Changes to the subcontractor's statement of work, subcontract terms and conditions and other commitments are resolved according to a documented project change management procedure
7. The client's or prime contractor's management team conducts periodic status / coordination reviews with the subcontractor's management team
8. Periodic technical reviews and interchanges are held with the subcontractor
9. Formal reviews to address the subcontractor's system engineering accomplishments and results are conducted at selected milestones according to the project plan
10. The client's or prime contractor's quality assurance group monitors the subcontractor's quality assurance activities according to a documented procedure
11. The client's or prime contractor's configuration management group monitors the subcontractor's configuration management activities according to a documented procedure
12. The client or prime contractor conducts acceptance testing as part of the delivery of the subcontractor's system products according to a documented procedure
13. The subcontractor's performance is evaluated by the client or prime contractor and reviewed with the subcontractor on a periodic basis

Multi-Cultural Training

In a May 2004 study entitled "Leading Causes of Outsourcing Failures," the Outsourcing Center[113] surveyed 305 buyers and providers in North America, Europe, Asia and India to assess their experiences and opinions about outsourcing failures. One-third of respondents were buyers, two-thirds were providers. They concluded that 25% of the reasons for outsourced project failures are due to poor communication (16%) and cultural fit (9%). If you believed 25% of your

---

[113] The Outsourcing Center is a wholly owned subsidiary of the Everest Partners, L.P.; Two Galleria Tower, 13455 Noel Road, Suite 2100; Dallas, TX 75240; PH: 214-451-3000 FAX: 214-451-3001; http://www.outsourcing-center.com/

outsourcing projects would fail because either you or your provider didn't understand each other, even though you both speak the same language, or innocently offended each other because you didn't understand each other's cultural mores, you would do something about it wouldn't you?

Multi-cultural or cross-cultural training is a key success factor when considering outsourcing. Gerard (Geert) Hendrik Hofstede is an influential Dutch sociologist whose life's work includes the study of the interactions between national cultures and organizational cultures. Hofstede defines five dimensions of culture in his study of national work related values which are:

- **Individualism vs. Collectivism**: measure of how greatly members of the culture define themselves apart from their group memberships
    - Individualist Cultures: people are expected to develop and display their individual personalities and choose their own affiliations
    - Collectivist Cultures: people are defined and act mostly as a member of a long-term group, such as the family, a religion, an age cohort, a town or a profession
- **Long vs. Short Term Orientation**: A society's "time horizon" or the importance attached to the future vs. the past and present
    - Long Term Oriented Societies: people value actions and attitudes that influence the future such as persistence, perseverance, thrift and shame
    - Short Term Oriented Societies: people value actions and attitudes effected by the past or present such as normative statements, immediate stability, protecting one's own face, respect for tradition and reciprocation of greetings, favors and gifts
- **Masculinity vs. Femininity**: the value placed on traditionally male or female values
    - Feminine Cultures: people, male or female, value relationships and quality of life
    - Masculine Cultures: people, male or female, value competitiveness, assertiveness, ambition and the accumulation of wealth and material possessions
- **Small vs. Large Power Distance**: A measure of how widely the less powerful members of society expect and accept that power is distributed unequally. Hofstede called this metric the Power Distance Index (PDI)
    - Small Power Distance Cultures: people expect and accept power relations that are more consultative or democratic. For example, in countries like Austria, Israel, Denmark, New Zealand, Ireland, Sweden and Norway:
        - People relate to one another as equals regardless of formal position
        - Subordinates are comfortable with and demand the right to contribute to and critique the decisions of those in power
    - Large Power Distance Culture: the less powerful accept autocratic or paternalistic power relations. For example, in countries like Malaysia, Guatemala, Panama, Philippines, Mexico, Venezuela and China :
        - Subordinates acknowledge the power of others based on their formal hierarchical positions

- **Weak vs. Strong Uncertainty Avoidance**: A metric of how extensively members of a society are anxious about the unknown and try to cope with anxiety by minimizing uncertainty
  - Strong Uncertainty Avoidance Cultures: people prefer formally structured activities and explicit rules about issues of life such as religion and food. Employees tend to remain longer with their present employer
  - Weak Uncertainty Avoidance Cultures: people prefer implicit or flexible rules or guidelines and informal activities. Employees tend to change employers more frequently

Hofstede mapped all of these dimensions to 66 countries. The following table[114] illustrates the relationship of the countries to one of the most significant of these metrics, the PDI. The number following the name of the country is its PDI.

Hofstede Power Distance Index Country Mapping			
Malaysia: 104	India: 77	Thailand: 64	Hungary: 46
Guatemala: 95	Nigeria: 77	Zambia: 64	Jamaica: 45
Panama: 95	Sierra Leone: 77	Chile: 63	United States: 40
Philippines: 94	Singapore: 74	Portugal: 63	Netherlands: 38
Mexico: 81	Brazil: 69	Uruguay: 61	Australia: 36
Venezuela: 81	France: 68	Greece: 60	Costa Rica: 35
China: 80	Hong Kong: 68	South Korea: 60	Germany: 35
Egypt: 80	Poland: 68	Iran: 58	United Kingdom: 35
Iraq: 80	Colombia: 67	Taiwan: 58	Switzerland: 34
Kuwait: 80	El Salvador: 66	Czech Republic: 57	Finland: 33
Lebanon: 80	Turkey: 66	Spain: 57	Norway: 31
Libya: 80	Belgium: 65	Pakistan: 55	Sweden: 31
Saudi Arabia: 80	Ethiopia: 64	Japan: 54	Ireland: 28
United Arab Emirates: 80	Kenya: 64	Italy: 50	New Zealand: 22
Ecuador: 78	Peru: 64	Argentina: 49	Denmark: 18
Indonesia: 78	Tanzania: 64	South Africa: 49	Israel: 13
Ghana: 77			Austria: 11

Figure 120 - Hofstede PDI Country Mapping

Having an understanding of the Hofstede PDI scale provides insight into one of the foremost causes of cross-cultural communication failures—the difference between high context and low context communication. This is very likely the primary cause of the communication difficulties that resulted in the 16% of outsourced project failures in the 2004 survey. The residents of large PDI countries use high context communication as opposed to small PDI countries where the

---

[114] Source: http://www.clearlycultural.com/geert-hofstede-cultural-dimensions/power-distance-index/; Accessed April 28, 2010.

residents use low context communication. To learn the difference between high and low context communication, let's examine two fictitious conversations.

Conversation #1:

Low context, small PDI manager: "Is everything ready to move the system to production?"
Low context, small PDI project manager: "No. There's going to be a 1 week delay because the server didn't pass its disaster recovery testing. The network technicians need to check the link between the primary and failover data centers. Once they've corrected the problem, QA will re-run the tests. We'll be ready to go as soon as the destructive testing phase passes."

This is a straightforward question with a detailed straightforward answer. The PM provides a lot of specifics. The manager does not have to make any assumptions about what the PM is saying because low context communicators speak their mind. For the next conversation, let's change things around. The same manager asks the same question of a PM overseeing a project that is outsourced to a high context country. The high context PM has the equivalent credentials, training and experience as the low context PM. The problem the high context PM is experiencing is identical to those of the low context PM.

Conversation #2:

Low context, small PDI manager: "Is everything ready to move the system to production?"
High context, large PDI project manager: "Yes, it seems so. The team is working very hard."

Not quite the same answer is it? Before we analyze the discussion, what do you think is happening?

The low context manager expects straightforward conversation. If there is a problem, s/he expects a straightforward answer with specifics as in conversation #1. When the high context PM doesn't specifically mention the problems being faced, the low context manager assumes everything is proceeding according to schedule and looks forward to a successful on-time and within budget implementation. The high context PM is simply observing the cultural norms of a high context country. In high context countries, subordinates acknowledge the power of others based on their formal hierarchical positions. The subordinates offer their superiors great respect. Out of respect, the high context PM doesn't directly inform the manager of the issues due to the concern that the manager may suffer an offense. The PM assumes that the low context manager either fathoms the statement "it seems so" and will explore its meaning through further questioning or realizes the target date is going to be missed. Now, what do you think would happen if this type of communication failure pervaded the SDLC and an entire project?

Neither person is doing anything wrong or being deliberately deceptive. They are each exhibiting the normal communication patterns of their societies. What did go wrong is that their companies entered into on outsourcing contract without training their employees to understand how to work effectively with each other.

The other issue the survey uncovers pertinent to this topic is cultural fit. There are more ways than can be counted that one person can innocently offend another person simply because of an ignorance of cultural norms, customs and taboos. As one example, a friend from the U.K. related this story after he asked me a question where the answer was simply the number two. I did not respond verbally, but instead raised my hand and lifted my fingers to indicate the number two. As an American, I do so by lifting my first and second fingers and forming the shape of the letter "V." He told me that if I were ever to make that gesture in the U.K., perhaps for example when ordering drinks, it would very likely be interpreted as highly offensive visual profanity. The reason behind this cultural norm extends all the way back to the French-English wars of the Middle Ages. When French soldiers captured English archers, the punishment was to amputate the first two fingers of the archer's bowstring drawing hand. Later, archers that managed to keep all of their digits intact would lift their first two fingers and wave them at their enemies in defiance. That's how it became an offensive gesture.

Effective cross-cultural training solves the issues that resulted in the survey's 25% of project failures. Preparing employees to work outside of their native country or to work with offshore outsourcers is extremely important for outsourced project success. Basic multi-cultural training includes:

- Action plan for living abroad
- Communication characteristics and role
- Doing business in the country
- Eating and drinking
- Education, studies and professional training
- Introduction to culture and history
- Laws, norms, taboos and values of the society
- Leisure activities and customs
- Social contacts, friends and acquaintances
- Relations at work and management
- Women's life and role in society

Now that we've looked at all of the ancillary best practices to implementation, let's move onto the implementation process steps which begin with the Implementation Readiness Review. These steps are generic. They do not assume that an organization has a configuration management practice or release manager. If your organization has reached a level of maturity where these practices are embedded in your processes, the activity diagram on the accompanying CD can easily be tailored for your particular purpose.

Implementation Readiness Review

> **Principle #11: "Complete all project artifacts before implementation"**

The Implementation Readiness Review (IRR) consists of the following process steps:

- Implementation Plan is reviewed to ensure that the system/application or situation is ready for implementation activities
- Verify the following can be or is already installed and configured in the production environment(s):
  - System hardware, networking, databases and/or custom software or commercial products such as:
    - If a non-government organization:
      - Commercial off-the-shelf (COTS)
      - Modified or modifiable off-the-shelf (MOTS)
      - Niche off-the-shelf (NOTS)
    - If a government agency or branch of the military, same as non-government plus:
      - Government off-the-shelf (GOTS)
      - Military off-the-shelf (MOTS)
      - NATO off-the-shelf (NOTS)
- Confirm all project documentation is complete, quality checked and ready for deployment to its intended audiences

Submit the Change Request

Before anything can be moved to production, it must be approved by the Change Advisory Board. Most project change management policies designate a lead time to be observed for standard change requests. Lead times generally run from 5-10 days which means the change request shouldn't be submitted at the last minute. Submit the change request and take advantage of the lead time to rehearse the deployments.

Train the Users

If end user training hasn't started yet, deploy the training now. Training may begin during Quality Assurance testing if there isn't a significant gap in time between when training takes and the system is in production. If training is given too far in advance of production, it is ineffective. Students won't remember what they've learned. Begin the production turnover process by training the operations, maintenance and tier 1 and tier 2 support teams.

Package the Release

Depending on the number of environments you have, the release may have already been packaged and migrated to a staging environment. If not, package the release now and prepare it for implementation. Make sure is locked in the version control system and nothing can be changed. The package is ready to be committed to production.

Rehearse the Deployment

Athletes do it. Entertainers do it. Politicians do it. Public speakers do it and a whole host of others do it too. What is it that they do? They rehearse, that's what they do. Our twelfth and final principle is "rehearse deployments" because practice makes perfect. More things go wrong during the actual implementation than at any other time in the SDLC. It is astounding how an entire project can seemingly progress perfectly over the course of many months and then have something go desperately wrong during the implementation when the eyes of the entire end user community are focused on the project team. Nothing can be more embarrassing or attract more disdain from senior management than implementation mistakes. Yet, for some IT organizations this is the status quo.

Principle #12: "Rehearse deployments"

Implementation plans are frequently written in a vacuum by a single individual intimate with the project's details. There are usually some informal reviews and the final implementation readiness review, but the problem that comes from these reviews is that implementation steps are often omitted. The reviews can't uncover these problems because the reviewers may not be familiar with the technical area where the step is missed. Rehearsing the deployment by stepping through all of the process steps with the implementation team ensures a much smoother deployment and reduces the likelihood of mistakes being made.

Get everyone involved in the implementation into one room and walk through the process like it is to be implemented. Ensure that everyone understands their roles and responsibilities, place on the timeline, entry and exit criteria, who they receive the handoff from, who they pass the baton to and escalation procedures if something legitimately goes wrong. Explore the questions: Are there any gaps in the process? Are we missing anyone on the communication list? Is this the right sequence of events? Is there anything else missing? Rehearse more than once if necessary until everyone fully comprehends the implementation steps and can recite their role perfectly.

Perform the Deployment

When all approvals are received and everyone is certain of their roles, deploy the system to production. Send frequent progress communications to the entire team and key stakeholders. Hold periodic review meetings or teleconferences with the project team after each major implementation step is completed. You can never over communicate, especially when implementations are performed overnight or require multiple days to complete.

Operational Readiness Review

The Operational Readiness Review (ORR) for new projects or the Production Readiness Review (PRR) for maintenance projects uses the Implementation Plan as a checklist to determine if the system was implemented correctly. It helps determine if any issues or problems occurred during the implementation that may affect the release of the system or, in the case of missed steps, inject a situation into the production environment that needs to be addressed by sustaining operations and maintenance support.

Operational Acceptance Testing

Operational Acceptance Testing is also known as operational readiness testing. This is the final quality assurance test conducted by the project team and end users before flipping on the full production switch. Once the system is deployed, it is tested as much as possible to ensure nothing got broken by the implementation. The test also ensures that processes and procedures are in place to allow the system to be used and maintained. This may include checks done to back-up facilities, procedures for disaster recovery, training for end users, maintenance procedures and security procedures.

Implementation Phase Activity Diagram

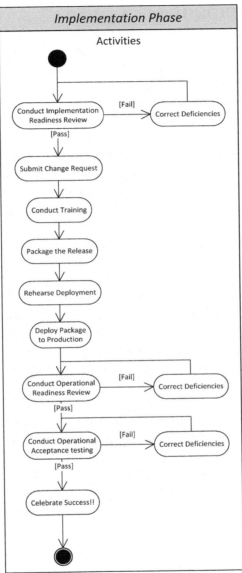

Figure 121 - Implementation Phase Activity Diagram

Continuous Improvement

In their book *"First Things First: to live, to love, to learn, to leave a legacy,"* authors Stephen R. Covey, A. Roger Merrill and Rebecca R. Merrill validate their understanding of fundamental human needs with wisdom literature dating as far back as 2500 BC. Wisdom literature is the genre of literature common in the Ancient Near East. The key principle of wisdom literature is to offer insight and wisdom about nature and reality using traditional story-telling techniques.

Virtually every major ancient culture has produced wisdom literature. In Ancient Egypt, wisdom literature was known as the sebayt (i.e. "teaching") written between 2080 BC and 1640 BC during the Middle Kingdom years. It later became canonical during the New Kingdom period of 1550-1069 BC. The poetry of Hesiod, a Greek oral poet often identified as the first economist, is an early adaptor of Near Eastern wisdom literature particularly in his *"Works and Days."* Another school of Hellenistic philosophy, the Stoics founded in Athens by Zeno of Citium in the early 3rd century BC, composed wisdom literature with a psychological essence. The Mirrors for Princes is a collection primarily composed of textbooks from the Early Middle Ages, Middle Ages and Renaissance periods that are best known for instructing kings or lesser rulers on certain aspects of rule and behavior. Mirrors for Princes books have been discovered in the Carolingian, Irish, Byzantine and Islamic cultures. Finally, the most widely known examples of wisdom literature are the books of Job, Proverbs, Psalms, Ecclesiastes and the Song of Solomon from the Bible; and the Wisdom of Solomon and Sirach from the Apocrypha.

One common thread running through all of this wisdom literature is the expression of an innate desire intrinsic to our human psyche to improve the circumstances in which we find ourselves. Our predisposition to improve our conditions extends to every aspect of our lives whether living environments, relationships, cultural or political situations, economic status or self. What person have you ever known goes to work on a Monday and does a great job and then wakes up on Tuesday and says, "I performed too well yesterday. I'm not going to do as good a job today as I did yesterday?" The answer of course is nobody. We are a competitive society and we all want to do better the next time than we did the last time, even if the only one we are competing against is ourselves. We strive for improvement.

If you recall from history, the great Industrial Revolution took place from the 18th to the 19th century. Major advances in agriculture, manufacturing, mining and transportation had a profound effect on socioeconomic and cultural conditions starting in the United Kingdom. While historians cannot determine any single specific catalyst for the Industrial Revolution, it marks a major turning point in human history influencing almost every facet of daily life as it spread throughout Europe, North America and eventually the world. Perhaps we can gain insight into a prevailing Industrial Revolution philosophy from Henry Ford, the famous American industrialist. Born in 1863 at the pinnacle of the Industrial Revolution, Ford said, "If you think of standardization as the best that you know today, but which is to be improved tomorrow; you get somewhere."

You may be wondering, "What has all of this all got to with the SDLC?" What all this illustrates at a macro level is what we must apply to the micro. As our customers and stakeholders demand better, cheaper and faster systems and efforts from us, we need to reach deeply within our essence to answer the call to continuously improve performance. Former President of ITT Corporation, Harold Geneen said, "It is an immutable law in business that words are words, explanations are explanations, promises are promises but only performance is reality."

Within the discipline of systems development, the SDLC is the standardization Ford speaks about. It is a collection of standard processes and practices that represent the very best we know today. But our best today may not be tomorrow's best; and for us to remain competitive we need to catch up, keep up or lead the charge. We can only do so when we embrace and own the concepts of continuous improvement. Bruce Hamilton, President of the Greater Boston Manufacturing Partnership (GBMP) and recipient of the coveted Shingo Prize for Operational Excellence, says, "Continuous improvement is not about the things you do well - that's work. Continuous improvement is about removing the things that get in the way of your work. The headaches, the things that slow you down, that's what continuous improvement is all about."

No SDLC is complete without addressing continuous improvement activities and metrics. Yet, this is the one area that most IT organizations fail to implement and then wonder why all of their processes and practices haven't brought them the productivity gains and bottom line value they envisioned. I have yet to work for a company where their IT department has successfully implemented a continuous improvement strategy. The pharmaceutical company came close, but still had a long way to go.

Continuous Process Improvement (CPI) is defined as "an ongoing effort to improve products, services or processes." CPI is a strategic approach for developing a culture of continuous improvement in the areas of reliability, process cycle times, costs in terms of less total resource consumption, quality and productivity. CPI therefore, is a framework that ensures continued improvement in an organization's performance. As with any process, business process improvement requires consistent and sustainable leadership and guidance. At times, this requires a radical change perspective, where the fundamental tenets of the process are under revision. At other times, the process undergoes cycles of continuous review and enhancement with minor adjustments considered. At all times, the process's core activities and their relationship (inputs and outputs) with other processes are to be understood, examined and challenged.

Processes are assets of an organization, much like people, facilities, equipment and information. Well managed and well understood processes pay off in terms of improved organizational performance and increased shareholder value. Processes, moreover, are somewhat special in that they are the transports that synchronize the other assets and aspects of change. They are the organizing framework, the glue for all other components.

CPI provides a structured context, tools, techniques and enablers for defining the Voice of the Customer (VOC), analyzing requirements and optimizing processes to align with organizational strategic objectives. Embedding CPI into an organization ensures that all organizational factors such as structure, roles and responsibilities, people and technology are not only integrated but are synchronized to deliver strategic goals and objectives. Figure 122 demonstrates what is needed to embed CPI in an organization.

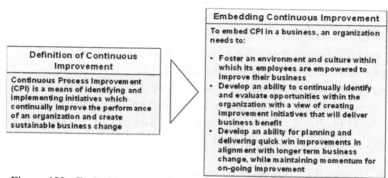

Figure 122 - Embedding Continuous Improvement into an Organization

As we take a deeper look into CPI, we'll build on what we've just discussed—that it is much more than implementing processes and metrics. It is an entire program designed and supported from the very top of the strategic pyramid to tie key processes together with their associated tools, techniques, supporting functions, enablers and business transformation governance. The SDLC only plays a small part in a holistic approach to CPI. And to fully appreciate the SDLC's role, we must first gain an understanding of what business transformation governance is and of some of the many philosophies, frameworks, practices, techniques, tools and models that have been developed over the years to address CPI initiatives which include:

- Benchmarking
- CMMI
- Kaizen
- Kanban
- Lean Six Sigma
- Learning-by-doing

- Overall Equipment Effectiveness
- Root Cause Analysis
- Scrum-ban
- Six Sigma
- Statistical Process Control

- Theory of Constraints
- TOC Lean Six Sigma
- Total Productive Maintenance
- Total Quality Management
- TRIZ

Business Transformation Governance

Business Transformation (BT) Governance is an enterprise framework of limits that define business rules and align work output units with organizational strategic goals. Governance is related to, but separate and distinct from management. Management is the supervision and direction of activities required to implement the business rules defined by the governance mechanism. Governance has three key components: policy, structure and process.

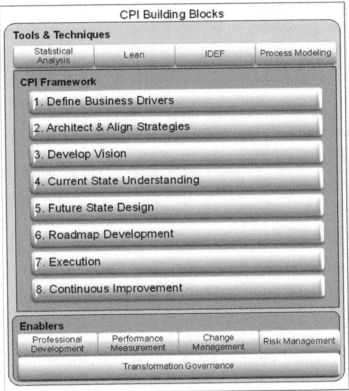

Figure 123 - CPI Framework Model

Governance policy embodies the business rules that guide BT decision-making from the strategic to the tactical level. The governance structure includes the roles and responsibilities of the forums and organizational entities involved in the process. Finally, the governance process identifies the specific activities, documents and information required by leadership for approval decisions regarding BT initiatives. Figure 123 is a public domain CPI framework model courtesy of the United States Army which illustrates transformation governance as the foundation for CPI.

The overarching goal of BT is to streamline or eliminate redundant operations to free financial and human resources and redirect them to the core company mission of providing value to its shareholders. With that goal in mind, the eight basic objectives of BT Governance are:

1. Identify the policies, business rules, roles and responsibilities through which BT is governed
2. Establish and maintain alignment between organizational strategic guidance and BT
3. Implement the decision processes, controls and enforcement necessary for BT
4. Integrate BT Governance with existing decision processes, and where necessary, modify existing processes
5. Establish performance management and metrics, timelines and milestones to track BT progress
6. Define Enterprise Process Portfolios that enable organizational capabilities and make decisions to approve, continue or terminate initiatives in the portfolios based on performance metrics and risk analysis
7. Baseline, simplify and ultimately optimize Enterprise Process Portfolios in support of organizational capabilities
8. Enable a culture of innovation in the organization that challenges the status quo and seeks Continuous Process Improvement

W. Edwards Deming on BT

On October 25, 1999 the Los Angeles Times ran an article titled "The 50: People Who Most Influenced Business This Century." In a special section of the home edition on page U-8, times staff writer Mark Magnier wrote *"Rebuilding Japan with the Help of 2 Americans."* The two Americans Magnier wrote about are General Douglas MacArthur and W. Edwards Deming. Magnier said, "Japan's path from post-war devastation to export powerhouse has involved many important factors, a lot of hard work and a bit of luck. But two Americans who played important parts in the world's greatest economic recovery story—a story that has altered lifestyles around the world and sent countless vehicles, VCRs and Walkmans into our homes—are Gen. Douglas MacArthur and quality guru W. Edwards Deming."

We've spoken about Deming before and his role as the "father of Total Quality Management" If you recall, TQM is designed to reduce errors produced during the manufacturing or service process, increase customer satisfaction, streamline supply chain management, aim for modernization of equipment and ensure workers have the highest level of training. TQM is frequently associated with systems required to support various business process improvement initiatives.

During his life, Deming wrote extensively about management theory, quality, continuous improvement and business transformation. Some of his BT principles fly in the face of traditional management theory. Among the most well-known are his 14 points for management in industry, education and government. Deming said his 14 points apply anywhere. The size of the organization doesn't matter, nor does the industry. They apply equally to a department, division or entire organization. But rather than write about them and lose something in the translation, let's hear it from the quality master himself. The following is an excerpt listing the 14 points from Chapter 2 of *"Out of the Crisis"* by W. Edwards Deming:[115]

1. Create constancy of purpose toward improvement of product and service, with the aim to become competitive and to stay in business, and to provide jobs.
2. Adopt the new philosophy. We are in a new economic age. Western management must awaken to the challenge, must learn their responsibilities, and take on leadership for change.
3. Cease dependence on inspection to achieve quality. Eliminate the need for inspection on a mass basis by building quality into the product in the first place.
4. End the practice of awarding business on the basis of price tag. Instead, minimize total cost. Move toward a single supplier for any one item, on a long-term relationship of loyalty and trust.
5. Improve constantly and forever the system of production and service, to improve quality and productivity, and thus constantly decrease costs.
6. Institute training on the job.
7. Institute leadership. The aim of supervision should be to help people and machines and gadgets to do a better job. Supervision of management is in need of overhaul, as well as supervision of production workers.
8. Drive out fear, so that everyone may work effectively for the company.
9. Break down barriers between departments. People in research, design, sales, and production must work as a team, to foresee problems of production and in use that may be encountered with the product or service.
10. Eliminate slogans, exhortations, and targets for the work force asking for zero defects and new levels of productivity. Such exhortations only create adversarial relationships, as the bulk of the causes of low quality and low productivity belong to the system and thus lie beyond the power of the work force.
    a. Eliminate work standards (quotas) on the factory floor. Substitute leadership.
    b. Eliminate management by objective. Eliminate management by numbers, numerical goals. Substitute leadership.
11. Remove barriers that rob the hourly worker of his right to pride of workmanship. The responsibility of supervisors must be changed from sheer numbers to quality.

---

[115] Source: http://deming.org/index.cfm?content=66; Accessed May 4, 2010.

12. Remove barriers that rob people in management and in engineering of their right to pride of workmanship. This means, inter alia, abolishment of the annual or merit rating and of management by objective.
13. Institute a vigorous program of education and self-improvement.
14. Put everybody in the company to work to accomplish the transformation. The transformation is everybody's job.

Some of Deming's 14 points are sure to raise eyebrows, for example, the statements he makes in 10b, "Eliminate management by objective. Eliminate management by numbers, numerical goals" or in point 12, "abolishment of the annual or merit rating and of management by objective." In another one of his works he goes on to describe the seven deadly diseases of Western Management. Number three on Deming's deadly disease list is "Evaluation of performance, merit rating or annual review." Regardless of whether you agree with Deming or not, he is a visionary with an incredibly successful track record. His management points are as relevant today as when he published them in 1989; and with the benefit of time, they are proven to be correct.

This may be a little off-topic for the SDLC, but if you are thinking about following Deming's advice and are wondering about what you should do in place of performance evaluations, you are not alone. Once, when Dr. Deming was lecturing[116] on the topic of eliminating performance appraisals, someone in the audience asked, "If we eliminate performance appraisals, as you suggest, what do we do instead?" Dr. Deming's reply: "Whatever Peter Scholtes says." To learn more about the alternatives to performance appraisals, read Chapter 9 - Performance without Appraisal in the *"The Leader's Handbook: Making Things Happen, Getting Things Done"* by Peter Scholtes.

Capability Maturity Model Integration

Capability Maturity Model Integration (CMMI) is a process improvement approach developed by the Software Engineering Institute (SEI). SEI is a federally funded research and development center headquartered on the campus of Carnegie Mellon University in Pittsburgh, Pennsylvania in the United States. The SEI operates with major funding from the U.S. Department of Defense and also works closely with academia and industry through research collaborations. The SEI conducts its research in three principal areas: management practices, engineering practices and acquisition practices. Corresponding to these three principle areas of practice are three CMMI models which vary in terms of their key process areas. The models are:

1. Product and service development—CMMI for Development (CMMI-DEV)

---

[116] Source: *"The Leader's Handbook"*, page 296

2. Service establishment, management and delivery—CMMI for Services (CMMI-SVC)
3. Product and service acquisition—CMMI for Acquisition (CMMI-ACQ)

The CMMI models designate what processes are implemented, but not how to implement them. How to implement any CMMI model is left up to the organization. However, each of the models can be implemented in either a staged or continuous representation. A continuous representation focuses on implementing specific processes important to an organization's present business objectives or those with a high degree of risk. A staged representation is a standard sequence of improvements and serves as a basis for comparing the maturity of different projects and organizations.

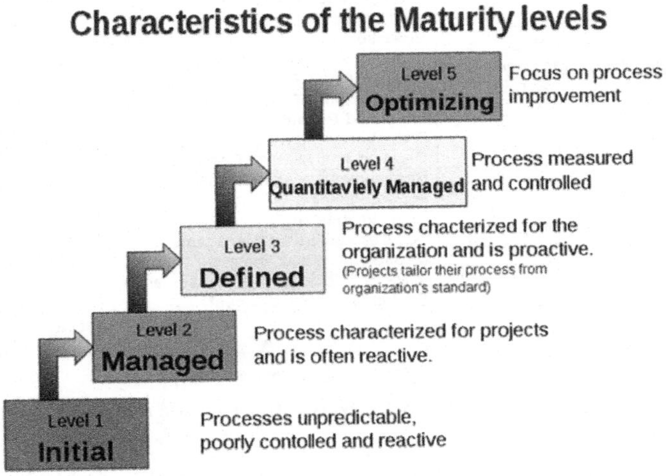

Characteristics of the Maturity levels

Figure 124 - CMMI Maturity Levels

Organizations implementing CMMI may determine the level of their process maturity by submitting themselves to a Standard CMMI Appraisal Method for Process Improvement (SCAMPI). A SCAMPI class "A" appraisal is the most formal type and can result in a maturity level rating. Maturity level ratings are awarded on a scale of 1 to 5. Figure 124 depicts the standard CMMI maturity rating scale.

The SEI tracks companies implementing CMMI and reports statistics that demonstrate measured performance increases in cost, schedule, productivity, quality and customer satisfaction where the median increase in performance varied between 14% (customer satisfaction) and 62% (productivity). But since the CMMI models don't explain how to implement their processes, there is no guarantee that other companies can achieve similar success due to the high degree of implementation variability. In fact, the SEI Process Maturity Profile published in March of 2006 establishes that as of year-end 2005, a small company with few resources is less likely to benefit from CMMI; 63.3% of small organizations with fewer than <25 employees are assessed at level 2: Managed, while 69.2% of the organizations with 1000-2000 employees are rated at level 3: Defined or higher. Figure 125 is another illustration of the CMMI maturity levels that includes their foci and process areas.

Capability Maturity Model—Integrated

Level	Focus	Process Areas	Result
5 Optimizing	Continuous process improvement	Organizational Innovation & Deployment Causal Analysis and Resolution	Productivity & Quality
4 Quantitatively Managed	Quantitative management	Organizational Process Performance Quantitative Project Management	
3 Defined	Process standardization	Requirements Development Technical Solution Product Integration Verification Validation Organizational Process Focus Organizational Process Definition Organizational Training Integrated Project Management Risk Management Decision Analysis and Resolution	
2 Managed	Basic project management	Requirements Management Project Planning Project Monitoring & Control Supplier Agreement Management Measurement and Analysis Process & Product Quality Assurance Configuration Management	
1 Initial	Competent people and heroics		

Public Domain Image Courtesy of NASA

Figure 125 - CMMI Levels with Process Areas

In 2002, academicians Richard Turner[117] and Apurva Jain[118] evaluated the components of CMMI for their support of agile methods and published their conclusions in a paper titled *"Agile Meets CMMI: Culture Clash or Common Cause?"* They conclude that while there are obviously large differences between CMMI and Agile methods, both approaches have much in common. Neither is the "right" way to develop software, but there are phases in a project where one of the two is better suited. They suggest combining the different features of the methods into a new hybrid model.

In 2007, Jeff Sutherland, Carsten Ruseng Jakobsen and Kent Johnson assert in *"Scrum and CMMI Level 5: The Magic Potion for Code Warriors,"*[119] that Scrum and CMMI together bring

[117] The George Washington University, Department of Engineering Management and Systems Engineering, School of Engineering and Applied Sciences, Washington, DC 20052
[118] University of Southern California, Center for Software Engineering, Computer Science Department, Los Angeles, CA 90089-0781
[119] Source: http://www.computer.org/portal/web/csdl/doi/10.1109/AGILE.2007.52; Accessed May 5, 2010.

a more powerful combination of adaptability and predictability than either one alone and suggest how other companies can combine them. In the abstract of their paper available on the IEEE web site, they say, "Projects combining agile methods with CMMI are more successful in producing higher quality software that more effectively meets customer needs at a faster pace. Systematic Software Engineering works at CMMI level 5 and uses Lean Software Development as a driver for optimizing software processes. Early pilot projects at Systematic showed productivity on Scrum teams almost twice that of traditional teams. Other projects demonstrated a story based test-driven approach to software development reduced defects found during final test by 40%."

In the 2006 Process Maturity Profile, SEI presented statistics on organizations adopting their earlier Software CMM. Since 1987, the median time for 200 organizations to move up from Level 1 to Level 2 is 23 months. The largest observed value in this category not classified as an outlier is 75 months. The median time for 274 organizations to move up from Level 2 to Level 3 is 20 months. The median time to move up from Level 3 to Level 4 is 25 months; and from level 4 to level 5 is 13 months. These latter categories represent 65 and 64 organizations respectively. For organizations that began their CMM-based effort in 1992 or later, the time to move up median times are somewhat improved:

- Maturity level 1 to 2 is 19 months
- Maturity level 2 to 3 is 19 months
- Maturity level 3 to 4 is 24 months
- Maturity level 4 to 5 is 13 months

The CMMI framework, when used together with the SEI's Team Software Process (TSP) methodology, are known to progress organizations from Level 1 to Level 4 in 30 months, less than half the average time it takes for the traditional approach. If you want to learn more about CMMI or read additional viewpoints about combining CMMI with Agile methods, you can do so by visiting the SEI website. CMMI is not a magic bullet. It is not going to solve all of an organization's continuous improvement problems. It is a difficult model to deploy because of the lack of implementation guidance.

Kaizen

Kaizen is a Japanese word that when translated means "improvement" or "change for the better." It is the philosophy behind the Toyota Production System discussed in the Lean Development section of Chapter 2. Its practices focus upon CPI in manufacturing, engineering, business processes and management. In Japan, it has been applied to virtually every industry. Kaizen is built on the effects of the Learning-by-doing method. Learning-by-doing is a concept of economic theory that refers to the capability of workers to improve their productivity by regularly repeating the same type of action. The increased productivity is achieved through practice, self-perfection and minor innovations.

As a daily activity, Kaizen humanizes the workplace, eliminates overly hard work (muri), teaches people how to perform scientific method experiments on their work and how to distinguish and eliminate waste in business processes. The key elements of kaizen are quality, effort, involvement of all employees, willingness to change and communication.

As for the humanizing aspect, Bunji Tozawa,[120] author of *"The improvement engine: creativity & innovation through employee involvement: the Kaizen teian[121] system,"* says, "The idea is to nurture the company's human resources as much as it is to praise and encourage participation in kaizen activities." In another book,[122] *"The Kaizen Blitz: accelerating breakthroughs in productivity and performance,"* authors Anthony C. Laraia, Patricia E. Moody and Robert W. Hall concur that a successful Kaizen implementation requires "the participation of workers in the improvement."

At Toyota, all manufacturing personnel are expected to stop their moving production line in the event of the discovery of any abnormality in the process. They then suggest an improvement, along with their supervisor, which may initiate a kaizen to resolve the anomaly. People at all levels of an organization participate in kaizen, from the CEO on down. At times, external stakeholders participate as well. Kaizen can be individual, group oriented or scale to cross-departmental levels. Kaizen activity can be thought of as continuous Plan • Do • Check • Act (PDCA) cycles which:

- Standardize an operation
- Measure the standardized operation
- Evaluate measurements against requirements
- Innovate to meet requirements and increase productivity
- Standardize the new, improved operations
- Continue cycle *ad infinitum*

---

[120] Source: Tozawa, Bunji; Japan Human Relations Association (1995). *"The improvement engine: creativity & innovation through employee involvement: the Kaizen teian system."* Productivity Press. pp. 34. ISBN 9781563270109. http://books.google.com/books?id=1vqyBirIQLkC&pg=PA34. Accessed May 5, 2010

[121] Teian = suggestion sheets used to communicate ideas to upper management, other departments or to record small breakthroughs in the way work is done.

[122] Source: Laraia, Anthony C.; Patricia E. Moody, Robert W. Hall (1999). The Kaizen Blitz: accelerating breakthroughs in productivity and performance. John Wiley and Sons. pp. 26. ISBN 9780471246480.

If you recall, the PDCA cycle is also known as the Deming Cycle or Shewhart Cycle. Figure 126 illustrates the Kaizen PDCA cycles.

Figure 126 - Kaizen PDCA Cycles

Interestingly, apart from the business world, two well-known self-help gurus have reportedly incorporated Kaizen principles into their personal development approaches: Anthony Robbins and Robert Maurer. Anthony Robbins is an American self-help author, motivational speaker and creator of Personal Power and Get the Edge. Robbins' books include *"Unlimited Power: The New Science of Personal Achievement"* and *"Awaken The Giant Within."* Dr. Robert Maurer is the Director of Behavioral Sciences for Family Medicine Spokane and a faculty member with the University of Washington School of Medicine. In his book *"One Small Step Can Change Your Life,"* Maurer describes Kaizen as a powerful technique for making positive improvements in work, health and relationships.

Theory of Constraints

Dr. Eliyahu Moshe Goldratt is an Israeli physicist who is the originator of the Optimized Production Technology, the Theory of Constraints (TOC), the Thinking Processes, Drum-Buffer-Rope, Critical Chain Project Management (CCPM) and other TOC derived tools. The TOC, also known as "Constraint Management," is an overall management philosophy introduced in his 1984 book titled *"The Goal"* written to help organizations continually achieve their goal.[123]

TOC assumes that organizations can be measured and controlled by variations on three measures: throughput, operating expense and inventory. Throughput is money (or goal units) generated through sales. Inventory is money the system invests in order to sell its goods and services. Operating expense is all the money the system spends in order to turn inventory into

---

[123] Cox, Jeff; Goldratt, Eliyahu M. (1986). *"The goal: a process of ongoing improvement."* [Croton-on-Hudson, NY]: North River Press. ISBN 0-88427-061-0.

throughput.[124] A constraint is anything that prevents a system from achieving more of its goal units. Goldratt contends that any manageable system is limited in achieving more of its goal units by a very small number of constraints and that there is always at least one; and by increasing flow through the constraint, overall throughput rises.

The TOC defines five focusing steps to ensure ongoing improvement efforts target an organization's constraints. TOC calls these steps the "Process of Ongoing Improvement" (POOGI). The POOGI's five steps are:

1. Identify the constraint:
    a. The policy, people or equipment that prevents the organization from obtaining more of the goal
2. Decide how to exploit the constraint:
    a. Make sure the constraint's time is not wasted doing things that it should not do
3. Subordinate all other processes to the exploit decision:
    a. Align the whole system or organization to support the exploit decision
4. Elevate the constraint:
    a. Permanently increase capacity of the constraint if required or possible
5. If, as a result of these steps, the constraint has moved, return to Step 1
    a. Don't let inertia become the constraint

The concept of "buffers" is critical to both the exploit and subordinate POOGI steps. Buffers are used to protect the constraint and allow for normal process variation. Buffers ensure that there is enough work in the queue before the constraint so that the constraint is never starved for capacity. The TOC assumption is that with only one constraint, all the other system work streams have the capacity to keep up with the constraint. The only instance in which a system is in danger is if the constraint in unable to complete its process due to a defect or buffer under run.

The Thinking Processes

The TOC led to the development of the Thinking Processes (TP). The TP are a set of tools to help achieve a buy-in process when initiating or implementing a project. This is sometimes referred to working through layers of resistance to a change. The TP may very well form the basis of an organizational change management strategy. There are five steps to the TP:

1. Gain agreement on the problem
    a. What to change?

---

[124] Goldratt, Eliyahu M.. *"Essays on the Theory of Constraints."* [Great Barrington, MA]: North River Press. ISBN 0-88427-159-5.

2. Gain agreement on the direction for a solution
   a. What to change to?
3. Gain agreement that the solution solves the problem
   a. How to cause the change?
4. Agree to overcome any potential negative ramifications
   a. Why change?
5. Agree to overcome any obstacles to implementation
   a. How to maintain the POOGI?

POOGI and TP have been successfully applied to Manufacturing, Project Management, Supply Chain / Distribution, Marketing, Sales and Finance. Despite its successes, TOC is not without its criticisms. Dan Trietsch, associate professor in the Department of Information Systems and Operations Management at The University of Auckland Business School, calls the TOC flawed and inferior to competing methodologies. [125][126] He says, "The five-step 'Theory of Constraints' as articulated and explained in Goldratt's books, is touted as 'not only beneficial but mandatory.' However, although it is indeed a useful focusing heuristic methodology with an impressive track record, it is not really a theory and it is certainly not mandatory. Furthermore, it involves a serious internal inconsistency that must be 'faced courageously:' to make drum-buffer-rope (DBR) work, Goldratt forbids balance, and yet Step 4 involves steps that tend to balance the system."

Other critics raise the claim of unacknowledged debt. They say the TOC is not based on Goldratt's original thinking and that he fails to acknowledge the true source of his work. Duncan (as cited by Steyn)[127] says that TOC borrows heavily from systems dynamics developed by Forrester in the 1950s and from statistical process control which dates back to World War II. Eric Noreen, Debra Smith and James T. Mackey, in their independent report[128] on TOC, point out that several key concepts in TOC "have been topics in management accounting textbooks for decades." Goldratt respond to these latter critics in papers, on his audio program called "Beyond the Goal" and in talks[129] called "Standing on the Shoulders of Giants."

---

[125] http://ac.aua.am/trietsch/web/MBC_to_MBC_II.pdf D. Trietsch, From *"Management by Constraints (MBC) to Management By Criticalities (MBC II)"*, Human Systems Management (24) 105-115, 2005
[126] http://ac.aua.am/trietsch/web/WorkingPaper281.pdf D. Trietsch, *"From the Flawed 'Theory of Constraints' to Hierarchically Balancing Criticalities (HBC)"*, Department of Information Systems and Operations Management, University of Auckland, Working Paper No. 281, May 2004
[127] Steyn, Herman (2000). *"An Investigation Into the Fundamentals of Critical Chain Project Scheduling."* International Journal of Project Management (19): 363–369.
[128] Eric Noreen; Debra Smith, James T. Mackey (1995). *"The Theory of Constraints and its implications for Management Accounting."* North River Press. pp. 149. ISBN 0-88427-116-1.
[129] Source: Standing on the Shoulders of Giants. http://www.youtube.com/watch?v=C3RPFUh3ePQ; Accessed May 5, 2010

Microsoft TOC Case Study

In November of 2005, David J. Anderson & Dragos Dumitriu of the Microsoft Corporation published a case study paper[130] entitled *"From Worst to Best in 9 Months: Implementing a Drum-Buffer-Rope Solution in Microsoft's IT Department."* The case study documents the effectiveness of the TOC's POOGI and the drum-buffer-rope production flow solution without having to resort to the TP or Critical Chain Project Scheduling. The paper is an excellent example of a TOC implementation and is interesting to read. Its abstract says in part:

The XIT Sustained Engineering team is part of one of Microsoft's eight IT groups. The department maintains over 80 applications for internal use worldwide by Microsoft employees. The team completes small change requests (often bug fixes) involving less than 120 hours of development work. The team was considered the worst performing in its business unit at the start of the 2005 fiscal year (July 2004). The backlog of work was exceeding capacity 5 times and it was growing every month. The lead time for a change request was typically 5 months. The due date performance was almost zero. The customers were unhappy. A new program manager stepped in to coordinate the efforts of XIT Sustained Engineering. He wanted to make some changes but was unclear whether they were the right changes and how effective they might be. By performing an analysis using the 5 focusing steps of TOC, David Anderson helped him to understand how his proposals fitted with a drum-buffer-rope and Throughput Accounting implementation. With no new resources, no changes to how the team performed software engineering tasks like design, coding and testing, the changes to how the work was queued and estimated resulted in a 155% productivity gain in 9 months. The lead time was reduced to a maximum of 5 weeks – typically 14 days. Due date performance improved to greater than 90%. The backlog was worked off and the department is no longer seen as an organizational constraint. Customers are delighted.

The XIT Sustained Engineering team is a CMMI Level 5 group located in Hyderabad, India. The constraint that led to the poor results is the requirement to provide a rough order of magnitude (ROM) estimate for every change request in order to triage and prioritize them. POOGI led the management team to the realization that ROMs were eating up 40% of the development teams' available capacity. The diagnostic process allowed the managers to conclude that to improve productivity they needed to apply two interventions: 1. Install buffers into the process; and 2. eliminate the ROM and related cost accounting practices. With these interventions, not only did they accomplish what is described in the abstract, but the cost of each change request dropped from approximately $7,500 to $2,500 and throughput increased from 17 to 56 change requests

---

[130] Source: http://www.agilemanagement.net/AMPDFArchive/From_Worst_to_Best_in_9_Months_Final_1_3.pdf; Accessed May 5, 2010

per quarter. In the second half of 2005, the XIT Sustained Engineering team won Microsoft's Engineering Excellence Award.

Kanban

Kanban is a Japanese word that means "signboard" or "billboard" and describes an embellished wooden or metal sign often representing a trademark or seal. Conceptually, Kanban is related to Lean and Just-in-time (JIT), an inventory strategy to improve a company's return on investment by reducing in-process inventory and its associated carrying costs. Taiichi Ohno is considered to be the father of the Toyota Production System. The Toyota Production System is one aspect of The Toyota Way. The Toyota Way is Toyota's overall management philosophy and is comprised of 14 principles. Section II of the Toyota Way is called "The Right Process Will Produce the Right Results." There are seven principles that are defined in this section:

1. Create a continuous process flow to bring problems to the surface
2. Use "pull" systems to avoid overproduction
3. Level out the workload
4. Build a culture of stopping to fix problems, to get quality right the first time
5. Standardized tasks and processes are the foundation for continuous improvement and employee empowerment
6. Use visual control so no problems are hidden
7. Use only reliable, thoroughly tested technology that serves your people and processes

Toyota invented the Kanban system to maintain a high rate of process improvements. While the word Kanban does not appear in this list, points 1, 2 and 6 are all descriptive of Kanban. Ohno is also credited with developing JIT. The JIT process relies on signals or Kanban between different points in the process to tell production when to make the next part. Kanban, therefore, is a signaling system that triggers an action.

In IT, Kanban acts to limit work-in-progress and focuses the team on achieving a continuous flow of value to the customer. It redefines accepted Agile system development practices by providing a cycle-less process with a regularly scheduled release cadence. How does it do that, you ask? Basically, with a white board and sticky notes, that's how. It's an incredibly simple process to use and can produce very powerful results. There are electronic Kanban systems that can be integrated into Enterprise Resource Planning (ERP) systems. E-Kanban systems help eliminate the rare but common problems of manual entry errors and lost sticky notes or cards.

To fully appreciate Kanban, think of the various system development work streams. Work streams are often referred to as pipelines or queues. In our homes, if a pipe gets clogged, water stops flowing or draining, backs up into the sink and the problem needs to get fixed. Work pipelines can also get clogged for various reasons and cause backlogs at various points in the process. With Kanban, work enters the pipeline in a controlled manner to reduce or prevent the backlog due to resource capacity constraints. In other words, no process receives more work into its queue than it has the capacity to complete it on schedule.

Figure 127 is an example of a basic Kanban board. Each sticky note signifies a work item as it flows through the lifecycle phases delineated by the columns. The names of the lifecycle phases make up the column headings. The numbers above the column headings are the number of work-in-process items permitted to be in a column at any one time. This number may vary from project to project or team to team based on available resources and lead time. Notice how some of the columns are divided by a dotted line. The left side of the dotted line is the actual work items still in-process for that phase. The space on the right side of the dotted line is for the items that have been completed in that phase and are waiting for the next phase to present an open slot.

Kanban practitioners code different types of work items by using a variety of colorful sticky notes. For example, one strategy could be:

- Yellow is a customer initiated enhancement or defect correcting change request
- Blue is a defect discovered in one of the testing cycles that needs to be fixed
- Red is constraint or exception that needs to be addressed because it is blocking a particular task from being completed
- White is a special category of work item known as a "silver bullet." Silver bullets are expedited requests that are hand carried through the system. They take priority over all other requests and may jump queues.
- Orange is a low priority, non-critical defect to be fixed and perhaps quality tested by developers on their slack time

The Kanban tickets themselves hold a lot of information that enable decentralized control and local decision making when determining which items to pull through the system. For example, there should always be some sort of ID number for traceability purposes. Tickets also include the date the work item was accepted, the hard delivery date, the assigned engineer and its SLA commitment. Issues impacting the work item are attached to the main note with additional red sticky notes.

The basic Kanban process really is this simple! But there's one question left to answer, "How do work items get put into the pending column in the first place?" There needs to be some type of governance or demand management process where work requests are triaged and prioritized. If we refer back to our generic IT governance model in Chapter 3 (Figure 36), demand management is handled by the IT Director, business unit steering committee or IT Governance Council depending on the estimated level of effort. With Kanban, you can either use the same governance structure or modify the model slightly to address backlogs with a different governance team known as a Prioritization Board (PB).

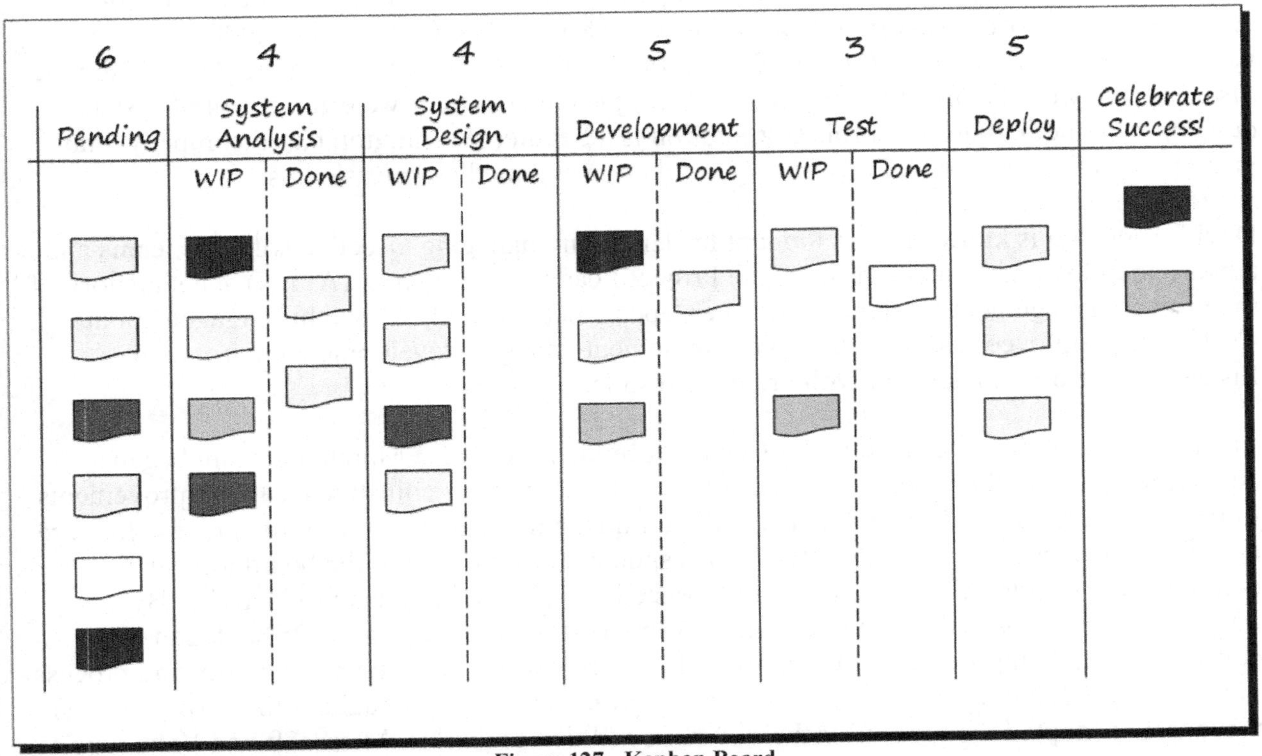

Figure 127 - Kanban Board

In one model from the gaming industry, the PB is composed of the VPs from 6 business units. They established a regular delivery cadence of two weeks per release. PB meetings are held every Monday and all content to be discussed is published 5 days earlier. The PB meetings are designed to answer one question, "Which items from the backlog do we want to move into the empty slots in the pending queue this week?" This means the selection decisions are made at the last possible moment, leaving open any additional options that may be available.

The one exception to this is the silver bullet. There should never be more than one silver bullet in the work stream at any particular time. This means silver bullets need to be justified by their business case, throughput, lead time and cost. Only the most critical items are considered as silver bullets. Silver bullets may include any work items related to regulatory compliance or other mandates such as a tax update for a payroll system.

Corbis Kanban Case Study

David J. Anderson is president of Modus Cooperandi. This is the same individual who co-authored the Microsoft Theory of Constraints Case Study. At QCon London 2008,[131] Anderson gave a presentation titled *"A Kanban System for Software Engineering."* In the presentation, he discusses the work he did at Corbis in introducing Kanban to their waterfall flavored system development methodology. Corbis Corporation is a Seattle, Washington based company who provides creative services for advertising, marketing and media professionals.

David Anderson is known for his thought leadership in managing effective software teams and is a board member and founder of the Agile Project Leadership Network (APLN) and signatory of the project management Declaration of Interdependence. When he began his engagement at Corbis, the employees assumed he would implement an Agile development environment. Instead, he introduced Kanban with dramatic results.

The implementation of Kanban took place in December, 2006. By March, the team began developing pride in the process and instinctively started making adjustments and improvements to fit their needs. By April they had revised their queue limits and extended the process forward to include business analysis. A waste bin was spontaneously added to the board to visually communicate rejected change requests that wasted energy and impeded productivity. By September, business analysis merged with system analysis and eliminated 25% of lead time consumed as queuing waste. Other teams within Corbis recognized the productivity and process improvements achieved by Anderson's team and Kanban spread throughout the corporation as those teams adopted the process as their own. In addition to Corbis, Microsoft and Yahoo are known to use Kanban.

Scrum-ban

Scrum-ban is a continuous improvement method that combines Scrum with Kanban. It maintains all the elements of Scrum but divides Kanban into sprints instead of its normal continuous, cycle-less pattern. By the end of each sprint, the Kanban board is empty.

Statistical Analysis Variants

The list of philosophies and frameworks from earlier in the chapter includes three variations of Six Sigma: Six Sigma, Lean Six Sigma and Theory of Constraints Six Sigma. The list also calls out Benchmarking (discussed in Chapter 9), Overall Equipment Effectiveness and Statistical

---

[131] Source: http://www.infoq.com/presentations/kanban-for-software; Accessed May 6, 2010

Process Control. The one point in common with all six of these methods is that they depend upon some form of statistical analysis to drive their continuous improvement processes.

Six Sigma

We touched briefly on the topic of Six Sigma in Chapter 9's discussion of Quality Models and Standards. Six Sigma and Statistical Process Control, pioneered by Walter A. Shewhart in the early 1920s, are very closely related. Both monitor their processes using control charts and diagrams, sometimes the same ones; and both seek to minimize process variation using statistical analysis. Because they are so closely related, we shall only discuss Six Sigma.

As mentioned in Chapter 9, a six sigma process is one in which 99.99966% of its outputs are free of defects. The two basic methodologies foundational to Six Sigma are inspired by Deming's Plan • Do • Check • Act model. Each of the methodologies is comprised of 5 phases. The methodologies are known by the acronyms formed by the first letter of the first word defining each of their phases. The acronyms are DMAIC and DMADV.

The phases of the DMAIC methodology are:

- **Define** the problem, the voice of the customer and the project goals
- **Measure** key aspects of the current process and collect relevant data
- **Analyze** the data to investigate and verify cause-and-effect relationships
  - o Ensure that all factors are considered
  - o Seek the root cause of the defect under investigation
- **Improve** the current process based upon statistical analysis
  - o Set up pilot runs to establish process capability
- **Control** the future state process to ensure that any deviations from target are corrected before they result in defects

DMADV is sometimes called DFSS which means "Design for Six Sigma." DMADV's five phases are:

- **Define** design goals that are consistent with customer demands and the enterprise strategy
- **Measure** and identify characteristics that are Critical to Quality (CTQ), product capabilities, production process capability and risks.
- **Analyze** to develop and define alternatives
  - o Create a high-level designs and evaluate their capability to select the best design
- **Design** details, optimize the design and plan for design verification
- **Verify** the design, set up pilot runs, implement the production process and hand it over to the process owner(s)

Six Sigma instructors often say, "If you can't measure it, why are you doing it?" usually paraphrasing Deming who is thought to have said, "You can't manage what you can't measure." Deming did not say this nor did he believe it. He saw it as a deadly disease of Western management. Number 5 on his list of seven deadly diseases is "Running a company on visible figures alone." Deming knew that not everything of importance to management can be measured and that many important factors are "unknown and unknowable." In spite of the philosophical dichotomy, Six Sigma has a proven track record of improving process quality.

Six Sigma works by measuring processes and then analyzing the measurements against the process mean and its nearest specification limit. Standard deviations are measured in terms of sigma units. If a process has six standard deviations or six sigmas (6σ) between the process mean and its nearest specification limit, virtually no items will fail to meet specifications. Figure 128 is a normal Six Sigma distribution curve.

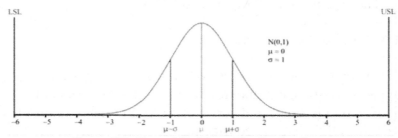

Figure 128 - Normal Six Sigma Distribution Curve

The Greek letter σ (sigma) marks the distance on the horizontal axis between the mean (μ) and the curve's inflection point. The greater this distance, the greater the spread of values encountered. For the curve shown in Figure 128, μ = 0 and σ = 1. The upper and lower specification limits (USL, LSL) are at a distance of 6σ from the mean. Because of the properties of the normal distribution, values lying that far away from the mean are extremely unlikely.

Studies[132][133] show that processes don't perform as well in the long term as they do in the short. The number of sigmas that fit between the process mean and the nearest specification limit may be observed to decrease over time whereby increasing process variation. To account for this, a 1.5 sigma shift is introduced into the calculation. The idea is that if a process fits six sigmas between the process mean and the nearest specification limit in a short-term, in the long term it will only fit 4.5 sigmas. This is either due to the mean moving over time or because the long-

132 Tennant, Geoff (2001). *"SIX SIGMA: SPC and TQM in Manufacturing and Services."* Gower Publishing, Ltd.. pp. 25. ISBN 0566083744.
133 Harry, Mikel J. (1988). *"The Nature of six sigma quality."* Rolling Meadows, Illinois: Motorola University Press. p. 25. ISBN 9781569460092

term standard deviation is greater than that of the short term; or it could be due to a combination of both. Referring back to Figure 128, even if the mean were to move right or left by 1.5σ at some point in the future, there is still a good safety margin.

Six Sigma is much more complex and far more detailed than can be represented in this chapter. And as with almost anything else, it is not without its critics. In an interview[134] conducted by Scott M. Patton, Joseph M. Juran, the noted quality expert, was asked "What do you think of Six Sigma?" Juran said "From what I've seen of it, it's a basic version of quality improvement. There is nothing new there. It includes what we used to call facilitators. They've adopted more flamboyant terms, like belts with different colors. I think that concept has merit to set apart, to create specialists who can be very helpful. Again, that's not a new idea. The American Society for Quality long ago established certificates, such as for reliability engineers."

Lean Six Sigma

Lean Six Sigma combines the principles of Lean with the methods of Six Sigma. The combination achieves what neither can do alone—provide a fastest rate of improvement in customer satisfaction, cost, quality, process speed and invested capital. The fusion of the Lean and Six Sigma methods evolved because:

- Lean cannot bring a process under statistical control
- Six Sigma alone cannot dramatically improve process speed or reduce capital investment
- Both enable a reduction in the cost of complexity

The two methodologies interact and reinforce one another, such that gains in Return on Investment Capital (ROIC%) are much faster if Lean and Six Sigma are implemented together. What sets Lean Six Sigma apart from its individual components is the recognition that you cannot do "just quality" or "just speed," you need a balanced process that can help an organization focus on improving service quality within a set time limit as defined by the customer.

Ironically, Six Sigma and Lean have often been regarded as rival initiatives. Lean enthusiasts note that Six Sigma pays little attention to anything related to speed and flow, while Six Sigma supporters point out that Lean fails to address key concepts like customer needs and variation. Both sides are right. Yet these arguments are more often used to advocate choosing one over the

---

[134] Source: Paton, Scott M. (August 2002). Juran: A Lifetime of Quality. 22. pp. 19–23. Accessed May 6, 2010 http://www.qualitydigest.com/aug02/articles/01_article.shtml

other, rather than to support the more logical conclusion of blending Lean and Six Sigma together.

TOC Lean Six Sigma

The third variation of Six Sigma combines the Theory of Constraints, Lean and Six Sigma into a holistic sequence of processes called TOC Lean Six Sigma (iTLS™®). Weber State University at Utah introduced iTLS to academia in May 2007 as a credible CPI alternative. It is part of the University's academic curriculum. iTLS as a CPI approach is growing in popularity with the experts. Goldratt acknowledged the significance of iTLS during the Theory of Constraints International Certification Organization (TOCICO) symposium in Nov 2007.

Dr. Reza (Russ) Pirasteh PhD., MBB, CLM. is founder of iTLS™ – ISO and originator of the iTLS approach to CPI. The iTLS international standards organization is a standardization body for the education, implementation and certification of iTLS worldwide. According to the iTLS™ – ISO, "iTLS™ is a unique approach that utilizes strengths of TOC, Lean and Six Sigma and applies them in a special order that the outcome financial benefits are typically 400-600% higher than if either one of TOC, Lean or Six Sigma were applied alone." The special order sequence is executed in the following order: 1. Apply TOC to focus on what needs to be fixed; 2. Apply Lean to eliminate waste; 3. Apply Six Sigma to optimize process variability and error

Program:	Theory of Constraints	Lean	Six Sigma
View of Waste:	Constraints drive waste	Non-value add is waste	Variation is waste
Application:	• Identify Constraint • Exploit Constraint • Subordinate Others • Elevate Constraint • Repeat Cycle	• Identify Value • Define Value Stream • Determine Flow • Define Pull • Improve Process	• Define • Measure • Analyze • Improve • Control
Tools:	Thinking processes	Visualization	Statistical Analysis
Focus:	Constraint	Process flow	Defects

Figure 129 - Six Sigma, Lean and TOC Comparison[135]

Figure 129 compares the major aspects of the three methodologies. It is clear to see that they compatibly address different issues and processes. Hence, it is safe to infer that iTLS is an effective CPI alternative to apply when the following assumptions are true:

- Every system has at least one constraint which limits its ability to get more of the goal

---

[135] Table based on one found in an article titled *"Six Sigma, Lean or TOC: What's the Difference?"* on http://learnsigma.com/; Author unknown. Accessed May 6, 2010

- o TOC is needed to manage the constraints
- Every system has non-value add waste
  - o Use Lean methods to eliminate them
- Every system exhibits process deviations
  - o Utilize Six Sigma to locate and eliminate them

iTLS™ – ISO conducted a study in which 105 projects were completed by using the three methods, either singly or in combination. Their findings: "TLS process improvement methodology appeared significantly more effective compared with the other two methodologies, Lean and Six Sigma, by delivering higher cost savings to the company. In this study TLS methodology application resulted in a contribution of 89% of the total savings reported, followed by 7% from Six Sigma and 4% from Lean applications."

All the Rest

So far we've discussed twelve of the sixteen CPI philosophies, frameworks, practices, techniques, tools and models listed earlier in the chapter. (TQM is discussed in Chapter 9.) The rest are either not applicable to systems development or discussing them in detail would not serve to add any value to what has already been presented. Two of these methods, Total Productive Maintenance and Overall Equipment Effectiveness, are very specific to manufacturing and won't adapt well to a system development CPI program. Total Productive Maintenance (TPM) is the first quality methodology Toyota used in the 1950s to improve its global position. Since we've already discussed Kaizen and Kanban, there's no need to explore TPM.

Overall Equipment Effectiveness

Overall Equipment Effectiveness is intriguing. Even though in its purest form it is not suitable for system development, it doesn't take too much of a stretch of the imagination to think it could be adapted to data center operations. Its two top level metrics are overall equipment effectiveness (OEE) and total effective equipment performance (TEEP). OEE quantifies how well a unit performs relative to its designed capacity during the periods it is scheduled to run. TEEP measures effectiveness against calendar hours, i.e.: 24 hrs./day, 365 days/yr., 24x7. TEEP could be a useful metric in a 24x7 data center. The problem with these metrics is that they are designed around manufacturing and the number of parts produced during a work shift. If you figure out an IT equivalent to substitute for the number of parts in the equations, you may be able to define some very useful performance measures.

Root Cause Analysis and TRIZ

Root Cause Analysis and TRIZ are generic problem solving techniques—tools that can be used within a CPI program. Root Cause Analysis is a reactive method of problem detection and resolution performed after an event has occurred. Its focus is to identify the root cause of a problem in order to create effective corrective actions that prevent it from re-occurring. TRIZ originates from Russia and is an acronym for Теория решения изобретательских задач (*Teoriya Resheniya Izobretatelskikh Zadatch*) which means "The theory of solving inventor's problems" or "The theory of inventor's problem solving." It is a methodology, tool set, knowledge base, model-based technology and algorithmic approach to the invention of new systems and the refinement of old systems. It is used for generating innovative ideas and solutions for problem resolution, system analysis, failure analysis and patterns of system evolution. A problem with TRIZ is that some of its features are in the public domain and some reside in knowledge bases held by commercial consulting organizations and are therefore unreachable to the general public without payment.

Whatever CPI approach an organization decides to use, there are few important lessons learned from all of the methods discussed in this chapter. When combined together, they represent a powerful collection of ideas and best practices that form the foundation of a successful organizational CPI program that develops people and improves process and technology. They are:

- From Kaizen:
    - Everyone in an organization is responsible for continuous improvement
    - Empower employees to improve the business
    - Create a culture of continuous learning
- From Kanban:
    - All work transpires in a series of interconnected processes
    - Fix problems in a sequential and disciplined fashion
    - Limit work-in-progress
- From the Theory of Constraints:
    - Manage constraints
- From Lean:
    - Eliminate process waste
- From Six Sigma:
    - Variation exists in all processes
    - Understand and analyze them

IT Performance Measurement

Performance measurement is the process by which an organization evaluates progress toward the accomplishment of specific, defined strategic organizational goals. Its purpose is to improve business performance and increase shareholder value. Successful organizations rely heavily on performance measures to operationalize strategic goals and objectives, quantify problems, evaluate alternatives, allocate resources, track progress and learn from mistakes. Managers responsible for executing an organization's performance measurement strategy must possess the expertise to set performance targets, design efficiency and effectiveness measures, systematically and accurately measure outcomes and then use the results for informed decision making.

IT products, services and delivery processes are critical resources for any results-driven program or operation. Managers, business customers relying on IT products and services and stakeholders often form partnerships to design, manage and evaluate IT systems that are critical to achieving improved business success. The one question they all want answered is "How are information technology products and services, including the infrastructure, supporting the delivery and effectiveness of the enterprise's programs?"

An effective performance measurement approach is not used for assigning blame or just to comply with reporting requirements. It is used to create and facilitate action to improve performance. Measures and performance information must link to strategic management processes. An effective performance management system produces information that delivers the following benefits.

- Provides an early warning indicator of problems and the effectiveness of corrective action
- Provides input to resource allocation and planning
    - Helps organizations prepare for future conditions that will likely impact program and support function operations and the demands for products and services:
        - i.e., decreasing personnel or financial resources or changes in workload
    - Metrics provide organizations with lead time to adjust for needed resources if conditions are known in advance
- Provides periodic feedback to employees, customers, stakeholders and the general public about the quality, quantity, cost, and timeliness of products and services

Perhaps most importantly, measures build a common results language among all decision-makers. Selected measures define what is important to an organization, what it holds itself accountable for, how it defines success and how it structures its improvement efforts.

There is no one "best" approach to IT performance management. How IT performance management is designed, implemented and sustained in each organization depends on many factors including:

- The organization's culture—whether leadership supports IT performance management and reflects their support in its program and employee appraisal and reward systems
- The importance of IT to program delivery
- The accepted value of IT in the organization
- The allocation of IT responsibilities in the organization, including whether IT is centrally managed or responsibility is dispersed
- The availability of resources (e.g., skills, people, tools, money) to support performance management

Factors such as these when taken together, are a complex environment affecting IT performance measurement. The greatest key success factor is top management ownership—their involvement in and use of IT performance information. Their attention, reinforcement and actions are critical to any organization's use of IT performance measures.

Performance Measurement Fundamentals

IT performance measurement and metrics are subsets of an overall performance management system. In structuring an effective approach to performance management, it is important to:

- Differentiate between IT's impact on intermediate vs. final program outcomes
- Use a good balance of diverse metrics
- Understand that measures may differ by management tier within an organization
- Evaluate both the overall performance of the IT function within an organization and the outcomes for individual IT investments

There are five practices that characterize IT performance management:

1. **Follow the IT results chain**: build and enforce a disciplined flow from goals to objectives to measures and individual accountability
   a. Define specific goals, objectives, and measures
   b. Use diverse metric types
   c. Describe how IT outputs and outcomes impact operational customer and enterprise program delivery requirements

2. **Follow a balanced scorecard approach**: translate organizational strategy and IT performance expectations into a comprehensive view of both operational and strategic measures to address:
   a. The strategic needs of the enterprise
   b. The needs of individual customers
   c. Internal IT business performance
   d. Ongoing IT innovation and learning
3. **Target measures, results, and accountability at different decision-making tiers**: match measures and performance results to various decision-making tiers or levels:
   a. Senior executives
   b. Senior to mid-level managers responsible for program or support units
   c. Lower-level management running specific operations or projects
4. **Build a comprehensive measure, data collection, and analysis capability**: give considerable attention to baselining, benchmarking and the collection and analysis of IT performance information:
   a. Use a variety of data collection and analysis tools and methods
   b. Keep stakeholders informed without imposing unnecessary reporting burdens
   c. Periodically review the appropriateness of their current measures
5. **Improve performance of IT business processes to better support strategic goals**: IT performance improvement begins and ends with IT business processes
   a. Map IT business processes and prioritize the processes which must be improved to support an enterprise and customers' business processes.

Developing performance measures that demonstrate the impact of IT on company performance requires management commitment, experience in constructing and evaluating metrics and a constant learning environment. If an organization has not demonstrated strong capability and sound performance in the basics of IT management, they will not be successful in attempting to develop a strategic or tactical impact measurement program. In other words, if an IT unit is not successful in delivering quality products and services to the organization, it has little credibility with senior management in measuring strategic contributions to business results.

SDLC Metrics

IT performance metrics cover a range of topics including cost, schedule, productivity, knowledge transfer, steady state, run time and quality. When determining which metrics to capture and report on, the basic premise is that if the metric does not support a management decision process, it is waste and should be discarded. Metrics that are typically captured include those that:

- Report the status of work activities in the organization
- Detail performance of the activities that are performed

- Detail a product's quality attributes
- Detail the quality attributes of the process

SDLC metrics are categorized into three broad classifications: Lifecycle Framework Metrics, Value Chain Metrics and Quality Assurance Metrics. Since every organization is unique, the 31 common metric and formula examples[136] presented here are simply suggestions to trigger the thinking process; or you can also use them to get yourself started with your own measurement program. These formulas have all been tested and produce the correct results in Microsoft Excel.

Lifecycle Framework Metrics

Cost of Quality (CoQ%): Four variables impact the Cost of Quality. They are Assessment, Engineering, Failure and Prevention

- **Assessment (A)**: Costs associated with determining the current state of a product
    o Includes reviews, testing and audits
- **Engineering (E)**: Costs associated with the effort involved in developing the system
    o Includes analysis, coding, design, documentation, environment and requirements
    o Don't double count efforts captured in any of the other three variables
- **Failure (F)**: internal failures detected prior to product delivery and external failures discovered post delivery
    o Includes rework and retesting
- **Prevention (P)**: Costs associated with efforts expended to ensure product quality
    o Includes defect prevention, metrics collection and analysis, process improvement and training

Formula:

$$CoQ\% = \left(\frac{A + F + P}{A + F + E + P}\right) * 100$$

Defects

- **Average Defect Age (ADA)**: average of how long it takes to uncover defects in terms of number of phases
    o Variables: Defect Found Phase (DFP), Originating Phase (OP), Phase Defects (PD), Total Defects (TD)

---

[136] Source: loosely based on metrics defined in *"QDGM Metrics"* by Viswanathan Sriram and Venkatraman Shanthi of Cognizant Technology Solutions

- o If ADA < 1, defect discovery is efficient. If ADA >= 1, defect discovery process needs improvement
- o Assumption: phases are sequentially numbered

Formula:

$$ADA = \left(\frac{\sum((DFP - OP) * PD)}{TD} \right)$$

- **Defect Density (DD)**: the ratio of Defects (D) to Size (S) or the ratio of Defects (D) to Effort (E)

Size Based Formula:

$$DD = \frac{D}{S}$$

Effort Based Formula:

$$DD = \frac{D}{E}$$

- **Defect Leakage (DL%)**: measure of efficiency of the review and testing processes. A high DL% for a particular phase indicates process inefficiency because detected defects are allowed to slip through to subsequent phases
  - o Variables: Number of defects uncovered in a phase attributable to a prior phase (PPD), Total Prior Phase Defects (TPPD)

Formula:

$$DL\% = \left(\frac{PPD}{PPD + TPPD} \right) * 100$$

- **Defect Removal Efficiency (DRE%)**: the efficiency of pre-delivery defect removal by internal review and testing processes
  - o Variables: Total Pre-delivery Defects (TD), Total Post-delivery Defects (TPD)

Formula:

$$DRE\% = \left(\frac{TD}{TD + TPD} \right) * 100$$

- **Review Efficiency (RE%)**: the efficiency of the review process expressed as a percentage
  - o Review defects include all stage reviews and testing cycles
  - o Any comments documented from a review are counted as defects

- Variables:
    - Phase Level: Current Phase Defects (CPD), Total number of defects detected in subsequent stages attributed to current phase (TSP)
    - Project Level: Total Review Defects (TRD), Total Testing Defects (TTD)

Phase Level Formula:

$$RE\% = \left(\frac{CPD}{CPD + TSP}\right) * 100$$

Project Level Formula:

$$RE\% = \left(\frac{TRD}{TRD + TTD}\right) * 100$$

Effort

- **Effort Variation (EV%)**: difference between Estimated (E) and Actual (A) effort compared to Estimated effort (E) expressed as a percentage
    - Work Completed (WC%) must be known
    - To calculate WC%, level of effort remaining (ER) must be known

Formulas:

$$WC\% = \left(\frac{A}{A + ER}\right) * 100$$

$$EV\% = \frac{A - \left(E * \left(\frac{WC\%}{100}\right)\right)}{E * \left(\frac{WC\%}{100}\right)} * 100$$

- **Load Factor (LF)**: ratio of Actual (A) effort expended to Available (Av) effort for a given time period
    - Available effort is a calculation of the number of available resources (R) for a given time period (T)

Formulas:

$$Av = R * T$$

$$LF = \frac{A}{Av}$$

- **Rework Effort (RE%)**: follow what's being taught in this SDLC and RE% should be 0, otherwise it is the total effort expended on rework (Re) divided by the actual (A) effort expended for the project expressed as a percentage

Formula:

$$RE\% = \left(\frac{Re}{A}\right) * 100$$

- **Work Efficiency Index (WEI)**: ratio of Work Completed (WC%) to Effort Expended (EE%)
    - Estimated (E) and Actual (A) effort must be known
    - Effort remaining (ER) must be known

Formulas:

$$WC\% = \left(\frac{A}{A + ER}\right) * 100$$

$$EE\% = \left(\frac{A}{ER}\right) * 100$$

$$WEI = \frac{WC\%}{EE\%}$$

Requirements

- **Requirements Leakage Index (RLI%)**: ratio of the number of missed requirements (MR) captured since baselining against the total number of baselined requirements (TBR) expressed as percentage figure

Formula:

$$RLI\% = \left(\frac{MR}{TBR}\right) * 100$$

- **Requirements Stability Index (RSI)**: measure of requirements elicitation effectiveness
    - Variables: Total Baselined Requirements (TBR), Requirements Modified Since Baselining (RM), Requirements Added Since Baselining (RA), Requirements Deleted Since Baselining (RD)

Formula:

$$RSI = \left(\frac{(TBR + RM + RA + RD)}{TBR} \right)$$

Schedule

- **Duration Variance (DV%)**: difference between Planned (P) vs. Actual (A) duration of a task, sprint, cycle, phase or activity expressed as a percentage
  - Variables: Planned Start Date (PSD), Planned End Date (PED), Actual Start Date (ASD), Actual End date (AED)

Formula:

$$DV\% = \left(\frac{(AED - ASD) - (PED - PSD)}{PED - PSD} \right) * 100$$

- **Schedule Variance (SV%)**: difference between the project's Actual End Date (AED) and Planned End Date (PED) vs. difference between Planned End Date (PED) and Planned Start Date (PSD) expressed as a percentage

Formula:

$$SV\% = \left(\frac{AED - PED}{PED - PSD} \right) * 100$$

Size Variance (SV%): Size is a generally a function point based metric although it can also be calculated as the number of lines of source code. A function point is a unit of measurement to express an amount of business functionality. To calculate function points, user requirements are categorized into one of five types: outputs, inquiries, inputs, internal files and external interfaces. Once categorized into types, the requirements are assessed for complexity and assigned a number of function points. If requirements are revised, as for a scope change or to capture a missing requirement, the size is recalculated.

Variables: Actual (A) and Estimated (E) size

Formula:

$$SV\% = \left(\frac{A - E}{E} \right) * 100$$

Value Chain Metrics

Knowledge Transfer

- **First Call Resolutions (FCR%)**: ratio of the number of incidents closed (IC) on the first call by Tier 1 resources against the total number of incidents (TI) logged for a system

  Formula:

  $$FCR\% = \left(\frac{IC}{TR}\right) * 100$$

Quality of Service

- **Application Availability (AppAv%)**: percentage of days the application was available at the scheduled time
  - Variables: Number of days application was started on time (OTS), total days of application availability (TAv)

  Formula:

  $$AppAv\% = \left(\frac{OTS}{TAv}\right) * 100$$

- **Maintainability (MTTR)**: Mean Time To Repair all production incidents and severity 1 post-production defects
  - Variables: Duration to close all incidents (Dur_y) of a specific type, total number of incidents (TI_y) for a specific type (y)

  Formula:

  $$MTTR = \left(\frac{\Sigma\left(Dur_y\right)}{TI_y}\right)$$

- **Reliability (MTBF)**: Mean Time Between Failures is the average time between failures for a given period; failures include all production incidents and severity 1 post-production defects
  - Variables: downtime (Dn), Uptime (Up), total number of incidents (TI_y) for a specific type (y)

  Formula:

  $$MTBF = \left(\frac{\Sigma(Dn - Up)}{TI_y}\right)$$

- **System Availability (SysAv%)**: system availability expresses as a percentage
  - Variables: MTTR, MTBF

Formula:

$$SysAv\% = \left(\frac{MTBF}{MTBF + MTTR}\right) * 100$$

Steady State

- **Average Duration Variance by Incident Type (iADV%)**:
  - Variables: Actual Duration (AD) to close incidents by type (y), Planned Duration (PD) to close incidents by type (y), Total Incidents (TI) by type (y)

Formula:

$$iADV\% = \left(\frac{\sum \frac{AD_y - PD_y}{PD_y}}{TI_y}\right) * 100$$

- **Maintenance Incident Duration Variance (MIDV%)**: difference between Actual Duration (AD) and Planned Duration (PD) vs. the Planned Duration for all closed maintenance related incident types for the specified period

Formula:

$$MIDV\% = \sum \left(\frac{AD - PD}{PD}\right) * 100$$

- **Residual Defect Density (RDD%)**: ratio of the number of production Defects to Size of the closed incident types
  - Variables: Total production defects (TPD) from enhancement requests, total size of enhancement requests (TSER)

Formula:

$$RDD\% = \sum \left(\frac{TPD}{TSER}\right) * 100$$

- **Turn Around by Incident Type (IRTA%)**: number of Incident requests by type (y) closed (cIR)during the given period vs. number of Incident requests by type (y) opened during the period (oIR)
  - Variable: total incident requests open at start of period (ToIR) by type (y)

Formula:

$$IRTA\% = \sum \left(\frac{cIR_y}{ToIR_y + oIR_y} \right) * 100$$

Quality Assurance Metrics

- **Automation Coverage (AC%)**: measures the percentage of automated test cases
  - Variables: number of automated test case (ATC), total test cases (TTC)

Formula:

$$AC\% = \left(\frac{ATC}{TTC} \right) * 100$$

- **Average Defect Retest Aging (avDRA)**: measures how fast defect fixes are retested
  - Variables: retest date (RD), fix release date (FRD), total number of defects (TD)

Formula:

$$avDRA = \frac{\sum(RD - FRD)}{TD}$$

- **Error Discovery Rate (EDR)**: ratio of defects per test cases
  - Variables: total defects found (TFD), total test cases executed (TCE)

Formula:

$$EDR = \frac{TFD}{TCE}$$

- **Quality of Fixes (QoF%)**: measures software regressions against reported fixes
  - Variables: defects reported as fixed (DRF), total reopened defects (TRD), total new defects (TND)

Formula:

$$QoF\% = \left(\frac{DRF - TRD}{DRF + TND}\right) * 100$$

- **Test Cases Passed (TCP%)**: percentage of test cases successfully passed
  - Variables: total test cases executed (TCE), total test cases passed (TCP)

Formula:

$$TCP\% = \left(\frac{TCP}{TCE}\right) * 100$$

- **Test Design Coverage (TDC%)**: measures the functional test coverage
  - Variables: Number of requirements (R) mapped to test cases, total number of baselined requirements (BR)

Formula:

$$TDC\% = \left(\frac{R}{BR}\right) * 100$$

- **Test Execution Coverage (TCE%)**: percentage of tests executed against plan
  - Variables: total test cases executed (TCE), total test cases planned (TCP)

Formula:

$$TCE\% = \left(\frac{TCE}{TCP}\right) * 100$$

The best advice that can be given right now is to take things slowly. Don't try to implement all these metrics in one big bang. It only leads to frustration and resistance. Start with a few metrics on small projects and see how it goes. Adjust the formulas to your liking.

Conclusion

This has been a long journey for us and it's my greatest hope that you've learned something that can benefit you in your career. Let's get serious for a moment. I have something I need to ask you. This is something I ask of everyone I've ever had the opportunity to mentor, teach or lead. If you've learned anything at all from me while reading this book, please share what you've learned with someone else and pay it forward!

Handy Desk Reference

You now have all the details necessary to create or mature your own best in breed System Development Life Cycle. All of the activity diagrams contained in this book are on the accompanying CD. They are yours to use within your own organization. Feel free to tailor them for your own needs. As you mature your own internal practices, especially in requirements elicitation, you will reap benefits and provide greater bottom line value to the organizations that employ you. You are well on the way to maturing into a world-class IT organization and gaining true advantage over your competitors.

The full best in breed SDLC drawing on the CD is 11 inches high by 48½ long, much too large to print on a standard printer or display in this book. If you don't have a plotter, the drawings are all provided in the individual form as well. This final chapter is intended to be used as a handy desk reference. The principles and the twenty-four most important tables and activity diagrams are here, one per page wherever possible. Instead of searching through the book to find a particular process activity, just look here. You'll find it more easily if it's right at your fingertips.

This has been fun for me and I wish you all the best in your pursuit of process maturity. Thanks for buying the *"The Ultimate Guide to the SDLC."* I hope it is of great value to you and your organization.

—*Victor*

The Principles

Principle #1: An effective organizational change management strategy is essential to the success of the SDLC.

Principle #2: Investment opportunities cannot be estimated accurately until the requirements are known.

Principle #3: The Project Management Method and the SDLC are complementary. They do not compete with each other.

Principle #4: Write requirements that are cohesive, complete, consistent, correct, feasible, modifiable, necessary, prioritized, reusable, testable, traceable, verifiable and unambiguous.

Principle #5: Model the requirements.

Principle #6: Quality Assurance begins at project inception

Principle #7: Keep the stakeholders engaged in the development process.

Principle #8: Build systems with minimal defects.

Principle #9: Make changes in the smallest steps possible

Principle #10: Always conduct acceptance testing

Principle #11: Complete all project artifacts before implementation

Principle #12: Rehearse deployments

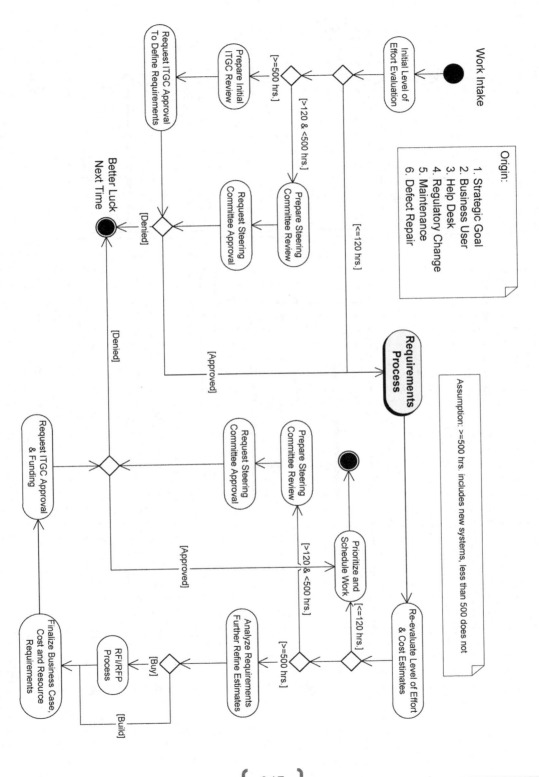

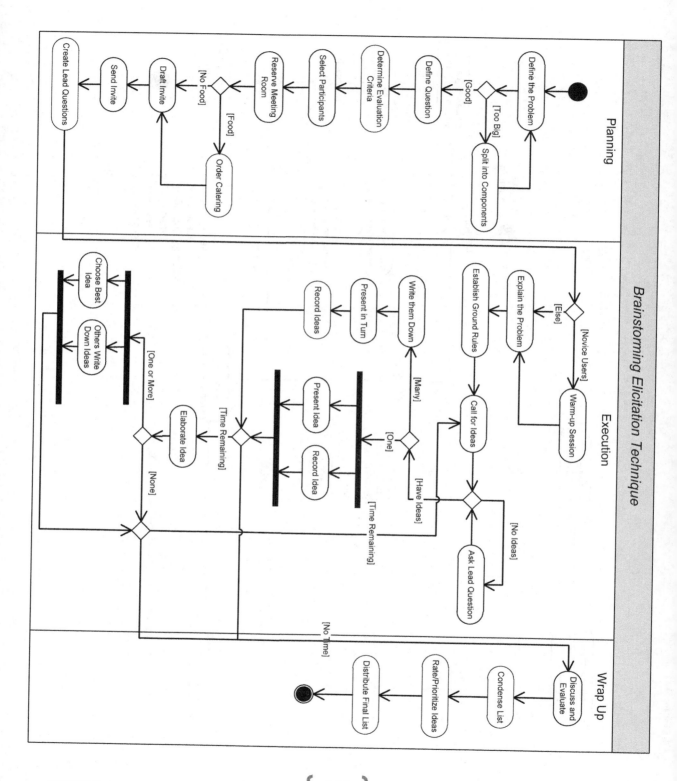

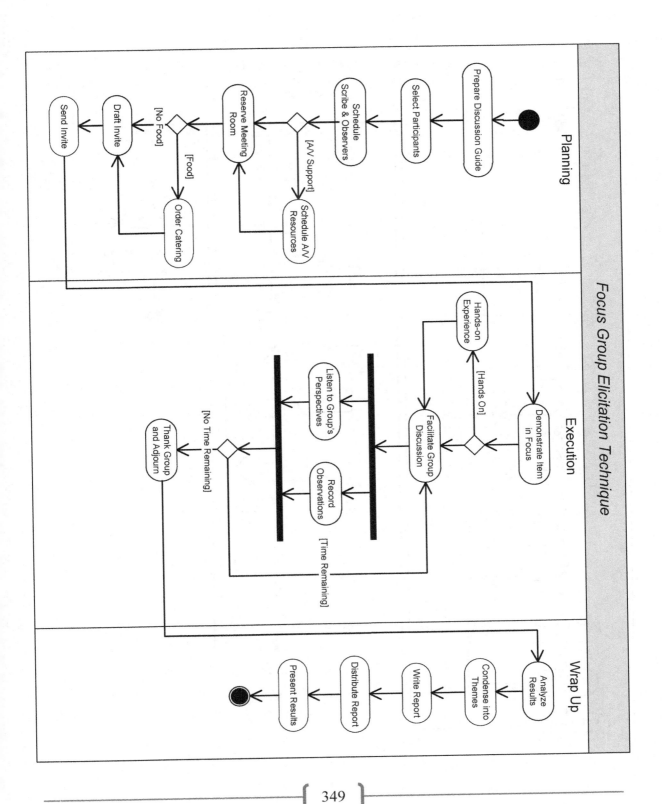

Focus Group Elicitation Technique

Planning

Prepare Discussion Guide → Select Participants → Schedule Scribe & Observers → [A/V Support] → Schedule A/V Resources → Reserve Meeting Room → [No Food] / [Food] → Order Catering → Draft Invite → Send Invite

Execution

Demonstrate Item in Focus → [Hands On] → Hands-on Experience → Facilitate Group Discussion → Listen to Group's Perspectives / Record Observations → [Time Remaining] / [No Time Remaining] → Thank Group and Adjourn

Wrap Up

Analyze Results → Condense into Themes → Write Report → Distribute Report → Present Results

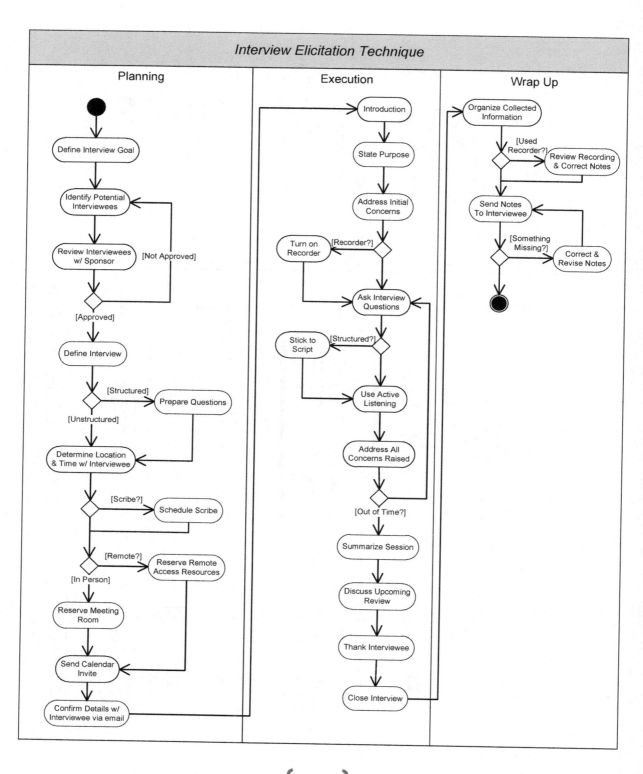

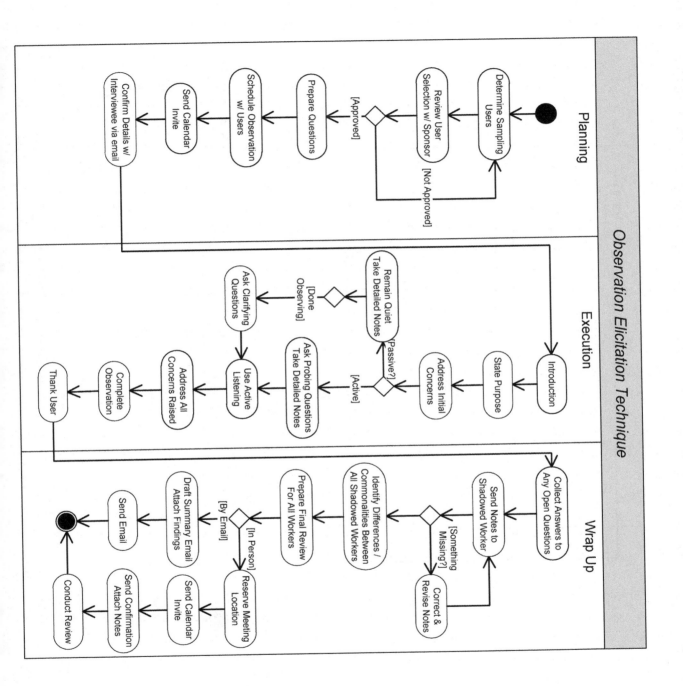

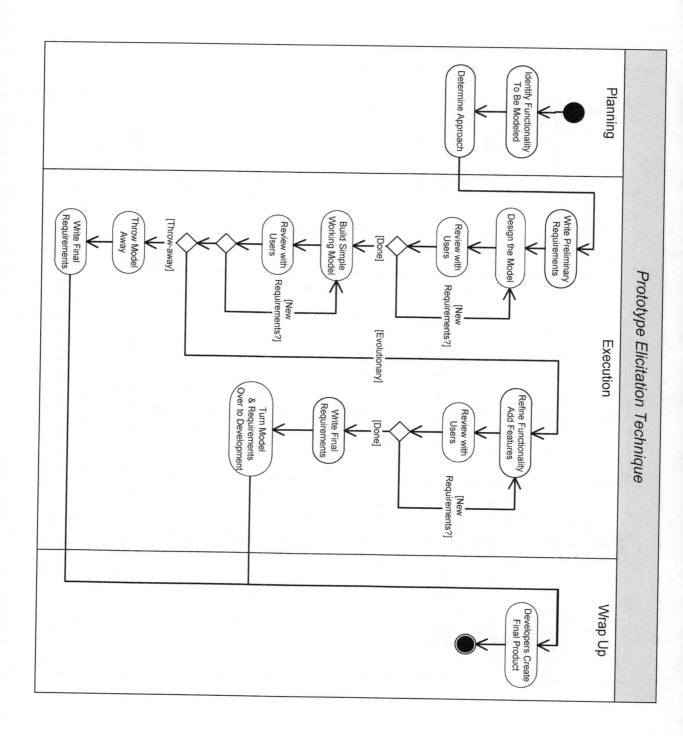

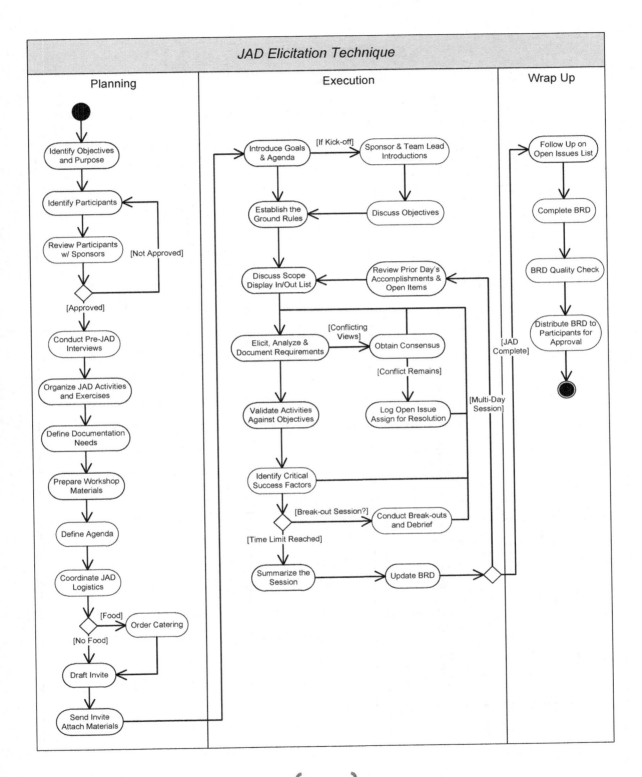

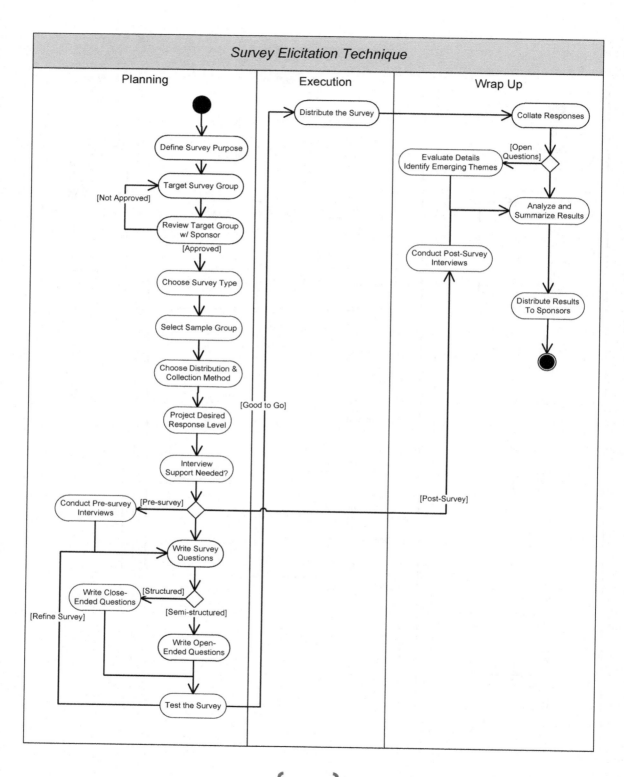

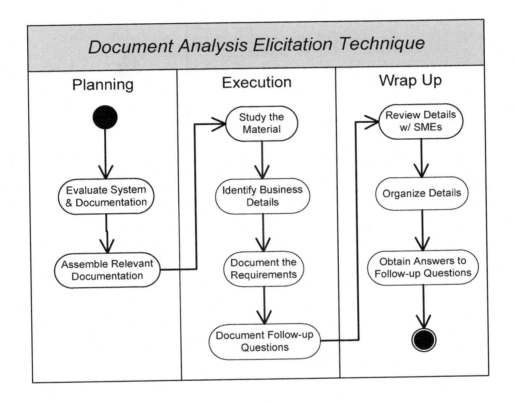

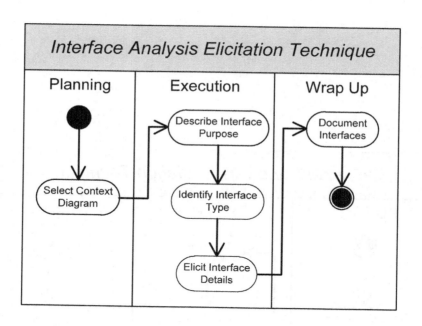

Good Requirements Quality Checklist

I.   **Cohesive**: A set of requirements is cohesive if it relates to only one thing. All requirements in a set or group support the overall purpose and scope of the system or component under discussion, whether that is a business process definition, business rule, information flow, data flow or so forth.

     1.   Are the requirements consolidated into groups such as products, components, use cases and user stories?

     2.   Do the requirements align with their process definitions and models?

     3.   Does each group contain 5 to 9 requirements? (Note: This is not a failing criterion if more than nine although, it may indicate the group can be divided.)

     4.   Do the grouped requirements flow logically from one to the next, from the more general to the more specific or from the least sensitive to the most sensitive?

II.   **Complete**: To be complete, all known relevant requirements are documented and all conditions under which a requirement applies are stated. A BRD is complete if, and only if, it includes the following elements:

- All significant requirements, whether relating to functionality, performance, design constraints, attributes, or external interfaces.
- Definitions of the responses of the system/software to all realizable classes of input data in all realizable classes of situations.
- Descriptive labels for and references to all figures, tables, models and diagrams in the BRD and definition of all business terms, acronyms and units of measure.

     1.   Does each requirement contain all the information necessary for the technical team to design, build and test that component of the solution?

     2.   Are all the inputs to the system/software specified, including their source, accuracy, range of values and frequency?

     3.   Are all the outputs from the system/software specified, including their destination, accuracy, and range of values, frequency and format?

     4.   Are all the communication interfaces specified, including handshaking, error checking and communication protocols?

     5.   Has analysis been performed to identify missing requirements?

     6.   Are the areas of incompleteness specified when information is not available?

     7.   Are the requirements complete such that if the product satisfied every requirement it would be acceptable?

     8.   Are all figures, tables, models and diagrams labeled in a descriptive manner?

     9.   Are all figures, tables, models and diagrams referenced within the document?

10. Are all business terms, acronyms and units of measure defined appropriately?

III. **Consistent**: Consistency demands that the requirement can be met without causing conflict or contradiction with any of the other requirements. Requirement should be stated in a way to allow the widest possible selection of implementation options.

7. Do the requirements avoid prematurely determining a solution?
8. Do the requirements avoid specifying a design?
9. Are the requirements specified at a consistent level of detail?
10. Should any requirements be specified in more detail?
11. Should any requirements be specified in less detail?
12. Are the requirements consistent with the content of other organizational and project documentation?

IV. **Correct**: Requirements must accurately describe the functionality to be built. Only the source of the requirements, the customers, users or stakeholders, can determine their correctness.

20. Do the requirements fulfill the original business need?
21. Has the scope of the system/software been bounded?
22. Have the overall function and behavior of the system/software been defined?
23. Has the required technology infrastructure for the system/software been adequately specified?
24. Are all the tasks to be performed by the system/software specified?
25. Can each requirement be allocated to an element of the solution design where it can be implemented?
26. Does each task specify the data/information content used in the task and the data/information content resulting from the task?
27. Is each requirement associated with a use case or process flow?
28. Have requirements for communication among system/software components been specified?
29. Have appropriate constraints, assumptions, and dependencies been explicitly and unambiguously stated?
30. Are the hardware requirements specified?
31. Are the physical security requirements specified?
32. Are the operational security requirements specified?
33. Is the maintainability of the system/software specified, including the ability to respond to changes in the operating environment, interfaces, accuracy, performance, and additional predicted capabilities?
34. Is the reliability of the system/software specified, including the consequences of failure, vital information protected from failure, error detection, and recovery?

35. Are internal interfaces such as software and hardware defined?
36. Are external interfaces, such as users, software and hardware defined?
37. Is each requirement relevant to the problem and its solution?
38. Is the definition of the requirement's success included? Of failure?

V. **Feasible**: Feasibility means each requirement is implementable within the existing infrastructure, budget, timeline and resources available to the team. The business analyst needs to work with the project team to make these determinations.

6. Are the requirements technically feasible and do they fit within the project funding and timing constraints?
7. If not, is the project able to develop the capability to implement the requirement?
8. Even if a requirement is technically feasible, it may not be attainable due to constraints. Are there any constraints that prevent the requirement from being attained?
9. Is it possible to implement each requirement within the capabilities and limitations of the technical and operational environment?
10. Is it possible to implement each and every requirement?

VI. **Necessary & Prioritized**: Requirements must be ranked for importance and/or stability. A necessary requirement is one that is essential to meet business goals and objectives. A priority is assigned to each functional requirement or feature to indicate how essential it is to a particular solution release. If all requirements are considered equally important, it is difficult for the project team to respond to budget cuts, schedule overruns, staff turnover or new requirements added during development. Ranking requirements for stability is in terms of the number of expected changes to the requirement. Stable requirements are ready to be developed.

4. Do requirements have an associated identifier to indicate either the importance or stability of that particular requirement?
5. Do conflicts exist regarding the importance and/or stability ranking of the requirements?
6. Are all requirements ranked the same?

VII. **Measurable, Testable, & Verifiable**: Verifiable means that the requirement states something that can be confirmed by examination, analysis, test or demonstration. A good requirement does not contain words that are not testable and measurable. If it is impossible to ensure that the requirement is met in the solution, it should be removed or revised.

- Testable requirements are designed to demonstrate that the solution satisfies requirements. Tests may include functional, performance, regression, and stress tests.
- The verification method and level (i.e., the location in the solution where the requirement is met) at which the requirement can be verified should be determined explicitly as part of the development of each requirement. Requirement statements that include words that have relative meaning are not verifiable. For example:

o Adequate	o Easy	o More efficient
o Better than	o Maximum	o Quality product
o Comparison	o Minimum	o Substantial

8. Are the requirements written in a language and vocabulary that anyone can understand? Do the stakeholders concur?
9. Is the expected response time from the user's point of view specified for all necessary operations?
10. Are other timing considerations specified such as processing time, data transfer and throughput?
11. Are acceptable tradeoffs between competing attributes specified? For example, between robustness and correctness?
12. Does each requirement capture a metric by which it can be measured?
13. Is each requirement testable?
14. Will it be possible for independent testing to determine whether each requirement has been satisfied?

VIII. Traceable: Requirements are traceable if their origin is known and the requirement can be referenced or located throughout the solution. The requirement should be traceable to a goal stated in the project charter, vision document, business case or other initiating document. Requirements are traceable backwards and forwards.

- Traceable backwards: each requirement can be traced back to specific customer, user or stakeholder input, such as a use case, a business rule, or some other origin. It can also be traced from any specific point in the life cycle back to an earlier phase, component or document.
- Traceable forward: each requirement should have a unique identifier that assists in identification, maintaining change history and tracing the requirement through the solution components.

5. Are requirements uniquely identified?
6. Can each requirement be traced to its origin or source, such as a scope statement, change request, business objective or compliance regulation?

7. Is each requirement identified such that it facilitates referencing in future development and enhancement efforts?
8. Has each requirement been cross-referenced to previous related project documents?

IX. Unambiguous: Requirements must be clear, concise, simple and free from ambiguity. They must be stated without technical jargon, acronyms (unless defined) or other obscure verbiage. Requirements express objective facts, not subjective opinions. Vague requirements are often misunderstood resulting in rework and corrective actions during the design, development and testing phases. If the requirement can be interpreted in more than one way, it should be removed or clarified.

- All readers of a requirement should arrive at the same interpretation of its meaning.
- All specialized terms and terms that might be subject to confusion should be well defined.

13. Are the requirements written with simple, short sentences?
14. Are the requirements specified clearly enough to be turned over to an independent group for implementation and still be understood?
15. Are functional requirements separated from non-functional?
16. Are requirements stated in a manner that avoids the likelihood of multiple interpretations?
17. Do all the requirements avoid conflicts with other requirements?
18. Do any of the requirements contain undefined acronyms?
19. Are all requirements stated in one place only?
20. Have redundant requirements been consolidated?
21. Has each requirement been specified separately, avoiding compound requirements?
22. Are the requirements written with proper grammar and correct spelling?
23. Do any requirements contain vague subjects, adjectives, prepositions, verbs and subjective phrases?
24. Do any of the requirements express negative statements?

Artifact	Artifact Type	Description	Phase
RACI Chart	Deliverable	Responsible, Accountable, Consulted and Informed Stakeholder Matrix	Requirements Planning
Communications Plan	Deliverable	Requirements process communications plan	Requirements Planning
Preliminary Elicitation Schedule and Work Breakdown Structure	Deliverable	Requirements activity schedule and resource assignments developed by the BA and PM and incorporated into the overall project plan	Requirements Planning
Business Requirements Definition (BRD)	Deliverable	Full Business Requirements Definition which includes both Business and Non-Functional Requirements.	Requirements Elicitation & Analysis
BRD Users Guide	Supporting Document	Users guide to learn how to use the BRD template.	Requirements Elicitation
Business Intelligence and Data Warehouse BRD	Deliverable	For BI and DW purposes only.	Requirements Elicitation & Analysis
Elicitation Technique Process Checklists	Supporting Documents	There is one process checklist available for each of the nine elicitation techniques.	Requirements Elicitation
Requirements Checklist	• Supporting Document (development stage) • Deliverable (inspection stage)	Checklist used by anyone writing, reviewing or testing the requirements document.	Requirements Elicitation & Inspection
Non-functional requirements Checklist	• Supporting Document (development stage) • Deliverable (inspection stage)	Checklist used by anyone writing, reviewing or testing the non-functional requirements document	Requirements Elicitation & Inspection
System Requirements Specification (SRS)	Deliverable	• High level architecture • High Level Development Plan • System Environments • List of impacted systems • Reusability • Service Oriented Architecture Governance • Methodology to follow • Test Strategy	Requirements Analysis
Traceability Matrix	Deliverable	Trace the requirements through all life cycle phases	Requirements Baselining

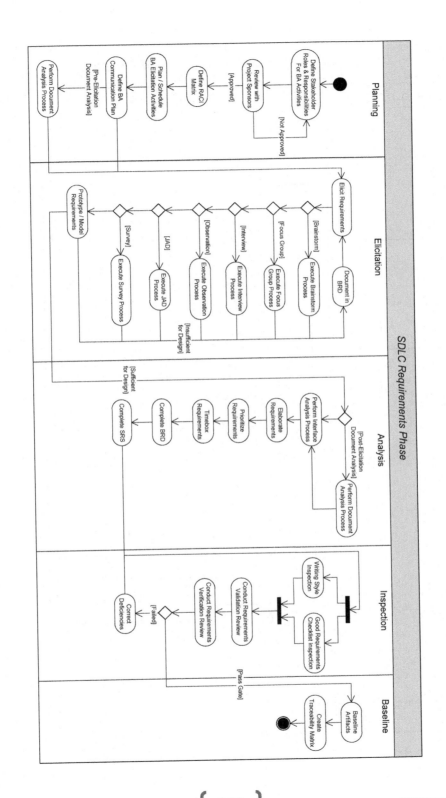

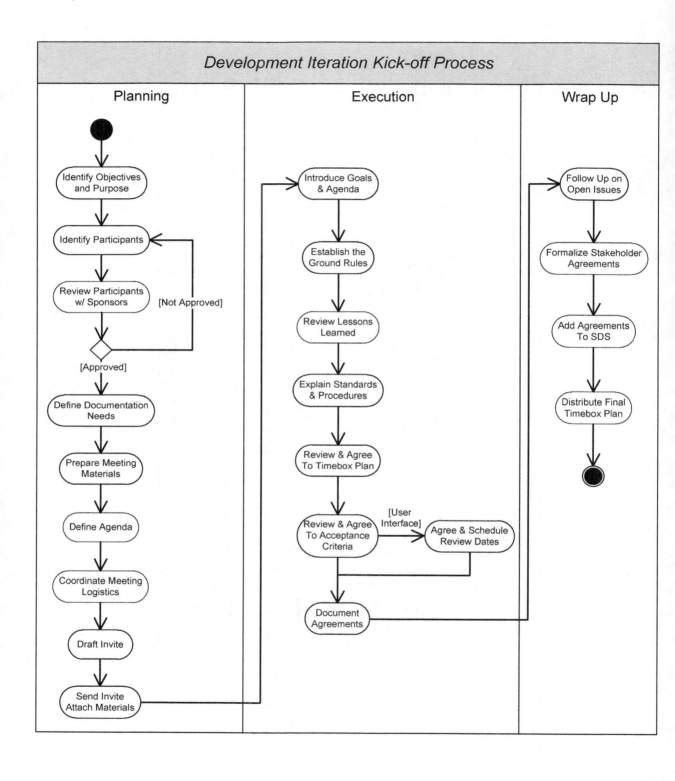

Development Iteration Kick-off Process

Planning

- Identify Objectives and Purpose
- Identify Participants
- Review Participants w/ Sponsors
  - [Not Approved]
  - [Approved]
- Define Documentation Needs
- Prepare Meeting Materials
- Define Agenda
- Coordinate Meeting Logistics
- Draft Invite
- Send Invite Attach Materials

Execution

- Introduce Goals & Agenda
- Establish the Ground Rules
- Review Lessons Learned
- Explain Standards & Procedures
- Review & Agree To Timebox Plan
- Review & Agree To Acceptance Criteria
  - [User Interface]
- Agree & Schedule Review Dates
- Document Agreements

Wrap Up

- Follow Up on Open Issues
- Formalize Stakeholder Agreements
- Add Agreements To SDS
- Distribute Final Timebox Plan

The Development Cycle

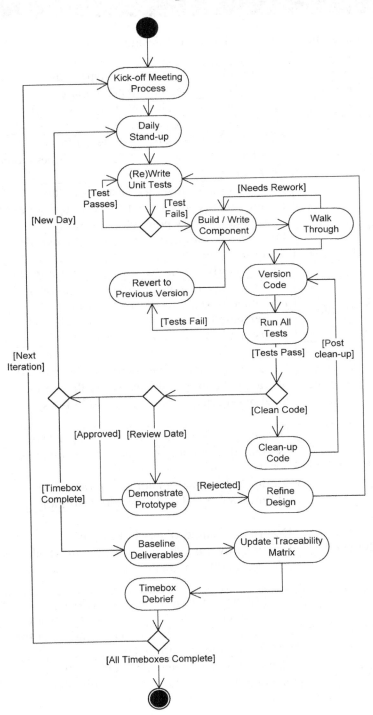

Artifact	Artifact Type	Description	Phase(s)
System Design Specification	Deliverable	The detailed system design	System Design, Development, Maintenance
Development and Coding Standards	Supporting Document	Organization and/or platform dependent standards for development and coding	Development
Unit Tests	Deliverable	Quality assurance tests design to test specific functionality of the components being created	Development
Implementation Plan	Deliverable	Describes how a system is to be deployed, installed and transitioned to a state of operational readiness	System Design through Implementation
Contingency Plan	Deliverable	Describes the strategy for ensuring system recovery in accordance with agreed to recovery times and recovery point objectives	Implementation, Production
Data Conversion Plan	Deliverable	Describes the strategies involved in converting data from an existing system/application to another hardware and/or software environment	Implementation
Maintenance Manual	Deliverable	Describes the sources of software components and other assets, how the architecture was implemented, the use of the architecture and assets and how it is to be maintained	Production Support
System Security Plan	Deliverable	Describes the actual managerial, technical and operational controls, documenting the current level of security implemented within the system	Requirements Analysis, System Design, Development, Test
Standard Operating Procedures	Deliverable	Documented procedures for performing tasks associated with equipment administration, network administration, application administration, system administration, data administration and database administration	Production Support
Release Plan	Deliverable	Describes what portions of the system functionality are to be implemented in which releases and the rationale for each release	Planning, Requirements Analysis, System Design, Implementation
Version Description Document	Deliverable	The primary configuration control document used to track and control versions of software being released to testing, implementation or the final operational environment	Implementation
Detailed Test Plan	Deliverable	Plan for conducting testing against both the functional and non-functional requirements	Test

Artifact	Artifact Type	Description	Phase(s)
Integration Test Plan	Deliverable	Test cases, datasets, procedures, scenarios and scripts for integration testing	Development, Test
System Test Plan	Deliverable	Test cases, datasets, procedures, scenarios and scripts for system testing	Test
System Integration Test Plan	Deliverable	Test cases, datasets, procedures, scenarios and scripts for system integration testing	Test
Regression Test Plan	Deliverable	Test cases, datasets, procedures, scenarios and scripts for regression testing	Test
Smoke Test Acceptance test Plan	Deliverable	Test cases, datasets, procedures, scenarios and scripts for smoke testing	Test
User Acceptance Test Plan	Deliverable	Test cases, datasets, procedures, scenarios and scripts for user acceptance testing	Test
Alpha Test Plan	Deliverable	Test cases, datasets, procedures, scenarios and scripts for Alpha testing	Test
Beta Test Plan	Deliverable	Test cases, datasets, procedures, scenarios and scripts for Beta testing	Test
System Performance Test Plan	Deliverable	Test cases, datasets, procedures, scenarios and scripts for system performance testing	Test
Load Testing Plan	Deliverable	Test cases, datasets, procedures, scenarios and scripts for load testing	Test
Stability Testing Plan	Deliverable	Test cases, datasets, procedures, scenarios and scripts for stability testing	Test
Usability Testing Plan	Deliverable	Test cases, datasets, procedures, scenarios and scripts for usability testing	Test
Security Test Plan	Deliverable	Test cases, datasets, procedures, scenarios and scripts for security or attack and penetration testing	Test
Localization Test Plan	Deliverable	Test cases, datasets, procedures, scenarios and scripts for internationalization and localization testing	Test
Destructive Test Plan	Deliverable	Test cases, datasets, procedures, scenarios and scripts for destructive testing	Test
Training Strategy	Deliverable	Plan for assessing end user needs, training goals, delivery methods, training materials, scaling and tailoring the program	Implementation
Lesson Plan	Deliverable	Details the target audience, by what means the training will be delivered and the schedule for training delivery.	Implementation and Production

Artifact	Artifact Type	Description	Phase(s)
End User Documentation	Deliverable	Any documentation required by the training strategy and lesson plan	Implementation and Production
End User Training	Deliverable	The materials, books, or CBT to be used for training users	Implementation and Production
Help Desk Scripts	Deliverable	Provides Tier 1 resources with details about how to troubleshoot potential issues to drive first call closure. Explains the escalation process if Tier 2 or higher support is required.	Implementation and Production
Service Level Agreements (SLA)	Deliverable	Formally defined service level contract between the stakeholders and project team.	Implementation and Production
Change Request (CR)	Deliverable	Change request to be authorized by CAB	All project phases including artifacts
Traceability Matrix	Deliverable	Updated to trace requirements to design elements, tests and documentation	All lifecycle phases after requirements are baselined
Quality Assurance Process Manual	Supporting Document	Comprehensive guide to all QA processes	All project phases
Change Process Manual	Supporting Document	Guide to the change management process	All project phases

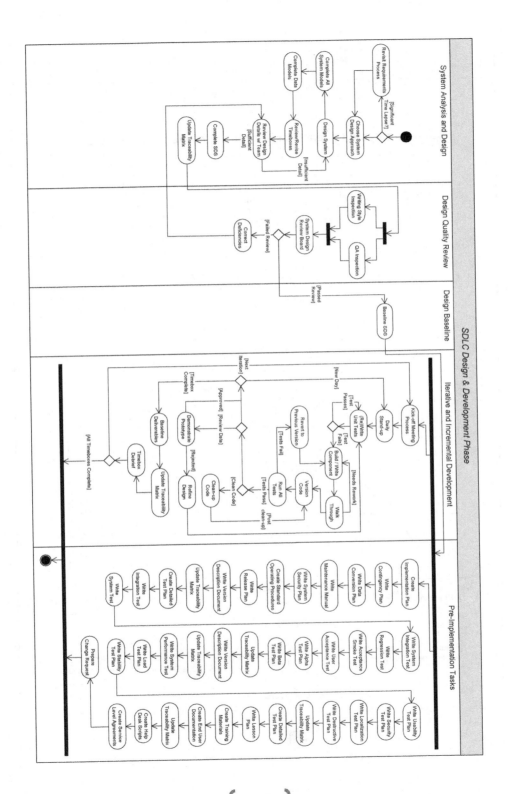

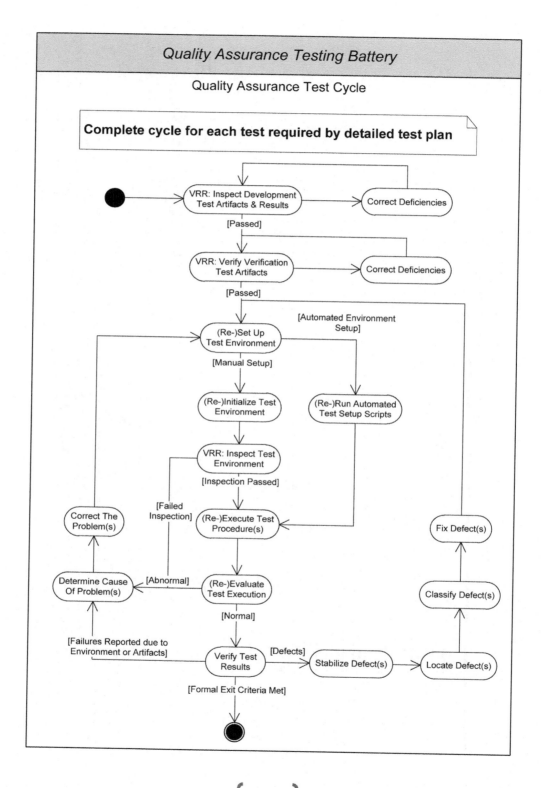

Quality Assurance Testing Battery

Quality Assurance Test Cycle

Complete cycle for each test required by detailed test plan

VRR: Inspect Development Test Artifacts & Results — Correct Deficiencies

[Passed]

VRR: Verify Verification Test Artifacts — Correct Deficiencies

[Passed]

(Re-)Set Up Test Environment

[Automated Environment Setup]

[Manual Setup]

(Re-)Initialize Test Environment

(Re-)Run Automated Test Setup Scripts

VRR: Inspect Test Environment

[Inspection Passed]

Correct The Problem(s)

[Failed Inspection]

(Re-)Execute Test Procedure(s)

Fix Defect(s)

Determine Cause Of Problem(s)

[Abnormal]

(Re-)Evaluate Test Execution

Classify Defect(s)

[Normal]

[Failures Reported due to Environment or Artifacts]

Verify Test Results

[Defects]

Stabilize Defect(s)

Locate Defect(s)

[Formal Exit Criteria Met]

370

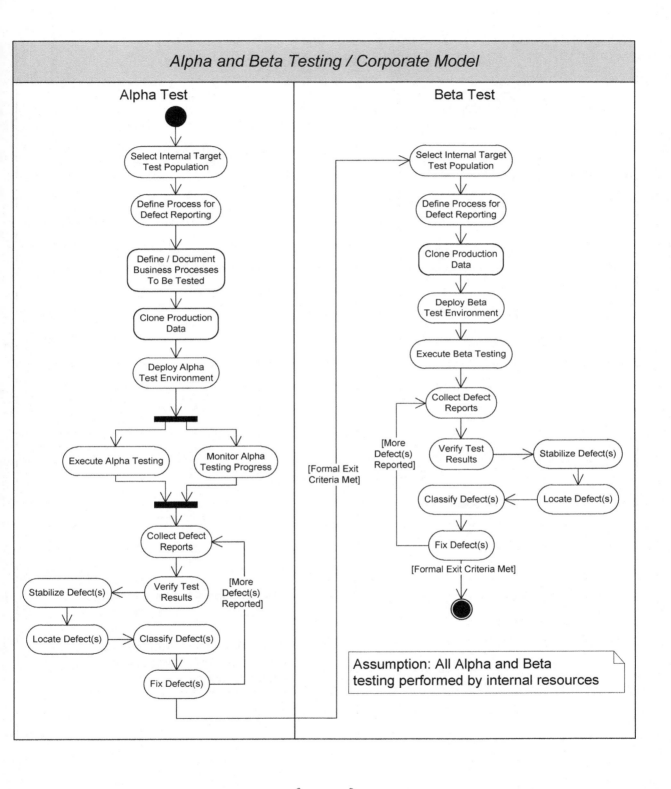

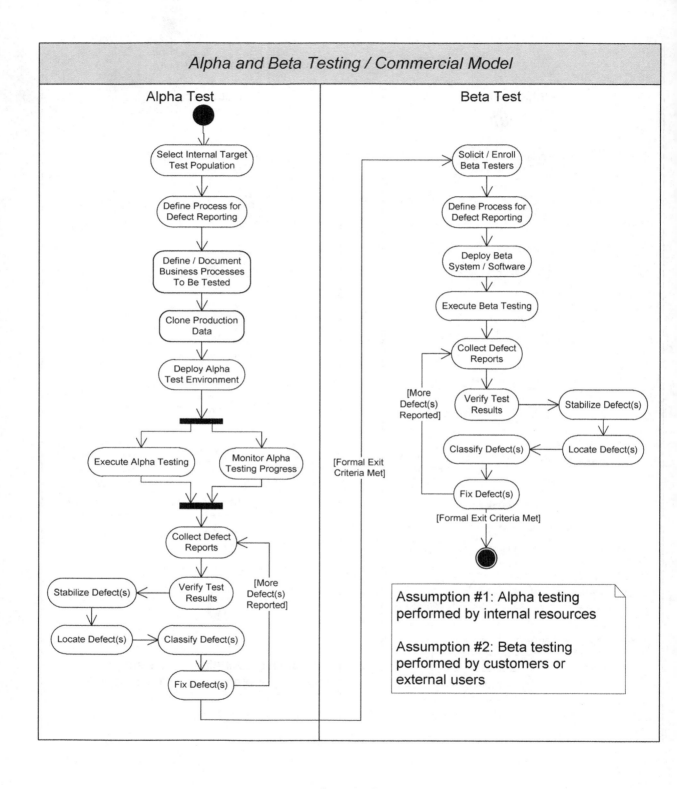

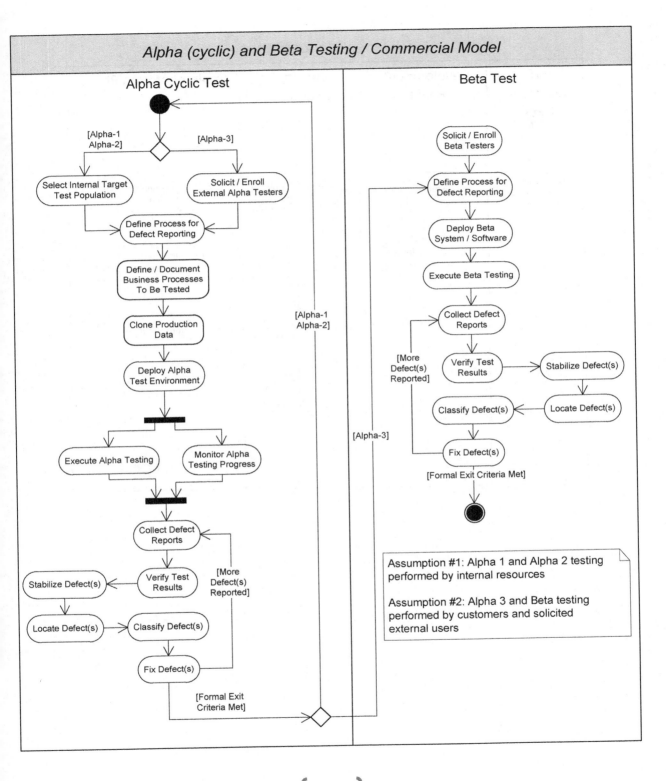

Alpha (cyclic) and Beta Testing / Commercial Model

Alpha Cyclic Test

[Alpha-1 Alpha-2]

[Alpha-3]

Select Internal Target Test Population

Solicit / Enroll External Alpha Testers

Define Process for Defect Reporting

Define / Document Business Processes To Be Tested

Clone Production Data

Deploy Alpha Test Environment

Execute Alpha Testing

Monitor Alpha Testing Progress

Collect Defect Reports

Verify Test Results

Stabilize Defect(s)

Locate Defect(s)

Classify Defect(s)

Fix Defect(s)

[More Defect(s) Reported]

[Formal Exit Criteria Met]

[Alpha-1 Alpha-2]

[Alpha-3]

Beta Test

Solicit / Enroll Beta Testers

Define Process for Defect Reporting

Deploy Beta System / Software

Execute Beta Testing

Collect Defect Reports

Verify Test Results

Stabilize Defect(s)

Locate Defect(s)

Classify Defect(s)

Fix Defect(s)

[More Defect(s) Reported]

[Formal Exit Criteria Met]

Assumption #1: Alpha 1 and Alpha 2 testing performed by internal resources

Assumption #2: Alpha 3 and Beta testing performed by customers and solicited external users

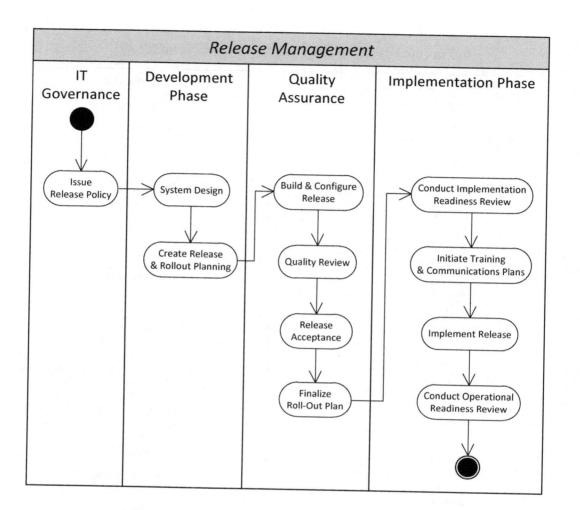

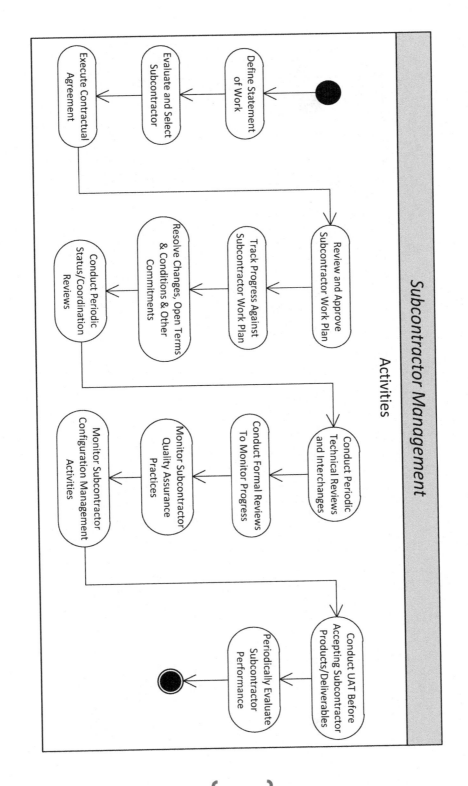

Subcontractor Management

Activities

- Define Statement of Work
- Evaluate and Select Subcontractor
- Execute Contractual Agreement
- Review and Approve Subcontractor Work Plan
- Track Progress Against Subcontractor Work Plan
- Resolve Changes, Open Terms & Conditions & Other Commitments
- Conduct Periodic Status/Coordination Reviews
- Conduct Periodic Technical Reviews and Interchanges
- Conduct Formal Reviews To Monitor Progress
- Monitor Subcontractor Quality Assurance Practices
- Monitor Subcontractor Configuration Management Activities
- Conduct UAT Before Accepting Subcontractor Products/Deliverables
- Periodically Evaluate Subcontractor Performance

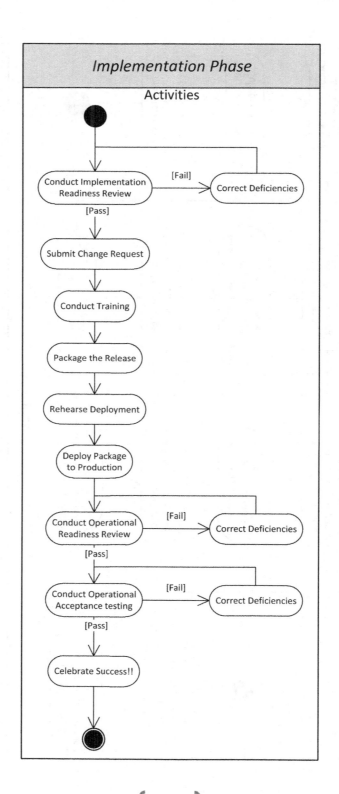

This page left intentionally blank

Table of Figures

Index

Other Fine Books from A FontLife Publication, LLC

The **Winning With WordPress** series is designed for all levels of user. All books cover WordPress up to the latest release.

Winning With WordPress Basics is for the beginner to intermediate user with little or no technical knowledge. In addition to learning the fundamentals for setting up and using WordPress to its full advantage, the author also shares tips, tricks, and search engine optimization (SEO) pointers will make your World Wide Web experience much easier and more enjoyable as your vision of a web presence becomes a reality.

Winning With WordPress Advanced covers such topics as multi-site, child themes, editing theme files, functions, performance tuning, and other advanced features not addressed in the Basics.

Winning With WordPress Security is the most technical book of the series. It covers the extent of hardening and securing your WordPress installations including modifying the Apache .htaccess file to prevent hacking attempts such as SQL injection and back door access.

CPSIA information can be obtained at www.ICGtesting.com
Printed in the USA
LVOW03s1953250115

424275LV00022B/935/P

9 780985 566647